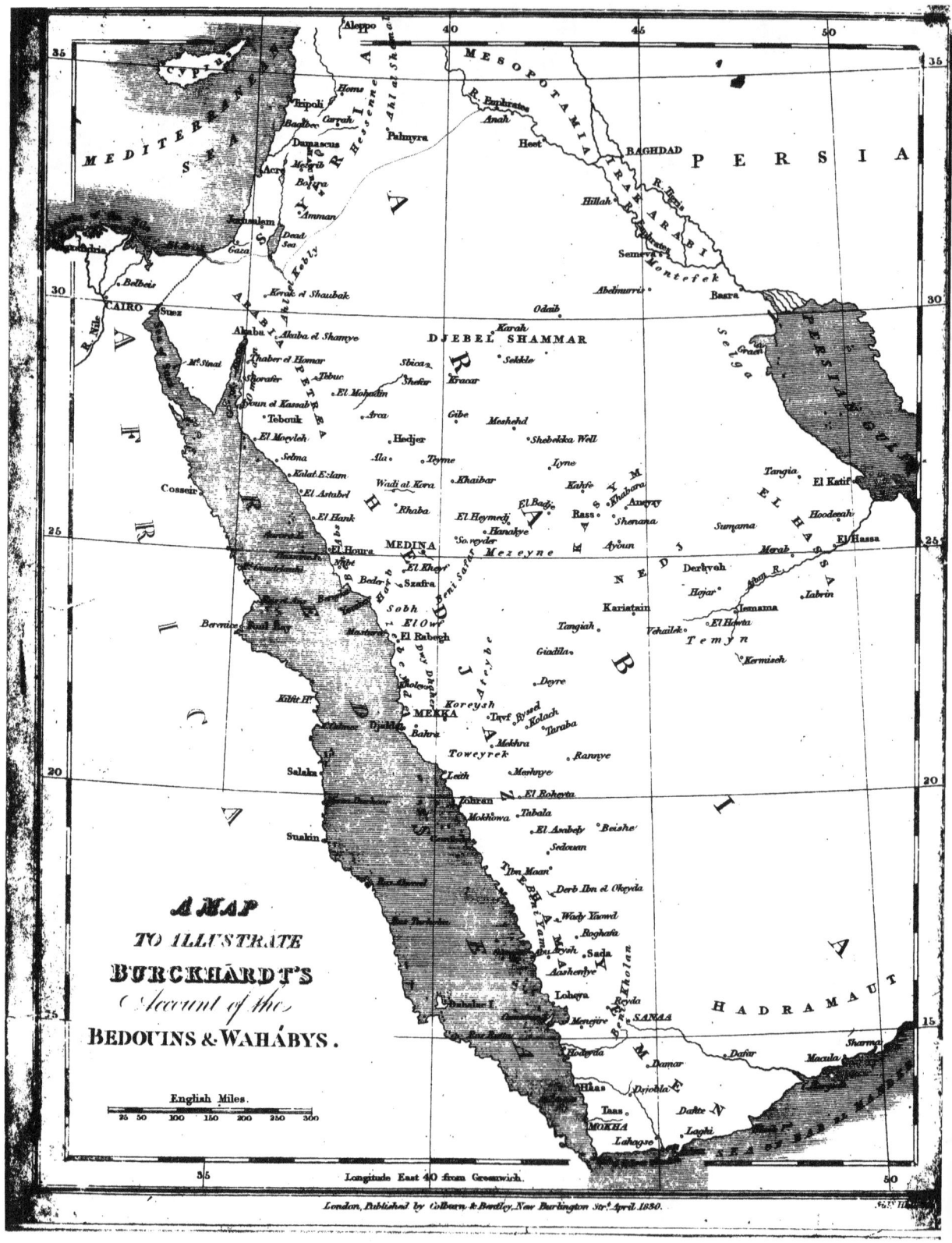

NOTES

ON THE

BEDOUINS AND WAHÁBYS,

COLLECTED

DURING HIS TRAVELS IN THE EAST,

BY THE LATE

JOHN LEWIS BURCKHARDT.

PUBLISHED BY AUTHORITY OF THE ASSOCIATION FOR PROMOTING
THE DISCOVERY OF THE INTERIOR OF AFRICA.

LONDON:
HENRY COLBURN AND RICHARD BENTLEY,
NEW BURLINGTON STREET.
1830.

PRINTED BY A. J. VALPY, RED LION COURT, FLEET STREET.

PREFACE.

To three volumes already published at different times, comprising the accounts of Burckhardt's Researches in Nubia, Syria, and Arabia, a fourth now succeeds, which will be found to contain, as was originally promised by Colonel Leake (the editor of the Nubian and Syrian Travels), "very copious remarks on the Arabs of the Desert, and particularly the Wahábys."[*]

This last-mentioned volume is here divided, after the author's own arrangement, into two parts, serving on many occasions for mutual illustration; yet each, in itself, forming a distinct and independent work; one part being merely descriptive, the other historical.

In the former we find not only an enumeration of the Bedouin tribes, and a statement of their various local establishments, numbers, and military force; but an account of their extraordi-

[*] Burckhardt's "Travels in Syria and the Holy Land." Pref. p. ii. 4to Edition, 1822.

nary customs, manners, and institutions; of their arts and sciences, dress, arms, and many other particulars relative to that interesting race of Arabs.

In the second portion of this volume, Burckhardt has compiled from such original information, both written and oral, as seemed on minute inquiry, most authentic, a history of those Mohammedan sectaries and fierce enthusiasts, the Wahábys; tracing them from their earliest appearance as reformers, in the last century, through all their wars with other Arabs and with the Turks, down to 1816, that year in which he returned from Arabia, the scene of action, to Egypt; where, not long after, a premature death terminated his literary career, and prevented the accomplishment of many important designs: his favourite object being to explore the interior and least-known regions of Africa.

In preparing this volume for publication, the editor must here declare, (as in his preface to Burckhardt's Arabia) that he has invariably adopted the plan of his ingenious friend, that accomplished scholar and antiquary, who superintended during their progress through the press, our lamented traveller's accounts of his Nubian and Syrian journies, in expressing with scrupulous fidelity the author's sentiments on all occasions, and in retaining, without any regard to mere elegance of style or selection of terms, his original language, wherever an alteration was not absolutely necessary to reconcile with our system of phraseology and grammatical construction, certain foreign idioms which had crept into his English writings.

The two works now offered, will sufficiently recommend themselves to readers of different tastes, by numerous anecdotes, curious and characteristic; but all must feel an interest in the account of those Arabs, respecting whom an eminent historian's words may here be quoted: "As the naked wilderness could not maintain a people of hunters, they rose at once to the more secure and plentiful condition of the pastoral life—the same life uniformly pursued by the roving tribes of the Desert; and in the portrait of the modern Bedoweens we may trace the features of their ancestors, who in the age of Moses or Mahomet dwelt under similar tents, and conducted their horses and camels and sheep to the same springs and the same pastures." (Gibbon's Roman Empire, chap. L.)

WILLIAM OUSELEY.

London, March 19, 1830.

CONTENTS.

ACCOUNT OF THE BEDOUIN TRIBES.

	PAGE
Classification of Bedouin Tribes that inhabit the Syrian Desert	1
Sketches.—Mode of Encamping	18
The Tent, and its different parts	21
Furniture of the Tent, and various Utensils	24
Bedouin Dress	26
Arms of the Bedouins	30
Diet of the Arabs	32
Arts and Industry	37
Wealth and Property of the Bedouins	39
Sciences, Music, and Poetry of the Bedouins	42
Feasts and Rejoicings	50
Diseases and Cures	52
Education	56
Religious Worship	57
Matrimony and Divorce	61
Government and Mode of Judicature	66
Warfare and Predatory Excursions	76
Blood-Revenge, or *Thár*	84
Robbery and Theft	89

CONTENTS.

	PAGE
Hospitality of the Arabs	100
Slaves and Servants	103
Moral Character of the Bedouins	104
Cattle of the Bedouins, and other Animals of the Desert	110
Vegetation of the Desert	126
Winds	127
Additional Observations.—Mode of Encamping	129
Dress of the Bedouins	131
Arms	134
Food and Cookery	135
Industry	138
The Arabs' Wealth	138
The Camel-driver's Song	146
Sciences, Music, Poetry, &c.	141
Feasts and Rejoicings	147
Diseases	148
Vaccination	148
Customs relative to Matrimony	149
Divorces of the Bedouins	154
Burial of the Bedouins	159
Religious Worship	160
Government	161
Warfare of the Bedouins	165
Blood-Revenge	177
Robbery and Thieving	184
The Traitor	186
Dakheil, or Protection	187
Hospitality	192
Domestic Relations	199
General Character of the Bedouins	203
Salutation	209
Language	211
Sagacity in Tracing of Footsteps; or *Athr*	212
General Reflections	214
Additions to the Classification of Tribes	217
Horses of Arabia	246
Camels	256
Locusts	268

MATERIALS FOR A HISTORY OF THE WAHÁBYS.

	PAGE
Introduction	273
Of Saoud's person and family	287
Wahaby Government	293
Administration of Justice	296
Revenues	304
Military Affairs of the Wahabys	311
Ghaleb, Sherif of Mekka, and the Turkish Pasha of Baghdád, at war with the Wahábys—The holy cities, Mekka and Medinah, taken by the Wahabys	321
Mohammed Aly, Pasha of Cairo, despatches his son, Tousoun Pasha, with a Turkish army to invade Arabia—Thomas Keith, a Scotchman, (Ibrahím Aga,) commander of Tousoun's Mammelouks—His intrepidity—Ahmed Aga, surnamed Bonaparte—Medinah taken by the Turks, and Mekka surrendered to them	342
Mohammed Aly Pasha proceeds from Egypt with an army of Turks—Arrives at Djidda and Mekka—Arrests Sherif Ghaleb, and sends him prisoner to Cairo—Ghaleb's troops assemble at Taraba	358
The Begoum Arabs headed by a woman, regarded as a sorceress by the Turks, who are defeated at Taraba—Mohammed Aly takes Gonfode—Discontent of the Turkish troops—Death of Saoud—His son Abdallah declared chief of the Wahabys	371
Distribution of the Turkish forces in Hedjaz—Massacre at Bahra—Mohammed Aly sends his son Tousoun Pasha to Medinah—The Turks defeated by the Wahabys in Zohrán—Mohammed Aly marches from Mekka towards Byssel—The Wahabys defeated there	383
Turks elated with victory—their cruelty—their distresses on the march from Beishe—Mohammed Aly returns to Mekka—Makes proposals of peace to Abdallah Ibn Saoud	401
Abdallah Ibn Saoud enters Kasym with an army—Negotiations between him and Tousoun Pasha—Peace concluded—Mohammed Aly returns to Cairo—Despatches his son, Ibrahím Pasha, with an army to renew the war in Hedjaz	412
Appendix, (comprising six articles)	423
Index of Arabic words	433

CORRIGENDA.

Page 46 for *Kouálek* read *Kouáleh,* قواله

50 after "warlike evolutions," insert يلعبو الطراد الخيل

224 for *Mowalle* read *Mowaze,* موازه

225   *Azayre*   *Azayze,* عزايزه

231   *Deyghám*   *Deygham,* ديغم

         Deyghámi   *Deyghami.*

267   *el fekeh*   *el fekek,* الفقق

ACCOUNT

OF

THE BEDOUIN TRIBES.

ACCOUNT

OF

THE BEDOUINS.

CLASSIFICATION OF BEDOUIN TRIBES THAT INHABIT THE SYRIAN DESERT.

THOSE tribes may be classed under two different heads: some who in spring and summer approach the cultivated parts of Syria, and quit them towards winter; and others who remain the whole year in the vicinity of the cultivated tracts. The first are the tribe of *Aeneze;* the latter are numerous tribes comprehended under the appellations of *Ahl el Shemál* and *Arab el Kebly*.

The *Aenezes* are the most powerful Arab nation in the vicinity of Syria, and, if we add to them their brethren in Nedjd, may be reckoned one of the most considerable bodies of Bedouins in the Arabian deserts. The Aenezes who live in the northern part of Arabia, generally take up their winter quarters in the *Hammad* desert, or the plain between the *Hauran* and *Heet*, a position on the Euphrates. The Hammad is without any springs; but in winter time the water collects there in deep grounds, and the shrubs and plants of the desert afford pasture to the Arab's cattle. The Aenezes have likewise been known to pass the Euphrates and encamp in Irak Arabi, and near Baghdad. In spring they approach the frontiers of Syria, and form a line of encampment extending from near Aleppo to eight days' journey to the south of Damascus. Their principal residence, however, during that time is the Hauran and its neighbourhood, where they encamp near and among the villages; while in the more northern country, towards Homs and Hamah, they mostly keep at a certain distance from the inhabited grounds. In these parts they spend the whole summer seeking pasture and water, purchase in autumn their winter provision of wheat and barley, and return after the first rains into the interior of the desert.

Their great strength has enabled them to levy a yearly tribute on most of the villages near the eastern limits of Syria. It is above fifteen years since all the Aenezes have been converted to the Wahaby faith. The profits which they derived from the pilgrim caravans to Mekka, have until now kept them on good terms with the Turkish governors, and even induced them to withhold the customary tribute paid to the Wahaby chief. But it is to be presumed, that if the Hadj do not soon regain its ancient splendour, they will again become tributary to the Wahaby, and in company with him, hereafter, lay waste the open country of Syria. The northern Aenezes, of whom alone I speak here, are divided into four principal bodies: *Would Aly, el Hessenne, el Raualla,* and *el Besher.*

I. *Would Aly.* These generally have their winter quarters on the Hadj road as far as Kalaat Zerka. Their sheikh is named *el Teyar:* he occupies the first rank among their chiefs, and is therefore styled *Abou el Aeneze,* or "Father of the Aenezes." The *Would Aly* are subdivided into five tribes.

1. *El Meshadeká*, comprising the *Arab el Teyár*, the great sheikh's own tribe, *el Merreykhat, el Lahhawein*.

2. *El Meshattá*, whose sheikh, *Dhouhy Ibn Esmeyr*, is at this moment the most powerful of the Aeneze chiefs, although inferior to the *Teyár* in rank. He derives his influence from an intimate connexion with the Pasha of Damascus, to whom he was in the habit of furnishing every year a vast number of camels for the pilgrim caravan. He seldom encamps, even in winter time, farther than eight or ten days' journey from Damascus. In his tent Yusuf Páshá took refuge after his flight from Damascus in 1810.

The larger tribes of the *Meshattá* are, *el Auadh*, wholly composed of the large family and relations of the Esmeyrs; *el Teyour, el Ateyfat, el Mekeybel*.

3. *El Hammamede*,—principally on the Mekka road, as far as Maan. They have two chiefs, originally of the same family, *Salem el Edda* and *Embarek el Edda*.

4. *El Djedaleme*, comprising two principal tribes, *el Kereynat* and *el Tourshat*, all at present following the fortunes of Ibn Esmeyr.

5. *El Tolouhh*. All the chief tribes of Would Aly are entitled to the *Szourra* or tribute from the hadjis or pilgrims on their passage through the desert; the amount is noted in the account-books of the Pasha of Damascus, or the *Emír el Hadj*, and in those of the *Kheznedar* (or treasurer) at Constantinople: but the Szourra increases on every passage as the Pasha pleases to tax the different skeikhs; a privilege he freely indulges for his own profit, bargaining with the Arabs for horses, camels, and sheep. The Toulouhh are the only tribe that receive their *szourra* at once from Constantinople.

II. *El Hessenne*—not so numerous as the other three great tribes of the Aeneze; they consist of two considerable tribes.

1. *El Hessenne*, properly so called: their sheikh, *Mehanna*,

usually encamps in the desert eastward of the route from Damascus to Homs; the Hessenne are proverbial for bravery, generosity, and hospitality. Their tribes are, *el Shemsy*, the noblest of the Hessenne, (a Shemsy Arab is said to possess all the virtues of a Nomade,) *el Keddaba, el Aueymer, el Refáshe, el Meheynat, el Hedjadj, el Sheraabe.*

2. *El Messaliekh*, who follow the banners of Mehanna, and are generally regarded as mercenaries, and who, though superior in numbers to the Hessenne, join them in all their expeditions only to partake of the chief's liberality. Their tribes are, *el Lehhetemy, Beni Reshoud*, called also *Beni Taleyhan, el Belsán,* and *el Semmelek.*

The *el Hessenne* are said to have once formed but a single tribe; they then divided under two brothers. Both the Hessenne and the Messaliekh take a tribute from the Basra and Baghdad caravan, which passes the desert on its way to Aleppo or Damascus; it amounts to about three shillings per camel load: they likewise take tribute from the villages on that road.

III. *El Raualla*—also called *el Djelaes*—a powerful tribe possessing more horses than any other of the Aeneze. In 1809 they defeated a body of six thousand men sent against them by the Pasha of Baghdad. They generally occupy the desert from Djebel Shammar towards the Djof, and thence towards the southern vicinity of the Hauran; but they frequently encamp between the Tigris and Euphrates. Like the other Aenezes, they had for many years refused the customary tribute to the Wahaby chief whose religion they had embraced: their courageous opposition to the Pasha of Baghdad caused a reconciliation between them and Ibn Saoud. In July 1810 they accompanied the Wahabys into the Hauran, and led Ibn Saoud to the most wealthy villages. The Raualla every spring pay a visit to the tribe of Ibn Esmeyr, to obtain, through his interference, permission from the Pasha that they may purchase in his territory wheat and barley. The Djelaes are not entitled either to the szourra from the Hadj, or to any tribute from the Baghdad and Basra caravans. Their principal tribes are, *el Souáleme, el Abdelle, Ferdja, el Belaaysh, el Bedour, Ibn Auydje, el Zerák, Sahhan, Hedjlis, Deraye.*

IV. *El Besher*, the most numerous of the Aeneze tribes. Their great chief is *Ibn Haddál*, who encamps with his tribe in the Nedjd, where most of the Besher tribe have taken up their abode. Ibn Haddál is at the same time one of the principal men at the court of Derayeh, if so may be styled the seat of Ibn Saoud. The Besher about fifty years ago began to claim passage-money from the Baghdad and Basra caravans; the Hessenne had received such toll from time immemorial. The Besher are divided into the following powerful tribes—*el Fedhaan, Ibn Imhyd, Ibn Ghebein,* (who conducted me to Palmyra in 1810), *Ibn Kay Shysh, Ibn Ghedhzour, el Zebaa.* In my way from Hamah to Tedmor, I found all the watering-places occupied by Arabs of this tribe: the greater part of them are in Nedjd; *el Mauaydje, el Metarcfe,* whose brethren are likewise in Nedjd; *el Seleymát, el Hossenny,* (not to be mistaken for the Hessenne,) *el Medheyán.* Thus far extends my knowledge of the greater *Aeneze* tribes. To detail all their minor branches or *towayefs*, would be to give an index of all their families, every large family with its relations constituting a small tribe in itself. It is difficult to ascertain the numbers of each tribe, from a prejudice which forbids them to count the horsemen, as they believe, like the eastern merchants, that whoever knows the exact amount of his wealth may soon expect to lose part of it. From some Damascus pedlars, who had passed their whole lives among the Bedouins, I learned particulars which induce me to state the force of the Aeneze tribes above mentioned, (their brethren in Nedjd not included,) at about ten thousand horsemen, and perhaps ninety or one hundred thousand camel-riders; a number rather over than under rated. The whole northern Aeneze nation may be estimated at from three hundred to three hundred and fifty thousand souls, spread over a country of at least forty thousand square miles.

Ahl el Shemál.

The Arabs so called, or the " Northern Nations," are those tribes who encamp during the whole year among the villages of Eastern Syria, partly in the once cultivated desert from Hauran towards Palmyra northward as far as Sokhne, a village five days from Aleppo on the Baghdad road. They inhabit the *Ardh el Shemál* or northern tract, while the Kebly and Nedjd Arabs generally reside in the more southern plains of Arabia. They never venture to the great Eastern desert. In proportion to their tents they have more horses, but fewer camels, than the Aenezes. Beginning from the north we may reckon,

1. The tribe of *el Maualy*, near Aleppo and Hamah: their emir or sheikh receives an annual sum from the governor of Aleppo, for which he protects the villages of the Pashalik against the other Arab tribes. They have about four hundred horsemen; they are reckoned treacherous and faithless. The father of their present chief, Mohammed el Khorfan, (whom Volney represents as a chieftain of thirty thousand horsemen, a number exceeding the amount of Arab cavalry between Syria and Baghdad,) treacherously murdered in his own tents, at a convivial feast, above two hundred Aeneze guests, that he might get possession of their mares. Of Maualy extraction, but now independent of them, are *el Turky, el Djemdjeme, el Akeydát*. The smaller tribes of *el Hadheyfa* and *el Medaheish* generally follow the Maualys, though not descended from them. Part of the *Akeydát* have become peasants, and cultivate the land about *Deir*, the ancient Thapsacus, on the Euphrates;

others of the same tribe encamp near Baalbec; and a third portion in the Djebel Heish, south-west of Damascus.

2. *El Hadedyein*, often at war with the Maualys, near whom they reside: in horsemen they equal that tribe, and are mostly armed with muskets: they breed great numbers of asses. Their women are celebrated for the fairness of their skin. In skirmishes between them and the Maualys, the vanquished party often seeks refuge among the garden walls of Aleppo. *El Seken*, a tribe of about six hundred tents, who cultivate part of the Djebel Hass, east and south-eastward of Aleppo. *El Berak* and *el Medjel* are of a Kourdy or Turkman origin; they rove about between Aintab and the Euphrates.

3. *El Turkman*. Several nomade tribes of Turkman origin wander about Hamah and Homs.

4. *El Arab Tahht Hammel Hamah*, or the Arabs who pay tribute to the Mutsellim of Hamah, an officer under the Pasha of Damascus: the tribute consists in sheep and butter, and some camels which they are obliged to furnish at a low price for the transport of the Hadj. These Arab tribes are *Beni Khâled*,—a branch of these reside in the neighbourhood of Basra,—*Beshakyn, Tokán, Abou Shaebán, Hauaeiroun, el Abou Azy, Beni Az, el Retoub, el Shekara, Ghanamat el Tel, el Kharashyein, el Rezeik, el Hadadeyn, el Turky, el Djemadjeme,* (see above,) part of the three last-mentioned tribes. The Beni Khaled have between two and three hundred tents, the others only from fifty to one hundred tents each.

5. The Arabs in the district of Baalbec, on the plain, about twenty hours northward towards Homs: they pay tribute of fifteen or twenty pounds of butter per tent, to the Emir of Baalbec, for their summer pasture in his territory. They are *el Turkmán Soueydieh*, who encamp likewise on the *Djourd el Sherky* or Anti-Libanon, belonging to the territory of Baalbec, a mountain re-

puted excellent for pasture. A few tents of *el Keydát, el Abeid*, chiefly near Harmel, between el Kaa and Homs: they date their origin from a black slave of the Harfoush, (the reigning Metaualy family of Baalbec,) who was emancipated and adopted the nomadic life; they have above eighty tents. *El Harb*, of the *Naym* (see below).

6. The Arabs in the fertile valley of Bekaa or Cœle Syria, where they pasture their cattle in summer only, paying tribute to the Emir Besheir, the chief of the Druses. Part of the *Faddhel* (see below), whose principal seat is in the Kanneitera, and *Djebel Heish*. Part of the *Naym*, in the same place as the former. *El Nemeyrát*, whose winter-quarters are in the district of *Szafad; el Zereykát*. To these may be added the Arabs *el Háib*, a small tribe who in winter pasture their cattle near the seashore between Jebail and Tartous. Some families of the Háib remain up in the mountains even during the winter months; their tents being pitched near the villages of Akoura or Temerin. In summer time the Háib ascend Mount Libanus, where I found them encamped, with their cattle, in September 1810, on the Ardh Lahlouh between Besherray and Akoura, near the highest summits of the mountain: besides camels, sheep, and goats, they breed cows, pay tribute to Tripoly, and are reputed to be great thieves.

7. *El Szoleyb*, a tribe of Ahl el Shemál, living dispersed among all the neighbouring tribes of Aeneze, as well as of the Arabs el Shemál, and on friendly terms with all, because they are poor: they possess neither horses, camels, sheep, nor scarcely tents. For separate families they construct miserable huts. Sometimes twenty or thirty families together shelter themselves from inclement weather in one large wretched tent. Their only property consists of a few asses, some cooking utensils, and a gun; their only means of subsistence, hunting and shooting. Men, women,

and children are clothed in gazelle skins, of which they likewise make the bags necessary for carrying their furniture. They go about as beggars among the Arabs, and with whatever alms they get, purchase powder and shot. The dried flesh of the gazelle is their food during the whole year.

8. *Ahl el Djebel*—the "Tribes of the Mountain."—So are called those Arabs who inhabit the mountains from Homs towards Tedmor, or Palmyra. There are two principal chains, *Djebel Abiadh*, and *Djebel Rouak*; both meet at Tedmor. These Arabs receive tribute from the villages of Ardh al Shemál, but on the other hand pay an annual tribute to the Aeneze tribe of El Hessenne. Their chief tribes are the *Amour*; forty or fifty of their tents are generally pitched among the huts of the peasants of Tedmor; and they have an excellent breed of horses.

Proceeding southwards, we find many Arab tribes dwelling in the territory of Damascus, principally about the country of Hauran. These tribes may be reckoned amongst the Ahl el Shemál; at least, the Aenezes include them within the number of the latter; but the Syrians regard them as occupying an intermediate station, between the Arabs El Shemál, and the Arabs El Kebly. Beginning with those Arab tribes who are tributary to the Pasha of Damascus, we may class them under four heads :—

1. *Arabs of the Hauran.*— *El Feheily*—about two hundred horsemen. The Pasha of Damascus invests their sheikh annually with a pelisse, and employs him to collect the tribute from all the Arabs of Djebel Hauran, and the district called Ledja. In return the Pasha expects a present of fifteen or twenty purses. The Feheilys receive an annual tribute from all the Hauran villages. They sometimes withhold the present from the Pasha, and are frequently at war with the governor of Hauran.

El Serdye.—Divided into two tribes, Arab *el Dháher*, and Arab *el Wáked*, each having two sheikhs. The Serdye have about one hundred and fifty horsemen, and an excellent breed of mares. The Pasha of Damascus presents to one of their chiefs every year a suit of clothes and arms, and receives in return a mare. The chief so honoured is then styled *Sheikh el Hauran,* and assists the Pasha's troops against any hostile invaders on the Hauran territory; but like the Feheilys, they are frequently at war with the Pasha, and receive a tribute from all the Hauran villages, sometimes twice as much as that taken by the Feheilys.

Ahl Djebel Hauran—several tribes, who live in peace with all their neighbours, and never forget their allegiance to the Pasha of Damascus. They never quit the mountain, but change their abode in search of pasture: they are the shepherds to the Hauran peasants, whose flocks of sheep and goats they pasture among the rocks of the mountain. In spring they send the flocks back to their owners, who retain them for three months in the villages in order to milk them, and make butter, and sell the young ones at Damascus. For their trouble, these Arabs receive one-fourth of the young breed, and the same portion of the butter. They carry charcoal to Damascus. Among them are *el Shenabele, el Hassan, el Haddye, el Sherfát, el Mezayd, Beni Adham, el Szammárát, el Kerád,* or the Kourds, who are an Arab tribe of Kourd origin. They have forgotten their national language, and have become Arabs in every respect. *El Raufae, el Gheiáth*—these are comprehended among the Ahl Djebel Hauran, although they seldom encamp upon that mountain. Their usual abode is in the country of *el Szafa,* one day and a half distant from the Djebel Hauran; the difficult approach to which enables them to defy the Pasha of Damascus, or the united Arab tribes. Szafa is a rocky level territory with excellent pasture land; the Gheiáth have about eighty horses. These tribes possess from eighty to one hundred tents each. The Shenabele are the most numerous.

2. *Arab el Ledja.* These wander about in the rocky but level country called *Ledja* at the N.W. foot of Djebel Hauran, extending one day's journey in breadth, and from two to three in length, and full of recesses equally difficult to be forced as those of Szafa. This circumstance often induces the Arabs to withhold their tribute from the Pasha, and causes a war, on which they sally forth and plunder the villages of Hauran; but, from the want of springs in their country, they are obliged to make peace towards the approach of summer. They pay, as tribute, (collected by the Feheilys) from ten to sixty piastres per tent, according to the wealth of the owners. Their chief tribes are—*el Szolout* and *el Medledj,* the two principal, having each about one hundred and fifty tents—*el Selmán, el Dhoueyhere, el Seyále*—their strength in horsemen amounting altogether to about sixty or eighty; but there is no tent without its firelock. These Arabs sell charcoal to the peasants of Hauran.

3. The Arabs of *Djolán.* This is a province extending from about eight hours' distance from Damascus, as far as three days' journey on a S.S.E. direction; its breadth is about ten hours. The Pasha of Damascus appoints an officer called *Hakim ed Djolán* to collect the *Miri* tax from the peasants, and the tribute from the Arabs. The tribes encamping on the plain of Djolán are—*el Dyáb, el Naym, el Woussie,* and *el Menádhere,* who live on the banks of the *Wady Hamy Sakar,* a torrent coming from Hauran, and changing its name into *Shereat el Mandhour* on its approach to the Dead Sea. Some of these Arabs are stationary, but continue to live in tents. On the banks of the river they cultivate fruit gardens, the produce of which is purchased by pedlars, and sold throughout the Hauran. *Beni Keláb,* called also *el Kelabát,* or *el Makloub,* in the S. of Djolán.

4. The Arabs of *Kanneitera* or of *Djebel Heish*. Kanneitera is a small village with a khan, two days from Damascus, in a S.W. direction, in the midst of a mountain called *Heish el Kanneitera*, (meaning the "Forest of Kanneitera," or simply *Heish*, a mountain) which extends from the foot of Djebel el Sheikh, under various denominations to the S.E. extremity of the Dead Sea, where it joins the mountains of Arabia Petræa. The Arabs inhabit the mountain to the distance of about four days S.W. of Damascus, and descend likewise on the mountain's western side into the plains N.E. of the lake Samachonitis, called by them *el Houle*, where some of their tribes are always to be found. An officer of the Pasha, the Aga el Kanneitera, collects the annual tribute from the Arabs, generally paid in kind, and deposited in the castle of Mezerib. All these Arabs live in uninterrupted peace. Their tribes are—

El Faddhel, whose sheikh (Ibn Hassan) takes the title of Emír. They chiefly reside in the Heish. I have already mentioned them amongst the Bekaa and Djolán Arabs. They have from two hundred and fifty to three hundred tents. They furnish Damascus with milk, sheep, and charcoal from the oak-trees which abound in the Heish. Their minor tribes are *el Herouk* and *el Adjremye*.

El Naym, a very powerful tribe of Arabs. Like the Faddhel, who occupy the same tract with them, they supply to the city of Damascus milk, *leben* (a kind of sour milk), butter and cheese, and charcoal. They regularly pay their tribute to the Pasha. Some cultivate ground in different parts of the mountain, others are nomades. They have few horses, but great numbers of sheep, which they sell at Damascus and in the mountain of the Druses and Libanus, during their summer residence in the Bekaa. The Naym have from four to five hundred tents; one of their minor tribes is called *el Harb*.

El Woussie. Some of these cultivate rice and dourra in the mountain, but live in tents and change their abode after every harvest. They have camels, sheep, and cows; and some, who live in Houle, breed buffaloes. They are divided into two tribes, *el Hamáse*, and *el Bakára*.

El Shouáya, el Dyáb, el Kebáere, el Djaatein, Beni Rabya, el Mehammedát, el Turkmán, who have a settlement of about one hundred and sixty tents in the Heish. They continue to speak Turkish, and few even understand Arabic. Their two small tribes are *el Nahayát* and *el Souadye*, so named, because all their sheep are black.

Beni Az, el Laheib, el Semake—so named, because they seldom quit the shores of Lake Houle, where they exercise the profession of fishermen,—*El Berkeyát, el Atbe, el Waheib, el Zegherye, el Seyád, el Azzye, el Aby Heya, el Daheywát, el Arakye, el Sherázyl, el Shám*. Most of these tribes possess from forty to sixty tents each. The *Dyab, Arakye*, and *Beni Az*, have each about one hundred tents. They all live on good terms with each other, and are in constant intercourse with Damascus; like the Bekaas they are styled *Arab ettaw*, or "subjected Arabs." Before I proceed to mention these subjected Arabs, it will be necessary to notice three tribes of free Arabs who generally encamp southward of the province Djolán; they are the *Beni Szakhr, el Serhhán*, and *Beni Ayssa*.

The *Beni Szakhr* rove on the plain from the fourth to the eighth station of the Hadj, and thence westward towards the mountain of *Belkaa*, a continuation of Djebel Heish; they also encamp in the Hauran. They do not pay tribute to the Pasha, but are much dreaded by his troops, the *Szokhouri* (plural of *Szakhr*) being celebrated for their bravery: they plundered the pilgrim caravan in 1755. Their manly persons, broad features, and thick beards, are no proofs of Bedouin origin; yet they pride themselves on being the only descendants of the *Beni Abs*, an ancient *Nedjd* tribe, famous in Bedouin history. They are almost constantly at war with the Aenezes, who approach their habitation in summer. The Arabic dialect of the Beni Szakhr has still more of a chanting expression than that of the Aenezes. Their force consists in about five hundred horsemen; they are divided into two tribes: 1. *El Tauwakka*, whose minor branches are *el Hakysh* and *el Bersán, Beni Zeyn* and *Beni Zeydán*. 2. *El Kaabene*, whose minor tribe is the *Beni Zeheyr*.

El Serhhán, or *el Serrahein* (both being plural). These generally encamp near the *Beni Szakhr*, with whom they live on good terms, and unite with them against the Aenezes. Two centuries ago, the Serhhán were masters of the whole Hauran; but the Serdye drove them into the desert as far as Djof, where they remained almost starving with their cattle for twenty years: they then returned and joined Beni Szakhr. Their force consists in about three hundred and fifty horsemen. They are reproached for a merely outward observance of the fast Ramadhán. Their women are celebrated for their fair complexions. The origin of this tribe is derived from Mesopotamia; they are divided into the tribes called *Ibn Ramle, Ibn Rafae, Ibn el Baly*, and the *Hebeyley*.

Beni Ayssa, equal in force to the Serhhán; like them, friends of the Szakhr and enemies of the Aenezes, they exact tribute from the Baghdad and Basra caravans.

Arabs of the Mountain Belkaa.

The Djebel Heish assumes the name of *Djebel Belkau* at five days S.S.W. of Damascus, to the W. of Fedhein, a village on the Hadj road. Here these Arabs reside, extending their camps as far as Kerak el Shaubak, on the S.E. corner of the Dead Sea, and descending on the west side of the mountain into the plains near that lake. They comprise above forty small tribes, amounting in all to between three and four thousand tents. Their common origin is from the tribe *Heteym*. Their great sheikh pays an annual tribute of two thousand sheep to the Pasha of Damascus; his allegiance however is very precarious: they take cattle for sale to Jerusalem; many have become cultivators, but continue to live in tents. Their principal tribes are *Beni Hassan* and *Ibn al Ghanam*, (the two most numerous,) *el Hatabye, el Abád, el Adjreme, el Bedeyát, el Djehawashe, el Auawathem, el Sheyrat, el Zefeyfa, el Resheyde, el Dadje, el Billy, el Khanatele*, and *el Meshalekha*.

Diverging from Belkaa towards the west, we find in the plains about the Dead Sea and the lake of Tabareya, many considerable tribes comprehended under the name of Arabs of the *Ghour* (all marshy ground being called *Ghour*). These are divided, according to their places of abode, into four classes.

The Ghour Arabs of *Tabareya*: of these are *el Sekhour*, (not to be confounded with Beni *Szakhr*, who in the plural are called *el Szekhour*,) *el Faut, el Bashatoue*.

The Ghour Arabs of *Beisán*, who have *el Ghezawaye, el Bauwatein*, and *Beni Fád*.

The Ghour Arabs of Jerusalem, (or *el Kodes*,) meaning those who live between the Dead Sea and Jerusalem. Their chief tribe is the *Mesoudy*, whose sheikh is styled *Emír el Kodes*, they levy considerable tribute from the Christian pilgrims going to Jericho and the Dead Sea.

The Ghour Arabs of *Rieha*: their tribes are *el Djermye*, and *el Tamere*. Many of the Ghour Arabs cultivate ground, and breed buffaloes, sell all their cattle at the Jerusalem market, and pay tribute to the Mutsellim of that place.

Returning from the west towards the southern parts of the Dead Sea, we find an Arab tribe encamped near Hebron (or, as the natives call it, *el Khalíl*). This tribe is named *el Djehalein*;

they cultivate land but reside in tents, have few horses but many firelocks.

Ahl el Kebly.

The following tribes are called *Ahl el Kebly,* or southern nations, in opposition to the northern, or *Ahl el Shemál.* To the south of the Belkaa tribes live the Arabs *el Kerak,* so named from the village of *Kerak el Shaubak,* near which they reside. This village has a castle on a mountain over the Dead Sea, at its S.E. corner, the ancient Nebo. (See the Book of Deuteronomy, ch. xxxiv. vs. 1.) The inhabitants of Kerak themselves, about six hundred Christians and as many Turks, are a kind of nomades, leaving their houses in summer, and wandering about with their families and cattle in search of pasture and watering-places. The Turks of Kerak are Wahabys; the Christians pay a yearly tribute to the Wahaby government. The Arab tribes of Kerak are *el Ammer*—they can muster about three hundred horsemen, and claim a *szourra* from the Hadj pilgrims; they frequently intermarry with the people of Kerak—*el Szoleyt*—about eighty horsemen and two hundred firelocks; they have but few camels—*Beni Hammeyde,* who cultivate the desert in many places.

To the S. of Kerak, the mountain once more changes its name and is called *Djebel Sherá,* the side branches of which extend towards Gaza. The mountain is peopled by the Arabs *el Hedjadje,* who are about four hundred horsemen strong. The peasants also cultivate grounds in the valley of the *Wady el Hassa,* a torrent that runs into the Dead Sea; and they pay as tribute to these Arabs half the produce of their fields. *Beni Naym* in the *Maan* district, the ninth station on the pilgrim road to Mekka.

El Haueytat, in the district of *Akabe el Shamye,* or Syrian

Akabe, which is the tenth pilgrim station from Damascus, situated at one day and a half's journey from *Akabe el Masry*, or the Egyptian Akabe, on the eastern branch of the Red Sea. They are about three hundred horsemen, but can furnish a large body of armed camel-drivers. They keep up a constant intercourse with Cairo. A caravan of more than four thousand camels every year sets out from these Arabs for Cairo, where they purchase wheat, barley, and articles of dress: this caravan is called *Kheleit*. In seasons of drought the Haueytat approach Gaza or Hebron. Of ten or twelve tribes, the principal are, *el Omrán, el Djásy, el Mesk,* and *el Resay*.

El Sherárát, in the sandy plain S. of the Akabe el Shamye and eastward of the Hadj route. Their numbers are considerable, and all are Wahabys. They have few horses, but innumerable camels; and most of them carry firelocks: they live on good terms with their neighbours; parties of them go every year into the Hauran and towards Gaza to sell camels and purchase wheat. They pay tribute to all the Aeneze tribes and several of the Kebly and Shemál Arabs. The Beni Szakhr take from the owner of each tent that passes, three piastres; el Teyar take one dollar. Among their numerous tribes are *el Kheyál, el Lehawy,* and *Beni Haueyny*.

South of the Sherárát on the E. of the Hadj road, as far as the vicinity of Mekka, the whole country is inhabited by Aenezes.

In the midst of the eastern desert, at twenty-five days from Damascus in the direction of Derayeh, the chief seat of the Wahabys, a chain of mountains running from W. to E. is called *Djebel Shammar*, where the powerful tribe Beni Shammar reside; these are mortal enemies of the Aenezes. Some of their tribe live in Irak Arabi, and are called there *el Djerba*, who, with the *Dhofyr*, are the most powerful tribes in the neighbourhood of Baghdad, and make frequent plundering incursions into the

Hauran. Of the Beni Shammar, some tribes are the following: *el Temeyát, el Menyát, Ibn Gházy, Bayr,* and *el Fesyany.*

Here may be named the principal tribes of Arabs who inhabit the banks of the Euphrates from *el Biri* down to *Anah.* The country on the right bank of the river between these two places is called *el Zor,* and the following are the *el Zor* Arabs: *el Akeydát, Abou Shaebán, Beni Sayd, el Woulde,* (this is the largest tribe, and divided into *Arabel Fahhel,* and *Arab el Dendel,*) *el Sabkha, el Bakara, el Djebour,* and *el Deleyb.* Many of these Arabs cultivate land, but live in tents; they pay tribute to all the chief Aeneze tribes, and furnish Aleppo with milk, butter, and cheese.

SKETCHES.

The following sketches relate exclusively to the Aenezes; these are the only true Bedouin nation of Syria, while the other Arab tribes in the neighbourhood of this country have, more or less, degenerated in manners; several being reduced to subjection, while the free-born Aeneze is still governed by the same laws that spread over the Desert at the beginning of the Mohammedan era.

Mode of Encamping.

The Aenezes are nomades in the strictest acceptation of the word, for they continue during the whole year in almost constant motion. Their summer quarters are near the Syrian frontiers, and in winter they retire into the heart of the desert, or towards the Euphrates. In summer they encamp close to rivulets and springs which abound near the Syrian desert, but they seldom remain above three or four days in the same spot: as soon as their cattle have consumed the herbage near a watering-place, the tribe removes in search of pasture, and the grass again springing up serves for a succeeding camp. The encampments vary in number of tents, from ten to eight hundred: when the tents are but few, they are pitched in a circle, and then called *dowár*; but more considerable numbers in a straight line, or a row of single tents, especially along a rivulet, sometimes three or four behind as many others. Such encampments are called *nezel*. In winter when water and pasture never fail, the mode of encamping is different. The whole tribe then spreads itself over the plain in parties of three or four tents each, with an interval of half an hour's distance between each party: to encamp thus, is called *fereik*. In the *dowár*, as in the *nezel*, the sheikh's or chief's tent is always on the western side; for it is from the west, that the Syrian Arabs expect their enemies as well as their guests. To oppose the former, and to honour the latter, is the sheikh's principal business; and as it is usual for a guest to alight at the first tent that presents itself in the camp, the sheikh's ought to be on the side from which most strangers arrive: it is even disgraceful that a wealthy man should pitch his tent on the eastern side.*

Every father of a family sticks his lance into the ground by the side of his tent, and in front ties his horse or mare (should he possess one); there also his camels repose at night. The sheep and goats remain day and night under a shepherd's care, who every evening drives them home.

When I was returning from Tedmor towards Damascus, I met, on the same day, two strong encampments moving slowly over

---

* The great nations among the Arabs are styled *Kabeile*, as the *Kabeile Would Aly*, &c. The branches of the Kabeile are styled *Fende*, as *Fende el Mesálikh*. The smaller tribes collected from various others, and from foreigners, are called *Asheire*, as *Asheire el Naym*. The Aeneze would think themselves degraded if their tribe were called Asheire. By the word *Tayfe* is expressed all those families of a tribe who can trace their origin to one common ancestor: they sometimes comprehend many hundred tents, sometimes but two or three. All Arab tribes are styled *Beni*, but this term is often lost under a more recent appellation; that is, every tribe derives its origin from one great-grandfather: thus amongst the Aenezes the Mesálikh, el Hessenne, and Would Aly, are all three of *Beni Waheb*, although never so entitled.

the sandy plain in search of water and pasture: their order of march was as follows. A party of five or six horsemen preceded the tribe about four miles, as a reconnoitring detachment (or *sulf*): the main body occupied a line of at least three miles in front. First came some armed horsemen and camel-riders, at a hundred or a hundred and fifty paces from each other, extending along the whole front; then followed the she-camels with their young ones, grazing in wide ranks during their march upon the wild herbage: behind walked the camels loaded with the tents and provisions; and the last were the women and children, mounted on camels having saddles made in the shape of a cradle, with curtains to screen them from the sun. The men indiscriminately rode along and amidst the whole body, but most of them in front of the line; some led horses by their halters: in depth their wandering bodies extended about two miles and a half. I had seen them encamped when on my way to Tedmor, and then estimated one at about two hundred, and the other at two hundred and fifty tents; the latter had above three thousand camels. Of all the Arabs I did not see one on foot, except a few shepherds, who drove the sheep and goats, about a mile behind the main body.

On a march the loaded camels belonging to one tent are called collectively *medhhour* or *dhaan;* and plurally, (meaning the whole marching body,) *medhaher* or *dhaoun*.

The expression for "pitching the tent" is *benoua al beiout* (they have built the houses); for "breaking up the tents," *heddoua el beiout*, or *terhhoua el beiout*: "they have broken up and are gone," *heddoua wa meddoua*. A flying camp of armed Arabs upon an expedition, whether mounted on horses or camels, they call *ghazou*. "The ghazou has encamped," *nowwakh el ghazou;* "the ghazou has broken up," *towwahh el ghazou*: but these expressions are unknown to the inhabitants of Syria who have no connexion with Bedouins.

The Tent, and its different parts.

The tent is denominated *beit* or house, never *kheime*, which is the common Syrian term. The covering of a tent, *zhaher el beit*, consists of pieces of stuff made of black goat's-hair, about three quarters of a yard in breadth, its length being equal to that of the tent; according to the depth of the tent, ten or more of these pieces (called *shauke*) are stitched together: this goat's-hair covering keeps off the heaviest rain, as I know from experience. The tent-poles are called *amúd*, or columns. It is usual to have nine poles or posts, three in the middle and an equal number on each side of the tent: of the three middle poles, the first or nearest to those who enter the tent, is called *makdoum*, that in the middle *wáset*, and the hindmost *dáfae*. Of the three side posts in the men's apartments to the left (of those entering the tent), the first is called *yed* or "hand," as likewise the hindmost; the middle one *kásere*. That these poles may be more firm when stuck into the covering of the tent, pieces of old *abbas* or woollen cloaks are stitched to the eight corners where the poles are to be fastened; these pieces are called *koum el beit*. The lower end of them is twisted about a short stick, to both extremities of which a leather string is tied called *kheroub*; each post has its *kheroub*, except the middle one (or *wáset*); and to these strings are fastened the ropes which secure the covering of the tent.

That the pieces of goat's-hair stuff of which the tent is composed may not be torn whenever the middle posts are forcibly drawn out, it is thought necessary to sew inside a narrow piece of the same stuff across the covering of the tent along the row of middle posts, which piece is called *matrek* or *sefife*. Its extremities are sewn to the *kheroub* of the *makdoum*, and the *dafae*. The back part of the tent is closed by the *rowák*, a piece of goat's-hair stuff from three to four feet high, to which a portion of some old cloak or *abba* is stitched (called *sefále*), and hangs down to the ground. The rowák and sefále keep out the wind; the rowák is fastened to the tent-covering by the three hind posts, and in winter is carried likewise round the side posts; along the back of the tent-covering runs a string (*mereis*) with many iron hooks (*khelle*), all or any of which may be fixed in the rowák, or taken out at pleasure, to admit or exclude air at the back of the tent. The ropes which are fastened to the eight kheroub are called *tenb* or *atenáb el beit*: the short sticks, to which the other ends of these ropes are fastened, are driven into the ground at three or four paces distant from the tent; these sticks or pins are called *wed* or *aoutád*: the middle post is bifurcated at the top, which fits into a short round stick (*kabs*), about which the *shaukes* are sewn and the *sefife* is drawn.

The tent is divided into two parts; the men's apartment, (*mekaad rabiaa*) and the women's (*meharrem*); the men's on the left of one entering the tent, the women's on the right: yet among the Arabs of Djebel Hauran I have seen the men's on the right, and the women's on the left. These apartments are separated by a white woollen carpet of Damascus manufacture, called *káteaa*, or *sáhhe*: this partition is drawn across the tent, and fastened to the three middle posts. If the woollen stuff be interwoven with patterns of flowers, it is called *markoum*. In the men's apartment, the ground is generally covered with a good Persian or Baghdad carpet; the wheat-sacks and camel-bags piled up round the middle post; and this pyramid, which often reaches almost to the top, is called *redjoud*. The camels' pack-saddles, upon which the sheikhs or the guests recline, are placed near the redjoud, or farther back, near the rowák: it is regarded as unpolite to place them near the kásere, or side-post. The women's apartment is the receptacle for all the rubbish of the tent, the cooking utensils, the butter and water-skins, &c.: all these things are laid down near the pole called *hadhera*, where the slave sits and the dog sleeps during the day. The corner end of the tent-covering always advances a little on that side over the *kheroub* of the hadhera, and hangs down floating in the wind; this corner is called *roffe*. Upon the ground under this, no man of good reputation would readily seat himself; and from the prejudice attending it is derived the expression متعدك الرفة "Your sitting-place is the roffe," denoting a mean despicable character. On the fore-post of the men's apartment hangs, likewise, a corner of the tent-covering, or roffe, which serves as a towel for wiping hands before or after dinner.

If the tent is to be broken up, (*remy el beit,*) the rowák is first taken off, then the partition, or káteaa, then the "hand," the makdoum, and the foot, after which the tent falls backwards behind the redjoud. Sometimes the redjoud is first taken off. The tent-poles are heaped together, and tied at both ends with two cords kept for that purpose, called *sheiaan*, and then hung on the side of a camel.

Such are the tents generally found among the *Ahl el Shemál;* whose chiefs, however, have always three posts in the middle, instead of one. Most of the Aenezes, on the contrary, have two middle posts, or *wasat*, and their sheikh's from four to five. In the latter case, whenever there are more than one waset, the others are placed, not behind each other, but along the tent lengthways; and there is then a corresponding number of *dafae* and *makdoums*, while the side posts are always the same in number.

In summer, the three front posts are sometimes not employed, and the tent is supported only by the middle and hind poles, being wide open in front. The height of the makdoum and wasat is about seven feet; that of the other posts about five feet. The tent, if it have two wasat, is between twenty-five and thirty feet; its depth or breadth (if all the poles are up), at most ten feet. The Aeneze tents are always of black goat's-hair. Among the *Ledja* Arabs in Haurán I saw several tents covered with goat's-hair stuff striped white and black.

The richest Aeneze has never more than one tent, unless he should happen to have a wife whom he does not wish to repudiate, but who cannot live on good terms with his other wife; he then pitches a smaller tent near his own. It may likewise occur, that if the Arab take his own married son's, or his deceased brother's family under his roof, he may find the tent too small for the whole number; he therefore pitches a side tent for them near his own.

Furniture of the Tent, and various Utensils.

The camel's pack-saddle (*hedádje*). The man's camel-saddle (*shedád*). The ladies' camel-saddle is of a different description; the *hesár* consists of a heap of carpets and abbas, rising about eighteen inches over the pack-saddle, so as to afford a commodious seat: this is used by the Ahl el Shemál. The Aeneze ladies ride in the *makszar*, a kind of cradle, which they cover with the *gharfe*, or red-tanned camel-skin: if the gharfe is of the smaller size, it is called *aybe*. The sheikh's ladies ride in the *ketteb*, a saddle much resembling the makszar in shape, but all over stuffed with red camel leather, and covered with similar skins of a large size, floating in the wind. Various-coloured cloth cuttings are sometimes hung round the ketteb. The halter used in guiding the camel is called *resen*, the common name in Syria: the ladies ornament them with cloth cuttings and ostrich feathers; and they are then called *rás*. The stick with which a camel is driven by the rider, is called *aaszy*, or *matrek*, if straight; but *aadján*, or *meshaab*, if it ends in a hammer. The small bells of iron that hang round the neck of camels yielding milk are called *tabl*; the small bag, into which is put the hair or wool that may fall from the camel or sheep on the road, is called *lebeid*.

The Arabs keep water for their horses in large bags made of tanned camel-skin; these are sewn up on the four sides, so as to leave two openings, the principal one above, the other near one of the lower corners, which they open on a march to allay their thirst, while it hangs on a camel's side. The shape of this water-bag may be thus sketched:—

Two of such skin-bags, called *ráwouye*, constitute a heavy load for a camel.

The goat-skins, in which the Arabs keep the camel's milk, are called *zeká*. A small goat-skin, used to hold camel's milk for the use of passing strangers, is called *sheráa*: and the same name is given to another skin, out of which the mares drink the camel's milk. Butter is made in a skin called *mamakhadh*, or *zeká*, and preserved in one called *mekrash*.

Wheat sacks, if made of wool, are called *udel* (plural *udoul*); if made of goat-hair, *udel harres*.

The leather in which camels are watered is called *hawdh*. Sometimes the Arabs only place sand, or a couple of stones, under the leather, to give it a degree of concavity, so that it may hold the water; it is then called *fursh*. The leather bucket which brings up water from deep wells is called *dellou* (the common Syrian name). The two sticks which cross the bucket, and to which the rope is fastened, are called *arká el dellou*. To supply the place of a cord or rope in drawing up the bucket, the Arabs use strips of camel leather twisted together; such a cord is named *mahhas*. A large copper pan used in cookery is called *keder*, a small pan *ghelie*. The mortar, wherein the women beat or pound wheat, is called *rahai*; and the same name denotes the hand-mill. The towel spread under the mortar, to save any flour that might fall, is called *tefál el rahai*. The wooden bowl into which the camels are milked, is named *kedehh*; the wooden water-cup *tás*; the wooden coffee mortar *mehabedj*; the coffee-pot *dellet el kahwe*. The three stones on which the pan is placed over the fire are called *khefaiedh*, or *houády*; the horse's feeding-bag *alýke*, and in Syria, *makhlye*. The iron chain which fastens the horse's fore-feet one to the other is called *hedeid el fers*. The horses thus chained pasture all day about the camp. *Merebet el fers* is a long chain, with an iron ring at one end, through which at night the mare's foot is passed and locked up; the owner secures the other end of the chain to an iron spike, which he drives into the ground at the place in his tent, where he proposes to sleep. It is therefore very difficult to steal the mare; yet robbers have sometimes succeeded in filing through the chain, and carrying off the prize.

Bedouin Dress.

In summer the men wear a coarse cotton shirt, over which the wealthy put a *kombar*, or long gown, as it is worn in Turkish towns, of silk or cotton stuff. Most of them, however, do not wear the kombar, but simply wear over their shirt a woollen mantle. There are different sorts of mantles, one very thin, light, and white woollen, manufactured at Baghdad, and called *mesoumy*. A coarser and heavier kind, striped white and brown, (worn over the mesoumy,) is called *abba*. The Baghdad abbas are most esteemed: those made at *Hamah*, with short wide sleeves, are called *boush*. (In the northern parts of Syria, every kind of woollen mantle, whether white, black, or striped white and brown, or white and blue, are called *meshlakh*.) I have not seen any black abbas among the Aenezes, but frequently among the sheikhs of Ahl el Shemál, sometimes interwoven with gold, and worth as much as ten pounds sterling. The Aenezes do not wear drawers; they walk and ride usually barefooted, even the richest of them, although they greatly esteem yellow boots and red shoes. All the Bedouins wear on the head, instead of the red Turkish cap, a turban, or square kerchief of cotton, or cotton and silk mixed; the turban is called *keffie*: this they fold about the head, so that one corner falls backwards, and two other corners hang over the fore part of the shoulders; with these two corners they cover their faces, to protect them from the sun's rays, or hot wind, or rain, or to conceal their features if they wish to be unknown. The keffie is yellow, or yellow mixed with green. Over the keffie, the Aenezes tie, instead of a turban, a cord round the head; this cord is of camel's hair, and called *akál*. Some tie a handkerchief about the head, and it is then called *shutfe*. A few rich sheikhs wear shawls on their heads, of Damascus or Baghdad manufacture, striped red and white; they sometimes also use red caps, or *tákie* (called in Syria *tarboush*), and under those they wear a smaller cap of camel's hair called *maaraka* (in Syria *arkýe*, where it is generally made of fine cotton stuff).

The Aenezes are distinguished at first sight from all the Syrian Bedouins, by the long tresses of their hair. They never shave their black hair, but cherish it from infancy, till they can twist it in tresses that hang over the cheeks down to the breast: these tresses are called *keroun*. Some few Aenezes wear girdles of leather, others tie a cord or a piece of rag over the shirt. Men and women wear from infancy a leather girdle around the naked waist; it consists of four or five thongs, twisted together into a cord as thick as one's finger. I heard that the women tie their thongs, separated from each other, round the waist.

Both men and women adorn the girdle with pieces of ribands, or amulets. The Aenezes call it *hhakou*; the Ahl el Shemál call it *bireim*. In summer the boys, until the age of seven or eight years, go stark naked; but I never saw any young girl in that state, although it was mentioned, that in the interior of the desert the girls, at that early age, were not more encumbered by clothing than their little brothers.

In winter the Bedouins wear over the shirt a pelisse made of several sheep-skins stitched together; many wear these skins even in summer, because experience has taught them, that the more warmly a person is clothed the less he suffers from the sun. The Arabs endure the inclemency of the rainy season in a wonderful manner. While every thing around them suffers from the cold, they sleep barefooted in an open tent, where the fire is not kept up beyond midnight. Yet in the middle of summer an Arab sleeps wrapt in his mantle upon the burning sand, and exposed to the rays of an intensely warm sun.

The ladies' dress is a wide cotton gown of a dark colour, blue, brown, or black; on their heads they wear a kerchief called *shauber* or *mekroune*, the young females having it of a red colour; the old, black. All the *Raualla* ladies wear black silk kerchiefs, wo yards square, called *shále kás;* these are made at Damascus.

Silver rings are much worn by the Aeneze ladies, both in the ears and noses; the ear-rings they call *terkie* (plur. *teráky*), the small nose-rings *shedre*, the larger (some of which are three inches and a half in diameter) *khezám*. All the women puncture their lips and dye them blue; this kind of tatooing they call *bertoum*, and apply it likewise in spotting their temples and foreheads. The Serhhán women puncture their cheeks, breasts, and arms, and the Ammour women their ankles. Several men also adorn their arms in the same manner. The Bedouin ladies half cover their faces with a dark-coloured veil called *nekye*, which is so tied as to conceal the chin and mouth. The Egyptian women's veil (*berkoá*) is used by the Kebly Arabs. Round their wrists the Aeneze ladies wear glass bracelets of various colours; the rich also have silver bracelets, and some wear silver chains about the neck: both in summer and winter the men and women go barefooted.

The Aenezes are easily distinguished from the Shemál Arabs by their diminutive size, few of them being above five feet two or three inches in height: their features are good, their noses often aquiline, their persons extremely well formed, and not so meagre or slight as some travellers have reported; their deep-set dark eyes sparkle from under their bushy black eye-brows, with a fire unknown in our northern climes; their beard is short and thin, but the black hair of all abundantly thick. The females seem taller in proportion than the men; their features in general are handsome, and their deportment very graceful. In complexion, the Arabs are very tawny, the children however at their birth are fair, but of a livid whiteness. As a physician, I had once an opportunity of seeing the naked arms of a sheikh's lady, which were as fair as those of any European beauty.

Arms of the Bedouins.

The most common arms of the Arabs are their lances. The Aenezes have two sorts, one called *remahh sán*, made of wood and brought from Gaza in Palestine; the other, (a more esteemed sort) called *remahh kennah*, brought from Irak and Baghdad; they are made of a kind of bamboo with many knots: the lightest lances are the most valued; the price of one varies from six to fifty piastres. The iron or steel pointed head is called *kentád;* I saw some covered with Persian workmanship in gold and silver; at the other end the iron spike that sticks the lance into the ground is called *harbe*, a name which the Syrians apply to the upper point. The lance is often without any ornament, but sometimes it has two balls or tufts of black ostrich feathers, as large as two fists, placed near its top; these are called *doube:* the upper tuft is fringed with short white ostrich feathers, called *ghalabe*, about the lance, between the two balls, are twisted strips of red cloth; these are called *toumán*.

The Arabs throw the lance but to a short distance, when they pursue a horseman whom they cannot overtake, and whom they are sure of hitting. To strike with the lance, they balance it for some time over their head, and then thrust it forward; others hold and shake the lance at the height of the saddle. If hard pressed by an enemy, the Arab continually thrusts his lance backwards to prevent the approach of his pursuer's mare, and sometimes kills either the pursuer or the mare by dexterously throwing the point of his lance behind. If any difficulty should occur, as sometimes happens, in drawing the lance from the wound, the Arab then has recourse to his sabre, or *seif*, which he carries on all occasions, even when he goes to sip coffee in a neighbour's tent. The Arabs esteem very highly the Persian blades, but are not qualified to judge of their real value, and often purchase from the travelling pedlars for eighty or a hundred piastres, blades of damasked steel not worth more than twenty. Besides his lance and sabre, every Arab carries in his girdle a curved knife called *sekín* (of which Niebuhr has given a delineation). Those who fight on foot use a short lance called *ketáa*, which they throw to a considerable distance.

Should a horseman be without a lance, he arms himself with a club or mace, of which they have various sorts: the *kenouaa*, with a wooden handle and round top of iron; the *dábous*, made wholly of iron; and the *kolong*, with a wooden handle and a hammer of iron at the top. The foot soldiers carry sometimes a target (*darake*); this is round, and about eighteen inches in diameter, made of wild ox skin and covered with iron bars.* The coat of mail, *dora*, is still used among the Arabs; the *Would Aly* have about twenty-five, the *Roualla* two hundred; the *Ibn Fadhel* and *Messaliekh* have between thirty and forty. The *dora* is of two sorts, one covering the whole body like a long gown from the elbow, over the shoulders, down to the knees; this is the *sirgh*; the other, called *kembáz*, covers the body only to the waist, the arms from the elbows downwards being covered with two pieces of steel, called *kaldjak*, fitting into each other, with iron fingers. Thus clad, the Arab completes his armour by putting on his head an iron cap (*tás*), which is but rarely adorned with

---

* The wild cow, *beker el wahkesh*, feeds on the herbs in the desert of the district of *Djof*, fifteen days journey from Damascus. It was described to me as resembling in shape both the cow and large-sized deer; its neck like that of the cow, its legs thicker than the deer's, and its horns short.

feathers. The price of a coat of mail fluctuates from two hundred to fifteen hundred piastres. The present chief of the Wahabys, Ibn el Saoud, has great numbers. Those of the best quality are capable of resisting a ball. The horseman clad in this *dora* armour is called *melebs* (plur. *melábeis*); if he wears a coat over the armour to conceal it, he is called *dáfen*. I have heard that the Arabs have coats of mail which partially cover the bodies of their horses, but I never saw any.

The Aenezes are well acquainted with the use of fire-arms; but the only guns that I saw among them were matchlocks, to discharge which a man couches upon his belly, and scarcely ever misses his aim. The Aenezes do not use pistols, but the Shemál Arabs frequently. The shepherds who tend flocks at a distance from the camp, are armed with the short lances, and also with slings, which they use very dexterously in throwing stones as large as a man's fist. The Aenezes have a kind of armour (called *lebs*) for their horses: this they use in war; it is made only at Aleppo, and consists of seven pieces of thick pasteboard of various sizes, covered with red cloth; two pieces hang on each side of the horse, two on its hinder parts, and one on the breast. The two side pieces are sewn together under the stirrups, and connected with the breast and hind pieces with steel buttons. Some men, who affect elegance, have the lebs embroidered: a pasteboard horse-covering of this kind costs from one hundred and fifty to two hundred piastres. It wards off the feeble thrust of a lance.

Diet of the Arabs.

The principal Bedouin dishes are,

Ftíta.—Unleavened paste of flour and water, baked in ashes of camel's dung, and mixed up afterwards with a little butter; when the whole is thoroughly kneaded, they serve it up in a bowl of wood or leather. If milk be mixed with the *ftíta*, the mixture is called *kháfoury*.

Ayesh.—Flour and sour camel's milk, made into a paste, and boiled: the camel's milk becomes sourish soon after it is put into the *zeka*, or goat-skin.

Behatta.—Rice or flour, boiled with sweet camel's milk.

Heneyne.—Bread, butter, and dates, blended together into a paste.

Khubz.—Bread; more commonly called in the Bedouin dialect *jisre*. It is of two sorts, both unleavened, one of which is baked in round cakes upon a plate of iron (*sádj*), as among the Syrian Fellahs: the other mode of making bread is, by spreading out in a circle a great number of small stones, over which a brisk fire is kindled; when the stones are sufficiently heated, the fire is removed, and the paste spread over the hot stones, and immediately covered with glowing ashes, and left until thoroughly baked. This bread is only used at breakfast, and is called *khubz aly el redháf*.

Burgoul.—Wheat, boiled with some leaven, and then dried in the sun. This dried wheat is preserved for a year, and, boiled with butter or oil, is the common dish with all classes in Syria.

Butter is made in the following manner. The goat's or sheep's milk (for camel's milk is never used for this purpose) is put into the *keder*, over a slow fire, and a little leben or sour milk, or a small piece of the dried entrails of a young lamb (*metefkhá*), thrown in with it: the milk then separates, and is put into the goat-skin, called zeka, which is tied to one of the tent-poles, and for one or two hours constantly moved backwards and forwards: the buttery substance then coagulates, the water is squeezed out, and the butter put into the skin, called *mekrash*: if after two days, they have collected a certain quantity of butter, they again place it over the fire, throw a handful of *burgoul* into it, and leave it to boil, taking care to skim it. After having boiled for some time, the burgoul precipitates all the foreign substances, and the butter remains quite clear at the top of the keder. The butter-milk is once more drained through a bag of camel's hair, and whatever remains in it of a butter-like substance is left to dry in the sun; and thus eaten it is called *aouket,* or *hhameid jebsheb.* The burgoul, cleared of the butter with which it was boiled, is called *kelláse,* and eaten by children. There are Aeneze tribes in the Nedjd, who seldom or never taste meat, but live almost wholly on dates and milk. Having taken off the butter, they beat the butter-milk again till it coagulates, and then dry it till it becomes quite hard; they then grind it, and each family collects in spring two or three loads of it. They eat it mixed with butter.

The Aenezes do not make any cheese, at least very seldom, but convert all the milk of their sheep and goats into butter. The Arabs of Ahl el Shemál, on the contrary, furnish cheese to most of the inhabitants of the Eastern Syrian plain.

Kemmáye, or *kemmá,* (or in the Bedouin dialect *djeme,*) a favourite dish of the Arabs, is a kind of truffle growing in the Desert, without any appearance of either roots or seeds; in size and shape the *kemmáye* much resembles the true truffle. There are three species of it: the red, *khelásy,* the black, *jebah,* and the white, *zebeidy.* If the rain has been abundant during winter, the *djemes* are found in the end of March. They lie about four inches under ground: the place where they grow is known by a little rising of the ground over them. If the fruit is left to attain full maturity, it rises above the earth to about half its volume. The children and servants dig it out with short sticks. They are sometimes so numerous on the plain that the camels stumble over them. Each family then gathers four or five camel-loads; and while this stock lasts, they live exclusively on *kemmáye,* without tasting either burgoul or ayesh. The kemmáyes are boiled in water or milk till they form a paste, over which melted butter is poured: they are sometimes roasted and eaten with melted butter. It is said that they produce costiveness. If they have been abundant, they are dried in the sun, and afterwards dressed for use like fresh ones. Great quantities are consumed by the people of Damascus, and the peasants of Eastern Syria. In general they are worth at Damascus about a half-penny per pound. They are brought to Damascus from the district near *Tel Zeykal* on the eastern limits of the *Merdj*. To Aleppo they are brought from the plain adjoining Djebel el Hass. Camels do not eat kemmáye. The desert *Hammad*, or the great plain between Damascus and Baghdad and Basrah, is full of *kemmáye*.

The Aeneze eat gazelles, whenever they can kill them. I heard that they regard the *jerboa*, or rat of the desert, as a great dainty, for its fine flavour. The interior of the desert abounds with jerboas.

The *ayesh* is the daily and universal dish of the Aenezes; and even the richest sheikh would think it a shame to order his wife to dress any other dish, merely to please his own palate. The Arabs never indulge in luxuries, but on occasion of some festival, or on the arrival of a stranger. For a common guest, bread is baked, and served up with the ayesh; if the guest is of some consideration, coffee is prepared for him, and *behatta*, or *ftíta*, or bread with melted butter. For a man of rank, a kid or lamb is killed. When this occurs, they boil the lamb with burgoul and camel's milk, and serve it up in a large wooden dish, round the edge of which the meat is placed. A wooden bowl, containing the melted grease of the animal, is put and pressed down in the midst of the burgoul; and every morsel is dipped into the grease before it is swallowed. If a camel should be killed, (which rarely happens,) it is cut into large pieces; some part is boiled, and its grease mixed with burgoul; part is roasted, and like the boiled put upon the dish of bourgoul. The whole tribe then partakes of the delicious feast. Camel's flesh is more esteemed in winter than in summer; and the she-camel more than the male. The grease of the camel is kept in goat-skins, and used like butter.

The Arabs are rather slovenly in their manner of eating; they thrust the whole hand into the dish before them, shape the burgoul into balls as large as a hen's egg, and thus swallow it. They wash their hands just before dinner, but seldom after; being content to lick the grease off their fingers, and rub their hands upon the leather scabbards of their swords, or clean them with the *roffe* of the tent (as above mentioned). The common hour of breakfast is about ten o'clock: dinner or supper is served at sun-set. If there is plenty of pasture, camel's milk is handed round after dinner. The Arabs eat heartily, and with much eagerness. The boiled dish set before them being always very hot, it requires some practice to avoid burning one's fingers, and yet to keep pace with the voracious company. Indeed, during my first acquaintance with the Arabs, I seldom retired from a meal quite satisfied. Among the Arabs of the desert, as those of the towns, the disgusting custom of eructation after every meal is universal. This I observe, to correct a misrepresentation of D'Arvieux.

The women eat in the *meharrem* what is left of the men's dinner: they seldom have the good fortune to taste any meat except the head, feet, and liver of the lambs. While the men of the camp resort to the tent in which a stranger is entertained, and participate in the supper, their women steal into the meharrem of the hostess, to beg a foot, or some other trifling portion of the animal killed for the occasion.

Arts and Industry.

Of the arts but little is known among the Aenezes: two or three blacksmiths to shoe the horses, and some saddlers to mend the leather-work, are the only artists found even in the most numerous tribes. These workmen are called *szona*: they are never of Aeneze origin, because their occupations are regarded as degrading to a free-born Aeneze. Most of them are from the villages of Djof, which are wholly peopled by workmen, some of whom, in spring, disperse themselves among the Bedouins, and return in winter to their families. An Aeneze never marries his daughter to a szona, or any descendant of a szona family; the latter intermarry among themselves, or take the daughters of the Aeneze slaves. The arts of tanning and of weaving are practised by the Aenezes themselves; the former by men, the latter by women. Their method of dying and tanning is this:—To render the camel's skin yellow, (no other skin is ever dyed,) they cover it with salt, which is left upon it for two or three days; they then steep it in a liquid paste, made of barley-meal mixed with water, where it remains for seven days; then they wash the skin in fresh water, and clear it easily of the hair. Next, they take the peels of dry pomegranates, (a fruit which they purchase in the Syrian towns, or from the Menadhere Arabs, or from the Fellahs on the Euphrates,) pound them, and mix them with water; they let the skin remain in that mixture three or four days: the operation is thus completed, the skin having acquired a yellow tint. They then wash and grease the leather with camel's fat, to render it smooth. If pomegranates cannot be obtained, they use the roots of a Desert herb called *oerk*: this is about three spans long, and as thick as a man's finger: the outer skin serves as a substitute for the pomegranate peel, and dyes the leather red. Of leather so prepared, the *ráwouye*, or large water-skins, are made; these are sometimes soaked a second, and even a third time, in the mixtures above described, a month after the first dying. For some time the ráwouye imparts to the water an astringent, bitterish taste; this, however, the Arabs like.

Among all the Bedouin tribes goat's hair constitutes the material of the coverings of tents, and of camel and provision-bags. The tent-covers are chiefly worked in Hauran, and the mountains of Heish and Belkaa, where goats abound more than among the Aenezes; who, on the other hand, fabricate of wool, wheat and barley-sacks, camel-bags, *rowáks* (or hind parts of tents), &c. The Arab women use a very simple loom; it is called *nutou*, (مرتك تنطا الشوقه) and consists of two short sticks, which are stuck into the ground at a certain distance, according to the desired breadth of the *shauke*, or piece to be worked. A third stick is placed across over them; about four yards from them, three sticks are placed in the same manner, and over the two horizontal cross-sticks, the woof (*sádouh*). To keep the upper and under woof at a proper distance from each other, a flat stick (called *mensebhh*) is placed between them.

A piece of wood serves as the weaver's shuttle, and a short gazelle's horn is used in beating back the thread of the shuttle. The loom is placed before the *meharrem*, or women's apartment, and worked by the mother and her daughters. The distaff (*meghezel el souf*) is in general use among the Aenezes. At Palmyra, I saw several men using the distaff; and among the Kebly Arabs all the shepherds manufacture wool.

Of camel's hair the Arab women make bags, with which the camel's udder is covered, to prevent the young ones from sucking: those bags are called *shemle*. The cords (*metrek*), with which these bags are tied, and *okál*, are the short strong cords with which the sitting camel's thigh and shin bones are fastened together, to prevent his rising up while loaded. Camel's hair is likewise used in knitting the *mearaka*, or bonnet worn by the men.

Some mix an equal quantity of wool and camel's hair, in the manufacture of their sacks, or bags: the poorest people only make the piece entirely of camel's hair, which is much less esteemed for its quality than goat's hair.

Wealth and Property of the Bedouins.

An Arab's property consists almost wholly in his horses and camels. The profits arising from his butter enable him to procure the necessary provisions of wheat and barley, and occasionally a new suit of clothes for his wife and daughters. His mare every spring produces a valuable colt, and by her means he may expect to enrich himself with booty. No Arab family can exist without one camel at least; a man who has but ten, is reckoned poor: thirty or forty, place a man in easy circumstances; and he who possesses sixty, is rich. I do not, however, make this statement as applicable to all the Arabs: there are tribes originally poor, like the *Ahl Djebel* Arabs; among whom, from the possession of ten camels, a man is reckoned wealthy. Some sheikhs of the Aenezes have as many as three hundred camels. The sheikh who was my guide to Tedmor was reputed to have one hundred camels, between three and four hundred sheep and goats, two mares and one horse. The price of a camel varies according to the demands of the Hadj or Mekka caravans. The Hadj not having taken place for the last four years, a good Arab camel is now worth about ten pounds. I once inquired from an Arab in easy circumstances, what was the amount of his yearly expenditure; and he said, that in ordinary years he consumed—

Four camel-loads of wheat	200 piastres.
Barley for his mare	100
Clothing for his women and children	200
Luxuries, as coffee, *kammerdin, debs,** tobacco, and half a dozen lambs	200
	700 piastres;

about 35 or 40 pounds sterling.

Among the Arabs, horses are not so numerous as might be supposed from the reports of several travellers, as well as of the country people in Syria, who indeed are but imperfectly acquainted with the affairs of the Desert. During my visits to Aeneze encampments, I could seldom reckon more than one mare for six or seven tents. The Aenezes exclusively ride their mares, and sell the male colts to the peasants and town's-people of Syria and Baghdad. The Arabs of Ahl el Shemál have more horses than the Aenezes, but the breed is adulterated in some instances

Wealth, however, among the Arabs is extremely precarious, and the most rapid changes of fortune are daily experienced. The bold incursions of robbers, and sudden attacks of hostile parties, reduce, in a few days, the richest man to a state of beggary; and we may venture to say, that there are not many fathers of families who have escaped such disasters. The details hereafter given, of Bedouin wars and robberies, will explain this assertion. It may be almost said, that the Arabs are obliged to rob and pillage. Most

---

* *Kammerdin,* dried apricot jelly from Damascus.—*Debs,* a sweet jelly made of grapes.

families of the Aenezes are unable to defray the annual expenses from the profits on their cattle, and few Arabs would sell a camel to purchase provisions; he knows, from experience, that to continue long in a state of peace, diminishes the wealth of an individual: war and plunder therefore become necessary. The sheikh is obliged to lead his Arabs against the enemy, if there be one; if not, it can easily be contrived to make one. But it may be truly said, that wealth alone does not give a Bedouin any importance among his people. A poor man, if he be hospitable and liberal according to his means, always killing a lamb when a stranger arrives, giving coffee to all the guests present, holding his bag of tobacco always ready to supply the pipes of his friends, and sharing whatever booty he gets among his poor relations, sacrificing his last penny to honour his guest or relieve those who want, obtains infinitely more consideration and influence among his tribe, than the *bakheil,* or avaricious and wealthy miser, who receives a guest with coldness, and lets his poor friends starve. As riches among this nation of robbers do not confer influence or power, so the wealthy person does not derive from them any more refined gratification than the poorest individual of the tribe may enjoy. The richest sheikh lives like the meanest of his Arabs: they both eat every day of the same dishes, and in the same quantity, and never partake of any luxury unless on the arrival of a stranger, when the host's tent is open to all his friends. They both dress in the same kind of shabby gown and *messhlakh.* The chief pleasure in which the chief may indulge, is the possession of a swift mare, and the gratification of seeing his wife and daughters better dressed than the other females of the camp.

Bankruptcy, in the usual acceptation of the word, is unknown among the Arabs. A Bedouin either loses his property by the enemy (it is then said of him *wakhad helâle*), or he expends it in profuse hospitality. In this latter case he is praised by the whole tribe; and as the generous Arab is most frequently endued with other nomadic virtues, he seldom fails to regain, by some lucky stroke, what he had so nobly lost.

Sciences, Music, and Poetry of the Bedouins.

On the subject of Bedouin science we shall not be long detained. There are whole tribes, such as the *Ibn Dhouahy*, of which not one person can read or write. A Damascus pedlar who resided with that tribe the greater part of the year, acting occasionally as secretary to the sheikh, assured me of the fact. It was mentioned as an extraordinary circumstance, that the children of Ibn Esmeyr had learned to write. On my journey towards Tedmor, I had taken with me a volume of the history of Antar, and sometimes read a striking passage from it to my companions; but I never met with one individual among them, who professed to know even as much as myself of Arabic reading. But little science can be expected among those, whose minds are constantly bent on war and depredation. I never saw, in the possession of the Aenezes, any book besides a few copies of the Korán. Their skill in medicine shall be mentioned hereafter. Their astronomical science consists in a mere nomenclature of the constellations and planets, with which most of the Aenezes are acquainted. The names, given by them to some of the lunar months, shall be noticed in the Appendix.

Poetry is still held in esteem among the Arabs: a poet is more frequently styled *saheb koul*, or *kouál*, than *shaará*. Their poetical talents are most commonly exerted in reciting verses, which celebrate the merits of their chiefs, or of some distinguished warrior (*el mediehh*), or the charms of their mistresses. Every kind of poetry is called *kaszíde*. Of ancient poetry, the History of *Antar*, (an excellent work,) and the History of *Selím el Zyr*, and three or four similar compositions in the true Bedouin style are known to a few individuals, and occasionally recited. Whenever an Aeneze recites verses, he accompanies his voice with the *Rebába* (a kind of guitar described by Niebuhr); the only musical instrument used in the Desert. The people of Djof are famous for their poetical and musical talents. Their poets visit the Aenezes from time to time, singing at the sheikhs' tents for a trifling remuneration; but the Aenezes themselves never accept any reward for having entertained the company. That the reader may judge of Bedouin poetry, I subjoin a true specimen of Desert production, a recent composition; which, although it may want grammatical precision, will perhaps be found interesting as a picture of Arab manners, drawn from real life, in the style employed by most Bedouins, when they celebrate the praises of their heroes, and in many parts exhibiting the true Bedouin dialect.

An Arab, against the advice of his sheikh, had sent his camels to pasture during the winter season with a foreign tribe; the camels died, and he addressed the following verses to his sheikh, who was thereby induced to repair the loss, by giving him some.

A Bedouin Poem.

"Soleymán! lend me the pen, and the white-coloured leaf, that I may compose my verses, the language of truth. Let me implore God's assistance; and may he have mercy upon our sins!

"Let us praise him with praises innumerable as the hoarded grains, as the cultivators of the earth; the *bedous* and the shepherds.

"And may the prophet before God intercede for us: our crimes may then be pardoned.

"O thou, who departest from me, mounted upon the clear-coloured camel, bearing upon its back the four-sided saddle,*

"And its bag and neck-leather,† and well-ground flour, with the coffee-beans, and the sweet-smelling Tombac.‡

"An honest youth he is, beloved by his companions, the young women's pride.

"The country paths he spies better than the night-swarming Kattas § do; and his eye sees farther than the eagle intent upon his prey.

"Thy way is towards the *Budje*; ‖ slowly thou proceedest, (for thou knowest not fear,) and rich booty thou wilt once obtain from the Hadj.¶

"The wandering robber thou must fight on thy road; and pursue him: but, friend, guard well thy camel, else the thief will leave thee to perish in the dreary plain.

"Let thy journey be at night, long after the time of sun-set, nor let the (far-appearing) fire hasten thy pace until thou hearest the dogs barking,

"And the songs of our people; the proudest women ** never discontinuing their songs in praise of the brother of *Waddha*.

---

* The *shedád*, or pack-saddle of the camel.

† The *marakah* is a piece of leather put upon the camel's neck, that it may serve to support the feet of the rider.

‡ *Tombac*, a kind of tobacco smoked in the argyle, or Persian pipe, after having been thoroughly washed.

§ The Katta abounds in the plains of Hauran.—See Russel's Natural History of Aleppo.

‖ The Budje is a fountain near Mezerib, two long days' journey south of Damascus.

¶ The Arabs pride themselves on robbing and pilfering among the caravans going to Mekka.

** The Arabs style *touámyh* those women who have quitted their husbands, but have not yet obtained a sentence of divorce.

"Amidst the flocks of the watchful shepherd,* thou mayst find Waddha's brother following the moving herd.†

"Mounted upon his snow-white mare;‡ with ease he overtakes each horseman; with her the booty that he takes is immeasurable.

"Who can count the heroes, the warriors whom he has slain! whose heart's blood has flowed upon the ground!

"They fly before his eye,—the warriors, like birds that have been slightly wounded.

"But he marks them, and at his war-cry § none dares to turn back; even the coward will fight for his booty.

"Has not his own kinsman felt the weight of his arm? a more praiseworthy deed none ever related. ‖

"And now when thou approachest the camp, songs of joy will be sung, and loud will be the shouting, and great will be the slaughter (of animals).

"Then come the girls with teeth bright as lightning, to learn the achievement of the brother of Waddha: rich are his Arabs. ¶

---

* As soon as the shepherd sees a man mounted on a horse or camel coming from a distance, he gives notice by loud cries to the Arabs of the camp.

† *El suhhet*, in the Bedouin dialect, is the herd of a whole encampment.

‡ *Khádhere*, a white mare.

§ Every Arab has some favourite expression, with which he animates in battle his own courage, and that of his friends. The famous horsemen generally use their own names to frighten and defy the enemy; thus one exclaims, *Aná ákhou Wáddha*—"I am the brother of Waddha." This war-cry is called *nekhouet*.

‖ The sheikh, to whom these verses are addressed, struck one of his own cousins with his mace, and knocked out some of his teeth, because he had behaved in a cowardly manner when the whole tribe was engaged in battle. The sheikh is praised for having thus forfeited, for the honour of his tribe, the sum which the Kadhy would sentence him to pay for the assault upon his cousin.

¶ His Arabs are rich, through their sheikh's generosity.

"His beard shining with virtue; his walk, not that of the wretched; and the darkness of night does not conceal any of his actions.

"His manly person stands clear of all base crimes, and proof against all reproaches.

"To him present my greetings and many blessings, and to his hand deliver my verses in his praise.

"And when thou enterest the tent, let every bad man retire: praise God and the prophet, and wealth will be thy lot.

"And thus saying, carpets will be placed for thee, and the boiling beans will diffuse their grateful odour,

"While dates and butter are dished up:* be sober, think on the sheep just slaughtered.

"Then after thou hast eaten and washed thyself,† he may ask thee where I live at present.

"Tell him, 'Jousef now lives in misery and distress: since the time when he slighted thy advice, he never has experienced good fortune.

"'His property is gone! neither lances nor enemies have taken it; but he is punished for inattention to thy advice.'

"God will amend the matter, my brother: his aid be always with thee; for if thou alone art left to me, O brother! I am still rich.

"O Fortune! accompany his steps; let verdure and roots, ‡ even in winter, sprout up before him, and bless his flock.

* The Arabs give the name of *kouálek* to the meal placed before strangers who arrive between the hours of breakfast and supper, or between ten in the morning and sun-set, during which time the Arabs seldom eat any thing.

† The Arabic original says, "clean washed with soap," in compliment to the sheikh, who does not grudge the expense of such a rare article as soap is in the Desert, that he may do honour to his guests.

‡ Here is meant the *kemmáye,* or truffle of the Desert, before mentioned.

"Whenever thou prayest to God, praise him with praises innumerable, like the beads of the shrub, and the hair of thy flock."

Besides the *kaszíde*, the Arabs have different national songs. Those of the Arab women are called *Asámer*. On occasion of feasts and rejoicings, the women retire in the evening to a place at some small distance behind the tents. They divide themselves into choruses of six, eight, or ten women: one party begins the song, and the other in turn repeat it; this is called *el benát yelaboua el asámer*. The song is always in praise of valour and generosity; and its never-varying tune is as follows:—

The movement is quick or slow, according to the pleasure of the singer. As a specimen of the words, I give the following:—

El kheil djeitna ya deiba—The warrior, O Deiba, advances!
El kheil djeitna hheteiba—The intrepid warrior advances!
El kheil Dhouhy ya deiba—Dhouhy, the warrior, O Deiba!

The first line of the song is repeated five or six times by the leading chorus, and then echoed by the other parties. In the same manner the second line is sung; but the third, which always contains the name of some distinguished warrior, is repeated as often as fifty times. The ladies, however, pronounce that name in such a manner, as to render it difficult for the men, who listen, to know who is the happy mortal.

The men's national songs are of a different description; the love-songs are called *hodjeiny*. The Arab's love is not enveloped in as much mystery as an European's: the object of his passion is known to all the tribe; and his only secret is the clandestine meeting with his beloved, much facilitated by the great number of *wádys*, or vallies, which the Desert affords in every direction. The wells, whence the women fetch water, are still the favourite places of appointment. If a lover cannot sleep at night, he goes to the men's apartment in the tent where his mistress resides, or to some friend's near it, and begins to sing his hodjeiny, which he continues till day-break, in unison with the friends who assemble around him. The girls, on their side, sometimes do the same; and their song is likewise called hodjeiny. Its tune never varies, but its melody and modulation are so different from all that Europeans hear of music, even in Turkish cities, that I was not able to note it down. Of the words of the men's hodjeiny, the following may serve as a specimen :—

يا ذيب يا اعلا من القعرَة

عاينت شوقي و دوارها

" O wolf! O thou who art taller than the *Kara*,*
I have seen my love, and her family's tents."

Another specimen is given in the subjoined lines—

يا عم قوم دنّي لي غامرَة

مالحد تشوق للخلاويه

حط عليها شداد الزين و الجربه جلد النجديه

ابغي عليها مع الزمال

" O cousin,† rise! bring me the camel,
The black camel, which the solitary maiden likes;
Cover it with its beautiful saddle, and the water-skins of *Nedjd* leather.
Let us proceed towards the fountain."

* *Kara*, a high hill in the district of Djof.

† عم instead of بنت عمي "daughter of my uncle." In the last line الزمال signifies the camel that carries the goat-skins of water.

A slight-formed camel (*dhámer*), and one of a dark grey, or blackish colour (*mólhhad*), are now in fashion among the Aeneze ladies; but camels of a brownish-red colour are more esteemed by the ladies of Beni Sakhr.

No one could give me a specimen of the women's hodjeiny, which is known to females only.

The men have a song, called *szahdje*, in praise of some chief. To sing this, half a dozen Arabs form a circle, and begin by repeating several times the word *hamoudé, hamoudé* (instead of *hamd*, "praise"); then one of them sings five or six words in praise of some individual; the *hamoudé* is again repeated with clapping of hands. A second then chants another stanza in praise of the same or some other man, and the final syllable of his verse is to rhyme with that of the former singer. The *szahdje* is in this manner continued for hours.

The war-song of the Arabs is called *hadou*. If a tribe march against an enemy, the first line is composed of horsemen, whom the camel-riders follow, and the Bedous on foot bring up the rear, armed with sticks, lances, *kolongs*, &c. If the enemy be near, the foot-soldiers accelerate their pace, and often run to come up with the advanced columns. On this occasion they sing the famous *hadou*:

يا موت خلّي السكرَ
يا موت حتي نتّرَ

"O death! suspend thy rage, O death, that (or until) we may take our blood revenge!"

The tune of this war-*hadou* is the same as that of the *asámer* before mentioned. The camel-rider's song they also call *hadou*; and it is well known, that the camel never moves with so much ease as when he hears his master sing—

يا رب سلمهم من التهديد
واجعد قوايهم عمد حديد

"O Lord, preserve them from all threatening dangers!
Let their limbs be pillars of iron!"

The طغرايط, cries, or shouts of rejoicing, are as often heard in the Desert as in the towns of Syria. The men think it beneath their dignity ever to join in such noises.

Feasts and Rejoicings.

Among the Arabs, the greatest festival is that of the circumcision. The boys at the age of six or seven years undergo this operation in all seasons of the year. On the morning fixed for the circumcision, the boy's father kills a sheep; his uncle, or nearest kindred, likewise brings a sheep ready killed to the tent; or, if they are poor, a large dish of cooked victuals; but there are generally five or six sheep killed. The makszar, or camel's saddle, is then placed before the tent, and some red cloth, or gown, or sherwal, thrown over it, and ostrich feathers stuck on the fore part. The women of the encampment now assemble near this display (which is called *moszana*), and amuse themselves with singing, while the men are at dinner in the tent. This meal being finished, the boy is circumcised; and the women accompany the operation with a loud song, or cry. The men now leave the tent, take their lances, and mount their mares, every one of them riding three times round the *moszana*; they then range themselves on both sides of the tent, at two or three hundred yards' distance, in two lines, and begin their warlike evolutions. A horseman gallops up to the opposite party, and defies one of them:

the latter immediately approaches him, and endeavours to pass his mare: arriving near his adversary's line, he in turn bids defiance, and thus the sport continues in rows, to and fro, for above an hour, in honour of the tent where the circumcision has taken place. The women all this time sing the *asámer*, and praise the best horseman, or the owner of the swiftest mare.

During the ramazán, the Arabs enclose a large square with walls of loose stones, and there perform their devotions, regarding this enclosure as a *mesdjed*, or chapel. After morning and evening prayers, they often exercise their horses in the manner above mentioned, on the plain before the chapel: but this occurs only in the holy month.

During the feast of sacrifice upon Mount Arafat (or the *ayd el dhahye*), a mesdjed of the same kind is constructed, and the horses regularly run, after prayers, for one hour. The daily fare during the festival is rather better than usual, even among those families that have no sacrifices to make for relations who have died in the course of the preceding year.

Besides the festivals above described, the Aenezes have no other; but they celebrate the arrival of every stranger with a banquet, to which all the friends of the host are invited. If the absence of a relation from home be protracted beyond a reasonable time, or if it be known that he is engaged in a dangerous expedition, his family make a vow (نذر) to place, at his return, some ostrich feathers upon the *makdoum* of the tent, that when seen from a distance, he may thus be complimented on his arrival; this they call رأيه لوجه الله. An Arab sometimes vows that he will sacrifice a camel to God, if his mare should bring forth a female: in this case he slaughters the camel, and its flesh serves as a feast to all his friends.

Diseases and Cures.

The small-pox (*djedry*) continues to make great ravages among the Bedouins; whole encampments have been depopulated by its violence: whenever a man or child is attacked by it, a tent is pitched for him at a considerable distance from the camp, and he is attended by a person only who has already been affected with the disease (نجي). Inoculation (دق الجدري) is well known among the Aenezes, and still more among the Shemál and Kebly Arabs. The operation is performed only by men, with a needle, held between the thumb and fore-finger; but the infected matter is seldom applied till the natural small-pox has made ravages in the tribe. Grown-up persons as well as children are inoculated. The Aenezes have learned inoculation from the peasants of Syria; but the Arabs in the interior of the Desert, such as the *Beni Shammar* and others, know nothing of it, and leave all to the will of God, as indeed do many of the Aenezes. Vaccination begins to extend itself in Syria; the vaccine matter was first brought to Aleppo by Mr. John Barker, his Britannic Majesty's consul at that place; he had received it from Vienna, and afterwards introduced it into the mountains of the Druzes, at the breaking-out of the late war between England and the Porte. Since that time, the greater portion of the Christian and Jewish families of Aleppo, Latikia, Tripoly, Beirout, the mountains of the Maronites, and the Druzes, and Damascus, have had their children vaccinated: in 1810 above nine hundred children were vaccinated at Damascus. The cow-pox has likewise been favourably received at Baghdad: the Turks follow slowly the example of the Christians, but will, without doubt, in a few years, know the importance and utility of vaccination.

The Arabs frequently complain of obstructions and indurations in the stomach: the constant drinking of camel's milk is supposed to be the chief cause of this disease; and they would suffer still more, did not the purging qualities of the brackish water relieve them. In these cases, and in rheumatic affections (*reihh*), the only mode of cure practised by the Arabs, is the *kei*, or burning of the skin all round the seat of pain with a red-hot iron. I have seen persons whose bodies were quite covered with the marks of similar operations; and it is certain that the *kei* has occasionally produced beneficial results. Instead of simply burning the skin, they sometimes take the skin up between two fingers, perforate it with slender red-hot iron, and pass a thread through the hole, so as to facilitate suppuration; this process is called *khelál*. They sometimes use, instead of the iron, the wood of the *sindián*, a species of oak that grows in great abundance upon the mountains of Heish and Belkaa. A branch of this tree (a very dry wood) is rubbed over a mill-stone, till it becomes quite hot; then they apply it to the invalid's body, in the same manner as the hot iron above mentioned.*

Fevers are not by any means excluded from the Desert: the inflammatory fever is called *khebye* (خبية), the intermittent, *szekhoun*; (but in Syria, the inflammatory fever is called *sekhouneh*, the intermittent, *dowwer*). If the kei, or burning, fail to cure, the patient is abandoned to the care of Providence.

Ophthalmic disorders are very common; and although nothing is ever done to check the evil, yet few Bedouins lose their sight in comparison with the numbers of blind persons found in the towns of Syria. The Arabs always sleep wrapped in their *meshlákh*; the town's-people, on the contrary, sleep in beds upon the high terraces of their houses, with their faces generally uncovered:

---

* I inquired whether two kinds of wood were known, which rubbed together would produce fire, but no one could give me any positive information on the subject.

this I think may account for the numerous cases of ophthalmia in Aleppo, and still more in Damascus.

The Arabs never bleed by opening a vein; but in cases of violent head-aches they draw a few drams of blood, by making, with a knife, small incisions in the skin of the forehead. Many of the Bedouins suffer from worms.

Venereal complaints are almost wholly unknown among the Aenezes; but the Ahl el Shemál frequently suffer from them. The Aeneze never indulges in debauchery when he enters a village or town, although Syria, in that respect, affords every facility. If one should be infected (a very rare occurrence), his family sends him to the hospital, or *murstan*, of Damascus or of Baghdad.

The leprosy (*áberz*), or at least a species of it, is still found amongst the Arabs; but during a practice of twelve years, a Frank physician at Aleppo had only seen one case of leprosy. I had no opportunity of seeing a leprous man in the Desert, but heard that the leprosy consists in white spots as large as one's hand, which appear on various parts of the body without rising above the skin, which remains quite clear and smooth. Some are born with the disease, others are attacked by it at the age of twenty or thirty years. If the white spots appear on the cheek, the beard most commonly (but not always) falls off; if other diseases cause the loss of the beard, it is regarded as a shame, and the person who has suffered that loss is styled *hetout*—a term denoting the itch or the mange under a horse's tail. The leprosy has never been cured. The Arabs declare, that if once confirmed in a family it can never be totally eradicated; but that it does not descend from the father immediately to the son, but from grandfather to grandson, passing the intermediate generation. Nothing can equal the notion of disgrace attached to the unfortunate sufferer: no Arab will sleep near a leper, nor eat from the same dish with him; nor will he permit his son or daughter to connect themselves by marriage with a leprous family. The tooth-ache is unknown among the Bedouins; all of whom have most beautiful teeth.

There are some, who know how to set or dress the broken leg of a man, by means of the *medjebber* (a kind of splint), which they also apply to the fractured limbs of sheep and goats.

The Bedouins use some of their Desert herbs as aperient medicines; a knowledge of these simples, and of the *kei* (before mentioned), constitutes all their medical science; but they have great faith in the efficacy of certain words written on slips of paper which the patient swallows with avidity. The great mass of a nation so temperate in eating and drinking may be supposed healthy; but the constant fatigues of a nomade life are beyond the strength of those advanced in years, and every traveller must remark the paucity of old men in the camps of those Arabs.

Their women suffer but little during parturition, and they often are delivered in the open air: when this occurs, the mother rubs and cleans the child, as soon as it is born, with earth or sand, places it in her handkerchief, and carries it home. If she feel symptoms of labour while mounted upon a camel, she alights and is delivered behind the camel, so that no person may see her, and then immediately remounts. She suckles the child until it is able to partake of solid food; but the Arab women have very little milk: during the last eight or ten days of pregnancy they drink profusely of camel's milk, in order to increase the quantity of their own; thus the infant is early accustomed to the taste of camel's milk, and even at the age of four months swallows it in copious draughts.

A name is given to the infant immediately on his birth. The name is derived from some trifling accident, or from some object which had struck the fancy of the mother, or any of the women present at the child's birth. Thus, if the dog happened to be near on this occasion, the infant is probably named *Kelab* (from *kelb*, a dog); or if the delivery should have been protracted during the night, until day-break, the name given to the boy is perhaps *Dhouyhhy* (from *Dhohhá*). Except *Mohammed*, which is not uncommon, true Muselman names, such as *Hassan, Aly, Mustafa, Fátme,* or *Aysha,* are seldom found among the genuine Bedouins. Besides his own peculiar name, every Arab is called by the name of his father, and that of his tribe or the ancestor of his family; thus they say, " *Kedoua Ibn Gheyán el Shamsy,*" *Kedoua,* the son of *Gheyán,* of the tribe of *Shamsy.*

With respect to education, a young Aeneze boy may be truly styled the " child of nature". His parents leave him to his own free will; they seldom chastise him, but train him from his cradle to the fatigues and dangers of a nomade life. I have seen parties of naked boys, playing at noon-day upon the burning sand in the midst of summer, running until they had fatigued themselves, and when they returned to their fathers' tents, they were scolded for not continuing the exercise.* Instead of teaching the boy civil manners, the father desires him to beat and pelt the strangers who come to the tent; to steal or to secrete in joke some trifling article belonging to them; and the more saucy and impudent they are, the more troublesome to strangers, and all the men of the encampment, the more they are praised as giving indication of a future enterprising and warlike disposition.

An Arab child never discloses to a stranger more than his own by-name, being instructed to conceal the name of his family, lest he should fall a victim to some enemy who had a claim of blood for the death of a relation, against the tribe: even grown-up Arabs never mention their family name to a stranger, of whatever tribe he may be.

---

* The Arabs in general can run a considerable distance with the greatest ease and celerity.

Religious Worship.

The Bedouins, until within a few years, had not any priests among them, neither *mollás* nor *imáms*: but since their conversion to the Wahaby faith, mollas have been introduced by a few sheikhs, such as el Teyar, and Ibn Esmeyr, whose young children have learned to write from one of them. The Aenezes are punctual in their daily prayers; they have no *khotbe* on Fridays. They observe the fast of Ramazan with great strictness; even during their marches in the middle of summer, nothing but the apprehension of death can induce them to interrupt the fast. There are but three things which the Bedouins consider themselves as forbidden to touch. These *harám*, or forbidden things are swine, dead bodies, and blood. They eat whatever kind of game they can take. On the day of *korbán*, the great sacrifice on Mount Arafat, each Arab family kills as many camels as there have been deaths of adult persons during the last year (نحي) in that family, whether the deceased were males or females. Though a dead person should have bequeathed but one camel to his heir, that camel is sacrificed; and if he did not leave one, his relations kill one of their own camels. Seven sheep may be substituted for a camel; and if the whole number cannot be procured for the *korbán* of the death-year, the deficiency may be supplied by killing some on the next or subsequent year. The korbán is therefore always a day of great feasting among the tribes.

On the death of an Arab, his body is immediately buried without any ceremony. When Soleimán died, who was elder brother of the famous Aeneze chief, Ibn Esmeyr, his body was thrown upon a camel, and entrusted for burial to a Fellah: no one, not even his brother, attended the corpse. If the camp in which an

Arab dies be near a ruined village, (and such abound in the Desert at four or five days east of Syria,) the dead man is buried among the ruins; but in the plain, if a ruined village be not near; and stones, piled over the grave, indicate it to the traveller, and at the same time serve to guard the body from wild beasts. On the death of a father, the children of both sexes cut off their *kerouns*, or tresses of hair, in testimony of grief. At the moment of a man's death, his wives, daughters, and female relations unite in cries of lamentation, (*welouloŭá*,) which they repeat several times. If the deceased has not left any male heir, and that his whole property is transferred to another family, or if the heir is a minor, and goes to live with his uncle or next relation, the tent-posts are torn up immediately after the man has expired, and the tent demolished (*khurbbeit*).

It is since their conversion to the Wahaby faith, (about fifteen years ago,) that the Aenezes have begun an observance of the regular prayers; knowing that the Wahaby chief is very rigid in punishing those who omit the practice. There are different opinions about the Wahabys' tenets, and I never met in Syria any person who even pretended to have a true knowledge of their religion. I think myself authorised to state, from the result of my inquiries among the Arabs, and the Wahabys themselves, that the religion of the Wahabys may be called the Protestantism or even Puritanism of the Mohammedans. The Wahaby acknowledges the Korán as a divine revelation; his principle is, "The Korán, and nothing but the Korán:" he therefore rejects all the *Hedayth* or "traditions," with which the Muselman lawyers explain, and often interpolate, the Korán. He regards Mohammed as a prophet, but merely as a mortal to whom his disciples pay too much veneration. The Wahaby forbids the pilgrimage to Mohammed's tomb at Medinah, but exhorts the faithful to visit the Kaaba, and, principally, to sacrifice upon Mount Arafat, sanctioning so far the objects of the pilgrims at Mekka. He reproves the Muselmans of this age, for their impious vanity in dress, their luxury in eating and smoking. He asks them, whether Mohammed dressed in pelisses, whether he ever smoked the argyle or the pipe? All his followers dress in the most simple garments, having neither about their own persons, nor their horses, any gold or silver; they abstain from smoking, which, they say, stupifies and intoxicates. They reject music, singing, dancing, and games of every kind, and live with each other (at least in presence of their chief) on terms of most perfect equality; because no respect, says the chief, is due to any but God, before whom all are equal; nor will this great chief allow any person to rise on his entrance, or to make room for him. He exclaims against any intercourse between his faithful people and the heretics, (*meshrekein*) as he calls the Muselmans. The Wahaby (as Ibn Saoud, the chief, is emphatically styled) propagates his religion with the sword. Whenever he purposes to attack a district of heretics, he cautions them three times, and invites them to adopt his religion; after the third summons, he proclaims that the time for pardon has elapsed, and he then allows his troops to pillage and kill at their pleasure. When the town of Mesdjed Aly was taken, his Arabs slaughtered all the inhabitants. A country once conquered by the Wahaby enjoys under him the most perfect tranquillity. In *Nedjd* and *Hedjáz* the roads are secure, and the people free from any kind of oppression. The Muselmans are forced to adopt his system; but the Jews and Christians are not molested in exercising the respective religions of their ancestors, on condition of paying tribute. A Wahaby priest, or molla, being asked why, in the assault of a town, the lives of honest Turks, Christians, and Jews, were not spared, replied, " If you wish to grind a heap of wheat in which you know that there are a few peas intermixed, do you not rather grind the whole together, than take the trouble of picking out the few peas one by one?"

A principal tenet of the Wahaby faith, is the obligation of paying tribute, (Zekawah, or Zeká,) due to the chief, by all his followers. In winter, the collectors of this tribute (mezekká) leave Deráyeh, and disperse themselves all over the Wahaby districts, exacting payment with great strictness: they then return to their chief with loads of gold and silver. The Aeneze pay annually, for every five camels, one Spanish dollar; and for every forty sheep or goats, the value of one. For every horse or mare, one *danab* (about seven shillings). I have reason to believe that the amount of tribute varies a little in different districts of Arabia. It is paid in cash. The chief for some time would only accept Spanish and Imperial dollars, but now is satisfied with Turkish coin. Ibn el Saoud disposes of his domains, (the grounds and palm-tree gardens belonging to himself personally,) on the same conditions which formerly gave origin to the feudal system in Europe. His tenants do not pay him any yearly rent, but hold their grounds as fees, being obliged to keep, always ready for marching, a certain number of armed camel-riders. Whenever he plans an expedition, he orders them to meet him, or his people, at some spot near the district which he means to invade; and they proceed accordingly, either in small parties, or singly, to the place appointed. This obligation of personal attendance prevails, as I have been informed, throughout all parts of Nedjd; the chief exacting one to attend him actually from every ten men, whether mounted on horses or on camels. This, however, is not the case with the Aenezes, who have never been conquered, but voluntarily consented to pay tribute.

To keep such fierce nations in perfect subjection is scarcely possible. They are always ready to shake off the yoke; the northern Aenezes have not paid any tribute for several years. All the Aenezes, whom I met in my journey through the Desert, were rebels; they still kept up an appearance of good understanding with the Wahaby. Their chiefs abstained from tobacco, and professed the Wahaby faith; but the common people care little about the new doctrine; they sing and smoke, but always mention the name of Ibn Saoud with respect.

Matrimony and Divorce.

Polygamy, according to the Turkish law, is a privilege of the Bedouins; but the greater number of Arabs content themselves with one wife: very few have two wives, and I never met with any person who could recollect a Bedouin that had four wives at once in his tent. The marriage ceremony is very simple among the Aenezes. When a man desires to marry a girl, he sends some friend of the family to her father, and a negotiation commences: the girl's wishes are then consulted; if they agree with those of the father, (for it is never supposed that she should be compelled to marry against her inclination,) and if the match is to take place, the friend, holding the father's hand, says, " You declare, that you give your daughter as wife to ——?" The father answers in the affirmative. The marriage day being appointed, (usually five or six days after the betrothing, which is called *talab*, not *kheteb*,) the bridegroom comes with a lamb in his arms to the tent of the girl's father, and there cuts the lamb's throat before witnesses. As soon as the blood falls upon the ground, the marriage ceremony is regarded as complete. The men and girls amuse themselves with feasting and singing. Soon after sun-set the bridegroom retires to a tent, pitched for him at a distance from the camp; there he shuts himself up, and awaits the arrival of his bride. The bashful girl, meanwhile, runs from the tent of one friend to another's, till she is caught at last, and conducted in triumph by a few women to the bridegroom's tent; he receives her at the entrance, and forces her into it; the women who had accompanied her then depart. The novelty of her situation naturally induces a young virgin to exclaim; and this is considered by the friends as a sufficient evidence of maiden timidity. They do not require any of those indelicate proofs, exhibited on such occasions among other Eastern nations. But if an Aeneze widow marry a second time, it would be regarded as highly improper, were she to utter such exclamations.

There is, in the vicinity of Nazareth, a tribe of El Ryer Arabs, among whom the two fathers negotiate the marriage of their respective children. Terms being concluded, the bridegroom's father presents to the bride's father a green leaf of some plant or vegetable, just at hand, and calls on all present to witness the donation.

Among the Aeneze it would be esteemed scandalous, if the bride's father were to demand money, or what is called " the daughter's price" (*hakk el bint*); although such is the universal custom in Syria, where every Turk, Christian, and Jew pays for his wife a sum proportionate to the rank of the girl's father. Among the *Ahl el Shemâl*, a father receives for his daughter the *khomse*, or " five articles," which, however, become the wife's property, and remain with her, even should she be divorced. The *khomse* comprehends a carpet, a large silver nose-ring, a silver neck-chain, silver bracelets, and a camel-bag of the Baghdad carpet manufacture. An Aeneze is permitted to bestow gifts on the object of his affections; nor is it reckoned indecorous for the girl to accept them. The lover sometimes makes presents to her father, or brother, hoping thereby to influence them in his favour; but this does not often occur the practice being reckoned disgraceful to those who receive such presents.

I have already mentioned that the Aenezes never intermarry with the *szona*, handicraftsmen or artisans; nor do they ever marry their daughters to Fellahs, or inhabitants of towns; but the *Ahl el Shemál* are less scrupulous in this respect.

If an Arab, on the consummation of his nuptials, should have reason to doubt whether he had found the bride in a state of virgin purity, he does not immediately expose her shame, being afraid of offending her family; but after a day or two he repudiates his wife, assigning, as a sufficient motive, that she did not please him. If an Arab has manifest evidence of his wife's infidelity, he accuses her before her father and brother; and if the adultery be unequivocally proved, the father himself, or the brother, cuts her throat.

Most Arabs are contented with a single wife; but for this monogamy they make amends, by indulging in variety. They frequently change their wives, according to a custom founded on the Turkish law of divorce, which, however, has been much abused among the Arabs; for when one of them becomes, on any slight occasion, dissatisfied with his wife, he separates himself from her by simply saying, *ent tálek*—" thou art divorced." He then gives her a she-camel, and sends her back to the tents of her family. He is not obliged to state any reasons, nor does this circumstance reflect any dishonour on the divorced woman, or her family: every one excuses him by saying, "he did not like her." Perhaps, on the very same day, he betroths himself to another female; but his repudiated wife, on the contrary, is obliged to wait forty days before she can become the wife of another man, that it may be known whether or not she is pregnant by the former husband. Divorces are so common among the Aenezes, that they even take place during the wife's pregnancy; and a woman is sometimes repudiated who has borne several children to her husband. In the former case, the woman nurses her child till it is able to run about, when the father takes it to his tent. When a man discards an old mother of a family, he sometimes allows her to live in his tent among her children; but she may retire to her parents. A woman who has been three or four times divorced, may nevertheless be free from any stain or imputation on her character. I have seen Arabs about forty-five years of age who were known to have had above fifty different wives. Whoever will be at the expense of a camel, may divorce and change his wives as often as he thinks fit.

The law allows to the wife also a kind of divorce; if not happy in her husband's tent, she flies for refuge to her father or kindred. The husband may induce her, by promises of fine clothes, ear-rings, or carpets, to return; but if she refuse, he cannot take her by force, as her family would resent the violence: all he can do is to withhold the sentence of divorce, *ent tálek*, without which the lady is not authorised to marry again. The husband is sometimes bribed, by a present of many camels, to pronounce the words of divorce; but if he persevere in refusing, the wife is condemned to a single life. A wife thus parted from her husband, but not regularly divorced, is called *támehhe*: of this class there are great numbers; but, on the other hand, there are not any old maids to be found among the Arabs.

If a young man leaves a widow, his brother generally offers to marry her; custom does not oblige either him or her to make this match, nor can he prevent her from marrying another man. It seldom happens, however, that she refuses; for by such an union the family property is kept together.

A man has an exclusive right to the hand of his cousin; he is not obliged to marry her, but she cannot, without his consent, become the wife of any other person. If a man permits his cousin to marry her lover, or if a husband divorces his runaway wife, he usually says, " She was my slipper, I have cast her off." * (كانت بابوجي وشلحتها)

Among the tribes of Ahl el Shemál, if it happens that an Arab elopes with another man's wife, and takes refuge in the tent of a third, this last kills a sheep, and thus marries the couple. In case of such an event among the Aenezes, the wife returns safely to her parents, and awaits the *talak*, or word of divorce, from her husband; her lover is likewise secure from personal danger, being *dakhul* of the family in whose tent he had taken refuge.

By this facility of divorce, every tie is loosened that should connect families; by the frequent change of wives, all secrets of parents and children are divulged over the whole tribe; jealousies are excited among the relations, and we may easily conceive its effect upon morals.

It must, however, be allowed that an Arab holds his parents in great respect; his mother, especially, he loves most affectionately; indeed he sometimes quarrels on her account with his father, and is often expelled from the paternal tent for vindicating his mother's cause.

When a son attains maturity, his father generally gives him a mare or a camel, that he may try his fortune in plundering excursions. Whatever booty falls to his lot, is reckoned his own property, and cannot be taken from him by his father. A favourite son, on occasion of his marriage, often receives a present of camels or money from his father: but this is not a general rule, and many young Arabs commence the matrimonial state with no other property than one camel to provide for the subsistence of his family. Sometimes the son is permitted to live with his young wife in the rather's tent. As to the girl, she never receives any thing from her father at the time of her marriage; the *khomse* (before men-

---

* See the Book of Ruth, iv. 7, 8.

tioned), given among the Ahl el Shemál by the husband to his wife's father, is by the latter often bestowed upon his daughter.

Government and Mode of Judicature.

The Arabs are a free nation; the liberty and independence of individuals among them almost border upon anarchy. From the experience, however, of ages, during which their political state has not suffered the smallest change, it appears that their civil institutions are well adapted to their habits and mode of life; although, at first view, they may not seem calculated to secure that grand object of legislation, the protection of the weak against the stronger.

Every Arab tribe has its chief sheikh, and every camp (for a tribe often comprises many) is headed by a sheikh, or at least by an Arab of some consideration: but the sheikh has no actual authority over the individuals of his tribe; he may, however, by his personal qualities obtain considerable influence. His commands would be treated with contempt; but deference is paid to his advice, if the people regard him as a man skilled in public and private affairs.

The real government of the Bedouins may be said to consist in the separate strength of their different families, who constitute so many armed bodies, ever ready to punish or retaliate aggression; and it is the counterpoise alone of these bodies that maintains peace in the tribe. Should a dispute happen between two individuals, the sheikh will endeavour to settle the matter; but if either party be dissatisfied with his advice, he cannot insist upon obedience. The Arab can only be persuaded by his own relations; and if they fail, war commences between the two families and all their kindred respectively. Thus the Bedouin truly says, that he acknowledges no master but the Lord of the Universe; and in fact, the most powerful Aeneze chief dares not inflict a trifling punishment on the poorest man of his tribe, without incurring the risk of mortal vengeance from the individual and his relations. The sheikhs, therefore, or *emirs,* as some style themselves, must not be regarded as princes of the Desert, a title with which some travellers have dignified them. Their prerogative consists in leading their tribe against the enemy; in conducting negotiations for peace or war; in fixing the spot for encampments; in entertaining strangers of note, &c.; and even these privileges are much limited. The sheikh cannot declare war or conclude terms of peace, without consulting the chief men of his tribe; if he wish to break up the camp, he must previously ask the opinions of his people concerning the security of the roads, and sufficiency of pasture and water in the districts to which he directs his view. His orders are never obeyed, but his example is generally followed. Thus, he strikes his tent and loads his camels, without desiring any one to do so; but when they know that the sheikh is setting out, his Arabs hasten to join him. It likewise happens, that if the sheikh encamps on a spot which his people do not like, they pitch their own tents a half day's journey from his, and leave him with only a few of his nearest relations. An Arab often leaves the camp of his friends, out of caprice or dislike of his companions, and joins another camp of his tribe.

The sheikh does not derive any yearly income from his tribe, or camp; on the contrary, he is obliged to support his title by considerable disbursements, and to extend his influence by great liberality. It is expected that he should treat strangers in a better style than any other person of the tribe; that he should maintain the poor, and divide among his friends whatever presents he may receive. His means of defraying these expenses are, the tribute which he exacts from the Syrian villages, and his emoluments from the Mekka pilgrim caravan. When a sheikh dies, he is succeeded in his dignity by one of his sons, or his brothers, or some other relation distinguished for valour and liberality: but this is not a general rule. If some other Arab of the tribe should possess those qualities in a more eminent degree, he may be chosen: the tribe is often divided; one party adhering to the family of the last sheikh, the other choosing a new one. A living sheikh is sometimes deposed, and a more generous man elected in his place.

The only form or ceremony attending the election of a sheikh, is the announcing to him that he is henceforward to be regarded as chief of the tribe. Among the Aenezes, those individuals who transact the business of the Pashas of Damascus and of Baghdad, are invariably sheikhs. The profits accruing to them from these connexions, are much greater than any which they might derive from plunder in war; and if the Pasha's agent allows his own friends to share in his profits, he is certain of being appointed chief.

In cases of litigation, the sheikh has not the power of executing any sentence: the parties sometimes agree to abide by his decision, or to choose umpires; but they cannot, on any occasion, be compelled to yield, and an adversary may be cited before the kady. Of those *kády el Arab*, so often mentioned by Arabian historians, a few still exist among the Bedouins. The *Would Aly* have three, the *Rowalla* and the *Bessher*, one each. These kadys, or judges, are men distinguished for their penetrating judgment, their love of justice, and experience in the customs and laws of their nations. They know not how to read or write, and refer to memory as a guide in the cases brought before them. A judge of this kind is called by the Arabs *kády el ferâa*, "the kady of customary laws," in opposition to the *kady el sheryaa*, or "kady of the written law," such as are found in the Turkish towns. They are not distinguished by dress, or any particular mode of living, from their fellow nomades. The office of kady generally continues in their family: the election of a new one depends upon the good opinions entertained of them by the other kadys of friendly Arab tribes, as well as by the people of his own tribe; in this election the sheikhs have not any influence. The costs paid to a kady in law-suits are very considerable. If a horse or mare be the object in dispute, the costs amount to a *bekra,* or a young she-camel; if the parties contend about a camel, the kady receives one *dahab* (about seven shillings). If a sum of money be in question, the kady's fees are twenty-five per cent. These fees are always paid by the person who gains the cause, never by the loser.

If a case occur presenting difficulties which human sagacity cannot unravel, (such as witnesses of equal credibility directly contradicting each other,) the kady sends the litigating parties before the *mebesshae,* who subjects them to the ordeal, a mode of trial resembling that used in Europe during the dark periods of the middle ages. To every one of the principal Aeneze tribes there is a chief judge, called *mebesshae* before whose tribunal all intricate cases are decided. Should his endeavours to reconcile the disputants prove vain, this judge directs that a fire should be kindled before him; he then takes a long iron spoon (used by the Arabs in roasting coffee), and having made it red hot in the fire, he takes it out, and licks with his tongue the upper end of the spoon on both sides. He then replaces it in the fire, and commands the accused person first to wash his mouth with water, and next to lick it as he had done; if the accused escape without injury to his tongue, he is supposed innocent; if he suffer from the hot iron, he loses his cause. The Arabs ascribe this wonderful escape not to the Almighty Protector of innocence, but to the Devil. Persons have been known to lick the red-hot iron (called *beshaa*) above twenty times without the slightest injury. The mebesshae receives for his trouble forty piastres, or a she-camel of two years. Whenever a person is accused of man-slaughter or murder, and denies the fact, or in any other cause which has, according to the Arabian expression, blood for its object, an appeal is always made to the mebesshae. In such a case the testimony of witnesses, however numerous, is not admitted, nor can the kady determine it; but when the accused denies, the plaintiff's only tribunal is the mebesshae's. If an Arab be dissatisfied with the sentence of his kady, he may apply to another, or to several; but these generally confirm the first sentence. If he should still think himself wronged, notwithstanding the decision of the kady and of the ordeal against him, he may refuse to obey the sentence, because in fact there does not exist any legal authority which can enforce it. In such cases, relations generally persuade him to make terms; but if he continue obstinate, they must not abandon him, lest blood should be shed, and revenge for it inflicted on them, although they may not have taken part in the affray.

Corporal punishments are unknown among the Arabs; the sentences of the sheikh, the umpire, the kady, and the mebesshae, founded on immemorial usage, always award pecuniary fines, of whatever nature the crime may be of which a man is accused. Every offence has its fine ascertained in the kady's court; and the nature and amount of those fines are well known to the Arabs; and the fear of incurring them preserves order and tranquillity in the tribe.

All insulting expressions,* all acts of violence, a blow, however slight, (and a blow may differ in its degree of insult according to the part struck,) and the infliction of a wound, from which even a single drop of blood flows, all have their respective fines ascertained. The kady's sentence is sometimes to this effect:—

---

* Such, as "You treat your guests ill;" (مطرود علي ضيفك); or "You are a slave" (انت عبد); or "You are a dog" (انت جعري); or "You are a Heteyme" (انت حتيمي), a tribe of the Kebly Arabs not held in much esteem; or "I know you well" (انا عرفتك); or "You are leprous," (انت ابرص).

Bokhyt called *Djolan* "a dog." Djolan returned the insult by a blow upon Bokhyt's arm; then Bokhyt cut Djolan's shoulder with a knife. Bokhyt therefore owes to Djolan—

For the insulting expressions . . . 1 sheep.
For wounding him in the shoulder . . 3 camels.

Djolan owes to Bokhyt,

For the blow upon his arm . . . 1 camel.

Remain due to Djolan 2 camels and 1 sheep.

Among the fines paid for certain crimes and aggressions, that paid for killing a watch-dog (حق الجعري) is remarkable. The dead dog is held up by the tail, so that its mouth just touches the ground; its length is then measured, and a stick (as long from the surface of the ground as the dog) is fixed into the earth: the person who killed the dog is then obliged to pour out over the stick as much wheat as will wholly cover it; and this heap of wheat is the fine due to the owner of the dog. I have heard that the kady of Constantinople exacts the same fine for the same offence, if the dog has not been killed by a man in self-defence.

If an Arab wants witnesses to any transaction between himself and another person, he calls upon all present, exclaiming *Ashehed yá fulán*, "bear thou witness, O * * *;" or it is deemed sufficient that he should touch their arms with his hand: this is considered as a summons to give testimony. If he does not observe either of those forms, should the transaction give rise to a law-suit, the kady immediately inquires whether the witnesses are *hadherein* (by-standers), or *sháhedein* (actual witnesses); if none appear but by-standers, the opposite party may reject their evidence. The *hadherein* may insist that the disputants should come with the kady to take their evidence at their own tents; while, on the other hand, custom obliges the actual witnesses (towards whom the above-mentioned forms have been observed) to present themselves in person before the kady, although he may be encamped at some days' distance. If a witness be unable from disease to perform such a journey, his sheikh takes his evidence, and communicates it either verbally or in writing to the kady, observing that he himself bears witness to the sick man's declaration. The bystanders, *hadherein*, are likewise called اولاد هلال or اولاد الخير or محضر. If there are any witnesses, the kady immediately gives his sentence; if there are none, he orders the accused party to swear a solemn oath professing his innocence; if he swears, he is considered as acquitted. The oath is never required of the claimant or prosecutor, but always of the defendant, according to the rule expressed in a common saying, "It is not proper that one should swear and eat" (ما يسير يحلف و ياكل). According to the same rule, the mebesshae never commands the plaintiff, who claims the price of a relation's blood, to try the red hot spoon, but leaves the benefit of that ordeal to the accused. There are several judicial oaths in use among the Arabs, distinguished by different degrees of sanctity and solemnity. One of the most common in domestic life is to take hold with one hand of the *wasat*, or middle tent-pole, and to swear "by the life of this tent and its owners."

و حياة هد* بيت و اصحاب البيت كذا و كذا

A more serious oath, often taken before the kady, is called the "oath of the wood" (يمين العود). To try the veracity of a person, a small piece of wood (or some straw), is taken up from the ground, and presented to him with these words—"Take the wood and swear by God, and the life of him who caused it to be green, and dried it up."

خذ العود و احلف بالله و حياة من خضره و يبسه

A still more solemn oath is the *yemein el khet* (يمين الخط), or "oath of the cross lines:" this is only used on very important occasions.

* هد for هذا

Thus, if a Bedouin accuses his neighbour of a considerable theft, and cannot prove the fact by witnesses, the plaintiff takes the defendant before the sheikh, or kady, and calls upon him to swear in his defence whatever oath he may choose to demand from him. If he complies readily, his accuser leads him to a certain distance from the camp, because the magical nature of the oath might prove pernicious to the general body of Arabs, were it to take place in their vicinity: he then with his *sekin*, or crooked knife, draws on the sand a large circle, with many cross lines inside it.

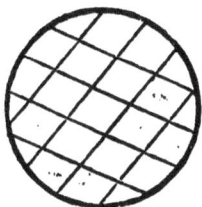

He obliges the defendant to place his right foot within the circle, he himself doing the same, and addressing him in the following words, which the accused is obliged to repeat—" By God, and in God, and through God, (I swear) I did not take it, and it is not in my possession."

و الله و تالله و بالله اني ما اخذته و ما هو عندي

Some persons enter the circle with both feet. It is said that Mohammed once made use of this oath; and to swear falsely by it, would for ever disgrace an Arab. To make it still more solemn, a *shemle* (or camel's udder-bag) and an ant (*el nemle*) are placed together within the circle; indicating that the accused swears by the hope of never being deprived of his camel's udder, and of never experiencing a time when he should want even the winter provision of an ant. Such is the *yémein el shemle we nemle*, or " oath of the shemle and nemle." (يمين الشمله و النمله) Another civil institution of the Arabs must here be mentioned, since it greatly contributes to maintain peace and tranquillity among a multitude of fierce and turbulent soldiers, who acknowledge no law but that of the strongest. This is the institution of the *wasy* (وصي), or "guardian." If an Arab wishes to provide for the security of his family even after his own death, he applies (though in the prime of life) to one of his friends, and begs that he will become guardian to his children. The ceremony on this occasion is that he should present himself, leading a she-camel, before his friend: then he ties one of the hanging corners of the *keffie* or kerchief of his friend into a knot, and leading the camel over to him, says, "I constitute you wasy for my children, and your children for my children, and your grandchildren for my grandchildren." If his friend accepts the camel, (and it is seldom refused,) he and his whole family become the hereditary protectors of the other man's descendants. The obligation of the wasy, and the claims of the protected, equally descend to their heirs, in the order of their institution: thus, A has made B wasy to his children; B's sons are wasy to A's grandchildren; B's grandsons to A's great grandchildren, &c.; but A's great grandchildren have no claim to the direct protection of B's children. Almost every Arab has his wasy in some other family, and is at the same time wasy to a third family: even the greatest sheikh is not without his guardian. The ward applies to his wasy whenever he thinks himself aggrieved, and in defending his ward the wasy's whole family co-operate with him. This system of guardianship is particularly beneficial to minors, to women, and to old men, who find it necessary to resist the demands of their sons. Thus it appears, that the Arabs constitute within their own families and those of the wasys so many armed bodies, which, by the fear they mutually entertain of each other, preserve peace in the tribe; and perhaps nothing but this institution could save a nation so fierce and rapacious from being destroyed by domestic dissensions.

The ceremony of tying a knot on the end of the wasy's keffie, is done that he may look out for witnesses to prove the act: the same custom is observed whenever any transaction is to be witnessed. The she-camel, ناقة, given to the wasy ought to be four years old: from a poor man, the wasy will accept of an *abba*, or mantle, instead of a camel.

The laws of inheritance among the Arabs are those prescribed by the Korán, and the property is divided among the male children in equal shares. If a father leaves at his death some children under age, the next relation takes them under his care; and if the father's tent should have been struck, he lodges them in his own, and becomes guardian of their property. The whole tribe knows, by the number of sheep and camels, the amount of the deceased's possessions; the minor cannot therefore be easily defrauded. The profits arising from the management of the property, furnish clothes &c. for the children. The boy takes it into his own hands as soon as he is able to know its value, i. e. at about the age of twelve years: before this time, the nearest relation exercises a certain influence over him; but should it be employed to the injury of the minor, an application is made to the wasy. If the creditors of the deceased make claims upon the heir, and that the debt consists of cattle, the due number is paid to the creditor: if the debt be for merchandise furnished, the creditor only receives the amount of the real value of the goods at the current price of the day, without any allowance for profit.

The Warfare and Predatory Excursions of the Bedouins.

The Arab tribes are in a state of almost perpetual war against each other; it seldom happens that a tribe enjoys a moment of general peace with all its neighbours, yet the war between two tribes is scarcely ever of long duration; peace is easily made, but again broken upon the slightest pretence. The Arab warfare is that of partisans; general battles are rarely fought: to surprise the enemy by a sudden attack, and to plunder a camp are chief objects of both parties. This is the reason why their wars are bloodless; the enemy is generally attacked by superior numbers, and he gives way without fighting, in hopes of retaliating on a weak encampment of the other party. The dreaded effects of "blood-revenge," which shall be hereafter noticed, prevent many sanguinary conflicts: thus two tribes may be at war for a whole year without the loss of more than thirty or forty men on each side. The Arabs, however, have evinced on some occasions great firmness and courage; but when they fight merely for plunder, they behave like cowards. I could adduce numerous instances of caravan-travellers and peasants putting to flight three times their number of Arabs who had attacked them: hence, throughout Syria, they are reckoned miserable cowards, and their contests with the peasants always prove them such; but when the Arab faces his national enemy in open battle, when the fame and honour of his tribe are at stake, he frequently displays heroic valour; and we still find among them warriors whose names are celebrated all over the Desert; and the acts of bravery ascribed to them might seem fabulous, did we not recollect that the weapons of the Arabs allow full scope to personal prowess, and that in irregular skirmishing the superior qualities of the horse give the rider incalculable advantages over his enemies. Thus we read in the history of Antar that this valiant slave, when mounted upon his mare *Ghabara*, killed with his lance, in a single battle, eight hundred men. However incredulous respecting the full amount of this statement, I may here be allowed to mention the name of a modern hero, whose praise is recorded in hundreds of poems, and whose feats in arms have been reported to me by many ocular witnesses. *Gedoua Ibn Gheyan el Shamsy* is known to have slain thirty of his enemies in one encounter; he prided himself in having never been put to flight, and the booty which he took was immense. But his friends alone benefited by this, for he himself continued always poor. His life at last was sacrificed to his valour. A war broke out in the year 1790, between the *Ibn Fadhel* and *Ibn Esmeyr* tribes, while most of the Aenezes engaged themselves on one side or the other. After many partial encounters, the two sheikhs, each with about five thousand horsemen, met near *Mezerib*, a small town on the Hadj road, nearly fifty miles from Damascus, on the plain of Hauran, and both determined on a general battle that should terminate the war. The armies were drawn up in sight of each other, and some slight skirmishing had commenced, when Gedoua (or, as the Bedouins in their dialect called him, *Djedoua*) formed the generous resolution of sacrificing his life for the glory of his tribe. He rode up to Ibn Esmeyr, under whose banners the Shamsy then fought, took off his coat of mail, and his clothes to his shirt, and approaching the chief, kissed his beard, thereby indicating that he devoted his life to him. He then quitted the ranks of his friends, and, without any arms besides his sabre, drove his mare furiously against the enemy. His valour being well known to the troops of both parties, every one waited with anxious expectation the result of his enterprise. The strength of his arm soon opened a way among the hostile ranks; he penetrated to their standard, or *merkeb*, which was carried in the centre; felled to the ground the camel that bore it by a stroke on its thigh; then wheeled round, and had already regained the open space between the two armies, when he was killed by a shot from a *metrás*, or foot-soldier.* His friends, who had seen the *merkeb* fall, rushed with a loud cheer upon their enemies, and completely routed them; above five hundred foot-soldiers having been slain on that day. Whenever the *merkeb* falls, the battle is considered as lost by the party to whom it had belonged.

I have already mentioned, that the usual mode of warfare is to surprise by sudden attacks. To effect this the Arabs sometimes prepare an expedition against an enemy, whose tents are at a distance of ten or twenty days from their own. The Aenezes are not unfrequently seen encamped in the Hauran, and making incursions into the territory of *Mekka*; or a party of the *Dhofyr* Arabs from the vicinity of Baghdad, plundering the Aeneze encampments near Damascus; or some of the *Beni Sakhr* tribe from *Djebel Belkaa*, seeking for pillage in the province of Irak Arabi. Whenever they resolve to undertake a distant expedition, every horseman who is to be of the party, engages a friend to accompany him: this *zammal*, or companion,† is mounted on a young and strong camel. The horseman provides camel-bags, a stock of food, and water. He mounts behind the *zammal*, that his mare may not be fatigued before the decisive moment (ساعت

---

* The *metrás*, (متراس), or foot-soldiers, are armed with fire-locks; they crouch down in front between the lines of horsemen, and place heaps of stones before them, on which they rest their muskets, that they may take a more certain aim.

† *Zammal*, زَمَل. Two men riding upon one camel are called *merdouf*, مردوف, frequently seen among Bedouins; a party of armed camel-riders they call *rukub*, ركب; a party of horsemen, *kheyáleh*, خياله.

الكسب) arrives. When the *ghazou* (غزو), or flying detachments, approach the enemy, their chief (عتير الغزو or كبير الغزو) generally appoints three meeting-places (ميعاد), where the zammals are to wait for the horsemen who push forward to the attack. The first meeting-place is seldom more than half an hour's distance from the enemy's camp, in a *wády* (or valley), or behind a hill. If, at the appointed time, their party does not return to them, the zammals hasten to the second meeting-place, and halt there for a whole day in expectation of their friends; thence they proceed to the third station, where they are to remain three or four days; this place being always at a long day's distance from the object of attack, the enemy's camp. If, after the expiration of that time, none of their people return, they hasten homewards as fast as possible. Should the expedition have proved successful in the taking of booty, the zammal is rewarded with a she-camel, even though his friend's share should not amount to more than a single camel; but if the horseman have been defeated, the zammal does not get any remuneration. It sometimes happens on distant expeditions, that all the horsemen are destroyed; if they are repulsed, and cut off from the zammals, who have with them the food and water, they must perish in the barren plain, or submit to be stripped and plundered.

Whenever an enemy comes from a distance to attack an encampment, he does not trouble himself about the property that may be in the tents, but drives away the horses and camels. If, on the contrary, the enemy's camp is near, the conquerors take away the tents, and all that they contain. In such case, a courageous woman may recover one of her husband's camels, if she run after the retiring enemy, and call out to their chief, "O noble chief, I beg my nourishment from God and from you!—we shall be starved!" (يا عقيد القوم اريد من الله و منك الاكل نحن مقطوعين) If she can keep up with the troop for any length of time, the chief will think himself bound in honour to give her a camel from his own share of the booty.

Whatever these Arabs take in a successful expedition, is shared according to previous agreement. Sometimes every horseman plunders for himself; at other times, an equal division is to be made. In the former case, whatever an Arab first touches with his lance is regarded as his sole property; thus, if a herd of camels be found, every one hastens to touch with his lance as many as he can before any other person, calling out as he touches each, "O N * * *, bear witness! O Z * * *, behold thou art mine." The chief of the *ghazou* (not always the sheikh of the camp, but some other respectable man of the tribe) generally stipulates for an extra portion of the booty; for instance, that all the male camels taken should be his, or one-tenth of the plunder above his ordinary share. If a large party take but a comparatively small booty, the chief on his return assembles the men, and the cattle that they had taken, before his tent, and then says to his companions, one after another, "Go thou and take one;" "and thou, go thou and take one," &c. When all have taken an equal share, should some few remain, which it would be difficult to divide among such numbers, the chief pronounces the word *máleha* (مالحة—which I am unable to explain, for it cannot here signify *salted*); on this signal, they all rush upon the remaining cattle, and whatever beast a man first seizes he retains as his own property.

The Aenezes never attack by night; this they regard as *boag* (بوق), or treachery; for, during the confusion of a nocturnal assault, the women's apartments might be entered, and violence offered, which would infallibly occasion much resistance from the men of the attacked camp, and probably end in a general massacre —a circumstance which the Arabs constantly endeavour to avoid. An exception, however, must here be made; for the *Shammar*

Arabs have a peculiar custom of attacking by night the enemy's camp, when it happens to be situated near their own. If they can reach it unobserved, they suddenly knock down the principal tent-poles; and whilst the surprised people are striving to disengage themselves from the tent-coverings which had fallen on them, the cattle is driven off by the assailants. This kind of attack they call *beyát* (بيات).

But the female sex is respected even among the most inveterate enemies, whenever a camp is plundered; and neither men, women, nor slaves, are ever taken prisoners. If the Arabs, after their camp has been plundered, receive a reinforcement, or can rally, they pursue the enemy; and whatever they can recover of the plundered property is returned to its original owner.

In the plundering of a camp, but few men are ever killed. As the camp is generally taken by surprise, defence would be useless against superior numbers; and an Arab never kills an unresisting foe, unless he has to avenge the blood of some relation.

The surprise of a camp often proves unsuccessful, in consequence of a previous intimation, either given by individuals who have settled among the enemy, or by one of the hostile tribe desirous of saving from ruin some intimate friend residing in the camp which is the object of attack: those who contrive to give such intimation are called *nezeir* (نذير).

If an Arab, pursued by an enemy, finds that the strength of his mare is nearly exhausted, he may save his life by throwing himself off (*howel* حول) and begging protection. To do this, however, is considered a disgrace, which nothing but extreme necessity can excuse; and the enemy will boast ever after, that such a person had leaped from his mare while he pursued him. Although life is spared on these occasions, a man loses his mare and all his clothes. If the flying party will not yield on the near approach of his pursuer, who calls out repeatedly "*howel!*

howel!" "get down! get down!" the pursuer wounds or kills him with a thrust of his lance.

It sometimes happens in a war between two tribes, that an Arab of one has some private business with a man of the other tribe which requires a personal interview. Upon this occasion, he convokes at his sheikh's all the principal men of his own tribe, and all the individuals of the enemy's, who may be resident in the camp, and taking a lance, or a hawk, he calls the whole company to witness that he designs one or the other as a present to the sheikh of the enemy's tribe, which he proposes to visit. When he arrives at the hostile camp, and delivers his present, he is allowed to continue there as long as his business may render his presence necessary. Should he be stopped on his return, and stripped by some of the enemy, his own sheikh will remonstrate with the enemy's, and the property taken will infallibly be restored.

Some of the great Aeneze chiefs use, in time of war, what may perhaps be styled the "battle banner;" for it is never displayed but in decisive and important actions, where the fall or the loss of it is regarded as a signal of defeat. This standard is of two sorts, one called *merkeb*, (مركب, or the "ship,") consisting in two stands of wood, about six or seven feet high; of which the annexed figure represents the shape.

These are placed one opposite to the other on a camel's back, so that above there is not more than a span's distance between them;

but below they are sufficiently separated for a person to sit in the midst on a saddle, and guide the camel: the upper part of this standard is covered with black ostrich feathers.

The other sort of banner is called *otfe* (عتفة); this consists of two side pieces of board, of an oblong square form, about five feet high, ornamented like the other with ostrich feathers. Such is now used by the *Teyar*, the chief of *Would Aly*.

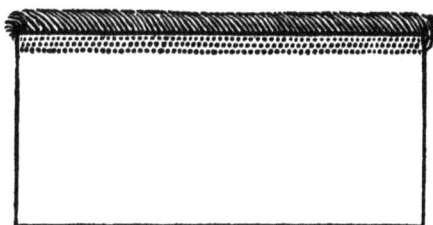

En Ibsmeyr, and *Ibn Fadhel*, have each a *merkeb*. The guide of the camel, that carries either a *merkeb* or an *otfe*, is never an adult free-born Arab, but a boy, an old woman, or a slave; for it is thought beneath the dignity of a man to sing or howl the cry called ظفرايا, with which the guide animates those who accompany the standard to battle. All the horsemen assemble around it; and the principal efforts of both parties are directed against the respective *merkeb* or *otfe* of the enemy. A captured banner is borne in triumph to the tent of the victorious sheikh.

Peace is concluded between two sheikhs under the tents of a third tribe friendly to both parties. The most frequent cause of war is a jealousy about watering-places and pasture grounds; but the dispute is soon settled, if one party be desirous of peace. If there be a domestic or internal discord among families of the same tribe and their *wasys*, the heads of the families soon effect a reconciliation. When a sheikh perceives that his people are not well satisfied with the terms of peace, he sends to the other party a written or verbal notification, that hostilities must be renewed. (مردود النقا)—the Bedouins use the word نقا for حرب)

To prevent the deadly effects of the "blood-revenge," or the *thár* (below mentioned), which is claimed by the relations of all who have been killed, even in open war, the sheikhs, by consent of the majority of their people, may conclude peace on condition of remitting, on both sides, whatever "price of blood," or private debts (arising from any cause except the *boag*, or treachery, before noticed) may be reciprocally due; and on this occasion they say, "The sheikhs have dug and buried." (الشيوخ احتلحوا و حفروا و دفنوا) But to these terms of peace the Arabs do not willingly assent.

The Aenezes no longer regard as sacred those months, during which, in ancient times, peace became a religious duty among all Arabs: they now attack their enemies even in the holy month of Ramazan. There are, however, in every lunar month, three days during which the Aenezes never fight; the sixth, sixteenth, and night of the twenty-first.*

The Blood-revenge, or Thár ثار

I am inclined to believe that this salutary institution has contributed, in a greater degree than any other circumstance, to prevent the warlike tribes of Arabia from exterminating one another. Without it, their wars in the Desert would be as sanguinary as those of the Mammelouks in Egypt; and as the principal causes of war exist as long as the nation continues its

---

* To express this they say,

كفى الله شرّ الست مع ست العشر و واحد العشرين يكفيك الكدي

The Aenezes likewise abstain from fighting on a Wednesday, superstitiously believing that they should lose the battle.

nomadic life, it can hardly be doubted that an uninterrupted state of war would soon reduce the most powerful tribes to little more than a name. But the terrible "blood-revenge" renders the most inveterate war nearly bloodless; and few subjects can be so interesting in a work that treats of Arabian manners and customs.

It is a received law among all the Arabs, that whoever sheds the blood of a man, owes blood on that account to the family of the slain person: this law is sanctioned by the Korán (II. 173.) which says—"O true believers, the law of retaliation is ordained to you for the slain; the free shall die for the free," &c. But the same book (XVII. 35.) says—"And whoever shall be unjustly slain, we have given to his heir the power of demanding satisfaction; but let him not exceed the bounds of moderation;" (فلا يسرف في القتل) viz. in putting the murderer to a cruel death, or avenging his friend's blood on any other person than the man who had actually killed him. The Arabs, however, do not strictly observe this command of their holy volume; they claim the blood not only from the actual homicide, but from all his relations; and it is these claims that constitute the right of *thár*, or the "blood-revenge."

This rests within the *khomse*, or fifth generation (the Arabs say الثار في الخمسه), those only having a right to avenge a slain parent, whose fourth lineal ascendant is, at the same time, the fourth lineal ascendant of the person slain; and, on the other side, only those male kindred of the homicide are liable to pay with their own for the blood shed, whose fourth lineal ascendant is at the same time the fourth lineal ascendant of the homicide. The present generation is thus comprised within the number of the *khomse*. The lineal descendants of all those who were entitled to revenge at the moment of the man-slaughter, inherit this right from their parents.

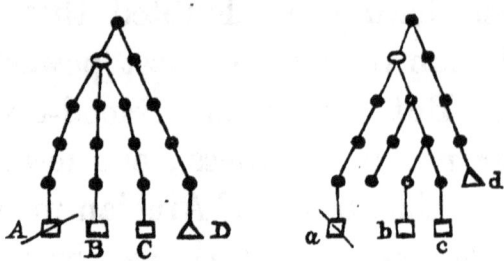

Thus, if A has killed a, B and C and their ascendants may be killed, but D is not comprehended within the *khomse*, and the *thár* does not reach him; b and c have claims to the thár, but d has not. The right to blood-revenge is never lost: it descends on both sides to the latest generations.

If the family of the man killed should in revenge kill two of the *dammawy's* (رجل دموي) or homicide's family, the latter retaliate by the death of one. If one only be killed, the affair rests there and all is quiet; but the quarrel is soon revived by hatred and revenge.

It depends upon the next relations of the slain person to accept the price of blood, which, among the Aenezes, is fixed by their ancient laws. If he will not agree to the offered price of blood, the homicide and all of his relations, who are comprised within the *khomse*, take refuge with some tribe where the arm of vengeance cannot reach them. A sacred custom allows to the fugitive three days and four hours, during which no pursuit after them is made. These exiles are styled *djeláwy* (جلاوي), and some of them are found in almost every camp.*

---

* Some of the *djeláwys* find themselves so pleased in the society of those Arabs who have protected them during their exile, that, even after the price of blood is settled, they do not return home, but remain with their new friends. They do not, however, join their new friends in battle against their own tribe, but if booty should be taken, and some of the djeláwy's property found (that had been left with the tribe), it will be returned to them.

In consequence of a single murder, it is sometimes necessary to remove many hundred tents. The djeláwys remain in exile till their friends have effected a reconciliation, and prevailed upon the nearest relation of the slain person to accept the "price of blood." Families of djeláwys are known to have been fugitives from one tribe to another (according as they become friendly or hostile to their original tribe) for more than fifty years; and it frequently happens that during the life of the son and grandson of the person killed, no compromise is made. To avenge the blood of a slain relation, all means are reckoned lawful, provided the homicide be not killed while he is a guest in the tent of a third person, or if he has taken refuge even in the tent of his deadly foe. In most cases, however, the price of blood is accepted; and the Aenezes do not censure the relations for making this arrangement: but it would reflect shame on the friends of the slain person if they were to make the first overture. When at last it is agreed to settle the matter, a man's blood is estimated in the following manner: If an Aeneze has killed an Aeneze, the price is "fifty she-camels, one *deloul* (a camel fit for mounting), a mare, a black slave, a coat of mail, and a gun." The last-mentioned five articles constitute what is called the *sola* (سلع). The fifty camels, with the *sola*, are called the *deey* (دية). If an Aeneze kills an Arab of a different tribe, or if a foreigner kills an Aeneze, the *deey* is regulated according to the custom prevalent in the stranger's tribe. Thus among the *Maualy, Serdye, Feheyly,* and others of the Arab el Shemál, the blood is worth one thousand piastres, or above fifty pounds sterling. Among the *Amour,* it is five hundred piastres. The quality of the articles comprised in the *deey* is not regarded; provided that the *deloul* be a good strong camel, the mare may be of the worst breed, and the gun not worth more than a few piastres. Still it is necessary that the *sola* should be paid. But the whole number of camels is seldom required. If the next relation of the slain man (to whom alone the *deey* belongs) declares himself ready to accept it, the friends of the dammáwy, with their wives and daughters visit the tent of their enemy, and every one begs of him to remit part of the *deey* for the sake of the petitioner. If he be generous, he then remits one camel for the sake of such and such a man, and two or three camels for the sake of a young pretty girl, &c. till there remains only a certain number, below which he will not descend. He never dispenses with the mare, the slave, and the gun. The dammáwy himself, or his principal friend, then comes with a she-camel to the tent of the adversary, before whom the animal is killed, and its blood is supposed to wash away that of the person slain. The camel is immediately eaten up by the friends of both parties, and is reckoned as part of the *deey*. At parting, the dammáwy, or his representative, ties a white handkerchief on the end of his lance, as a public notification that he is now *free from blood*. (بانه خلص من الدم) Part of the *deey* is paid immediately, the remainder in two or even three years after. The whole family of the dammáwy generally contributes to make up the *deey*.

If a person kills his own kinsman, the nearest relatives of the latter demand the price of blood from the individuals of their own family; in this case, the *deey* is usually collected without delay, and paid off. It is said, that if a slave has been killed, the master avenges his death as if he had been a freeman, and is therefore entitled to receive the *deey* himself: of this I am not quite certain; but an emancipated slave has all the claims of *thár*, or "blood-revenge," that a free Arab enjoys.

For those killed in wars between two tribes, the price of blood is required from the persons who were known to have actually killed them. If peace is made without the condition of "digging and burying," (above mentioned,) the blood must be avenged, even if the relations know only from vague report, who were the killers of their friends. As it is very difficult to ascertain by what individual a horseman has been killed, an appeal is made to the *Mebeṣshae* (above mentioned), if the person accused denies the slaughter. For blood shed in battles it is not customary to admit the testimony of witnesses before the kády; the fiery spoon alone can decide.

In time of war it necessarily happens that there is always "blood" among the tribes (or, as the Arabs say, بيننا دم). But even here a distinction must be made. If this blood-debt arise from men killed in the heat of skirmishing, and that the life of all who gave themselves up to the victor is spared, the Arabs say, for instance, "Between the *Fedhaán* and *Mauálys* there is blood." (بين الفضعان و الموالي دم) If, on the contrary, some individuals of one contending tribe begin to kill their enemies in a manner against the law of nations (بغير طريق الناس), that is, by cutting their throats with knives while they lie wounded on the ground, or by killing them after they have dismounted; in such cases the Arabs say, "Between us there is slaughter" (بيننا ذبح); and the aggrieved party retaliates by killing a double number of their enemies with the same circumstances of cruelty. This produces great animosity among the tribes: I heard, however, that of horsemen so slain, the number seldom amounts on both sides to more than fifteen or twenty, though the war may have lasted for some years. The Mauály Arabs are generally accused of treachery in slaughtering their enemies, whose relations never fail to claim the right of blood-revenge.

Robbery and Theft.

Having noticed the expeditions undertaken by the Arabs against their enemies, I must now give some account of their clandestine warfare, and of those depredations to which both friends and enemies are equally exposed. The Arabs may be styled a nation of robbers, whose principal occupation is plunder, the constant subject of their thoughts. But we must not attach to this practice the same notions of criminality that we entertain respecting highwaymen, house-breakers, and thieves, in Europe. The Arabian robber considers his profession as honourable; and the term *harámy* (robber) is one of the most flattering titles that could be conferred on a youthful hero.

The Arab robs his enemies, his friends, and his neighbours, provided that they are not actually in his own tent, where their property is sacred. To rob in the camp, or among friendly tribes, is not reckoned creditable to a man; yet no stain remains upon him for such an action, which, in fact, is of daily occurrence. But the Arab chiefly prides himself on robbing his enemies, and on bringing away by stealth what he could not have taken by open force. The Bedouins have reduced robbery, in all its branches, to a complete and regular system which offers many interesting details. If an Arab intends to go on a predatory excursion (غزو or جيش or ظلم), he takes with him a dozen friends. They all clothe themselves in rags. Each takes a very moderate stock of flour and salt, and a small water-skin; and thus slenderly provided they commence, on foot, a journey of perhaps eight days. The *harámys* (حرامي), or *robbers*, are never mounted. When they arrive, about evening, near the camp which is the intended object of their enterprise, three of the most daring are despatched towards the tents, where they are to arrive at midnight, a time when most Arabs sleep: the others are to await their return within a short distance of the camp. Of the three principal actors, each has his allotted business. One of them (styled *el mostambeh* المستمبح) stations himself behind the tent that is to be robbed, and endeavours to excite the attention of the nearest watch-dogs. These immediately attack him; he flies, and they pursue him to a great distance from the camp, which is thus cleared of those dangerous guardians. Another of the three, called emphatically *el harámy* (الحرامي), or "the robber," now advances towards the camels, that are upon their knees before the tent; he cuts the strings that confine their legs, and makes as many rise as he wishes. (It must here be remarked that an unloaded camel rises and walks without the least noise.) He then leads one of the she-camels out of the camp; the others follow as usual. The third adventurous companion (styled *kayde*, تعيبد) places himself meanwhile near the tent-pole, called "the hand," holding a long and heavy stick over the entrance of the tent, ready to knock down any person who might come forth, and thus give time for the *harámy's* escape. If the robbery succeed, the *háramy* and *kayde* drive the camels to a little distance; each then seizes by the tail one of the strongest camels, which they pull with all their might; this causes the beasts to gallop, and the men thus dragged, and followed by the other camels, arrive at the place of rendezvous, from which they hasten to join the *mostambeh*, who has, in the mean time, been engaged in defending himself from the dogs. It often happens that as many as fifty camels are stolen in this manner. The robbers, travelling only at night, return home by forced marches. To the chief of the party, and the three principal actors, an extra share of the booty is allowed.

But very different effects attend a failure of their project. If any neighbour of the tent attacked perceives the *harámy* and *kayde*, he awakens his friends, they surround the robbers, and he who first seizes one of them makes him his prisoner or *rabiet* (ربيط). The Bedouin laws concerning the *rabiet* are very curious, and show the influence which custom, handed down through many generations, (although not connected with religion,) may exercise over the fiercest characters among the wildest sons of liberty. The *rabát* (رباط, or he who seizes the *rabiet*) asks his captive on what business he had come, and this question is generally accompanied by some blows on the head. "I came to rob, God has overthrown me," is the answer most commonly given. The prisoner is then led into the tent, where the capture of a *harámy* occasions great rejoicing. The next act of the *rabát* is to clear the tent of all witnesses; then, still holding his knife, he ties the prisoner's hands and feet, and afterwards calls in the people of his tribe. Some one of them, or the rabát himself, then addresses the *harámy*, saying, *Neffa*, (نفِّ) or "renounce;" and the *harámy*, dreading a continuation of the beating, is induced to answer, "*Beneffa*," (بنفِي, or *yeneffa*, ينفِي) "I renounce." This ceremony is founded on a custom of the dakheil, which I shall here explain. It is established as a law among the Arabs, that as soon as a person is in actual danger from another, and can touch a third Arab, (be the last whoever he may, even the aggressor's brother,) or if he touch an inanimate thing which the other has in his hands, or with which any part of his body is in contact, or if he can hit him in spitting or throwing a stone at him, and at the same time exclaims, *Ana dakheilak*, (انا دخيلك) "I am thy protected," or *Terany ballah wa bak ana dakheilak*," (تراني بالله وبك انا دخيلك) he is no longer exposed to any danger, and the third is obliged to defend him: this, however, is seldom necessary, as the aggressor from that moment desists. In like manner the *harámy* would be entitled to the same privilege, could he find an opportunity of demanding it. On this account, the persons entering the tent desire him to "renounce" (that is, the privilege of *dakheil*), and his reply, "I do renounce," makes it impossible for him to claim any further the protection due to a *dakheil*. But this renunciation is only valid during the present day; for, if the same persons on the next day should enter the tent, the same form of renunciation would be necessary, and in general it is repeated whenever any person enters the tent. That the *harámy* may not easily escape, or become the *dakheil* of any one, a hole is formed in the ground of the tent, about two feet deep, and as long as the man: in this hole he is laid, his feet chained to the earth, his hands tied, and his twisted hair fastened to two stakes on both sides of his head. Some tent-poles are laid across this grave, and corn-sacks and other heavy articles heaped upon them, so as to leave only a small opening over the prisoner's face through which he may breathe.

If the camp is to be removed, a piece of leather is thrown over the harámy's head; he is then placed on a camel, his legs and hands always tied: wherever the camp is pitched, a hole or grave is prepared, (as above described) for his prison. Thus buried alive, the prisoner does not yet resign all hope of escaping; this constantly occupies his mind, while the *rabát* endeavours to extract from him the highest possible ransom. If the former belongs to a rich family, he never tells his real name, but declares himself a poor beggar. If he be recognised, which generally happens, he must pay as a ransom, all his property in horses, camels, sheep, tents, provisions, and baggage. His perseverance in pleading poverty, and in concealing his real name, sometimes protracts an imprisonment of this kind for six months; he is then allowed to purchase his liberty on moderate terms, or fortune may enable him to effect his escape. Customs long established among the Bedouins contribute much to that effect. If from the hole, which may be called his grave, he can contrive to spit into the face of a man or child, without the form of renunciation above mentioned, he is supposed to have touched a protector and liberator; or if a child* give him a morsel of bread, the *harámy* claims the privilege of having eaten with his liberator; and although this person may be the *rabát's* near relation, his

---

* From this rule, however, is excepted the rabát's own child.

right to freedom is allowed, the thongs which tied his hair are cut with a knife, his fetters are taken off, and he is set at liberty. Sometimes he finds means to disengage himself from his chains, during the rabát's absence; in this case he escapes at night, and takes refuge in the nearest tent, declaring himself *dakheil* to the first person he meets, and thus regains his freedom; but this seldom happens, for the prisoner always receives so very scanty an allowance of food, that his weakness generally prevents him from making any extraordinary effort, but his friends usually liberate him either by open force, or by contrivance in the following manner:—

A relation of the prisoner, most frequently his own mother or sister, disguised as a beggar, is received in the character of a poor guest by some Arab of the camp in which the *harámy* is confined. Having ascertained the tent of his *rabát*, the disguised relation introduces herself into it at night, with a ball of thread in her hands, approaches the hole in which he lies, and throwing one end of the thread over the prisoner's face contrives to guide it into his mouth, or fastens it to his foot; thus he perceives that help is at hand. The woman retires, winding off the thread until she reaches some neighbouring tent; then awakens the owner of it, and applying the thread to his bosom, addresses him in these words: " Look on me, by the love thou bearest to God, and thy own self, this is under thy protection." (تراني بالله و بک هذا دخيلک) As soon as the Arab comprehends the object of this nocturnal visit, he rises, and winding up the thread in his hands, is guided by it to the tent which contains the *harámy*. He then awakens the *rabát*, shows him the thread still held by the captive, and declares that the latter is his *dakheil*. The *harámy* is then released from his fetters, the *rabát* entertains him as a guest newly arrived, and he is suffered to depart in safety. What I relate here is not a romantic or fictitious tale; the facts are

..y true, as most of the enterprising robbers among the Arabs could authenticate from their own experience.

The *rabiet* is sometimes liberated in another manner; his friend remains in the camp till the Arabs strike their tents, when the prisoner, tied on a camel, is removed with the baggage of the family. His friend then contrives some opportunity of separating the camel which carries the prisoner from those of the family, and drives it towards some other Arab, who becomes the *rabiet's* protector and deliverer.

If, however, no means can be devised for effecting the prisoner's escape, he must at length conclude some terms of ransom. A sum being fixed, it generally happens that among the *rabát's* tribe some settlers of his own tribe are found who become responsible for the amount. He is then consigned to those friends, one of whom accompanies him to his own home, and receives from him the stipulated ransom, camels or other articles, which he delivers punctually to the *rabát*. If the liberated robber cannot collect among his friends the full amount of the ransom, he is bound in honour to resign himself up into the hands of his *rabát*, and thus again become a captive. There are but few instances of the *rabiet's* refusing to pay, or to return; if his friendly bail cannot enforce the payment, he must satisfy the *rabát* from his own property; but he can inflict a severe punishment on his false friend, a punishment so dreaded that the Arabs very seldom incur it. The bail has only to denounce the other as a traitor (*yeboagah* يبوقه) among all the tribes of his (the bail's) nation; after this, if the denounced person should come, in peace or war, to any tent of that nation, he cannot claim the privilege of a guest or of a *dakheil*, but may be stripped even by his host of all his property. The claim of *boag* (for so the Arabs pronounce بوق) ceases, whenever the traitor returns the stolen goods; his conscience or his own interest will at last bring him to terms; he cannot be forced by the sheikh, or even by the persuasions of his own family, to restore the property. In the traitor's own tribe the *boag* has no effect, although the man will be subject to contempt for having incurred it.

If the father of a family (or a son) resolves upon a predatory expedition, however dangerous, he never mentions it to his nearest friends, but orders his wife or sister to make a provision of flour and salt in a small bag. To any inquiry respecting the object of his journey, he either replies, "That's not your business," or gives the favourite Bedouin reply, "I go where God leads me;" (علي باب الله).

A father whose son has been taken prisoner (as a *rabiet*), often sacrifices his whole property for the ransom, because he considers it an honour that his son should be a *harámy*; and hopes that he will soon repay him by the result of a more successful expedition.

The *rabiet* is sometimes liberated without any ransom, or for one very moderate; this generally happens if his life is endangered by imprisonment: if he dies in fetters, his blood falls upon the *rabát's* head. A high-minded and generous Arab scorns to make his enemy a prisoner in the manner above described, but instances of this generosity are not very numerous.

Arabs never approach a hostile camp on foot, or in small numbers, but for the sake of robbing. To make an open attack, they come mounted on horses or camels; and though their attempt fail, they will be treated like fair enemies, not as robbers; stripped and plundered, but not detained. On the contrary, when an Arab meets an unarmed enemy on foot, he knows him to be an *harámy* coming with the intention of robbing; he is therefore authorised to make him his *rabiet*, provided he can seize him in a place from which it is possible that he can return to his own camp before sun-set, or reach the tents of some friendly tribe.* In this case, the presumption is that the enemy intended that very night to rob the camp; but if the place where he meets the enemy be at a greater distance than one day's journey, or as far as one can march during the remainder of the day, (counting from the time of meeting till sun-set,) he is not justified in making him *rabiet*, but must treat him as a common enemy. Women are never imprisoned as *rabiet*.

Should a man be seized at the moment when he is endeavouring to release his captive friend or relation, he is himself made *rabiet*, provided that he arrived directly from the Desert; but if he has been received as a guest in any tent of the camp, or if he has even drunk some water, or sat down in one of the tents, and pronounced the salutation, *Salám aleyk!* ("Peace be to you!") he must be protected by the owner of the tent, and not molested, although his generous design has failed.

If the successful *harámys*, returning home, are overtaken with their booty by Arabs of the plundered tribe, or their friends, the stolen camels are retaken, but become the property of him who retakes them, and are not restored to the original owner; and whoever can seize a *harámy*, claims him as *rabiet*.

The *harámys*, while in the act of robbing, sometimes perceive that they are detected, or that day-light is near, which would expose them to danger, or that one of the party is disabled, and cannot follow; in these cases, they abandon the enterprise altogether, and, entering any of the tents, awake the people in it, and declare, "We are robbers, and wish to halt" (نكن حرامي و نريد)

---

* I learned, however, from some Arabs, that even among the Aenezes there are certain tribes, such as the Fedhan, who treat as *rabiet* all the enemies they can take indiscriminately, whether engaged in robberies or fighting in open warfare.

نتحول) "You are safe" (سلمتوا), is the reply. A fire is immediately kindled, coffee prepared, and a breakfast placed before the strangers, who are entertained as long as they choose to stay. At their departure, provision is given to them sufficient for their journey home. Should they meet on their return a hostile party of the tribe which they had intended to rob, their declaration, "We have eaten salt in such or such a tent" (نحن مالحين), is a passport that ensures them a safe journey; or, at all events, the testimony of their host would release them from the hands of any Arabs, whether of his own or some friendly tribe. But if the harámys, having been hospitably entertained by their protector, should on their return be so base as to rob some other Arabs of the hostile tribe, they forfeit the privilege of the *dakheil*; the individual robbed applies to their host, who immediately despatches a messenger to the sheikh of the robbers' tribe, claiming the stolen property, as having been stolen contrary to the laws of honour and justice. If the *harámys* restore the booty, all is settled. Should they refuse, their former host proceeds himself to meet them, bringing with him the copper dish, out of which they had eaten when he received them as guests. When he arrives at the tent of the robbers' sheikh, the whole tribe assembles: he tells the *harámys*, "this is the dish out of which you have eaten, (the token of the protection granted when you were in peril); return, therefore, the stolen cattle." If they comply, the affair ends amicably; if they persist in refusing, the Arab takes up the dish (called *makarah* مَقَرة), and publicly tells them, "You are traitors, and shall be every where denounced as such." (مبوقين) The effects of this declaration are similar to those above mentioned, in the case of *boag*, or treacherous conduct.

On the conclusion of peace between two tribes, their sheikhs having "digged and buried" (as above mentioned), whatever "treachery" debts may be due to individuals on both sides continue due even after the peace, the efforts of *boag* never ceasing till the account is completely settled.

The reception of a *dakheil* is voluntary; it may be, but seldom is refused. The Arabs say that the *dakhal*, or man soliciting protection, comes upon us by surprise; we have no merit in complying with his request; but on some occasions the right of *dakheil* is only partially granted. If in battle, where there is "slaughter," (see above,) a pursued enemy can find an opportunity of throwing himself on the favour of an Arab who happens to be a friend of the pursuer, the Arab will perhaps tell him, "I protect your life, but not your horse, nor your property:" these, of course, are taken by the pursuer.

Women, slaves, even strangers, may receive a *dakheil*. They transfer him immediately—a woman, to her father, her husband, or relation—a slave, to his master—and a stranger, to his host. I have observed that, under certain circumstances, the *rabiet*, by touching any person, may declare himself his *dakheil*; but it must be understood, that no one, by voluntarily touching the *rabiet*, can himself liberate him. This is a necessary precaution of the law, because the man to whom the prisoner belongs has always some secret enemy in his own tribe, who would endeavour to defraud him of the ransom; he must, therefore, be constantly on his guard, and either force his prisoner to renounce the privilege of *dakheil*, or else prevent the admission of any visitors. The *rabat*, if much occupied, may consign his prisoner to the care of some trusty friend, who guards him in his (the friend's) own tent, and receives in advance, for his trouble, a she-camel.

If any man should hurt or molest the *dakheil* of another, (a circumstance that rarely happens,) his whole property would not be thought by the kady sufficient to atone for such an offence—greater than if he had injured the protector himself. To express that "my *dakheil* has been wronged by a third person," the Arab says, "my ground has been cut up or trampled on;" "my honour has been injured." (كسرت عرضي or قطعت ارضي)

So far I have only noticed the robberies committed in hostile camps; but the Arabs do not restrict their depredations to the tents of enemies, they often rob people of their own, or some friendly tribe. Such a robber, taken in the very fact, is condemned by the ancient law to forfeit his right hand; but custom allows him to redeem this at the price of five she-camels, payable to the person whom he proposed to rob. Those who practise such depredations on their friends are never made *rabiet*; they are called *netál* (نتَال, not *neshál*, نشال, the common term in Syria for " a thief ").

Hospitality of the Arabs.

After what has been related, it is scarcely necessary to say, that among the Aenezes a guest is regarded as sacred; his person is protected, and a violation of hospitality, by the betraying of a guest, has not occurred within the memory of man. He who has a single protector in any one tribe, becomes the friend of all the tribes connected in amity with that. Life and property may with perfect security be entrusted to an Aeneze; and wherever he goes, one may follow him; but his enemies become the enemies of the man whom he protects. The messengers between Aleppo, Baghdad, and Basrah, are always Aenezes. They formerly accompanied English gentlemen, returning from India or going there, through the Desert; and although some few instances have occurred, of travellers being plundered on the road by strange tribes, it is certain that their Aeneze guides, however importunate in their demands for money, faithfully observed the engagement which they had made. I here may state a fact from my own experience.—In June 1810, I set out from Aleppo with a sheikh of the *Fedhán*: he had been plundered near Hamah by some Maualy Arabs, with whom the Aenezes were then at war. Most of his property, and the camels of his Arabs, having been restored through the influence of the mutsellim of Hamah, the sheikh continued his journey; but took fright on the Wahaby's approach to Damascus, near which city his family was encamped; he therefore refused to accompany me as far as Tedmor, but gave me a single guide to conduct me among the ruins, and proceeded on his way towards the south. I feared, at that time, that the sheikh had betrayed me; but it soon appeared that the single guide was a sufficient protector in every respect. All the Arabs whom we met received me with hospitality; and I returned with him across the Desert to Jeroud, twelve hours distant from Damascus.

A guest, as well as the host himself, in an Arab tent, is liable to nocturnal depredation; certainly not from any individual of the host's family, but from *harámys*, or *netáls*. Knowing, however, that such is the case, and jealous lest any circumstance should excite a suspicion of his own integrity, the host takes particular care of the stranger's mare or camel; and if rich and generous, should a robbery occur, he indemnifies the stranger for whatever loss he may sustain while under the protection of his hospitality.

Strangers, who have not any friend or acquaintance in the camp, alight at the first tent that presents itself: whether the owner be at home or not, the wife or daughter immediately spreads a carpet, and prepares breakfast or dinner. If the stranger's business requires a protracted stay, as for instance, if he wishes to cross the Desert under protection of the tribe, the host, after a lapse of three days and four hours* from the time of his arrival,

---

* It may be remarked, that the same space of time is allowed to the *djeláwy* for his escape. (See p. 86.)

asks whether he means to honour him any longer with his company. If the stranger declares his intention of prolonging his visit, it is expected that he should assist his host in domestic matters, fetching water, milking the camel, feeding the horse, &c. Should he even decline this, he may remain, but will be censured by all the Arabs of the camp: he may, however, go to some other tent of the *nezel* (see p. 19), and declare himself there a guest. Thus every third or fourth day he may change hosts, until his business is finished, or he has reached his place of destination. The Arabs of a tribe in Nedjd welcome a guest by pouring on his head a cup of melted butter; and among the *Merekedes* (مرقده), a tribe on the frontiers of Yemen, custom requires that the stranger should pass the night with his host's wife, whatever may be her age or condition. Should he render himself agreeable to the lady, he is honourably and hospitably treated; if not, the lower part of his *abba*, or cloak, is cut off, and he is driven away with disgrace. When the *Merekedes* became Wahabys, they were obliged to discontinue this custom; but a drought happening soon after, they regarded the misfortune as a punishment for having abandoned the good old practice of their forefathers, and applied to the Wahaby chief (*Abd el Azyz*) for permission to honour their guests as before, which he accordingly granted.* To tell an Arab that he neglects his guest, or does not treat him well (انت با شع علي ضيفك or مطرد ضيفك), is one of the greatest insults.

* Burckhardt, in his Arabian Travels, (Appendix No. II.) mentions this extraordinary custom of the Merekede tribe, and says that, "some female of the family—most commonly the host's own wife," was assigned to the stranger as his companion during the night; but, that "to this barbarous system of hospitality, young virgins were never sacrificed." Whatever doubts he entertained concerning the truth of such a report, were removed by the evidence of several persons who had witnessed the fact, however inconsistent with our notions of the respect in which female honour is held by the Arabs.

Slaves and Servants.

Black slaves are very common among the Arabs: every powerful sheikh procures annually five or six male slaves, and some females, who come from Baghdad (whither they are brought by the Mascat and Yemen merchants), or from Mekka or Cairo. The Aenezes always abstain from cohabitation with their female slaves, but, after a service of some years, give them their freedom, and marry them to their male slaves, or the descendants of slaves, established in the tribe. The male slaves are emancipated in presence of witnesses; and in token of emancipation are allowed to shave their heads. Ibn Esmeyr has above fifty tents belonging to persons who were once his slaves, and owe their good fortune wholly to the liberality of that sheikh. He cannot now exact from them any yearly tribute, as they are reckoned free Arabs; but he demands their daughters in marriage for his newly-purchased and emancipated slaves; and if in time of war those black men should acquire considerable booty, the sheikh may ask from them a fine camel, which they never refuse to give. The slaves, though emancipated, still retain the stamp of servile origin, and must not marry a white girl; neither does a free Arab ever marry a black girl. The descendants of slaves intermarry among themselves, and among the szona, or workmen, who have settled in their tribe. They gradually lose some of the negro appearance, especially in the hair, but still retain in their features manifest proofs of their origin. It may be truly said, that the Syrian Desert contains whole camps of negroes, who occasionally change their situation.

The rich are often attended by Arab servants: the slaves are treated with kindness, and seldom beaten, as severity might induce them to run away. A servant would resent any blow or insult as from an equal. To every tent, or to every two or three tents, there is a shepherd, or person to attend the cattle, either a younger son, or a servant; he receives wages for ten months. During the two first spring months the cattle feed around the tents without the care of any person. The wages consist in a *howár*, or young camel, which remains with its dam until one year old; and with the camel, a *khomse*, or set of five articles, viz. a pair of shoes (زربول), a shirt (توب), a keffie, or kerchief, an abba, or cloak, and a sheep-skin: the *khomse* being altogether worth about twenty-five shillings.

Moral Character of the Bedouins.

From the perusal of these pages, the reader will probably have discovered some contradictory circumstances in the moral character of the Bedouins, which it would be extremely difficult to reconcile. In speaking of the Arabs generally, a strong distinction must be made between the Bedouins, the indigenous inhabitants of the country or *Fellahs*, and the Turks, or Osmanlys, who subdued the country, and have settled in all the government towns. We now treat merely of the Bedouins, but must remark in justice to the *Fellahs*, that the two distinctions above mentioned should be strictly observed in describing the Syrian character.

An inordinate love of gain and money, forms a principal feature in the Levantine character; it pervades all classes, from the *pashá* to the wandering Arab, and there are few individuals who, to acquire wealth, would not practise the meanest or most illegal act. Thus with the Bedouin, the constant object of his mind is gain; interest the motive of all his actions; and the account of their judicial institutions will have shown that this spirit is promoted by their laws. Lying, cheating, intriguing, and other vices arising from this source, are as prevalent in the Desert as in the market-towns of Syria; and on the common occasions of buying and selling, (where his *dakheil* is not required,) the word of an Arab is not entitled to more credit than the oath of a broker in the *bázár* of Aleppo. The Arab displays his manly character when he defends his guest at the peril of his own life, and submits to the reverses of fortune, to disappointment and distress with the most patient resignation. He is, besides, distinguished from a Turk by the virtues of pity, and of gratitude, which the Turk seldom possesses. The Turk is cruel, the Arab of a more kind temper, he pities and supports the wretched, and never forgets the generosity shown to him even by an enemy. Not accustomed to the sanguinary scenes that harden and corrupt an Osmanly's heart, the Bedouin learns at an early period of life, to abstain and to suffer, and to know from experience the healing power of pity and consolation.

The Arab is free, sprightly, jocose, and decent, in his familiar conversation. The Turk is insinuating, grave, cautious, in discourse; he seldom laughs, and is fond to excess of obscene or indelicate allusions. The Arab is not by any means that silent being which some travellers represent him; on the contrary, I found him a merry companion. It must, however, be owned, that on a journey, the Arabs talk but little; for they have observed, that during the fatigue of travelling in the heat of summer, much talking excites thirst, and parches up the palate; but when they assemble under their tents, a very animated conversation is kept up among them without interruption. I have had frequent opportunities, however, of ascertaining the truth of an observation, that the Bedouin in a town appears to be a very different man from the same person in the Desert. He knows that the town's-people, whom he despises, entertain absurd notions respecting his nation, and therefore he endeavours to impose on them, by affecting an air of silent penetration, and of determined resolution. The phraseology that he adopts is calculated to show the immutability of his opinions; but this character, assumed for the purpose of promoting his business, he lays aside at his return to the Desert. Still it must be allowed, that the conversation of a Bedouin has more originality than is found in the Arabic used among the inhabitants of towns, who, like the Turks, employ much circumlocution to convey a meaning which the Bedouin forcibly expresses by two or three words; although he sometimes, when in a town, makes a display of sentences which he never uses (at least I never heard a Bedouin use them) in the Desert. The wandering Arabs have certainly more wit and sagacity than the people who live in towns; their heads are always clear, their spirits unimpaired by debauchery, and their minds not corrupted by slavery: and I am justified in saying, that there are few nations among whom natural talents are so universally diffused as among the Bedouins. In sensual enjoyments, they are very moderate and abstemious. If an Arab has a sufficiency of food, he cares but little about its quality, or about those luxuries which we call " pleasures of the table." With respect to women, he is generally content with his own wife; instances of conjugal infidelity are very rare, and public prostitution is unknown in the Arab camps. The Bedouins are jealous of their women, but do not prevent them from laughing and talking with strangers. It seldom happens that a Bedouin strikes his wife; if he does so, she calls loudly on her *wasy*, or protector, who pacifies the husband, and makes him listen to reason.

In his tent, the Arab is most indolent and lazy; his only occupation is feeding the horse, or milking the camels in the evening, and he now and then goes to hunt with his hawk. A man, hired for the purpose, takes care of the herds and flocks, while the wife and daughters perform all the domestic business. They grind wheat in the hand-mill, or pound it in the mortar; they prepare the breakfast and dinner; knead and bake the bread; make butter, fetch water, work at the loom, mend the tent-covering, and are, it must be owned, indefatigable; while the husband or brother sits before the tent smoking his pipe, or, perceiving that a stranger has arrived in the camp, by the extraordinary volume of smoke issuing from the *moharrem* (or women's apartment) of the tent, where the stranger has been received as a guest, to that tent he goes, salutes the stranger, and expects an invitation to dine and drink coffee with him.

The Arabs salute a stranger with the "*salám aleyk!*" (peace be to you!) this they address even to Christians: if the stranger is an old acquaintance, they embrace him; if a great man, they kiss his beard. When the stranger has seated himself upon a carpet, (which the host always spreads out for him on his arrival,) it is reckoned a tribute of politeness due to the whole company that he should ask each individual how he does. The phrase used on this occasion is, "Perhaps you are well?" or "I hope you are well" (لعلك طيب which they pronounce, "*allek toy*"). The conversation then becomes animated; they ask the stranger for news of his tribe and his neighbours, and the politics of the Desert are discussed. The continual movements of the Arabs cause news of every kind to be soon dispersed throughout the Desert; and it is really surprising to find what accurate information the Aenezes obtain respecting the affairs of Nedjáz, Hedjáz, Derayeh, and Irák, in a country where there is scarcely any intercourse by letters. During my stay in Hauran, I learned from a Druze chief that some Aenezes, a few months before, had brought intelligence, that the Franks, called *Indjeleis*, (so the Bedouins pronounced *English*,) had made a descent on the Arabian coast of the Persian Gulf, had taken the fort of *Rás el Kheymè*, killed many of the Arabs there, and that among the slain was a cousin of Ibn Saoud. The people of Haurán would not, at first, give credit to this news. "We know," said they, "that the English came to Acre from the westward, how is it possible that all at once they could make their appearance so far eastward from us?" When I explained the circumstance, they repeatedly said, "We know that there must be some truth in the report, for the Aenezes do not spread news over the Desert without good foundation."

Notwithstanding the general excellence of D'Arvieux's valuable work on Arabian manners, I may venture to declare that the Bedouins are not, by any means so austere as he represents them; and that they frequently spit. He is certainly right in his account of the horror which is excited among them, by a certain gross violation of decorum in society, and I was assured that an Arab known to have so offended frequently in company, is no longer deemed worthy of being admitted as a witness before the kády.

In their private dealings, the Arabs cheat each other as much as they can; usury is secretly practised among them.

In spring, when the Arabs approach the confines of Syria, about twenty pedlars leave Damascus on a visit to the different tribes. They take with them for sale whatever goods of town production the Arabs want; articles of dress, powder and ball, nails, iron, horse-shoes, sabres, coffee, tobacco, sweetmeats, spices, harness for the sheikh's horses, &c. Of these petty merchants, each pays a small yearly tribute to the sheikh of the tribe which he frequents; thus he is protected by them, and enjoys all the privileges of a free Arab. The whole capital employed in this trade does not exceed the amount of five or six thousand pounds sterling. Every merchant has his own tent, and his own camels, and when several of them visit the same tribe, they pitch their tents close to each other, and establish in this manner a kind of market-place. They follow the camps wherever they go, and are exposed to almost as many casualties as the Arabs themselves; but as their property consists chiefly in goods, should the camels be driven off at night by the enemy, they still retain whatever is in their tents. I knew one of these pedlars who had lost all his property four different times; he recovered it once, because he knew the person who had taken it during the tumult caused by the nocturnal attack, and as that man happened to be of a tribe whose sheikh received tribute from the pedlar, and with whom of course he was on brotherly terms, the robber was compelled by the protector of the pedlar to restore the stolen goods. These merchants allow one year's credit for all they sell, and on the following year they take in return for their merchandise, butter and sheep, of which they dispose on their arrival at Damascus, in winter.* Should an European traveller wish to visit the interior of the Desert between Damascus and the Persian Gulf, he may best contrive to accomplish his design through the assistance of these pedlars. They are men of probity and in good esteem among the Bedouins. Half of them are Christians, and enjoying the same protection from the Arab sheikhs, that they accord to the Turks; for those Arabs are not fanatical Muselmans, and make little distinction between sects.

The principal tribes of the Aenezes exact tribute from the villages of Eastern Syria, near which they encamp in summer. By having one man in a tribe to which the tribute is paid, security is obtained from any depredation by the Arabs of that tribe, except the nocturnal robber, who does not feel himself

---

* The Arabs who encamp on the south-eastern limits of Haurán, bring to Damascus loads of salt, which they collect at the small salt lake called Ezrak, six days' journey from Damascus, in the direction of S.S.E. There is a ruined castle near it, and several springs of sweet water, with numerous palm-trees.

bound to refrain. The tribute is generally paid to the sheikh or some respectable man of the tribe, who becomes "brother" to the villagers, and calls the village his "sister." From this appellation the tribute is called *khoue* (خوه), or "brotherhood." When this is first agreed upon between a village and an Arab, (قطع الخوه or عاقد الخوه) the latter requires that part of the stipulated annual sum should be paid down immediately; out of this he purchases some eatables, which he divides among his friends, that they may be witnesses of the compact, as having eaten part of the *khoue*. Whatever the Arab may ask in the course of the year as a trifling present from his tributary, (in addition to the stipulated *khoue*,) he enforces the next year as a due; and the small gift which he asks the second year becomes, in like manner, a due on the third year. This also is the case with the *szurra*, or tribute paid to the Aenezes and other Arab tribes from the Hadj (or body of pilgrims), which amounted in the last year of the Hadj, to between fifty and sixty thousand pounds.

The Cattle of the Bedouins, and other Animals of the Desert.

The camel of the Syrian Desert is smaller than the Anatolian, Turkman, or Kurdy camel; it bears heat and thirst better than the latter, but is much affected by cold, which kills many of them even in the Desert. The Anatolian camel has a thick woolly neck; it is larger and stouter than the camel of the Desert, carries heavier loads, and is most useful in the mountains of Anatolia, but never thrives in the Desert. The Anatolian breed is produced between an Arab she-camel, and the double-humped male dromedary imported from the Crimea. The camel produced between a she Arab and male Turkman, is called *kufurd* (كفرد),

a weak animal unfit for fatigue. The male and female Turkman camels produce the *dály,* or "mad," so styled from its intractable nature. A dromedary and she Turkman camel produce the breed called *táous* (طاوس), a very handsome but small camel, with two small humps, one of which the Turkmans cut off immediately on the birth of the creature, to render it more fit for bearing a load. This breed has a very thick growth of long hair under the neck, reaching almost to the ground. The dromedary and a she Arab camel, produce the *máyá* (مايا) and *beshrak* (بشرك), or the common Turkman, or Anatolian camel. She-dromedaries are never brought to Anatolia, nor are the male dromedaries ever used as beasts of burden, being kept merely for breeding. The Arabs have not any dromedaries with two humps, nor did I ever see or hear of one in Syria.

In the beginning of the second year, the young camels are weaned, they are prevented from sucking, though not from feeding on the herbage of the Desert, by a piece of wood about four inches long and sharp pointed, which is driven up the palate and comes out at the nostrils. For the same purpose the Turkmans fasten across the young camel's nostrils a piece of wood, sharp at both ends, which pricks the mother, and causes her to kick and go away: that the young camel may suck only at proper times, some of the mother's teats, or perhaps all, are fastened up in a bag made of camel's wool, and called *shamle* (شمله). The string which fastens this, passes about the camel's whole body, and remains on it generally, even after the *shamle* is removed: I observed it on most of the she-camels in the Desert. Some people, instead of the *shamle,* cover the teats with a thin round piece of wood. In years of scarcity the camels always prove barren. A camel of one year is called *howár* (هوار); of two years, *meferoud* (مفرود), or *mekhloul* (مخلول), or *mekhlál* (مخلال); one of three years, *hhudj* (حُج); a she-camel of four years is called *rebáa* (رباع); a he-camel of four years, *jedá* (جدا). In its fourth year the camel begins to breed; after the first birth it is called *bekr* (بكر), after the second, *thanne* (ثنّة): camels are known to attain the age of forty years. The Arabs ride on the male camel in preference to the female, although the latter is said to move more expeditiously. Should a male camel become ungovernable, (as sometimes happens in the breeding season,) they perforate one of his nostrils, through which they pass a thread made of the hair of a camel's tail (حُلب *hulb*); to this a cord is tied, and the rider is thus enabled to quiet the camel; (a camel under those circumstances they call دلول مخزوم). In a camel the brown colour is not esteemed; reddish, or light grey, or a reddish grey is preferred. When a camel is to be killed, the Arabs choose a female that does not breed. If a camel happen to break its leg, it is immediately killed, the fracture being deemed incurable. The Arab camels feed upon the herbage of the Desert. The Syrian peasants, like the Turkmans, give to their camels every evening a ball made of barley paste and water; this ball is called *maabouk* (معبوك). The Aeneze and Ahl el Shemál tribes do not make butter of their camels' milk; they drink it themselves, and give some also to their horses. The camel's wool is easily taken off the skin by a person's hand at the end of spring; a camel has seldom more than two pounds of wool. I have already mentioned the uses made of the camel's wool. The Turkmans fabricate coarse carpets from the wool of their camels, which is stronger and of better quality than that of the Arabs.

All the Bedouin camels are marked with a hot iron, that they may be recognised if they straggle away, or should be stolen. Every tribe and every *taifé*, or fami'y of a tribe, has its own particular mark. This is generally placed on the camel's left shoulder, or its neck. The following may serve as specimens of those marks:—*

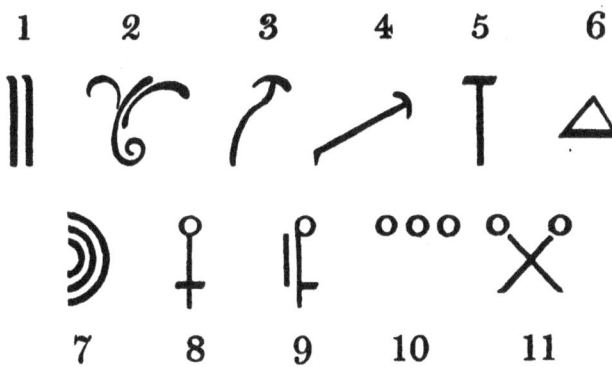

Should a camel run away, the owner traces it by its footsteps for many hours (مسك الاثر). The Arabs also know, by what has fallen from th camel on the road, how many days previously it had been there, even as far back as five or six days. The place where a camel has lain down is called مبرّق.

The camels of the Desert are liable to many diseases, but none epidemic. Their most dangerous diseases are three: the first is a stiffness and hardness of the neck, which turns to one side or the other: the animal so affected is called مطيور; it refuses nourishment, and dies in a few days. The second disease (*mehmour*, مهمور) is a violent diarrhœa, which attacks the two-year-old camels, and always proves mortal. The third dangerous disease is called *medjaoum* (مجعوم), caused by the camel's swallowing with herbage some of the dung left by sheep and goats the preceding year: this produces colic, which generally ends in death. This disease only affects camels of full growth; against it, as against the two former, the Arabs know not any remedy; but they believe that the Jews, in their sacred books, have remedies mentioned, which

---

* 1. Ibn Dhouehy.—2. Ibn Esmeyr.—3, 4. El Teyár.—5. El Hessene.—6, 7. Besshr. —8, 9. Beni Sakhr.—10, 11. Naym.

they withhold through hatred and malice. Of less dangerous diseases, I may notice the جدري or small-pox, which appears in small pustules about the camel's mouth, particularly those of two years; it is not, however, attended with much inconvenience. The اضبط *ádhbet* is a violent swelling of the camel's legs. The *ákawa* (اكوه), a stiffness in its fetlocks. A camel is styled *ákherd* (اخرد), when in walking it throws its fore legs very far sideways, and describes a large circle before it puts them down again.

Sheep and Goats.—The *Ahl el Shemál* Arabs are most rich in goats, the Aenezes in sheep. The Arab sheep have not the fat tails that are found in some countries: their ears are rather larger than those of the common English breed. The goats are mostly black, and they have long ears. A sheep in its first year is called خاروق; in the second, ترتوي; and in the third year, كبش. The goat in its first year is called سخله; in its second year, معزه or ثنيه. The sucking lambs and kids are called بهم *baham*. A ewe or a she-goat, at the time when she loses her milk, is called *gharzeh*, غرزه. The sheep and goats are milked during the three spring months in the morning and evening: they are sent out to pasture before sun-rise, while the lambs and kids remain in or near the camp. About ten o'clock the herd returns; the young are allowed to satiate themselves, after which all the ewes belonging to one tent are tied to a long cord, and milked one after another. When a ewe is feeble in health, her milk is left wholly for the lamb, which is then called مهجل. The same process occurs at sun-set. From one hundred ewes or goats (the milk of which is always mixed together) the Arabs expect, in common years, about eight pounds of butter per day, or about seven hundred weight in the three spring months. An Arab family uses in the year about two quintals of butter, the rest is sold to the peasants and town's-people. The male lambs and kids are sold or slaughtered, except two or three, which the Arab keeps for breeding. In years of scarcity, both sheep and goats prove altogether barren. The milk of camels, sheep, and goats is in the Desert called *leben* (لبن); sometimes, also, *haleib*. The Syrians give the name of *leben* to a kind of sour milk, found but seldom among the Aenezes, who call it خاثر. The Aenezes shear their sheep once a year, near the end of spring: they usually sell the wool before the sheep are shorn, at so much for the wool of a hundred sheep.

Epidemic diseases are rare and seldom violent among the Aeneze herds: the Kourd sheep, on the contrary, which come from Mesopotamia, and supply the markets of Aleppo, partly of Damascus, and the Druze mountains, are very subject to epidemic diseases; and in the spring of 1810 above thirty thousand of them died on a pasture ground of Mount Libanus. When at peace with the Wahabys, many Aenezes were accustomed to go every year into Nedjd, loaded with dollars and merchandize, to purchase camels and sheep. These sheep (called *rakheymy* رخيمي) are for the greater part black, having the head and neck, or sometimes only the forehead white, with a long but not fat tail. The Aenezes set out with them from Nedjd in winter, that they might reach Syria early in spring, when they immediately sold them to the butchers of Damascus, and of the Druze mountains, who killed them without delay, knowing, from experience, that almost all the sheep left to fatten in Syria died suddenly about a month after their arrival.

Horses.—I allude here merely to the horses of the Desert. Turkish horses are treated very differently; and the Osmanlys are generally much more scientific jockies than the Bedouins. There are three breeds of horses in Syria; the true Arab breed, the Turkman, and the Kourdy, which is a mixture of the two former. The Arab horses are mostly small; in height seldom exceeding fourteen hands; but few are ill formed, and they have all certain characteristic beauties, which distinguish their breed from any other. The Bedouins count five noble breeds of horses, descended, as they say, from the five favourite mares of their prophet. *Taueyse,* (طويسه), *Manekeye* (معنكيه), *Koheyl* (كحيل), *Saklâwye* (سقلاويه), and *Dujlfe* (جلفه). These five principal races diverge into infinite ramifications. Every mare particularly swift and handsome, belonging to any one of the five chief races, may give origin to a new breed, the descendants of which are called after her; so that the names of different Arab breeds in the Desert are innumerable. On the birth of a colt of noble breed, it is usual to assemble some witnesses, and to write an account of the colt's distinctive marks, with the names of its sire and dam. These genealogical tables (*hhudje,* حجة) never ascend to the grand-dam, because it is understood that every Arab of the tribe knows by tradition the purity of the whole breed. Nor is it always necessary to have such genealogical certificates, for many horses and mares are of such illustrious descent, that thousands might attest the purity of their blood.

The pedigree is often put into a small piece of leather, covered with waxed cloth, and hung round the horse's neck. The following may serve as a specimen :—

"GOD

" Enoch

"In the name of the most merciful God, the Lord of all creatures; peace and prayers be with our Lord Mohammed, and his family, and his followers, until the day of judgment; and peace be with all those who read this writing, and understand its meaning. The present deed relates to the greyish-brown colt, with four white feet, and a white mark on the forehead, of the true breed of *Saklâwy,* called *Obeyán,* whose skin is as bright and unsullied as milk, resembling those horses of which the prophet said, 'True riches are a noble and fierce breed of horses;' and of which God said, "The war-horses, those which rushed on the enemy with full-blowing nostrils; those which plunge into the battle early in the morning." And God spoke the truth in his incomparable book. This *Sakláwy* grey colt was bought by *Khoshrún*, the son of *Emheyt*, of the tribe of *Zebaa*, an Aeneze Arab. The sire of this colt is the excellent bay horse called *Merdján*, of the breed of *Koheylán*: its dam is the famous white *Sakláwy* mare, known by the name of *Djeroua*. According to what we have seen, we attest here upon our hopes of felicity, and upon our girdles, O sheikhs of wisdom, and possessors of horses! that this grey colt above mentioned is more noble even than his sire and dam. And this we attest according to our best knowledge, by this valid and perfect deed. Thanks be to God, the Lord of all creatures!

"Written on the 16th of *Safar*, in the year 1223.

"Witnesses, &c. &c."

This is faithfully translated from the original Arabic deed, in the hand-writing of the Bedouins. The Mohammedan year 1223, in which it is dated, corresponds to the year 1808 of our era.

The Arabs almost exclusively ride their mares, and sell the horses to town's-people or *Fellahs*. The price of an Arab horse in Syria, is from ten pounds to one hundred and twenty: this latter price is the highest that I have known. Since the English at Baghdad and Basra purchase Arab horses, which they send to India, the prices have risen considerably. The late Dutch consul at Aleppo, Mr. Masseyk, bought in 1808 above twenty of the finest Arab horses for Bonaparte, paying for each between eighty and ninety pounds. An Arab mare can scarcely be obtained under sixty pounds; and even at that price it is difficult for town's-people to purchase one. The Arabs themselves often pay as much as two hundred pounds for a celebrated mare, and the price has amounted even to more than five hundred pounds. The present sheikh or emir of the Maualys has a Nedjd mare for the *half of whose belly* (in Arab phraseology) he paid four hundred pounds. If an Aeneze has a mare of remarkable breed, he never, or very seldom, consents to sell her without reserving for himself one half or two thirds of her. If he sells half, the buyer takes the mare, but is obliged to let the seller have the mare's next filly, or else to return the mare and keep the filly for himself. If the Arab has sold but one third of his mare, the purchaser takes her home, but must give to the seller the fillies of two years, or else one of them and the mare. The fillies of the third year, and all subsequent, belong to the buyer as well as the male colts, whether produced in the first or any following year. This contract the Arabs call " selling half or one third of the mare's belly;" and thus it happens that most of the Arab mares are the joint property of two or three persons, or even half a dozen if the price of a mare be very high. The Ahl el Shemál usually sell one half of their mares, and take half of all the male as well as female offspring: a mare is likewise sold on condition that all the booty obtained by the man who rides her should be divided between him and the seller.

Until the end of the first year the filly is called طريح; during the second year, حوليه; the third, جدع; the fourth year ربعا or ربعيه; then فرس, or else they count on ساد سه, خامسه, &c. The male colt is called مهر or فلو.

Immediately after the birth of a colt, the Arabs tie its ears together over its head with a thread, that they may assume a fine pointing direction: at the same time they press the tail of the colt upwards, and take other measures whereby it may be carried high. The only care taken of the dam after she has produced her colt, is to wrap a piece of cloth or linen round her body; this cloth is removed on the next day. If the mare is only partially possessed by an Arab, he is obliged, on the ninth day after she has produced a filly, to assemble some witnesses, and to declare before them his intention of giving the new-born filly to the seller of the mare, or to keep the filly, and return the mare to her former owner (قسم و شهد). Having once made this declaration, he is bound to abide by it. The colts remain with the mother thirty days, after which the Arabs always wean them; and then either give them to the seller of the mare, or rear them themselves upon camel's milk. For the space of one hundred days after the colts have been weaned, it is not permitted to give them any other food than camel's milk; even water is not allowed. After that time, the colt receives a daily portion of wheat diluted with water; at first only a handful: this quantity is gradually increased, but milk still continues to be the colt's principal food. Such is the colt's diet for one hundred days more; during the latter of which he is permitted to feed upon the grass near the tents, and to drink water. The second period of one hundred days having elapsed, barley is given to the colt; and if camel's milk be abundant in the owner's tent, a bucket of it is given every evening along with the allowance of barley.

Among the Aenezes, the usual method of rearing the colts is this:—The Arab who brings a colt of two or three years to market in Syria, swears that the colt has never tasted any food but camel's milk. This is a palpable falsehood, because the Arab colts in the Syrian Desert are never fed exclusively on milk beyond the first four months. The Nedjd Arabs, on the contrary, give neither barley nor wheat to their horses, which feed upon the herbs of the Desert, and drink plenty of camel's milk, and are besides nourished with a paste of dates and water. To a favourite horse the Nedjd Arab, and sometimes an Aeneze, gives the fragments, or leavings of his own meals.

It is well known that the Arabs are not so nice in the choice of a stallion as the European breeders; for they ascribe the good qualities of the colt rather to the dam than to the sire. I have heard, however, of Arabs who took their mares a journey of several days that they might breed by some celebrated horse; the price paid on such an occasion is usually one dollar or a sheep.

During the whole year, the Arabs keep their horses in the open air; I never saw one even in the rainy season tied up under the tent of its owner, as may frequently be observed among the Turkmans. The Arab horse, like its master, is accustomed to the inclemency of all seasons, and, with very little attention to its health, is seldom ill. The Arabs never clean or rub their horses, but are careful in walking them gently whenever they return after a ride. From the time that a colt is first mounted, (which is after its second year,) the saddle is but seldom taken off its back; in winter time a sack-cloth is thrown over the saddle, in summer the horse stands exposed to the mid-day sun. Those Arabs who have no saddles, ride upon a stuffed sheep-skin, (called مفتع) and without stirrups; they all ride without bridles, guiding the horse with a halter. This will not astonish the European reader, when he learns that the Bedouin horse is extremely good-tempered, without any viciousness, and more the friend than the slave of his rider. The Arabs do not practise the game of the *djerid*, which often ruins the Turks' horses before they acquire perfect strength. The Arabs indeed are unacquainted with the Turkish mode of horsemanship, and those evolutions of which the Osmanlys are so vain. But their habits of riding without stirrups or bridle, of throwing the heavy lance in full gallop, and of balancing themselves, from early infancy, upon the bare back of a trotting camel, give to the Bedouin a more firm seat on his horse than the Osmanly can boast, although the latter may ride more gracefully.

The Arabs are ignorant of those frauds by which an European jockey deceives a purchaser; one may take a horse on their word, at first sight or trial without any risk of being cheated; but few of them know how to ascertain a horse's age by its teeth. I once looked into the mouth of a mare, whose owner and many other Arabs were present: at first it was apprehended that I was practising some secret charm; and when the owner heard that by such inspection the mare's age might be ascertained, he seemed astonished, and wished that I should tell his own age by an examination of his teeth.

The Arabs believe that some horses are predestined to evil accidents; and, like the Osmanlys, they think that the owners of other horses must, sooner or later, experience certain misfortunes, which are indicated by particular marks on the horses' bodies. Thus, if a mare has a star on the right side of the neck, they believe that she is destined to be killed by a lance; if the star be on one of the shank-bones, the owner's wife, they think, will prove unfaithful to her husband, and the orthodoxy of the latter as a Muselmán is liable to suspicion. There are above twenty evil marks of this kind, which have, at all events, the bad effect of depreciating the horse's value by two thirds or more.

The Arabs do not mark their horses as some imagine; but the hot iron which they frequently apply in curing a disease, leaves an impression on the skin that appears like an intended mark.

The Arabs call a white horse ابيض or اشهب or خاضر—a grey horse ازرق, a dark grey صنر, a black ادهم, a bay اخمر; a bay without any white mark اخمر صحّه, a sorrel اشقر, a dark chesnut اخمر محروق; a horse spotted with different colours حبش; a bay with four white feet اخمر محجّل; a horse having three white feet, and the left fore-leg of the same colour as the body, محجّل الثلاث و مطلوق اليمين.

Subjoined are the Bedouin names of some diseases incidental to horses.

مغاص Gripes.

سَراجَه The Farcy; regarded by the Arabs as almost incurable.

حروق Poll evil; they burn the flesh all round the swelling.

عُقر السُرا Navel Gulls. For this disease they have not any remedy.

عُقر الصفها Warbles. They open the tumours, and put on them lint made of untwisted rope, which they change several times: they then wash the wound with soap and water, rub it well over with salt, till the blood which comes from the wound dries up; they then wash it once more, and put on it a dry plaster made of pounded pomegranate peels, and the leaves of *Henne*.

مكمور Surfeit. If this is caused by the horse's drinking too much cold water after violent exercise, the Arabs despair of a cure. If it is caused by a superabundance of food, they bleed the horse's feet, and wrap the skin of a sheep just killed round its body; they also take some eggs, (if such be within their reach,) break them upon that part where the horse seems to suffer most, and rub it with the contents of the eggs.

متطوع القلب Broken wind.

مصفور Jaundice.

سقاوة Strangles. They burn some blue linen, (which has been dyed with indigo,) and let the smoke ascend into the horse's nose; this occasions a copious discharge. They rub the tumours with a paste, made of barley-chaff and butter.

جرب The mange.

خنزير The Stag-evil.

نعورة Violent head-ache.

حنوت Mange under the horse's tail.

باش Watery swellings upon the horse's stomach.

Burning is the most general remedy for the diseases of horses, which in this circumstance, as in many other respects, are treated by the Arabs as if they were human creatures. The Arabs never ride their horses unshod; the horse-shoes are called حدو. The whole set of four shoes طباقه حدو; two of them صدر; a single shoe وطبه. The bridle is called صروغ; the bridle with a bit, عنار; the leather strap or cord, with which the halter is tied over the horse's head, عذار; the saddle-cloth طراهه: but all these are Bedouin terms. The Syrians express the same things by a very different vocabulary.

Whenever a mare becomes old and unfit for war, the owner sells her to a village sheikh or some town's-man, always reservng for himself one half or two thirds of her future breed.

Ostriches.—These inhabit the great Syrian Desert, especially the plain extending from Hauran towards the Djebel Shammar and Nedjd. Some of them are found in Hauran, and a few are taken almost every year, even within two days' journey of Damascus. The Arabs call the male ostrich اضليم; the female, ربده. The male has black feathers, with white ends, except the tail feathers, which are wholly white. But the feathers of the female are spotted grey. This bird breeds in the middle of winter, and lays from twelve to one-and-twenty eggs. The nest (مدحه) is generally made at the foot of some isolated hill. The eggs are placed close together in a circle, half buried in sand, to protect them from rain, and a narrow trench is drawn round, whereby the water runs off. At ten or twelve feet from this circle, the female places two or three other eggs, which she does not hatch, but leaves for the young ones to feed upon immediately after they are hatched. The parent birds sit on the eggs in turn; and while one is so employed, the other stands keeping watch on the summit of the adjacent hill, which circumstance enables the Arabs to kill them. When they descry an ostrich standing in this manner on a hill, they conclude that some eggs must be near: the nest is soon found, and the ostriches fly away. The Arab then digs a hole in the ground near the eggs, puts his loaded gun into it, having fastened to the lock a long burning match, the gun being pointed towards the eggs; he covers it with stones, and retires. Towards evening the ostriches return, and not perceiving any enemy, resume their places, generally both at once, upon the eggs: the gun, in due time, is discharged; and the Arab finds, next morning, one of the ostriches, or frequently both, killed upon the spot. Such is the usual method of killing these birds, for the hunting of them is not practised in the Northern Arabian Desert. It has been supposed that the sun alone hatches the ostriches' eggs; but this opinion is proved to be erroneous, by the statement above given, which shows that the ostrich sits during the rainy season on its eggs; and the young ones are hatched in spring, before the sun has acquired any considerable degree of heat.

The inhabitants of the district called *Djof* eat the ostrich's flesh, which they purchase from the *Sherarát* Arabs. The eggs are sold for about one shilling each: the Arabs reckon them delicious food. The town's-people hang up the shells as ornaments in their rooms. Ostrich feathers are sold at Aleppo and Damascus; principally at the latter city. The people of Aleppo sometimes bring home ostriches which they had killed at the distance of two or three days' journies eastward. The *Sherarát* Arabs often sell the whole skin with the feathers on it; such a skin in the year 1810 was sold at Damascus for about ten Spanish dollars; the skin itself is thrown away as useless. At Aleppo (in the spring of 1811) the price of ostrich feathers was from 250 to 600 piastres the *rotolo* (about 2*l.* 10*s.* to 6*l.* per pound). The finest feathers are sold singly, at from one to two shillings each.

Gazelles.—These are seen in considerable numbers all over the Syrian Desert. On the Eastern frontiers of Syria are several places allotted for the hunting of gazelles; these places are called مصياده (*masiade*). An open space in the plain, of about one mile and a half square, is enclosed on three sides by a wall of loose stones, too high for the gazelles to leap over. In different parts of this wall gaps are purposely left, and near each gap a deep ditch is made on the outside. The enclosed space is situated near some rivulet or spring to which in summer the gazelles resort. When the hunting is to begin, many peasants assemble and watch till they see a herd of gazelles advancing from a distance towards the enclosure, into which they drive them; the gazelles, frightened by the shouts of these people, and the discharge of fire-arms, endeavour to leap over the wall, but can only effect this at the gaps, where they fall into the ditch outside, and are easily taken, sometimes by hundreds. The chief of the herd always leaps first, the others follow him one by one. The gazelles thus taken are immediately killed, and their flesh sold to the Arabs and neighbouring *Fellahs*. Several villages share in the profits of every *masiade*, or hunting-party, the principal of which are near *Kariatein*, *Hassia*, and *Homs*. Of the gazelle's skin, a kind of parchment is made, used in covering the small drum or *tabl* (طبل), with which the Syrians accompany some musical instruments or the voice.

Wild Asses.—In the country adjoining the district of *Djof*, between *Tobeik*, *Sauán* and *Hedrush*, and to the south of these places, the wild ass is found in great numbers. The Sherarat Arabs hunt them, and eat their flesh, but not before strangers. They sell their skins and hoofs to the pedlars of Damascus, and to the people of Hauran. The hoofs furnish materials for rings, which are worn by the peasants on their thumbs, or fastened under the arm-pits, as amulets against rheumatism.

Wild dog.—According to the description given by some Arabs, there is a species of wild dog called *derbown* (دربون), of a black colour, found in the country near *Djof*, the Fellahs of which district eat them.

Lizard.—A kind of this creature, called *dhab* (ضب), is seen in the same district; it is about eighteen inches long, with a tail of six inches. I have not hesitated to call it a lizard, according to the accounts given by different persons. The Arabs eat them, and keep their butter in the skins, which are scaly.

Besides the animals above described, hyænas, ounces, wolves, jackalls, and wild cats, inhabit the Desert; there are also a few foxes. The wild boars are very numerous, but not in the heart of the Desert. The Amour Arabs who live near Tedmor, are famous for killing them with the lance.

The eagle called *rakham* (رخم), the stork, the wild goose, the partridge, the *katta*, and lark, are the birds most commonly found in the Desert. The kattas are so numerous, that they actually appear like a cloud at a distance; they breed in the stony districts of *Djebel Haurán, el Szafa, el Ledja,* and *Djebel Belkaa.* The katta lays three eggs, as large as a pigeon's, of a greenish black colour. The Arabs collect great quantities of these eggs, which they eat fried with butter.

Vegetation of the Desert.

The Desert at the distance of four or five days' journies, from the eastern limits of Syria, in most parts consists of arable earth, and still exhibits evident signs of former cultivation. Farther on towards the interior of the Desert, the soil becomes sandy; but even there the Arabs find in winter a great variety of herbs which contribute to the food of their cattle. In the Desert it rarely happens that different kinds of herbs are found together; but every district seems to have its peculiar plant, which grows where no other is found. The Arabs call herbs in general عُشب; the green plants just growing up ربيع; the herbs withered by the sun (a favourite food of the camels) هُمري. The plants which grow to a certain height are called "trees," or اشجار. The following herbs are products of the Desert, according to information that I received.

Routa, روتَه, about three feet high, the best food for camels. *Fers* (فرس). *Shieh* (شِح); this the camels eat only when it is dried up in summer. Its seeds are used with success as a vermifuge. *Sous* (سوس), *oerk* (أرك), *akoul* (عقول), grow in the Desert near Damascus. The *akoul* is likewise found in Irák Arabi and Mesopotamia. *Serr* (سرّ); this is very like the *shieh*, and the Arabs eat the stem of it in spring. *Ghadha* (غضي), in the district of Dhahy. *Harbak* (هرَبك). *Kaltaf* (قتنف), which always grows in low grounds. *Shaumár* (شومار); something like fennel; the Arabs eat its stem. *Etel* (اتل), which grows to the height of six feet. *Merár* (مرار). *Wasbe* (وسبه); this has a yellow stalk, that stains the camel's mouth black. *Násy* (ناسي), chiefly in sandy districts. *Shaured* (شورد) resembles the basilisk. The Desert truffle, or *kemmaye*, is generally found in spring, on the spot where this herb grows if the winter rains have been abundant.

Winds.

The north wind in the Desert, whether it be hot or cold, is always considered pernicious to the health of man and beast. The west wind (*gharby*, غربي) is the most usual in summer. The south wind is reckoned favourable to the earth, and the sprouting herbs. The east wind is the hottest of all; the Arabs call it *kásy* (قاسي): every hot wind is called *samoum*. When it comes from the east, it dries up the water in the water-skins; and therefore the wandering Arabs sometimes die of thirst, but not by the immediate effect of the wind. The Arabs cannot foretell by any particular signs the approach of this *samoum*. If during the *samoum* a camel happens to lie upon the ground, he hangs down his head to alleviate the injurious effects of the wind; if a camel happens to be walking at the time, he continues his pace without any halt. The Arabs cover themselves with a second mantle, or some sackcloth, to prevent the wind from parching their skins.

ADDITIONAL OBSERVATIONS.

Mode of Encamping.

In countries where security reigns, the Bedouins often encamp the whole year round, occupying but two or three tents together, at the distance of several hours from any other members of their tribe. I have seen such solitary inhabitants of the Hodeyl tribe in the mountains east of Mekka, and some of the Sowaleha and Mezeiyne tribes in the mountains of Sinai.

It may be here remarked that all the wealthy Bedouins have two sets of tent-coverings—one new and strong, for winter—the other old and light, for summer.

On the Syrian and Arabian plains the Bedouins encamp in summer (when rain-water cannot be found in pools), near wells, where they remain often for a whole month; while their flocks and herds pasture all around, at the distance of several hours, under the guard of slaves or shepherds, who bring them every second or third day to the well for water. It is on these occasions that the Arabs make attacks upon other tribes; for it becomes known that such or such people are encamped near a certain well, and may be easily surprised. If an attack of this kind be apprehended, the men of the encampment are in constant readiness for defence, and for the rescue of their cattle, which the enemy often strives to carry off. The Sherarat Arabs, who, living on the

Syrian Hadj route, are much exposed to invasion, constantly have a saddled camel before their tents, that they may the more readily hasten to the assistance of their shepherds. Most wells in the interior of the Desert, and especially in Nedjd, are exclusive property, either of a whole tribe, or of individuals whose ancestors dug the wells. During the Wahaby government many new wells have been made by the chief's order. If a well be the property of a tribe, the tents are pitched near it, whenever rain-water becomes scarce in the Desert; and no other Arabs are then permitted to water their camels there. But if the well belongs to an individual, he repairs it in summer time, accompanied by his tribe, and receives presents from all strange tribes who pass or encamp at the well, and refresh their camels with the water of it; and these presents are particularly required if a party pass on its return home, which has been seen taking plunder from an enemy. The property of such a well is never alienated; and the Arabs say, that the possessor is sure to be fortunate, as all who drink of the water bestow on him their benedictions. In spring and winter it is more difficult to carry off the cattle, because in those seasons they find sufficient food close to the tents, and are, therefore, easily protected. There are tribes which encamp in spring time far from any streams or wells, on fertile plains, where they remain for several weeks without tasting water, living wholly upon milk; and their cattle can dispense with water as long as green and juicy herbage affords them nourishment: this, however, is not the case with horses. Considerable numbers of the Beni Shammar thus encamp every spring, for upwards of a month, in the waterless desert between Djof and Djebel Shammar.

In travelling, strong parties only can venture to encamp at night near a well, where they may naturally expect visitors. Weaker parties water their beasts, fill their water-skins, and encamp at a distance from any road leading to the well.

Dress.

In every province, almost in every tribe, a difference may be perceived in the dress of the Bedouins. The striped woollen mantle, or *abba* (in Syria called *meshlah*), the head-kerchief, or *keffie*, with yellow and green stripes, for the men; and the blue gown for the women, are universal in all the tribes north of Mekka. The Wahabys in Nedjd carefully perfume the keffie with civet, or with the odoriferous earth named *ares*, which is brought from Aden, and much used in the Desert. Near Mekka and Tayf, and beyond those places southward, in the direction of Yemen, men and women dress usually in leather: the men fasten a leather apron round their loins, and at night and in winter cover themselves with an abba, but walk about in the warm season quite naked. The women have a similar apron, but larger than that of the men, reaching down to their ancles, and an upper cloak, with narrow sleeves, made also of leather; this is well tanned, neatly worked and sewn, and adorned with many tassels, which give it a gay appearance. They rub it frequently with butter, to render it soft. Over the apron both men and women wear leather girdles, consisting of long slender thongs, tied in a dozen or more folds round the body. The women wear similar thongs, fastened upon the bare skin of the stomach under the apron; and this is a general custom all over the Desert. The Bedouins affirm that Mohammed wore the same. It is reckoned shameful that a male Bedouin should wear drawers: these form no part of a man's dress throughout the Desert; they are considered as fit only for women. About the head, over the keffie, the Mekka and Yemen Bedouins wear, instead of the woollen rope with which the northern Bedouins tie the keffie, a circle made of wax, tar, and butter, strongly kneaded together; this is pressed down to the middle of the head, and looks like the airy crown of a saint. It is about the thickness of a finger; and they take it off very frequently to press it between their hands, so that its shape may be preserved. The Arabic name of this article I have forgotten. The southern Bedouins wear over the right elbow a ring of yellow metal, which cannot be taken off without difficulty. I have seen one almost hidden by the flesh of the arm growing over it.

All Bedouin women are equally fond of ear-rings, nose-rings, finger-rings, ankle-rings, and bracelets. The poor have their ornaments made of horn; some wear common glass beads; but the richer use articles of silver, amber, coral, or mother-of-pearl. The male Bedouins care little about their own dress, but love to decorate their wives, and dress them in good clothes, which they think reflect honour upon themselves. These women do not put by their fine dresses and ornaments to wear them only at feasts or visits, like the ladies who live in towns: the Bedouin females deck themselves every day with whatever they regard as the most valuable in their wardrobe; having often five or six bracelets on the same arm, and two or three rings in the same ear. It may be here remarked, that about Mekka several of the Bedouins wear blue shirts, made very short, and with narrow and short sleeves.

The women's hair-dress varies in almost every tribe. In Hedjaz and Yemen they wear their hair in plaits, much like those of the Nubian females. The Arab women of Sinai tie it in a thick bunch, projecting over the forehead. In Arabia (proper), they perfume their hair, as the men perfume the keffie. Among the

Arabs of Sinai, all unmarried girls, as soon as they attain the age of puberty, are permitted to wear an ornament called *shebeyka*, composed of different pieces of mother-of-pearl, about three or four inches long, and a quarter of an inch broad, fastened to a string, and tied in such a manner to the head, that they hang down over the cheek and forehead, the latter being moreover decorated with a round piece of the same substance, about two inches in diameter. The bridegroom takes away the *shebeyka* by force on the nuptial night; and a married woman can never wear that ornament again. The same women (of Tor Sinai) adorn their leather girdles with a great number of small sea-shells. In the interior of the Desert, even in Hedjaz, and, as I understood, likewise in Yemen, the Bedouin women usually go unveiled. All the Bedouins who are connected in intercourse with Egypt, oblige their women to wear veils before strangers.

I have already mentioned, that several of the Aenezes allow their hair to grow, and wear it falling in locks upon the cheek, as do most of the Hedjaz Bedouins. The tribes of *Sobh* and *Owf* (belonging to the *Harb* tribe) wear their thick locks in tresses down to the breast. The Wahaby chief had prohibited his Arabs from wearing their hair in this fashion, which he thought degrading to a man, and fit only for such as desired to affect an appearance of effeminacy. Among the *Maazy* Arabs, who occupy the mountains between the Nile and the Red Sea, as far as the latitude of Cosseir (and who have come within the last century from Arabia, their mother country), it is an established and remarkable custom, that those young men only are allowed to shave the hair of the head, who have brought home some booty from an enemy. It becomes then a festival in the family, whenever one of the sons for the first time has his head shaved; while young men are sometimes met among them whose hair still covers their heads.

Arms.

Matchlocks are scarce among the Syrian Bedouins, and in general among all of them northward of the Akabas. Every Bedouin in the Nedjd country, in Hedjaz and Yemen, is armed with a matchlock. The Wahabys' principal force consists in this infantry. Their fire-arms are of very coarse workmanship: they procure them from the towns in their neighbourhood. In Hedjaz, however, I saw many fine Persian barrels. They esteem the barrels in proportion to their size and weight; the heavier and larger being the most valued. The best guns are distinguished by particular names, and descend from father to son as a kind of entailed property, with which the possessor would never part but on occasions of extreme necessity. The Bedouins are expert marksmen, especially those of Nedjd, and the mountains of Hedjaz. Matchlocks are generally most numerous in the mountains; while in the plains, camel-riders armed with lances are more common. A European would think it almost impossible to take a sure aim with an instrument so rude as the Arab matchlock, which is often not worth more than one dollar. Yet, by means of such guns, loaded with balls, I have seen crows, and even partridges killed. In numerous encounters between the Turks under Mohammed Aly Pasha, and the Bedouins, the latter invariably defeated the enemy whenever they fought in rocky districts, by the mere fire of their musketry, but were constantly defeated wherever the Turkish cavalry had room to act. The Bedouins every where make their own powder. Salt-petre and charcoal are found in many districts; the salt-petre is purchased in towns. The matchlock, it would seem, is a much safer, though less handy weapon than our gun, for it can never miss fire. The Bedouins prefer it; and when they get a common musket have it altered into a matchlock.

In the southern deserts of Arabia, and in the mountains of Hedjaz, short lances (*mezrák*) are very common; they are twisted round with yellow wire like those of the Nubian Arabs. The Bedouins sometimes use them in close combat, or throw them, like javelins, to a distance.

Coats of mail are seen in every part of Arabia, but no where in great numbers; the price of them being considerable. The late Wahaby chief, Ibn Saoud, constantly wore one under his shirt. The Wahabys esteem highly the coat of mail (درع). Saoud had in his possession an ancient and celebrated coat of mail, which once belonged to the famous Orar el Deyghemy, the owner of the horse *Mashhour*, a hero well known in Arabian history. A coat of mail of the finest quality (which is called *Daoudy*) costs from five hundred to a thousand dollars. Such coats are of antique workmanship, and belonged probably to the European knights of the Crusades.

Food and Cookery.

Throughout the Desert there is a great sameness in the Bedouin dishes; for they every where consist chiefly of flour and butter. In every province, however, different names are given to the same dish; thus what the Aenezes call *ftita*, the Arabs of Sinai denominate *medjelleh*, or, if milk be mixed with it, *merekeda*. The *djereisha* is a very common dish in the interior of the Desert, boiled wheat which has been coarsely ground, and over which butter is poured; with the addition of milk it becomes *nekaa*. The custom of telling the landlord to take away the meat for the women (لحم القرش), is prevalent among the Sinai Arabs, although not known in Hedjaz. In such parts of the Desert as are far distant from any cultivated districts, the consumption of corn is much less than in others. Thus the Arabs on the eastern coast of the Red Sea, between Yembo and Akaba, use but little wheaten bread. It is the want of corn that obliges all Bedouins to keep up any intercourse with those who cultivate the soil; and it is a mistake to imagine that the Bedouins can ever be independent of the cultivators. The frontier villages of Syria and Mesopotamia, the towns of Nedjd; Yembo, Mekka, and Djidda, and the cultivated vallies of Hedjaz and Yemen, are frequented for provisions by all the Bedouins at a distance of ten or fifteen days from those points: there they sell their cattle, and take in return wheat, barley, and clothes. It is only when circumstances force them, that Arabs content themselves with a diet of milk and meat alone.

Of camels' milk, neither butter nor cheese is ever made; it abounds among the Aenezes. The sheep and goats are milked every morning by the women before day-break; the milk is shaken for about two hours in skins, and thus becomes butter; and the butter-milk constitutes the chief beverage of the Arabs, and is much used in their dishes: it is generally (but not always) called *leben*, while fresh milk is distinguished by the term, *haleib*.

A lamb is sometimes roasted or baked in the earth; a hole being made for that purpose, heated and covered with stones. Many Bedouins have a custom of boiling certain herbs in butter, which is then poured off into the skins containing their provisions. This butter becomes strongly impregnated with the odour of those herbs, and is much liked by the Arabs. The herb *shyh* is often used in this manner; the herb *baitherán* (a species of thyme) is commonly applied to this purpose in Nedjd.

On their journeys, the Bedouins live almost wholly upon unleavened bread baked in the ashes, and mixed with butter: this food they call *kurs*, *ayesh*, and *kahkeh*.

I have elsewhere remarked that the Arabs of Kerek regard it as extremely shameful to sell any butter. Among the Bedouins near Mekka to sell milk is considered as equally degrading, and the poorest Arab would not expose himself to the opprobrious nickname of *lebbán*, or " milk-seller," although, during the pilgrimage, milk is excessively dear. It forms a curious exception to this rule, that the Beni Koreish, who esteem themselves the most noble race of Arabian Bedouins, freely sell their milk, with which Mekka is supplied from the tents of that tribe, generally pitched about Djebel Arafat and Wady Muna.

In Hedjaz the usual dish of the Arabs is Indian rice, mixed with lentils and without any bread; this they find cheaper than corn, and equally nutritious; but wherever dates grow, that excellent fruit constitutes their chief diet. In Nedjd, Hedjaz, and Yemen, the Bedouins use butter to excess. Whoever can afford such luxury, swallows every morning a large cupful of butter before breakfast, and snuffs up as much into his nostrils (this is also a favourite practice among the people of Mekka): all their food swims in butter. The continual motion and exercise in which they employ themselves strengthen their powers of digestion, and for the same reason an Arab will live for months together upon the smallest allowance; and then, if an opportunity should offer, he will devour at one sitting the flesh of half a lamb without any injury to his health.

In the interior of their deserts, the Bedouins never make any cheese; their butter is made of sheep's or goats' milk. I have never seen any butter made from the milk of camels, although I understood that this was sometimes the case on particular occasions of necessity; many Arabs with whom I conversed had never tasted any.

Throughout the Desert when a sheep or goat is killed, the persons present often eat the liver and kidney raw, adding to it a little salt. Some Arabs of Yemen are said to eat raw not only those parts, but likewise whole slices of flesh; thus resembling the Abyssinians and the Druses of Libanon, who frequently indulge in raw meat, the latter to my own certain knowledge. The Asyr Arabs, and those south of them towards Yemen, eat horse-flesh; but this is never used as food among the northern Bedouins.

Industry.

The chief specimens of Bedouin industry are the tanning of leather; the preparing of water-skins, the weaving of tents, sacks, cloaks, and *abbas*. The leather is tanned by means of pomegranate juice, or (as more commonly over the whole Desert) with the *gharad* or fruit of the *Sant*, or else with the bark of the *Seyale*, another mimosa species. The women sew the water-skins which the men have tanned. They work in Hedjaz very neat neck-leathers for the camels, upon which their husbands ride; these are a kind of net-work, adorned with shells and leather tassels, called *dawîreh*. The distaff is frequently seen in the hands of men all over the Hedjaz; and it seems strange that they should not regard this as derogating from their masculine dignity, while they disdainfully spurn at every other domestic employment.

The Arabs' Wealth.

The only Bedouins that can be reckoned wealthy, are those whose tribes pasture their cattle in the open plains, which have been fertilized by the rains of winter. To them belong innumerable herds of camels: the richest Bedouins of the southern plains are the *Kahtan* tribe, on the frontiers of Yemen. The father of a family is said to be poor among them, if he possess only forty camels; the usual stock in a family is from one hundred to two hundred. The tribes of poor Bedouins are all those who occupy a mountainous territory, where the camels find less food, and are not so prolific. Thus the Bedouin inhabitants of that whole chain of mountains, that extend from Damascus across Arabia Petræa, and along the coast of the Red Sea, as far as Yemen, are all people of little property in cattle, while all the tribes of the eastern plains possess great numbers. The account which I have already given of an Arab's yearly expenses, must be understood only of a man above the common class; many respectable families spend only half that sum. To give a specimen of the means adopted by a poor Arab to gain his livelihood, and furnish his family with provisions, my journal of an expedition in the Sinai mountains may be consulted. Poor Bedouins come from thence to Cairo, bringing their camels loaded with coals. Such a load, which requires the labour of one man for ten or fifteen days to collect, is sold at Cairo for about three dollars, after a journey of ten or eleven days. With these three dollars, the man then purchases half a load of wheat, some tobacco for himself, and a pair of shoes or handkerchief for his wife, and returns the same distance to his tent; having been above five weeks employed, together with his camel, in procuring this scanty supply for the family. On such occasion a Bedouin will gladly forfeit the only sensual pleasure he can enjoy on the road, (eating butter and smoking tobacco,) rather than return to his home without some small present for his family, for the purchase of which he sacrifices, if necessary, even his butter-skin and tobacco-pouch.

Some Arab families pride themselves in having only herds of

camels, without sheep or goats; but I never heard that there existed whole tribes without the latter. Those who have camels alone are mostly families of sheikhs; and in case strangers arrive for whom a lamb is to be killed, then the Arabs usually bring one for that purpose to the sheikh's tent. In some encampments, the Arabs will not permit their sheikh to slaughter a lamb on any occasion, but furnish by turns the meat for his tent. The families who have camels only are called *ahel bel* (اهل بل), in opposition to the *ahel ghanem* (اهل غنم).

But in the most desperate circumstances, without camels or sheep, a Bedouin is always too proud to show discontent, or much less to complain. He never begs assistance, but strives with all his might, either as a camel-driver, a shepherd, or a robber, to retrieve his lost property. Hope in the bounty of God, and a perfect resignation to his divine will, are deeply implanted in the Arab's breast; but this resignation does not paralyse his exertions so much as it does those of the Turks. I have heard Arabs reproach Turks for their apathy and stupidity, in ascribing to the will of God what was merely the result of their own faults or folly, quoting a proverb which says, "He bared his back to the stings of mosquitos, and then exclaimed, God has decreed that I should be stung." The fortitude with which Bedouins endure evils of every kind is exemplary: in that respect they are as much superior to us as we exceed them in our eager search after pleasing sensations and refined enjoyments. Wise men have always thought that the amount of evil in this world was greater than that of pleasure; it seems therefore that he is more truly a philosopher who, although he knows but few refinements of pleasure, laughs at evil, than the man who sinks under adversity, and passes his happier moments in the pursuit of visionary enjoyments.

The secret hopes and expectations of the Bedouin are much

more limited than those of the Arab who dwells in a town. His chief desire during a state of poverty is to become so opulent that he may be enabled to slaughter a lamb on the arrival of every respectable guest at his tent, and in this act of hospitality to rival at least, if not to exceed, all the other Arabs of his tribe. If fortune grant him the accomplishment of this desire, he then looks out for a fine horse or dromedary, and good clothes for his females: these objects once attained, he feels no other wish but that of maintaining and increasing his reputation for bravery and hospitality. For this reason it may be safely affirmed that there are among Bedouins, an infinitely greater number of individuals contented and happy with their lot, than among other Asiatics, whose happiness is almost always blighted by avarice, and the ambition of rising above their equals.

The Bedouin is certainly unhappy when he feels himself so poor that he cannot entertain a guest according to his wish; he then looks with an envious eye upon his more fortunate neighbours; he dreads the sneers of friends and of enemies, who regard him as unable to honour a stranger: but whenever he can contrive to display hospitality, he feels himself upon a footing of equality with the richest sheikh, towards whom he bears no envy on account of his more numerous flocks and herds, the possession of which does not procure to him any increase either of honours or enjoyments.

Sciences, Music, Poetry, &c.

Of reading and writing, all the Bedouins throughout Arabia are equally ignorant. The Wahaby chiefs have taken pains to instruct them; they have sent Imáms among the different tribes to teach the children, but their efforts have had little effect;

and the Bedouins remain, as might be expected, a most illiterate people. In the mountains of Hedjaz and of Yemen, where many Bedouin tribes have become agriculturists, more persons are found who can read, and know something of their laws and learned language, than among those encamped on the plains. This is also the case in Nedjd, where the Wahabys have established schools in every village, and oblige the fathers of families to superintend the instruction of their children. At Derayeh many learned persons of the first class among eastern men of letters have collected very valuable libraries from all parts of Arabia, and some of their olemas have composed treatises on religious and judicial subjects. Among their books are great numbers of historical works, which seem to be in particular request at Derayeh. Whatever manuscripts of that description could be found at Mekka and Medina, and in the towns of Yemen, have been purchased by them and carried off. The library of Saoud is unquestionably the richest, at present, in Arabic manuscripts on historical subjects.

How much eloquence is still admired among the Bedouins, I have already noticed. A sheikh, however renowned he may be for bravery, or skill in war, can never expect to possess great influence over his Arabs without the talent of oratory. A Bedouin will not submit to any command, but readily yields to persuasion.

Through every part of the Arabian desert, poetry is equally esteemed. Many persons are found who make verses of true measure, although they cannot either read or write; yet as they employ on such occasions chosen terms only, and as the purity of their vernacular language is such as to preclude any grammatical errors, these verses, after passing from mouth to mouth, may at last be committed to paper, and will most commonly be found regular and correct. I presume that the greater part of the early poetry of the Arabs which has descended to us, is derived from similar compositions. Ibn Saoud had assembled the best poets of the Desert at Derayeh; he delighted in poetry, and very liberally rewarded those who excelled in it. According to Arab custom, if a reputable poet address some verses to a sheikh, or a distinguished warrior, he will receive a camel or some sheep as a present. The largesses which in former times were bestowed on poets by Arabian chiefs, are still the subject of frequent conversation among the Bedouins; but no one is inclined to imitate the ancient generosity. The people of *el Hassa*, near the Persian Gulf, are celebrated for their poetical genius above all other Arabs of Nedjd or Hedjaz.

The *rababa* (a string-instrument) is common all over the Desert, although not always of the same shape. In Nedjd, as among the Sinai Arabs, it is reckoned disgraceful to play on the rababa before a numerous company. Slaves alone perform on it in that case: and if a free Arab wish to acquire some degree of execution on that instrument, he must practise at home, and in the bosom of his family. But, on the other hand, I have seen in Hedjaz Bedouins play on the rababa before company.

The songs called *asamer* require a more detailed description. They are heard all over the Desert; but each tribe varies in the performance of them. During my stay in the mountains of Sinai, I had frequent opportunities of hearing those songs, and of witnessing the performance in the dead of the night.

About two or three hours after sun-set, either the girls and young women, or the young men, assemble upon an open space before or behind the tents and begin to sing there in choruses until the other party joins them. The girls then place themselves either in a group between the men, who range themselves in a line on both sides, or if the number of the females be but small, they occupy a line opposite to that of the men, at a distance of about thirty paces. One of the men then begins a song (*kâszyde*) of which only one verse is sung, repeating it many times, always with the same melody. The whole party of men then join in the chorus of the verse, accompanying it with clapping of hands, and various motions of the body. Standing close together, the whole line inclines sometimes towards one side, sometimes towards the other, backwards and forwards, occasionally dropping on one knee, always taking care to keep time by that movement, in measure with the song. While the men do this, two or three of the girls come forth from the group, or line of their companions, and slowly advance towards the men. They are completely veiled, and hold a mellaye, or blue cloak, loosely hung over both their outspread arms. They approach with light steps and slight bows, in time to the songs. Soon the motions of the girls become a little more lively, while they approach within two paces of the men; but still dancing (as it is called), continuing to be extremely reserved, strictly decent, and very coy. The men endeavour to animate the girls by loud exclamations, with which they interrupt their song from time to time. They make use for this purpose of exclamations and noises, with which they are accustomed to order their camels to halt, to walk, and trot, to drink, and eat, to stop, and to lie down. They do not address the girl by her name, which would be a breach of politeness, according to Bedouin manners, but style her "camel," affecting to suppose that she advances towards them in search of food or water. This fiction is continued during the whole dance. "Get up, O camel;" "walk fast;" "the poor camel is thirsty;" "come and take your evening food:" these, and similar expressions, are used on the occasion, added to the many guttural sounds in which camel-drivers talk to their beasts. To excite the dancer still more, some of the gay young men spread before them upon the ground their own turbans, or head-kerchiefs, to represent food for the camel. If the dancing girl approach near enough to snatch away any article of dress, she throws it behind her back to her companions; and when the dance is finished, the owner must redeem it by a small fee paid to the girl. I once released a handkerchief by giving to the girl a string of pretty beads made of mother-of-pearl, observing that it was meant as a *halter* for the camel; with this she was much pleased, and hung it round her neck. After the dance has continued five or ten minutes, the girl sits down, and another takes her place, beginning like the former and accelerating her movements according as she herself feels interested in the dance. If she seems animated and advances close to the men's line, the latter evince their approbation by stretching out their arms as if to receive her; this dance, which continues frequently for five or six hours, and till long after midnight, and the pathetic songs which often accompany it, most powerfully work upon the imagination and feelings of the Arabs, and they never speak of the mesamer but with raptures. The feelings of a lover must, on this occasion, be carried to the highest pitch. The veiled form of his mistress advances in the dark, or by moonlight, like a phantom, to his embraces; her graceful, decent steps, her increasing animation, the general applause she receives, and the words of the song, or kaszyde, which are always in praise of beauty, must create the liveliest emotions in the bosom of her lover, who has, at least, the satisfaction of being able to give full scope to his feelings by voice and gestures, without exposing himself to any blame.*

If the girls of the encampment have any cause to be angry with the young men, the latter attend for many nights, but no females appear to sing the mesamer: on the other hand, I have

---

* The decent and romantic nature of this dance places it widely in contrast with the vulgar and licentious motions and contortions of the Egyptian dancing-girls, and is even preferable, in a high degree, to the Egyptian or Syrian ladies' dance.

heard the girls sing, although none of the young men came from the tents to join them.

The mesamer are general throughout the Desert, but almost every tribe differs in the mode of singing them. The song is often composed extempore, and relates to the beauty and qualities of the girl who dances: if the young men are at home in the camp, they continue the like mesamer, for months together, every night. Married men and women sometimes join; young men often walk at night a distance of some hours, and back again, that they may enjoy the mesamer of a neighbouring camp. I may here remark that *mesámer* must not be confounded with *Mezámer*, which in Arabic signifies the Book of Psalms.*

The Camel-driver's Song.

In Hedjaz and in Egypt I have heard the following words, which seemed to be the favourite burden of this song:—

"None can perform long journies but the stout and full-grown camel."

---

* The women of the Aleygat tribe in the Sinai mountains sing their own praises in the following verse:

"O women of Aleygat! nothing is found to equal us,

Excepting heaven; (but) men are the earth (upon which we tread)."

I have heard the Maggrebyn Bedouins sing in the mesamer, a verse of which the the oddity deserves mention. Addressing a mistress named *Ghalye*, the lover exclaims:—

"O Ghalye, if my father were a jack-ass, I would sell him, that I might be able to purchase Ghalye."

Feasts and Rejoicings.

It is generally so arranged by those who have families in a camp, that all the young boys should be circumcised on the same day. Every man then kills at least one sheep in honour of his son—sometimes three or four, and all the members of the tribe, besides the strangers who come for the purpose, feast together during a whole day. On the festival of Ramadhan, and of the sacrifice of Arafat, those Arabs who have no horses, run races upon their camels, while the women amuse themselves by singing loudly. Among the Sinai Arabs, the girls are permitted, on those occasions, to let their faces be seen by the young men of the tribe, who ride by swiftly on their camels, the girls at that moment raising their veils, so as to allow a hasty glance. It has been remarked, that immediately after these feasts the girls are demanded in marriage from their fathers. The most prudish or coy among the girls do not join their companions in this raising of the veil, but remain in the interior of their tents.

There are few Bedouin tribes within whose territory, or at least within a little distance from it, the tomb of some saint or reverend sheikh is not found; to him all the neighbouring Arabs address their vows. These tombs are usually visited once a year by great numbers of Arabs, who there slaughter the victims they had vowed during the preceding year. These vows are made with the hope of obtaining male issue, or a numerous breed of horses or camels.* The day of visiting the saint's tomb becomes

* The veneration in which these Bedouins hold a saint, almost borders on idolatry: they certainly believe that he can influence heaven in their favour, both here and in the other world. Against this superstition, and the killing of victims in honour of saints, the Wahabys have exerted themselves in sermons. The saints' tombs are generally placed on the summits of mountains.

a festival for the whole tribe, and all the neighbours. The women then appear clothed in their finest dresses, and mounted upon camels, the saddles of which their husbands take great care to adorn. Upon every occasion the Bedouin endeavours to show off his wife under her most advantageous appearance; and he seems desirous that she should exceed all her female acquaintances in clothes and rings, while he himself wears scarcely more upon his body than is absolutely necessary to protect him from the inclemency of a hot or rainy season.

Diseases.

Among the Bedouins of Hedjaz, particularly those in the neighbourhood of Mekka and Medina, many suffer occasionally from their intercourse with public women, in whose dwellings some Bedouins may be at all times seen, which is never the case either at Aleppo or Damascus. But even in Hedjaz, public women are excluded from the Arab encampments. Those Bedouins also who visit Cairo, have frequently reason to repent of their acquaintance with the ladies of that city.

Vaccination.

After various efforts to introduce it in Egypt, it was only in the winter of 1816 that a Syrian physician succeeded in rendering it general among the Christians. No country in the east requires it more than Egypt, especially Upper Egypt, where the small-pox is often almost as pernicious as the plague, and more to be dreaded, because it occurs more frequently. Among the Hedjaz Bedouins, inoculation is very little practised. It was proposed to

Mohammed Aly Pasha, that he should command his subjects in the open country to be vaccinated; but, like other Turkish governors, he only listens to beneficial schemes when they can tend to promote his own interests. The most ridiculous and extraordinary remedies for diseases are always those to which the Asiatics resort with implicit confidence in their efficacy. I have seen an Arab immediately on his rising in the morning swallow whole draughts of camel's urine, because a physician (i. e. a barber) of Mekka had advised him to do so, as a certain remedy for oppression on the breast. Another, in the last stage of a consumption, was directed to eat, for one fortnight, nothing but the *raw* liver of a male camel. It being summer time, and fresh liver not every day attainable, the man persisted in feeding upon the same putrid liver for several days together, until death proved the fallaciousness of this prescription.

Customs relative to Matrimony.

What I shall add on this subject refers principally to the Bedouins of Mount Sinai, with whom I lived for nearly two months in the spring of 1816, while the plague raged at Cairo. The terms being settled between the girl's father and the man desirous of marrying her, the father gives to the suitor a branch of a tree or shrub, or something green, which he sticks in his turban and wears for three days, to show that he has taken a virgin in matrimony: if he marry a widow, this is not done. The girl is seldom acquainted with the change that is to take place in her condition, for no one thinks it necessary to consult her inclination; and even if she should dislike the bridegroom, she must yield, at least for the first night, to his embraces, but is at liberty the next morning to retreat from his tent. But among the wealthy Arabs of the eastern plain, the Aenezes, the Meteyr in Nedjd, and the Ateybe in Hedjaz, the father never receives the price of the girl, and therefore some regard is paid to her inclinations.

Among the Arabs of Sinai, the young maid comes home in the evening with the cattle. At a short distance from the camp she is met by the future spouse, and a couple of his young friends, and carried off by force to her father's tent. If she entertains any suspicion of their designs, she defends herself with stones, and often inflicts wounds on the young men, even though she does not dislike the lover; for, according to custom, the more she struggles, bites, kicks, cries, and strikes, the more she is applauded ever after by her own companions. She is then taken to her father's tent by those young men who place her in the women's apartment; and one of the bridegroom's relations immediately throws over her an abba, or man's cloak, completely enveloping her head, and exclaims, " None shall cover thee but such a one," mentioning the bridegroom's name. Till that moment, the girl is often unacquainted even with the name of the person to whom she is betrothed. After this ceremony she is dressed by her mother and female relations in the new clothes provided for her by the bridegroom, and a camel is brought before the tent, ornamented with tassels and shreds of cloth, according to the wealth of the husband. Upon this camel she is mounted, although still continuing to struggle in a most unruly manner, and held by the bridegroom's friends on both sides. Thus she is led three times round his tent, while her companions utter loud exclamations; after which, she is taken to a private recess which the bridegroom has prepared for her in his tent, with curtains, in the interior of the women's apartment.

If the bride belong to a distant camp, she is placed upon a camel immediately after the abba has been thrown over her, and led to the husband's camp, attended by women: during this procession decency obliges her to cry and sob most bitterly. While she is left in the husband's tent with one woman only, the other females assemble before the tent, singing in praise of the young couple. Several sheep, in the mean time, have been killed;* and the guests who flock to the feast eat *bread* (for this is a circumstance absolutely necessary on such nuptial occasions) and *meat*. Late at night, when the bridegroom can with decency escape from the congratulating crowds of his friends, he enters the bride's recess, and the marriage is completed, the bride still continuing to cry very loudly.† The husband, when he enters the nuptial recess, leaves his shoes before the door, to show that he is within.

On the next morning every father of a family in the encampment brings a goat as a present to the bride; two or three goats are killed, and after a plentiful dinner the ceremony is concluded.

If the girl has been married wholly against her inclination, she is allowed on the following morning to take shelter in her father's tent, which neither he nor any body else can prevent her from doing. The rich sheikhs seldom refuse their daughters to a poor

---

* That the blood of sheep should flow upon the ground is considered by the Beni Harb, in Hedjaz, as necessary to the completion of a marriage; but all the Bedouins are not of that opinion. In Egypt, the Copts kill a sheep as soon as the bride enters the bridegroom's house, and she is obliged to step over the blood flowing upon the threshold, at the door-way.

† It sometimes happens, as I have been assured, that the husband is obliged to tie his bride, and even to beat her, before she can be induced to comply with his desires. The want of civilisation is more evident in the relation between males and females, than in any other circumstance. Among the Arabs of Upper Egypt, there is a particular custom. On the wedding-night, the bridegroom, when he approaches his bride, is accompanied by two women, who, on coming out from the nuptial chamber, bear witness to the virgin state in which he had found the new-married girl, whom he must not again visit before the third night.

Arab, provided he can pay the price demanded for her, and is stout and active enough to keep her from starving.

But the marriage of a widow or divorced woman is not attended with so much ceremony or rejoicing. The lady is not wrapped in an abba, nor does she offer any resistance when the friends conduct her to the husband's tent; and if the latter has been a married man already, no feast whatever takes place; if, however, he has not been married before, she is led in pomp from her tent to his. But even then, no guest will come to eat of the nuptial bread; which, indeed, is only distributed on the marriage of a virgin: for the Arabs regard every thing connected with the nuptials of a widow as ill-omened, and unworthy of the participation of generous or honourable men. For the space of thirty days, or a whole month, the husband will not eat of any provisions belonging to his wife, nor even use any of her vessels at meals. During that time she herself, and every thing appertaining to her, are stigmatised as being *gerán* (قران); and the Arabs believe that any infraction of this custom would be the sure road to perdition. If the husband make coffee for the Arabs, every one of his guests brings with him his own cup, that he may not drink out of one belonging to the new-married widow.

It is thought decent, that on the nuptials of a virgin she should remain at least one fortnight in the interior of her tent, leaving it only at night. If her husband absent himself on a journey before the expiration of that time, she may abridge the period of her confinement. The marriage ceremony among the Bedouins generally takes place on a Friday evening.

The price of a girl varies according to circumstances, and is never exactly stipulated in a tribe. Among the Arabs of Sinai it is from five to ten dollars, but sometimes amounts to thirty, if the girl is well connected and very handsome. Part only of the money is paid down, the rest standing over as a kind of debt.

The father receives the money; or, if he is dead, the brother, or nearest male relation. Whoever has a right to receive this money is styled the maid's master. The price of an *azeba*, or widow, is never more than half of what is given for a virgin; generally no more than one third. It likewise is paid into the hands of her masters.

A singular custom prevails among the Mezeyne tribe, within the limits of the Sinai peninsula, but not among the other tribes of that province. A girl, having been wrapped in the abba at night, is permitted to escape from her tent, and fly into the neighbouring mountains. The bridegroom goes in search of her the *next* day, and remains often many days before he can find her out; while her own female friends are apprised of her hiding-place, and furnish her with provisions. If the husband finds her at last (which is sooner or later, according to the impression that he has made upon the girl's heart), he is bound to consummate the marriage in the open country, and to pass the night with her in the mountains. The next morning the bride goes home to her tent, that she may have some food; but again runs away in the evening, and repeats these flights several times, until she finally returns to her tent. She continues there, never entering her husband's tent until she becomes far advanced in pregnancy: then she goes, and not before that circumstance, to live with him. If she does not become pregnant, she must remain in her own family tent a full year (counted from the wedding-day), after which she may join her husband. I heard that the same custom prevailed among the Mezeyne Arabs, related to those who live in another part of Hedjaz, and in the vicinity of Nedjd. Among the Djebalye, a small Sinai tribe, of modern origin, the bride remains after marriage three full days with her husband, and then runs off to the mountain, and never returns until her husband finds her out.

Divorces.

I have already mentioned, that divorces are very frequent among all Bedouins, as well as among those of Sinai. Should a Bedouin belonging to the latter tribes divorce his wife without being able to allege any valid reason, or to prove her guilty of any misconduct, he must give her, when she goes from him, six or eight dollars, a goat, a copper boiler, a hand-mill, and several other articles of kitchen utensils; and, at the same time, he forfeits the price which he had paid for her. If the wife leave him of her own accord, she receives nothing, and her masters even forfeit that portion of her price which was not paid down in cash; but they retain the part received; for it is just, say the Arabs, that some amends should be made to the masters for having now a widow under their tent instead of a virgin.

Among the Sinai Arabs a forsaken husband seldom refuses to his run-away wife the sentence of divorce, which alone enables her to marry again. But he sometimes obliges her friends to find for him another wife, and to pay the price of this latter, before he pronounces the two desired words "*Ent taleka*"—" Thou art divorced." Among some Arabs of Upper Egypt it is the law, that if a wife oblige her husband to give a divorce, her dowry and all her clothes are taken away; and the husband shaves her head completely before he dismisses her.

All Arabian Bedouins acknowledge the first cousin's prior right to a girl; whose father cannot refuse to bestow her on him in marriage, should he pay a reasonable price; and that price is always something less than would be demanded from a stranger. The Arabs of Sinai, however, sometimes marry their daughters to strangers in the absence of the cousins. This happened to a guide whom I had taken from Suez. When we arrived at his encampment, one day's journey distant from the convent of Sinai, he expected to marry a cousin of his own; and during the whole journey he had extolled to me the festivities which I should witness on that occasion. He, too, had brought with him some new clothes for his intended bride; and was therefore exceedingly disappointed and chagrined on his arrival, when he learned that, three days before, the girl had been married to another. It appeared that her mother was secretly his enemy; and had contrived matters in such a manner, as to render him ridiculous in the eyes of his companions. He bore his misfortune, however, like a man; and, instead of evincing any signs of displeasure, soon turned the tide of ridicule upon the mother herself, and her son-in-law. To prevent similar occurrences, a cousin, if he be determined to marry his relation, pays down the price of her as a deposit into the hands of some respectable member of the encampment, and places the girl under the protection of four men belonging to his own tribe. In this case she cannot marry another without his permission, whether he be absent or present; and he may then marry her at his leisure, whenever he pleases. If, however, he himself break off the match, the money that had been deposited is paid into the hands of the girl's master. This kind of betrothing takes place sometimes long before the girl has attained the age of puberty.

Bedouins are perhaps the only people of the East that can with justice be entitled true lovers. The passion of love is, indeed, much talked of by the inhabitants of towns; but I doubt whether any thing is meant by them more than the grossest animal desire; at least, I have never witnessed among them any instance of persevering affection amidst misfortunes; while, on the contrary, many persons daily evince the most perfect indifference immediately after enjoyment. The seclusion of women forbids the possibility of becoming acquainted with the beloved object's character, as the first interview with her leads invariably to possession; and where the minds cannot understand each other, it is scarcely possible that sentiments of friendship should assume any degree of sublimity; which, I imagine, constitutes the difference between animal and rational love. In the amorous verses which a townsman addresses to his mistress, this sentiment of inferior love may be easily distinguished. Instead of exalting the qualities of her mind and her heart, he merely describes the beauties of her person, or his own eager desire to possess her; and among the Arabic love-verses of modern composition, there are very few which a high-minded European would not reject with disdain. But the Bedouins have more frequent opportunities of becoming acquainted with the daughters of their neighbours: their love is often conceived in their youthful days, and fostered during a series of years; and such is the prudery of a Bedouin girl, that whatever may be her sentiments with respect to a lover, she will seldom condescend to let him know them, and still less to suffer any personal liberties, however convinced of a reciprocal affection. The firm assurance of her honour and chastity must powerfully influence his heart; and as a Bedouin's mind and imagination are always strong and sound, not pampered into sickly sensibility, or a depraved fancy like the townsman's, it is to be supposed that virtuous impressions being once made, take a firm hold. The custom of divorce, we must acknowledge, does not speak much in favour of any lasting attachment; but I would rather ascribe it to the unruly temper of those wild sons of the Desert, than to any want of feeling in their character.*

* Last year (1815) a Bedouin of Sinai shot himself at the nuptials of a wife whom he had divorced, and who had married another man. Just when the new husband entered the closet of his wife, the former husband, in a state of distraction, put an end to his own existence, while he was sitting among the company. Another proof of Bedouin feeling occurred above twenty years ago, near Wady Feiran in the

A quarrel happens between a man and his wife; and as nothing is done within doors among Bedouins, the neighbours soon learn the nature of the quarrel, and take part on one side or the other. Affairs become serious; the eloquence and loquacity of the wife (which are not exclusively the property of European ladies) very often triumph over the just cause of the husband; but the latter cannot bear to see himself slighted before his companions, and much less to be ridiculed and overpowered by the tongue of a woman: he therefore, in a moment of irritation, sometimes pronounces the words, *Ent taleka*," which constitute a divorce, and cannot be revoked. On such occasions the by-standers exclaim, "Well done! now we perceive that you are a man!" and this compliment banishes whatever remains of cool judgment might still exist in his mind. Instead of blaming his hasty act, the Bedouins commend it, saying, that a man should forget his private feelings in avenging a wrong done to him publicly. Such fits of anger frequently cause divorces. Sometimes a Bedouin marries from no other motive but that he may pass a few pleasant weeks with his new wife, whom he sends away when his desires are gratified, in which real love had no concern; but innumerable instances are likewise known of man and wife continuing faithful to each other during their whole lives.

It is usual in the Eastern towns and deserts to use the expression, "*Aley et talak*," (I shall divorce, i. e. my wife,) in order to confirm an assertion the more strongly. If the person who makes use of this expression should be in the wrong, and that he has vehe-

---

Desert of Sinai, where a mountain is shown from which two young girls precipitated themselves, having the ringlets of their hair twisted together; thus they dashed themselves to pieces, because on that evening they were to be married, by an arrangement of their friends, to men whom they disliked. The summit from which they threw themselves is still called *Hadjar el Benát*, or the "Damsels' Rock."

mently insisted upon that assertion in the presence of several witnesses, the law can oblige him to divorce his wife immediately. The Wahaby chief has exerted all his authority to render divorces less frequent among the Arabs: he disgraces at his court the man who has divorced his wife; and he punishes severely any person whom he hears using that expression, "*Aley et talak.*"

It is not usual, but happens sometimes, that an Arab, after a couple of years, takes back the woman whom he had divorced; and who, during that time, may have had several other husbands.

Polygamy is seldom found among the Bedouins. None but the rich sheikhs can afford to maintain many establishments; the necessary consequence of a plurality of wives; as two women, lawfully wedded to the same man, will never remain long together in one tent.

It may be said, that in Egypt the peasant girls are sold in matrimony by their fathers to the highest bidder; a circumstance that frequently causes the most mean and unfeeling transactions.

In Hedjaz, as among the Arabs of the Red-Sea, elopement with the wife of another man is an event which happens but seldom, and entails very severe punishment. Among the Red-Sea Arabs if an unmarried girl elope with her lover, the seducer may be lawfully slain by her relations on the very day of the elopement, without exposing themselves to the penalty of "*blood-revenge.*" But if they kill him after that day, his blood is upon them, and they must account for it.

A Tyaha Arab had eloped with a married woman of that tribe; he was overtaken in his flight by the injured husband's brother, and severely wounded; yet he recovered, and the affair was settled by arbitration among the contending parties; and it was decided that the seducer should pay sixty camels, one male and one female slave, one free girl instead of her who had eloped: which girl the husband might marry without paying her price, a fine poniard, and the dromedary upon which the guilty pair had fled. Such articles paid as damages are comprised under the term *ghurreh*, which does not include money. The man and his relations being obliged to pay these damages, were completely ruined. So that the penalty for criminal conversation with another man's wife is not unknown in the Desert. If an injured husband kill the seducer of his wife, he is exempted by the Bedouin laws from blood-revenge, or retaliation from the friends of the deceased.

Burial.

The Arabs of Hedjaz, of the Red-Sea coast, and of the neighbourhood of Southern Syria and Egypt, have within their respective territories burial-grounds, to which they bring the bodies of their friends, wheresoever they may have died within the limits of their district. This seems to be an ancient custom. These burial-grounds are generally on or near the summits of mountains. The same custom also is observed by the Nubian Bedouins.

I have seen among ancient Arab tribes in Upper Egypt the female relations of a deceased man dance before his house with sticks and lances in their hands, and behaving like furious soldiers. As an appearance of mourning, the only instance I recollect is that among some Arabs in Upper Egypt, of the *Rowadjeh* and *Djaafere* tribes, who live about Esne. If any person of the family die, the women stain their hands and feet blue with indigo; which demonstration of their grief they suffer to remain for eight days, all that time abstaining from milk, and not allowing any vessel containing it to be brought into the house; for they say that the whiteness of the milk but ill accords with the sable gloom of their mind.

Some Bedouins of the Sherkyeh, or eastern provinces of the Delta, bury with the dead man his sword, turban, and girdle.

From scarcity of linen the Bedouins are sometimes buried, an abba only being wrapped about the body. I know a sheikh of the Omran Arabs, on the eastern gulf of the Red Sea, who entertains such apprehensions of not being properly buried, that he constantly carries with him on his journies a winding-sheet prepared for himself.

Religious Worship.

The Bedouins throughout Arabia have very just notions of the Deity, but are little addicted to the precepts of their religion. The Wahabys have endeavoured in vain to render them more orthodox. The dread of punishment might induce some tribes who were under the immediate control of the Wahabys to observe the forms of their religion with more regularity; but it was a forced compliance; and as soon as the Wahaby power had suffered a diminution, in consequence of the attacks made by Mohammed Aly Pasha, all the Bedouins relapsed into their former religious indolence. While many Arab settlers in Nedjd and Yemen adopted with enthusiasm the Wahaby doctrines, very few, or perhaps no Bedouins, were ever reckoned among their favourers, although some adhered faithfully to the system of government established by the new sect, and were obliged to assume an appearance of zeal, and even of fanaticism, with the hope of promoting their own political interests. Now that, in Hedjaz at least, the Wahaby influence is for the present destroyed, the Bedouins affect still more irregularity than before; and, to prove that they have quite renounced the Wahaby tenets, they never pray at all. The Bedouins are certainly the most tolerant of Eastern nations; yet it would be erroneous to suppose that an avowed Christian going among them would be well treated, without some powerful means of commanding their services. They class Christians with the foreign race of Turks, whom they despise most heartily. Both Christians and Turks are treated in a manner equally unkind, because their skins are fair, and their beards long, and because their customs seem extraordinary: they are also reckoned effeminate, and much less hardy than the tawny Bedouin.

I have elsewhere had occasion to observe, that wherever Christians are found who have adopted the manners at least, if not the religion of Arabs, as the people of *Salt*, of *Kerck*, and of *Wady Mousa*, and the Christian pedlars who visit the Aenezes in the Syrian Desert, all such persons are sure to experience kind treatment from the Bedouins; while among the haughty and fanatic Osmanlys they are reduced to an abject condition.

Those Bedouin sheikhs who are connected with the government towns in the vicinity of their tribes, keep up the practice of prayer whenever they repair to a town, in order to make themselves respected there. But the inferior Arabs will not even take that trouble, and very seldom pray either in or out of town.

Government.

All the preceding remarks concerning Bedouin government are applicable in their fullest force to every tribe that I have had an opportunity of seeing. The sheikh has no fixed authority, but endeavours to maintain his influence by the means which wealth, talents, courage, and noble birth afford. The different family clans into which his tribe is divided, are independent of each other; their chiefs form the effective council of the tribe: and while the great sheikh may take upon himself to decide questions of minor importance, the opinion of every distinguished individual in the tribe must be ascertained, and his consent obtained, when matters of general interest, or of public importance, are to be discussed. It is certain that those sheikhs who are connected with the governors of towns in Syria, Egypt, or Hedjaz, and derive from that connexion considerable gains, and still more such as have become tributary to those governments, or dependent upon them, have found means to extend their authority over their tribes, so much that an Arab will not readily oppose their wishes, knowing that the enmity of a sheikh can interfere with the profits which he might derive from the town's-people, and principally by the transport trade: but even here the sheikh has not any means of enforcing his commands; and daily experience teaches him to respect the individual independence of his Arabs. I know that there are tribes of Arabs domiciliated, but still living under tents in Egypt, among whom the sheikh is authorised to inflict bodily punishment. These, however, cannot properly be classed with the true Bedouin tribes, who constitute the subject of these pages. It is, besides, a custom among Bedouins, when a party of them with their sheikh visit any neighbouring town, to express great deference towards him, representing themselves as being completely under his control. This they do, that the governor of the town with whom they have to treat may be inspired with a high opinion of the sheikh's great power and authority; an opinion which often causes more favourable terms to be granted, than the Bedouins could otherwise have obtained. This deception is easily practised, as the governors of towns are generally ignorant Osmanlys, or Turks, who cannot even imagine the existence of any chief without the possession of despotic power. But as soon as the party returns to their Desert the mask is thrown off, and the sheikh mixes again with the crowd of his people, not venturing even to scold any one of them without exposing himself to a reproachful and vituperative reply.

Mohammed Aly Pasha learned from his own experience the truth of what I have just mentioned. When he established his head-quarters at Tayf, eastward of Mekka, he was occupied during six months in collecting camels for the transport of his provisions from Djidda, and in gaining over to his party the sheikhs of the neighbouring tribes. Among these sheikhs he distributed great sums of money, yet found to his astonishment that the Bedouin sheikhs do not possess absolute power at home. Not one camel could they drive away without the owner's consent: not one Arab could they force to enlist under the banners of a foreign chief, equally despised as disliked by the Bedouins. His efforts, therefore, proved ineffectual; although several sheikhs were gained over by bribery, and disposed to serve him. His money was taken; but such Arabs only could be assembled with their camels, whose vicinity to Mekka and Tayf exposed them to the attacks of the Pasha's cavalry, and whose principal means of subsistence were derived from the Pasha's granaries at Djidda and Mekka.

As the office of sheikh among the Bedouins is inherent in the same family, although not hereditary, the sheikh's family by this means being able from time immemorial to acquire great influence and power, the Wahabys found it necessary to change the sheikhs of almost every tribe which they subjected to their domination; well convinced that in leaving the main influence in the hands of the ruling family, the tribe would never become sincerely attached to the new supremacy. They therefore usually transferred the sheikhship to an individual of some other considerable family; who, as might be supposed, had entertained secret jealousies against the former sheikh, and was, from private motives, inclined to promote and strengthen the Wahaby interest. This line of policy generally succeeded, and was universally adopted by the Wahabys. When Mohammed Aly Pasha subjugated Hedjaz, he replaced the ancient families and former sheikhs in their long-accustomed rights, and thus created a formidable opposition to the Wahabys.

The Bedouins had formerly kadhys throughout the Desert. Saoud, the Wahaby chief, knowing the great partiality and injustice of their decisions, and their readiness to accept bribes, abolished them all over his dominions, and sent to the Bedouins, in their place, kadhys from Derayeh, well-informed men, paid out of the public treasury, and acknowledged even by their enemies to be persons of incorruptible justice. Those tribes who have not submitted to the Wahabys, still retain their kadhys; thus the Arabs of Sinai have two or three in every tribe. If disputes happen among individuals, the decision of three kadhys may be taken one after another; but that of the third cannot be annulled; and both parties must abide by it, if they do not wish to let the quarrel become an affair of open force, and an appeal to arms; for nothing but the sword ultimately settles some disputes and litigations; although it must be confessed, that to this tribunal recourse is not often had, when civil affairs only are the subjects of discussion.

If two disputants appear before a kadhy, it is usual that they should deposit with him whatever arms they may carry, as a proof that they suspend, for the time, their right of deciding the quarrel by personal combat.

The office of kadhy is universally inherent in one family; and in some tribes hereditary, in others not; but if the kadhy happens to be a dull or stupid person, that man of the tribe who is most clever and eloquent becomes the true kadhy, and is chosen arbiter in most differences.

The trial before the *mebeshae*, a kind of ordeal, seems an institution peculiar to the Aeneze tribe; at least, I know not that it exists among any other Bedouins whom I have visited. It was said, however, that the Meteyr Arabs, who live between Medinah and Nedjd, had formerly the same custom; but they were obliged to relinquish it by express orders from the Wahaby chief. In Hedjaz the *mebeshae* is quite unknown.

To take an oath of any sort is always a matter of great concern among all the Bedouins. It seems as if they attached to an oath consequences of a supernatural kind; and as if they believed that the Almighty would resent having his name made subservient to earthly purposes, should the oath even be perfectly true. A Bedouin, even in defence of his own right, will seldom be persuaded to take a solemn oath before a kadhy, or before the tomb of a sheikh or saint, as they are sometimes required to do; and would rather forfeit a small sum than expose himself to the dreaded consequences of an oath. In their dealings with each other they pronounce the name of God a hundred times in a day, to give strength to false assertions; but as long as the oath is not solemnly administered, they apprehend no danger from it.

The institution of the *wasy*, or **guardian**, is not general throughout the Desert; but all the Arabs of Nedjd observe it.

Warfare.

The Bedouins who live in mountainous districts have fewer camels and horses than those of the plains, and therefore cannot make so many plundering expeditions into distant quarters, and are less warlike than the others. Mountain warfare is moreover liable to many difficulties and dangers unknown in the open country: plunder cannot be so easily carried off, and the recesses of the mountains are seldom well known to any but their own inhabitants. Still there are very few tribes who are ever in a state of perfect peace with all their neighbours; indeed, I cannot at present recollect that this was the case with any one among the numerous tribes that I knew. The Sinai tribes were in 1816 at peace with all the Arabs in their neighbourhood except the Sowaraka, a tribe dwelling near Gaza and Hebron.

I may here confirm what has been said respecting the martial spirit of the Bedouins; their cowardice when fighting for plunder only; and their bravery when they repel a public enemy. Of the last, they have given repeated proofs, during their wars with the Turks in Hedjaz, whom they defeated in every encounter; for the great battle of Byssel, in January 1815, was merely gained by the stratagems of Mohammed Aly Pasha. In that action whole lines of Bedouins, tied by ropes fastened to each other's legs, were found slaughtered, having sworn to their women at parting that they would never fly before a Turk. To adduce instances of personal valour among the Bedouins would be easy; but such instances are not altogether conclusive as to the character of a whole nation. Whoever has known the Bedouins in their deserts must be perfectly convinced that they are capable of acts displaying exalted courage, and of much more steadiness and cool perseverance, in cases of danger, than their enemies, the Turks.

The most renowned warrior in the southern parts of Arabia was, during my residence in Hedjaz, *Shahher*, of the Kahtan tribe. He alone once routed a party of thirty horsemen belonging to the Sherif Ghaleb, who had invaded the territory of his Arabs. Ghaleb, who was himself a man of considerable bravery, said on this occasion that, "since the time of the *Sword of God* (this is one of Aly's surnames), a stronger arm than Shahher's had not been known in Arabia." At another time, the Sherif Hamoud, governor of the Yemen coast, was repulsed with his escort of eighty mounted men by Shahher alone.

The sheikh of Beni Shammar, in Mesopotamia, whose name is *El Djerba*, or, as he is otherwise entitled, *Beney*, has also obtained great celebrity for his courageous deeds. When the troops of the Pasha of Baghdad were defeated in 1809, by the Rowalla Arabs, Beney, with his cousin Abou Fares, covered their retreat; and these two horsemen fought against a multitude of the enemy's cavalry. In the Desert, valour must alone be sought among the chiefs, who are generally as much distinguished for bravery as for the influence which they possess.

There is one circumstance that greatly favours the chance of a foreign general in his contests with the Bedouins.* They are but little accustomed to battles in which much blood is shed. When ten or fifteen men are killed in a skirmish, the circumstance is remembered as an event of great importance for many years by both parties. If, therefore, in a battle with foreign troops several hundred are killed in the first onset, and if any of their principal men should be among the slain, the Bedouins become so disheartened, that they scarcely think of further resistance; while a much greater loss on the side of their enemies could not make a similar impression on mercenary soldiers. But even the Arabs would only feel this impression at the beginning of a severe contest; and they would soon, no doubt, accustom themselves to bear greater losses in support of their independence, than they usually suffer in their petty warfare about wells and pasture-

---

* But this must not flatter him with the hope of reducing them to perfect subjection; and if it be asked what could induce a foreign chief to attempt such a conquest, the answer may be given in a quotation from the letter of Abdallah Ibn Saoud, to the Grand Signor:—" Envy does not spare even those whose dwellings are miserable huts in deserts, and upon barren hills."

grounds. Of this, the Asyr Arabs, who were principally opposed to Mohammed Aly in the battle of Byssel, afford a striking example. Having lost fifteen hundred men in that action (from which their chief Tamy escaped with only five men), they recovered sufficient strength to be able, about forty days after, to meet the Turkish soldiers in another battle, in their own territory, a battle less sanguinary, although better contested than the former; but it ended, after two days' fighting, in the defeat and subsequent capture of Tamy.

Whenever a tribe engages in an expedition, their troops are headed by the *agyd*, of whose rank and power I had no correct knowledge, and had partly overlooked it when I composed my former account of the Bedouins. It is a remarkable circumstance in Bedouin history and policy, that, during a campaign in actual warfare, the authority of the sheikh of the tribe is completely set aside, and the soldiers are wholly under the command of the agyd. Every tribe has, besides the sheikh, an agyd; and it rarely happens that the offices of both are united in one person, at least no instance of such a case is known to me; although some Arabs mentioned, that they had seen a sheikh acting as agyd among the Basrah Arabs. The office of agyd is hereditary in a certain family, from father to son; and the Arabs submit to the command of an agyd, whom they know to be deficient both in bravery and judgment, rather than yield to the orders of their sheikh during the actual expedition; for they say that expeditions headed by the sheikh are always unsuccessful.

If the sheikh join the troops, he is for the time commanded by the agyd, whose office ceases whenever the soldiers return home: the sheikh then resumes his own authority. All Bedouin tribes, without exception, have their agyd. The same person acts on some occasions as agyd to two neighbouring tribes, if they are small and closely allied. Thus, among the Arabs of Sinai, a family of Oulad Sayd is in possession of the agydship for all the tribes of the peninsula. The person of the agyd, and still more his office, is regarded with veneration. He is considered by the Arabs as a kind of augur or saint. He often decides the operations of war by his dreams, or visions, or forebodings: he also announces the lucky days for attack, and names other days that would be unlucky.

When the agyd is doubtful about the measures that should be adopted against the enemy, he consults with the principal men of his army, if he think fit to do so; but the Arabs never refuse to follow him, even though he should act wholly according to his own judgment.

They believe that even a child of the ancient agyd family may be a proper leader, supposing him to act by a kind of heavenly inspiration. It is related, that in the tribe of Beni Lam, of Nedjd, no males remained in the family of their agyds, but one young orphan, who lived with his elder sister. From want of a proper and genuine agyd, the tribe had been headed, on several occasions of warfare, by the sheikh, and always without success. After many losses, the Arabs agreed in opinion, that without their true agyd they should never be fortunate; and it was therefore resolved, that they should ascertain how far that child, to whom the office hereditarily belonged, was capable of commanding the tribe on a military expedition. They accordingly directed his sister to prepare a camel, and to mount it herself, desiring her brother to take his seat behind her, that so he might join the troops who were then on the eve of commencing their march. Had he consented to mount behind his sister, the Arabs would not have thought him sufficiently old or manly to assume the command. When his sister desired him to take his place, as had been suggested, the boy endeavoured to strike her, and exclaimed, with indignation, "Am I a slave?—Must I sit behind a woman?

No, you must mount behind me." The Arabs accepted this exclamation as a favourable omen. They followed him in battle, the girl guiding the camel from behind her brother, and the expedition proved successful.

The agyd's share of plunder is not the same among all tribes; sometimes he has two, sometimes three shares: but whenever the sheikh joins the party, his share is like that of all the other Arabs. The agyd, as I have already observed, is found in every tribe of Arabia. Even in Nubia, the Ababde and Djaalein Bedouins have retained this ancient institution of their forefathers. Thus, for instance, in the large Aeneze tribe of Fedhan, the great sheikh is Dhoehy Ibn Ghobeyn, and the agyd is Hedjres Ibn Ghasel, in whose family the office of agyd constantly remains. Among the Wold Aly (another tribe of Aenezes), the sheikh is Ismeyr, and the agyd, El Teyar.

If the agyd be a man of remarkable valour and sagacity, he retains great influence over the affairs of his tribe, even in time of peace: his vote, however, is not equivalent to that of the sheikh; but he is consulted on intricate matters, and circumstances of difficulty, and much deference is paid to his opinion. But in this respect he has no advantage over the other Arabs of his tribe who unite the qualities of sagacity and valour.

If an Arab, accompanied by his own relations only, has been successful on many predatory excursions against the enemy, he is joined by other friends; and if his success still continue, he obtains the reputation of being "*lucky;*" and he thus establishes a kind of second, or inferior agydship in the tribe. Of this, advantage may be taken on partial expeditions; but whenever the whole tribe is engaged, the true and regular agyd must be the leader.

The agyd possesses no more coercive power over his Arabs than the sheikh. All are at perfect liberty to join him, or to act by themselves; but if they once join him, they must submit to his commands, or else expect that he will discard them, as not worthy to form a portion of his corps: in this case they forfeit all claim to any share of the booty which may be taken by the whole army.

This institution of the agyd owes its origin undoubtedly to the wise policy of that legislator who established rules for the wild shepherds of Arabia. He wished by this institution to check any increase of power in the person of the chief of the tribe. By preventing him from commanding his Arabs in time of war, he rendered it difficult for him to engage in feuds merely from private motives, and effectually hindered him from exercising any undue influence in the division of plunder, which would most probably have been the case, had he, as military chief, the opportunity of augmenting his own wealth in a degree disproportionate to that of his Arabs; and this wealth might, in process of time, induce and enable him to assume arbitrary power.

We have seen in the histories of different western nations, that when sovereigns put themselves at the head of armies, their subjects had reason to lament, in the loss of many rights, the heroism of their kings. These notions of sound policy, however, do not strike the untaught mind of a Bedouin. He has no idea of the agyd being a salutary balance to the sheikh's power; because he cannot even imagine that, as long as his mare is able to carry him, or while his arm can wield a lance, any successful attempt could be made to enslave him, or even to curtail the smallest of his rights. They revere the agyd as a kind of heaven-inspired leader in their wars: and they return in peace to the guidance of their sheikh with the same fearless indifference and consciousness of independence that the Romans felt, when, in the better periods of their history, they entrusted their commonwealth to the care of consuls, or sometimes to the will of a dictator.

The Wahaby chief has left this institution in full force throughout his dominions: he has even employed it in favouring his own projects; having assembled at Derayeh many agyds of tribes in whose obedience he could not confide, he thus paralyses, on one side, the efforts they might make to throw off his yoke, and increases, on the other, the dread of his own power, because where so many agyds are united, it is supposed that operations will always succeed.

Besides the agyd, some tribes setting out on an expedition select one of the most respectable men of the tribe, to whom they give the title of *kefyl*. The duty of this person is to settle among them all disputes arising from the division of booty, and to watch that no part of it be secreted from the common stock by individuals. He shares in the booty always, in the same proportion with the agyd. The *kefyl* is not found in many tribes; there is always such an officer among the Djeheynes of Hedjaz.

Nocturnal attacks upon camps are very common in Hedjaz, although the Aenezes regard them as disgraceful. In order to surprise a tribe, the enemy generally contrives his march in such a manner that he may fall upon the party to be attacked about one hour before the first dawn, when he is certain of finding every body asleep. The Bedouins have no idea of any night-watches, and still less of sentinels, however necessary such precautions appear to be in their particular mode of life and warfare. If they apprehend an immediate attack, all the males in the encampment, or all the soldiers on an expedition, remain together, watching by their fires during the whole night. The Wahaby chiefs, with the usual foresight and wisdom that appear in all their regulations, establish sentinels whenever troops are on a march. The person who was sent in 1815, by Tousoun Pasha, to negotiate with Abdallah Ibn Saoud, told me that he has met single sentinels, followed by reliefs of guards and small detachments at two miles' distance from the camp of Abdallah; and the

Wahaby escort which he had with him gave the watch-word to every sentinel that passed; the watch-word for that night was "*Nasser,*" "Victory." The Turkish camp, at a distance of only six hours, was exposed to sudden attacks; for, notwithstanding their frequent wars with Europeans, the Osmanly chiefs and even Mohammed Aly have not yet learned this most important and necessary precaution against an active and enterprising enemy.

Whether camps are plundered by day or by night, the women are generally treated with respect; so far, at least, that their honour is never violated; not a single instance of the contrary has ever come to my knowledge. Sometimes, however, in case of inveterate hostility, they may be stripped of their ornaments, which the plunderers oblige them to take off themselves. This rule is invariably observed by the Wahabys whenever they obtain possession of an enemy's camp: they order the females to strip off whatever articles of clothes or valuable trinkets they may happen to wear; and during this time they stand at some distance from the women, to whom they turn their backs. In a skirmish between the Maazy Arabs and those of Sinai, in 1813, the former by chance wounded a woman of the latter, who, however, soon recovered. In the year following, the Sinai Arabs made an incursion into the Maazy territory, surprised an encampment near Cosseir, killed eight or ten men, and were going to retire, when one of them recollected the wound that had been inflicted on a female in the preceding year; he therefore turned upon the Maazy women, who were sitting before their tents weeping, and with his sabre wounded one of them, to avenge the blood of his country-woman. His companions, although they applauded what he had done, acknowledged they should not like to imitate his example. This is the only circumstance of such a nature that ever was mentioned to me.

The Bedouins of Sinai have a peculiar custom in commencing a great expedition against the enemy. They assemble at the first meeting-place, and, with the agyd at their head, pile up a quantity of loose stones together in a heap, giving to it the coarse appearance of a camel, in a crouching position; they next recite the Fateha, or opening chapter of the Koran, while assembled around it, and then, at the command of the agyd, they rush at once precipitately towards their camels, which they hastily mount, and suddenly gallop off without looking behind till they are at a considerable distance. I have not been able to learn the precise meaning of this practice, which the Bedouins regard as a kind of mystical incantation.

When two hostile parties of Bedouin cavalry meet, and perceive from afar that they are equal in point of numbers, they halt opposite to each other out of the reach of musket-shot; and the battle begins by skirmishes between two men. A horseman leaves his party and gallops off towards the enemy, exclaiming, "O horsemen, O horsemen, let such a one meet me!" If the adversary for whom he calls be present, and not afraid to meet him in combat, he gallops forwards; if absent, his friends reply that he is not amongst them. The challenged horseman in his turn exclaims, " And you upon the grey mare, who are you?" the other answers, " I am * * * the son of * * *." Having thus become acquainted with each other, they begin to fight; none of the bystanders join in this combat, to do so would be reckoned a treacherous action; but if one of the combatants should turn back, and fly towards his friends, the latter hasten to his assistance, and drive back the pursuer, who is in turn protected by his friends. After several of these partial combats between the best men of both parties, the whole corps join in promiscuous combat. If an Arab in battle should meet with a personal friend among the enemy's ranks, he turns his mare to a different side, and cries out, " Keep away! let not thy blood be upon me!"

Should a horseman not be inclined to accept the challenge of an adversary, but choose to remain among the ranks of his friends, the challenger laughs at him with taunts and reproaches, and makes it known, as a boast, during the rest of his life, that such a one * * would not venture to meet such a one * * in battle.

If the contest happen in a level country, the victorious party frequently pursue the fugitives for three, four, or five hours together at full gallop; and instances are mentioned of a close pursuit for a whole day. This would not be possible with any but the Bedouin breed of horses, and it is on this account that the Bedouin praises his mare, not so much for her swiftness as for her indefatigable strength.

It is an universal law among the Arabs, that if, in time of war or in suspicious districts, one party meet another in the Desert, without knowing whether it be friendly or hostile, those who think themselves the stronger should attack the other; and sometimes blood is shed before they ascertain that the parties are friends; but this is not the case in the Wahaby dominions, where a strong party must pass a weak one without daring to molest it.

The Bedouin mode of fighting is most ancient. The battles described in the two best heroic romances (the History of *Antar*, and that of the tribe of *Beni Helál*) consisted principally in single combats, like those above mentioned. It is more congenial with the disposition of Bedouins, who are always anxious to know by whom a man has been killed—a circumstance which in a promiscuous attack cannot easily be ascertained.

If two neighbouring tribes of Bedouins are at war with each other, and a third foreign tribe should come in the mean while to take possession of the territory, or watering-place, of one of the two contending tribes; these latter often conclude a sudden peace, and unite against the foreign invader. The attacked tribe then applies to some neighbours, saying, "We demand from you the loan of one day, (meaning assistance for one day in battle,) which we shall repay to you whenever you require similar assistance." An affair of this kind happened in the spring and summer of 1812, when a severe conflict took place in the Syrian Desert, eastward of Homs, between the tribes of Ahsene on one side, and the Fedan and Sebaa on the other. The two latter had for several years endeavoured to seize upon the pasture grounds of those plains, and the tribute which the villages on the Syrian frontiers pay to the Bedouins. Melhana el Melkem, chief of the Ahsene, severely pressed by the superior number of his enemies, applied for assistance to the powerful Djelae, (a tribe of Nedjd which, until very lately, was unknown in the Syrian deserts), and offered to them a share in the tribute, provided they would co-operate with him against the Fedan. For twenty successive days the united armies fought in constant skirmishes, being encamped within a distance of only a few hours from each other. Sahhan the son of Deraye, one of the principal sheikhs of the Djelae, had been in the Hedjaz, to fight under the banners of Abdallah and Ibn Saoud against Mohammed Aly Pasha. From them he went to Nedjd, and, as such expeditions are considered parties of pleasure by Bedouins, he returned to Syria with his forty horsemen just in time to have a share in the battles above mentioned.

The Fedan, apprehensive of being overpowered, now in their turn applied for assistance to Djerba, the sheikh of Beni Shammar in Mesopotamia, with whom they were actually at war: they offered him terms of peace, and begged that he might join them against the Djelae, a foreign tribe, (although one of the Aeneze nation,) who, they said, had no just right to pasture their cattle on the Syrian borders. Djerba immediately accepted the offers of peace, and proceeded with fifteen hundred horsemen in support of the Fedan; but he was repulsed by the Djelaes, and the Fedan were soon afterwards obliged to abandon Syria, and to retreat again towards Nedjd. The Beni Shammar now say to the Fedan, " You owe us a day."

The battle-banners, called *merkeb otfa*, are unknown in Hedjaz; I believe that they are only used among the Aenezes.

In concluding the terms of peace, an agyd can give but his single vote, like any other individual of the tribe. The condition " to dig up and to bury," is common all over the Desert, and is a matter of stipulation, whenever the tribes entertain a sincere desire for peace. Those Arabs who are not satisfied with this condition, (several of their relations having, perhaps, been slain in the contests,) leave their own tribe, and settle with some other for the time; where they are at liberty to seek revenge, which they cannot do if their own tribe has once annulled the claims of revenge. I have found, in general, very few tribes without some of those implacable enemies, whose thirst for revenge exists even after a declaration of peace, when a most friendly intercourse is immediately established between the other members.

Blood-Revenge.

The fundamental laws of blood-revenge are the same, and universal throughout the whole Arabian desert. The right to it exists every where within the *khomse*: Arabian tribes residing in foreign parts have invariably carried this institution with them. We find it among the Libyan Bedouins, and all along the banks of the Nile, up to Sennar: wherever true Arabs are settled, there is a law, that for blood an atonement must be made by blood, or by a severe fine, if the family of the person slain or wounded will agree to such a commutation. They have rendered this independent of the public administration of justice, and hav given the blood-revenge into the hands of the sufferer's friends, or of his friends, persuaded that a judicial punishment would not satisfy a person who had been so seriously hurt and insulted in private, and to whom the law of nature gave the right of revenge. The system of the Arabs' political corporation would prevent the arising of any public disorder from the retaliation between individuals; every clan would stand forward in protection of any of its members unjustly persecuted; and it seems, that in a rude state of society, whenever the security of the whole is not affected, each person has full right to retaliate an injury upon his neighbour. The Arab regards this blood-revenge as one of his most sacred rights, as well as duties; no earthly consideration could induce him to relinquish it: and even among the degenerate and enslaved race of Egyptian peasants, trembling under the iron rod of Mohammed Aly, a Fellah plunges his dagger into the breast of the man who has murdered his brother, although he knows that his own life must be forfeited for the deed; for that Pasha has endeavoured, by all the means in his power, to suppress every remaining spark of independent feeling among his subjects.

The stronger and the more independent a tribe is, the more remote from cultivated provinces, and the wealthier its individuals, the less frequently are the rights of the *Thar* commuted into a fine. Great sheikhs, all over the Desert, regard it as a shameful transaction to compromise in any degree for the blood of their relations; but when the tribe is poor, and infected by the paltry spirit of neighbouring settlers in cultivated districts, the fine (or *dye*) is frequently accepted. To give up the right of personal revenge as well as of this fine, is a matter of which they cannot even form any notion, and the Arabs have a proverbial saying, "Were hell-fire to be my lot, I would not relinquish the *Thar*."

The fine for blood varies in almost every tribe. Among the Beni Harb, in Hedjaz, it is eight hundred dollars. The same sum has been fixed by the Wahaby chief, following the rule prescribed in the time of Mohammed, when Abou Beker declared the price of a free man's blood to be one hundred she-camels. Saoud has estimated every she-camel at eight dollars, and thus made it a sum of eight hundred dollars. He has done all in his power, to induce the Arabs throughout his dominions to give up this long-established right of private revenge, and to accept the fine in its stead. But he has seldom been able to prevail over their ancient prejudices: and the Bedouins feel much ill-will towards him for his endeavours to abrogate a law, which they regard as sacred.

Whenever an Arab has entered into a compromise with the family to whom he owes blood, he addresses himself to his relations and friends, soliciting from them some contributions in sheep and lambs, that he may be enabled to make up the sum required. Among some tribes it is a custom, that contributions should be made, in proportionable shares, by all the individuals comprised within the khomse, and who are therefore liable themselves to suffer from the blood-debt, in case no payment of another kind be accepted. But this is not a general rule; and the dammawy in many tribes must make up the sum himself, with his brothers and father only.

But in those tribes where ontributions are made, the Arabs evince great liberality, when the man who asks their assistance is liked by his people. Their gifts are so abundant from every quarter, that he is not only enabled to make up the sum required, but is often enriched by the surplus; which, the debt being paid, remains with him as his own property. On such occasions, they likewise go about among their friends of foreign tribes soliciting assistance. This is seldom refused. A similar kindness is expected in cases of emergency; and there is no circumstance in which the Bedouins more fully prove the affection which they entertain for each other, as members of one great nation, than when they are thus called upon for their contributions. They may indeed be considered, on such occasions, as partners belonging to one extensive company, in the gains and losses of which every individual is more or less interested.

The same demand for assistance is made, whenever the cattle of an Arab has been driven off by the enemy. His friends never hesitate to contribute towards the reparation of his loss, although not always so liberally as in the cases mentioned above; when, besides their friendship for the sufferer, they are impelled by a national feeling: for a tribe esteems itself honoured by enumerating among its individuals, men who have slain enemies, and are therefore supposed to be persons of valour. If the sheikh of a tribe should happen to lose his property, by the attack of an enemy, all his Arabs voluntarily hasten to his relief; and if he be a favourite, they soon reinstate him to the full amount of the cattle which he had lost.

When an atonement for blood is to be made among the Arabs of Sinai, the relations of the dammawy appoint a place of meeting with the family of the man who has been killed, that an arrangement may be settled; the killed man's friends having consented to the meeting. At the time fixed, both parties repair to the place appointed, with their wives, children, and all other relations: there they pass several days in feasting, and every guest that arrives is treated with great hospitality. Those, to whom the blood is due, then make their claims. As there does not exist any certain fine, or *dye*, among these Sinai Arabs (nor indeed among several other tribes), the sum at first demanded is exorbitant;

but all the persons in company immediately agree in soliciting a diminution. For instance, a woman presents herself before the nearest relation of the deceased, and conjures him, by the head of his own infant child, to grant, for her sake, an abatement of two or three dollars. A respectable sheikh then declares, that he will not eat any food, until an abatement of one camel shall have been made for his sake; and, in this manner, all who are present crowd about the man who claims the fine for blood, and who at first assumes a very lofty tone, but allows himself to be flattered into a display of generosity, gradually remitting dollar after dollar, until a sum is at last mentioned which all parties agree in thinking a fair equivalent: this is paid in instalments at monthly intervals, and always punctually discharged. Among those Arabs, twenty or thirty camels generally suffice to settle the business. They likewise give, on such occasions, in payment, some of the date-trees which abound in the vallies of Sinai occupied by Bedouins.

It may be agreed perhaps to accept for the blood a fine comparatively small; but in this case the debtor (that is, he who killed the man) must acknowledge, that himself and his family are *hhasnai* (or persons in a state of obligation) to the other's representative: a declaration which gratifies the pride of one party, as much as it mortifies the other, and is therefore not often made, although it is not attended by any other consequence; in fact it is merely a nominal obligation. If adopted, it remains for ever in the two families. The Omran and Heywat Arabs observe this custom.

The Oulad Aly, a powerful Libyan tribe of Bedouins, inhabiting the Desert between Fayoum and Alexandria, make it a rule never to receive the price of blood, unless the homicide, or one of his nearest kindred, should brave the danger of introducing himself into the tent of the person slain, and then say to the relations, "Here I am, kill me, or accept the ransom." The nearest relation may do as he pleases, without incurring any blame; for the stranger has voluntarily renounced the right of *dakheil,* which all the Libyan Bedouins hold as sacred as the Arabian. A man who gives himself up in this manner is called *mestatheneb.* If the enemy should meet him before he reaches his tent, an attack is almost always the result. If he enter the tent, a ransom is most commonly accepted; but instances to the contrary sometimes happen.

The two tribes of Omran and Heywat act upon a rule, which forms an exception to the general Bedouin system of blood-revenge remaining within the "khomse." When one of their people is killed by an unknown hand of a known tribe, they think themselves justified in retaliating upon any individual of that tribe, either innocent or guilty; and if the affair be compromised, the whole tribe contribute to make up the *dye,* or fine, in proportion to the respective property of each tent. For this reason, the Arabs say, that "the Omran and Heywat strike sideways"—a practice which is much dreaded by their neighbours.

Among several other tribes, the blood of those who fall by the unknown hand of a known tribe is demanded from the sheikh, who pays the fine, to which his Arabs contribute. This practice, however, is not by any means general; and among the warlike tribes of the Eastern parts, whoever perishes by an unknown hand cannot be avenged by any legal proceedings; although the Bedouins say, that two tribes will never be on terms of sincere friendship, as long as they know that blood continues unavenged between them.

The Arabs entertain such notions respecting the solemnity and sacredness of an oath, that when a man is even falsely suspected of having killed another, and the relations of the person slain tender to the accused an oath, by taking which he might free himself from the imputation, he sometimes agrees to pay the fine rather than swear. Whatever may be the consequences of taking an oath, it is considered as a permanent stain on the reputation of an Arab to have ever sworn a solemn oath. The formula, by which a charge of homicide is denied, I shall here set down:—

"Wallahy inny ma shageytou djeldou,
Wa ma yettemtou woldou."

"By God! I have not pierced any skin,
Nor rendered orphan any boy."

If a man be wounded in a scuffle, and should afterwards kill his antagonist, no allowance is made for the wound, but the full fine for killing a man is imposed, even though the slain person may have been the aggressor. Had not the man been killed, the wounded person would have received a considerable fine, as a recompense for the injury which he had suffered.

Among the Arabs of Sinai, when a murder happens, the aggressor either flies, or endeavours to compromise the affair by paying a fine; he therefore places himself under the protection of some venerable man of his tribe. To this protection the friends of the deceased pay due respect during the space of thirty days. If, before the lapse of that time, he should not be able to effect an arrangement, he must fly, or expect that his life will be sacrificed to the deadly vengeance of his enemies.

What I have already said of "slaughter" (*dhebahh*), is applicable to all tribes of Bedouins. In their wars with each other they make a distinction between "blood" and "slaughter," having recourse to the latter only in cases of considerable irritation. It frequently happens, and especially among the mountain Arabs, (whose wars are always more sanguinary and inveterate than those among the inhabitants of plains, perhaps because less frequent,) that one tribe puts to death all the males of their enemies whom they can possibly seize, without inquiring what number of their own people had been slaughtered by their adversaries. These, of course, retaliate, whenever an opportunity offers.

The general slaughter, where no one ever asks, or ever grants quarter, is still in practice among the Red-Sea Arabs, those of Southern Syria, and of Sinai; but peace is usually soon concluded, and causes a cessation of the bloodshed. An Arab would be censured by his tribe, were he not to follow the general practice, or allow himself to be influenced by the dictates of humanity, should his companions resolve upon the slaughter. I believe that the cruel Israelitish slaughter of the captive kings (that is, Bedouin sheikhs, for so the word *emír*, or *malek*, must be translated,) may be traced to a similar custom prevalent in former times; and the chiefs might have insisted upon a strict adherence to the ancient usage, apprehending that a dereliction of it would tend to weaken the martial spirit of their nation, and render them less respected among their neighbours. Even now, Bedouins would be severely reproved by others for sparing the lives of individuals belonging to a tribe that would not show mercy to them.

Robbery and Thieving.

It may easily be conceived, that those Bedouins have the boldest spirit of enterprise, who are the most exposed to attacks from others, and most frequently engaged in wars. This is the case with the Bedouins inhabiting rich pasture plains; while those whose territory lies among mountains, or is sheltered by local circumstances from frequent chances of invasion, or is remote from warlike tribes, are of a much less daring disposition. We find, on this account, the profession of the haramy in much repute among the great eastern tribes; while among those more limited in the territories near Egypt, and towards Mekka, robberies are not so frequently practised; and whoever there attempts to steal in the tents of his own tribe, is for ever dishonoured among his friends.

Among the Arabs of Sinai, robberies are wholly unknown: any articles of dress, or of furniture, may be left upon a rock without the least risk of their being taken away. Some years ago, an Arab of Sowaleha laid hold of his own son, carried him bound to the summit of a mountain, and precipitated him, because he had been convicted of stealing corn from a friend. I have witnessed, in every part of the Desert, as complete and absolute security from robbers, as in the Swiss mountains, properly so called, while the northern part of the peninsula is of dangerous access.

The rabiet is taken by all Arabs of the eastern Desert; even those who inhabit the towns of Nedjd and Kasym are accustomed to put the haramy, whom they can surprise, into close confinement. This is not usual among the Hedjazi Arabs. The tribe of Beni Harb, who dwell in the districts between Medinah and Nedjd, take the rabiet; but this practice is rejected by the other tribes of Harb, southward of Medinah. The Wahaby chief has left it in full force among his subjects, as he has invariably endeavoured to check private robberies.

The following anecdote, which I often heard related, shows the manner in which a closely confined rabiet found means to escape. He had been severely beaten by his master in presence of an Arab, who pitied and resolved to liberate him. The Arab broke a date into two parts, ate one, and gave the other to a woman who was employed in grinding corn before the tent, begging her, in a few words, to contrive that it should fall into the prisoner's hands. With much ingenuity and art, she immediately began a song, such as those which serve to amuse the women while they work; and introduced certain words which indirectly alluded to the subject in question. When she had reason to believe that the prisoner understood this mysterious communication, she threw the piece of date unseen, upon the hole in which he lay, his hands at that time being untied. The prisoner swallowed a small portion of the broken date, and when he saw many persons assembled before the tent, called loudly upon them, demanding to be liberated, as he had eaten with such a one, naming the man who had divided with him the date. His master hastened to the spot, denied the truth of his assertion, and beat him; but the person who had befriended him appeared and confirmed the fact. It was then required that the prisoner should produce a portion of the food in proof of his assertion, when he immediately exhibited the broken date, which he had secreted in a manner of which decency will not allow a more particular mention: he had so concealed it, apprehending a discovery before his deliverer could arrive. Having thus satisfactorily proved that he had eaten of the same date with another Arab of the tribe, his master was obliged to liberate him.

The Traitor.

Should he not restore the goods stolen or treacherously obtained, and if his tribe should not force him to do so, nor expel him from their encampment, they incur the penalty of being all declared *báikeh*, or "treacherous," and the other Arabs will not respect the *dakheil* of any individuals belonging to this tribe until the stolen goods are restored.

Dakheil, or Protection.

A common expression for *dakheil* among the Arabs, is *zeben;* they say *tezebbenet* instead of *dakhelet,* and the tribe with which a man has found protection is called *mezbene.* The *melha* which gives a claim to the dakheil, consists in eating even the smallest portion of food belonging to the protector. If the rabiet can extricate himself from confinement so as to mount the mare or camel of his rabbat or master, and escape upon it to the tent of another Arab in search of protection, the mare or camel upon which he effected his escape is assigned to him by ancient custom, as well as the chain which he may have worn upon his neck.

It may easily be imagined that all Arabs do not hold the law of dakheil as sacred as they ought to do, when their own immediate interests are concerned. Among the great Aeneze tribes, and other wealthy clans of the extensive plains, few if any instances are recorded of an Arab having proved false to the dakheil, yet they may show themselves rather slow in granting it, according to circumstances.

When Yousef Pasha of Damascus was obliged, in 1810, to abandon the town, and had scarcely time for effecting his escape with a dozen followers, he retreated into the Hauran, where the numerous tribe of Wold Aly had pitched their tents. Ibn Ismeyr, the chief sheikh of these Arabs, who, during the government of Yousef Pasha, had always professed himself a friend, and had often received proofs of his generosity, was, of course, the man to whom Yousef applied: but he received him very coolly, being apprehensive of incurring the displeasure of his successor, and told him, after a repast, that he would not advise him to remain in his camp, which, being only distant three days' journey from Damascus, might not afford him effectual security. The Pasha understood this hint, and with a few guides proceeded northwards, in the direction of the Desert, east of Homs, where he alighted at the tent of Mehanna el Melhem, the sheikh of Ahsenne, another Aeneze tribe with which he had always been on bad terms, and frequently at war, because he was jealous of the partiality which the Pasha had constantly evinced to Ibn Ismeyr. From Mehanna he experienced the kindest reception. "My tent," said he, "is the secure asylum of persons in distress, and has had the honour before now of affording shelter to great men. Let your successor, Solyman Pasha, cut all the throats of the Melhems; he shall never be able to drive you from this spot." He entertained Yousef hospitably during several days, and then escorted him, with a body of armed men, to Rieha, in the neighbourhood of Aleppo, whence the Pasha repaired to Antioch.

Some years before, when the same Yousef commanded a corps of cavalry in the service of Ibrahim Pasha of Damascus, having been defeated by the Arabs in the Desert, he fled for refuge to the tent of the chief of the Mowalys, a tribe residing near Aleppo, notorious for their treacherous propensities, and now much fallen to decay. Gendje, the chief, treated him with hospitality, but obliged him at parting to leave behind his fine cashmere shawl, his purse, and his sword. Such examples rarely happen among Arabs, never among the great tribes. With their power and martial spirit, even Bedouins sometimes lose their honour.

An Arab's sentiments concerning the sanctity of the *dakheil*, are well expressed in a letter of the Wahaby chief, Abdallah Ibn Saoud, to Tousoun Pasha. In this letter he says, "Ask the Bedouins,—they will tell you, that were they even to kill one of Saoud's family, and that I should promise them security, they would trust to my word." In another letter, the same Abdallah says to the Pasha, who suspected his good faith, "Were one of your people even to carry the head of one of my brothers in his hands, he should have nothing to fear from me." Similar assertions can never be credited by an Osmanly (or Turk), who boasts of entrapping his enemy by a violation of the most sacred pledges.

The dakheil has lost much of its power among all those tribes, whose geographical situation and mode of subsistence bring them into contact with Turkish governments as well as settlers. With them the *dakheil* is of no efficacy, unless the tent of an Arab has been actually entered; for the fugitive is not entitled, they say, to protection, who can only claim it from having eaten with him, or touched him or any thing that he held in his hands.

If strangers are seen approaching a tent with an apparent intention of alighting there, and if the owner of the tent suspect that they belong to a hostile tribe, induced by untoward circumstances to fly for refuge, which must not be refused, he cries out to them from afar :—" If you belong to a hostile tribe, you shall be stripped." After this warning, they are not entitled to claim the right of *dakheil* from that person, but may endeavour to find it at another tent.

Instances are mentioned, when even the entering of a tent did not suffice to protect a man from his pursuers. Whenever we find the laws of *dakheil* thus slighted, it may be admitted as a certain fact, that the tribe has lost its national importance and part of its independence. The treachery of the Turkish governors and the Mamelouks had made all the feeble tribes in the eastern Desert bordering upon Egypt forget their ancient laws, and become degenerate. Instances, like those recorded by Lord Valentia of Shedeid's wife, (instances very common among the Aeneze tribes,) will rarely be found in those parts, where the Arabs have made it a general rule not to protect individuals pursued by great or powerful men. On the contrary, the Libyan Bedouins, or, as they are called in Egypt, the Maggrebyn Bedouins, maintain those laws in all their strictness, and the *dakheil* is with them as rigidly observed and as easily obtained as among the Aenezes. The occupation of Hedjaz by the Turkish troops, has had in this respect a very bad effect upon the Bedouins. They might console themselves for the loss of independence, by hoping that it was only a temporary privation; but they will never be able to retrieve the loss of their reputation and national integrity, which they exchanged for the gold of Mohammed Aly, and which no power or conquests can restore. Examples have become frequent in Hedjaz of fugitives given up by Bedouins, although the latter were not within immediate reach of the Pasha's troops. The prospect of certain gain, and not fear, induced them to act thus basely; and they did not consider that the circumstance not only reflects dishonour upon themselves, but is, according to Bedouin notions, a lasting stain upon the whole tribe, and that it must inevitably lead to other infractions, when the individuals of a nation have once become indifferent about their public character.

Two of the principal Wahaby chiefs, Othman el Medhayfe, and el Medheyan, were both treacherously delivered up by the owners of those tents in which they had taken refuge; the first by a man of the Ateybe tribe near Tayf, and the other by one of the Beni Harb near Beder. They were remunerated for their treachery by ample rewards, and endeavoured to excuse their conduct by saying, that the fugitives who had sought their protection were heretics, and on that account not entitled to the rights of hospitality; but an Aeneze will not only protect a fugitive sectary of his own religion, but even a Christian or a Jew, with the same noble courage that he exerts in the cause of a brother Aeneze. No vice or crime is more deservedly stigmatised as infamous among Bedouins, than treachery. An individual in the great Arabian Desert will be forgiven if he should kill a stranger on the road, but eternal disgrace would be attached to his name, if it were known that he had robbed his companion, or his protected guest, even of a handkerchief. Whoever has had an opportunity of seeing various tribes, must have observed, that the boldest highway robbers are invariably those who regard as most sacred the rights of *dakheil*, and most vehemently abhor every act of treachery; as if they would grant to the rest of mankind, with whom they are at war, the best mode of defence against their own depredations.

Among the Arabs of Sinai, the *dakheil* is only granted when the fugitive can contrive to eat or sleep in a tent; and protection is continued to him, his goods, and cattle, for three days and eight hours after he has left the tent. So that, if within that space of time he should be robbed by other Arabs, the owner of the tent which had protected him, would think himself bound to insist upon the restoration of his property. This allowance of three days and one third, is consecrated to hospitality throughout the Desert.

Tribes may be at peace with each other, yet not sufficiently amicable to allow that an individual should protect a man, belonging to a hostile tribe, passing through their territory. Thus, in the year 1811, going from Deyr on the river Euphrates to Sokhne, under the protection of an Arab of Sebaa, I fell into the hands of some Rowalla Arabs, and was robbed, but my guide was not molested. The Rowalla and Sebaa tribes were then actually at peace, but not on such terms of friendliness as would authorise them mutually to protect enemies; and I, being a reputed townsman, was consequently regarded as a national enemy by all Bedouins.

Arab tribes often make a kind of petty or clandestine war upon each other, infringing upon the respective rights of *dakheil*, and robbing fugitives who had been protected, &c. for several months, until open war is at last declared; and instances are therefore not unfrequent, of two tribes being nominally at peace, while every body knows, that the individuals of those tribes rob each other on the road.

Hospitality.

To be a Bedouin, is to be hospitable; his condition is so intimately connected with hospitality that no circumstances, however urgent or embarrassing, can ever palliate his neglect of that social virtue. It cannot, however, be denied, that in some instances their hospitality proceeds from vanity, and a desire of distinguishing themselves among their equals in the tribe. But if we could minutely examine the true motives of action in most men, we should find that virtue is seldom practised merely for its own sake, and that some secret accessory spring is often necessary to prompt the heart; charity, and the consciousness of our own frailty, thus teach us to respect even this secondary merit; and we must value a person for his virtuous actions, were they even dictated by policy. Where all foreigners are so much disliked, as among the Bedouins, we cannot wonder that their hospitality should be principally exercised towards each other; but I should myself be guilty of ingratitude for many proofs of kindness and commiseration, bestowed on me in the Desert, were I to deny that the hospitality of Bedouins extends to all classes, and is combined with a spirit of charity that eminently distinguishes those Arabs from their neighbours, the Turks: it is also better suited to the morals of a religion which they are taught to curse, than to the religion which they acknowledge.

As the Turks possess very few good qualities, it would be unfair to deny that they are in a certain degree charitable, that is, they sometimes give food to hungry people; but even this branch of charity they do not extend so far as the Bedouins, and their favours are bestowed with so much ostentation that they lose half their merit. After an acquaintance of two or three days, a Turk will boast of the many unfortunate persons whom he has clothed and fed, and the distribution of his alms in the feast of Ramadhan, when both law and fashion call upon him for charity; and he offers a complete picture of the Pharisee in the temple of Jerusalem. It must, however, be allowed, that charity towards the poor is more generally practised in all parts of the East than in Europe; while, on the other hand, an honest but unfortunate man, ashamed to beg, yet wanting more than a scanty dish of rice, will probably find assistance in Europe sooner than in the East. Here, it seems to be the rich man's pride that he should have a train about him—a train of needy persons whom he barely keeps from starving, while they go almost naked, or blazon in the town his wonderful generosity, whenever he distributes among them some of his old tattered clothes.

The influx of foreign manners, by which no nation has ever benefited, seems to be pernicious in its effect upon the Bedouins; for they have lost much of their excellent qualities in those parts where they are exposed to the continual passage of strangers. Thus, on the pilgrim road, both of the Syrian and Egyptian caravan, little mercy is ever shown to *hadjys* in distress. The hospitality or assistance of the Bedouins in those places can only be purchased by foreigners with money; and the stories related by pilgrims, even if not exaggerated, would be sufficient to make the most impartial judge form a very bad opinion of Bedouins in general. This is also the case in Hedjaz, and principally between Mekka and Medinah, where the caravan-travellers have as little chance of obtaining any thing from the hospitality of the Bedouins on the road, as if they were among the treacherous inhabitants of the Nubian Desert.

Yet, even in those places, a helpless solitary traveller is sure of finding relief; and the immense distance of space between Mekka and Damascus is often traversed by a poor single Syrian, who trusts altogether to Bedouin hospitality for the means of subsistence during his journey. Among such poor people as Bedouins generally are, no stronger proof of hospitality can be given than to state, that, with very few exceptions, a hungry Bedouin will always divide his scanty meal with a still more hungry stranger, although he may not himself have the means of procuring a supply; nor will he ever let the stranger know how much he has sacrificed to his necessities.

The instances recorded by ancient writers of Arabian hospitality, seem frequently to me much exaggerated, or to describe a foolish prodigality, which neither honours the heart nor the head of the donor. To alight from one's horse, and bestow it upon a beggar who asks alms, and perhaps to give him also one's clothes, is a kind of whimsical ostentatious profusion that partakes more of folly than of generosity. This may be recognised in the late Mourad Bey of Egypt, loudly celebrated for munificence because, not happening to have any money about him, he gave to a beggar his poniard, mounted with jewels, and reckoned worth three thousand pounds. Similar acts generally answer their purpose in the East, where people's minds are dazzled rather than convinced; but they as little answer the purpose of well-directed charity, as the bags of money which the miser deposits in a secret chamber.

It cannot, however, be denied, that even now frequent instances occur among Bedouins, which evince hospitality carried to a pitch that might almost appear unnatural or affected, even to a generous European, but which is strictly consistent with the laws established in the Desert; and I find the more pleasure in mentioning an anecdote on that subject, from its resemblance to a story related of Hatem el Tay, the most generous of ancient Arabs. Djerba, the present powerful sheikh of Beni Shammar in Mesopotamia, who is intimately connected in politics with the pashalic of Baghdad, was, many years ago, encamped in the province of Djebel Shammar, in the Eastern Desert, at a time when Arabia suffered most severely from dearth and famine. The cattle of himself and of his Arabs, had already mostly perished from want food, as no rain had fallen for a considerable time: at length there remained, of all the cattle, only two camels, which belonged to him. Under these circumstances, two respectable strangers alighted at his tent, and it was necessary to set a supper before them. No provisions of any kind were left in his own tent, nor could the tents of his Arabs furnish a morsel: dry roots and shrubs of the Desert had for several days served as food to these people, and it was impossible to find either a goat or a lamb for the strangers' entertainment. Djerba could not bear the thought of allowing his guests to pass the night without supper; or that they should retire hungry to sleep. He therefore commanded that one of his two camels should be killed. To this his wife objected, alleging that their children were too weak to follow the camp next morning on foot, and that the camels were absolutely necessary for the removal of his own family and of some of his neighbours' wives and children. "We are hungry, it is true," said one of the guests, "but we are convinced of the validity of your arguments; and we shall trust to the mercy of God, for finding a supply of food somewhere to-morrow: yet," added he, "shall we be the cause that Djerba's enemies should reproach him for allowing a guest to be hungry in his tent?" This well-meant remark stung the noble-minded sheikh to the soul, he silently went out of the tent, laid hold of his mare, (the only treasure he possessed besides his camels,) and throwing her on the ground, was engaged in tying her feet that he might kill her for his guests, when he heard from afar the noise of approaching camels; he paused, and soon had the satisfaction of seeing two camels arrive, loaded with rice, which had been sent to him as a present from the province of Kasym. Of this anecdote I cannot doubt the truth, having heard it related frequently by Arabs of provinces totally different.

Whoever travels among Bedouins, whether rich or poor, and wishes to be on friendly terms with them, must imitate, as far as he can, their system of hospitality—yet without any appearance of prodigality, which would inspire his companions with a belief that he possessed immense wealth, and would render his progress difficult, in proportion to their increasing demands of money. He must likewise condescend (if it can be called condescension) to treat the Bedouins on terms of equality, and not with the haughtiness of a Turkish grandee, as travellers too frequently do. A Bedouin will be sociable, and prove himself a pleasant companion, without ever becoming insolent or impertinent, which is always the case with Syrians or Egyptians, whenever they are admitted to familiarity. That they may learn respect, it is necessary to keep them at a proper distance; and they easily submit to this treatment, because they are not accustomed to any other. But, in living with a Bedouin, his feelings must not be wounded; he must be treated with friendliness; and in return he will seek for an opportunity of proving to you, that in his own Desert he is a greater man than yourself. And why not treat kindly a man, who, if you were in the most abject and forlorn condition, would certainly treat you as a brother.

As a hint to travellers, I must here add, that letters of recommendation to *independent* Bedouin sheikhs are of very little use. If one of these sheikhs should once promise to conduct a person in safety, he will keep his word, without considering how the traveller comes recommended to him; and a letter of the strongest recommendation, even if it were written by a Pasha (provided that the latter have no direct influence over the tribe), is but little regarded. The more a stranger is recommended, the more he must pay, and the more insatiable becomes the sheikh. Therefore, a traveller will do well to go amongst Bedouins as a poor man, or else to pay for his passage through their country by dint of money, without foreign aid.

Many tribes have the national reputation of being generous; others are reckoned stingy. Among the latter is the Beni Harb, a considerable tribe in the Desert of Hedjaz. The great profits which they derive from the Hadj caravans have perhaps rendered them parsimonious in proportion as they became more desirous of wealth. The same reputation of stinginess is attached to the Bedouins about Mekka, especially to the Koreysh, now a full tribe of from two to three hundred matchlocks. In the mountains of Sinai, stinginess is the reproach of a tribe called *Oulad Sayd*, a branch of the Sowaleha Arabs; and their neighbours have a proverbial saying in rhyme, which advises a person thus—" Sleep alone, rather than among the Oulad Sayd."

> "Abeyt waheyd
> Wa la aned Oulad Sayd."

Generous men belonging to these stigmatised tribes, have at least the advantage of rendering themselves easily conspicuous and distinguished amongst the rest; and therefore it is said by the Arabs, that generosity is principally found among tribes re puted avaricious.

The guest who enters an encampment of the Nedjd Bedouins usually alights at the first tent on the right side of the spot where he entered the dowar, or circle of tents. If he should pass that tent and go to another, the owner of the slighted tent would think himself affronted.

Among the Arabs of Sinai there is a custom which, I believe, is common to several other tribes on the southern limits of Syria; that, if a stranger be seen from afar coming towards the camp, he is the guest for that night of the first person who descries him, and who, whether a grown man or a child, exclaims, " There comes my guest." Such a person has a right to entertain the guest that night. Serious quarrels happen on these occasions; and the Arabs often have recourse to their great oath—" By the divorce (from my wife) I swear that I shall entertain the guest;" upon which all opposition ceases. I have myself been frequently the object of such disputes, in which the Bedouin women took a very active part, assembling in the females' apartment of the tent where I sat, defending the rights of their husbands with all the loquacity that their lungs could supply. It is a received custom in every part of the Arabian Desert, that a woman may entertain strangers in the absence of her husband. Some male relation then does the honours, representing the absent owner of the tent.

The Serudje Arabs, in the plain of Hauran, southward of Damascus, permit their wives and daughters to drink coffee with the strangers upon their arrival, while they sit in the men's apartment, provided the owner of the tent be present. Such a circumstance is never known among other Arabs in the Northern Desert, where a woman will never drink coffee, nor eat before men. In the mountains south of Mekka, towards Yemen, where manners appear very different from those in Nedjd and the northern plains of Arabia, women are said to entertain a guest in the absence of her husband, and to sit up with the stranger. Guests do not always remain in the tent of their host, if it happen to be small; the host leads the stranger to a more roomy and commodious tent belonging to some acquaintance, where he, and not the owner of the tent, entertains the guest.

Domestic Relations.

Among people who assign to their women exclusively all the duties and menial offices of the tent, it cannot be supposed that the female sex meets with great respect. Women are regarded as beings much inferior to men, and, although seldom treated with neglect or indifference, they are always taught to consider that their sole business is cooking and working. While a girl remains unmarried, she enjoys, as a virgin, much more respect than a married woman; for the fathers think it an honour, and a source of profit, to possess a virgin in the family. Once married, a Bedouin female becomes a mere servant, busily occupied the whole day, whilst her husband lies stretched out in his own apartment, comfortably smoking his pipe. This arrangement he justifies by saying, that his wife should work at home, as he undergoes so much fatigue on journies. Nothing distresses the Bedouin women so much as fetching water. The tents are but seldom pitched very close to a well; and if this be only at half an hour's distance from the camp, the Bedouins do not think it necessary that the water should be brought upon camels: and when asses are not to be procured, the women must carry the water every evening on their backs in long water-skins; and they are sometimes obliged to seek a second supply at the well.

Among the Arabs of Sinai and those of the Egyptian Sherkieh, it is an established rule, that neither men nor boys should ever drive the cattle to pasture.* This is the exclusive duty of the

---

* Among the Sinai Arabs, a boy would feel himself insulted were any one to say,

unmarried girls of the camp, who perform it by turns. They set out before sun-set, three or four together, carrying some water and victuals with them, and they return late in the evening. Among other Bedouins, slaves or servants take the flocks to pasture.

Thus early accustomed to such fatiguing duties, the Sinai women are as hardy as the men. I have seen those females running barefooted over sharp rocks where I, well shod, could with difficulty step along. During the whole day they continue exposed to the sun, carefully watching the sheep; for they are sure of being severely beaten by their father, should any be lost. If a man of their tribe passes by the pasturing ground, they offer to him some sheep's milk, or share with him their scanty stock of water, as kindly as their parents would have treated him in their tent. On other occasions, the Bedouin women, seeing a man pass on the road, sit down and turn their backs towards him; nor will they ever receive any thing from the hands of a stranger (who is not a relation) into their own hands, unless some friends be present. I have frequently passed women on the road who asked for biscuit or flour to make bread; this was set near them upon the ground, while their backs were turned towards us; and they took it up when we had retired a few paces. It has always appeared to me, that the more a tribe is connected with the inhabitants of towns, the stricter they are with respect to the seclusion of women. In the Mekka and Sinai mountains, a woman, if addressed by any stranger, will seldom return an answer: on the contrary, in the distant plains, I have freely conversed and joined in laughter with Aeneze, Harb, and Howeytat women. Their morals probably may be rated in an inverse proportion to the pains taken for preserving them.

" Go and drive your father's sheep to pasture;" these words, in his opinion, would signify, " You are no better than a girl."

The respect which Bedouins bear to their mothers is much more exemplary, than that which they evince towards their fathers. Among the poor tribes, where the tent depends for subsistence on the exertions of its master, and not solely upon the fecundity of the cattle, as among the wealthy eastern tribes, a man grown old frequently loses the means of procuring for himself the necessary supply of daily food: his sons are married, and have their own families to support, and the old man often remains alone. Bedouin laws do not oblige a son to maintain his aged parent, although such is generally the case. But I have likewise known instances of old men living upon the charity of the whole camp, while their sons were in affluent circumstances, and might easily have supported them. The sons' excuse was, that when they married, their fathers would not assist them with the smallest sum; and that whatever they possessed was entirely due to their own industry and exertions. The daily quarrels between parents and children in the Desert constitute the worst feature of the Bedouin character. The son, arrived at manhood, is too proud to ask his father for any cattle, as his own arm can procure for him whatever he desires; yet he thinks that his father ought to offer it to him: on the other hand, the father is hurt at finding that his son behaves with haughtiness towards him; and thus a breach is often made, which generally becomes so wide that it never can be closed.

The young man, as soon as it is in his power, emancipates himself from the father's authority, still paying him some deference as long as he continues in his tent: but whenever he can become master of a tent himself, (to obtain which is his constant endeavour,) he listens to no advice, nor obeys any earthly command but that of his own will. A boy, not yet arrived at puberty, shows respect for his father by never presuming to eat out of the same dish with him, nor even before him. It would be reckoned scandalous were any one to say, "Look at that boy, he satisfied his appetite in the presence of his father." The youngest male children, till four or five years of age, are often invited to eat by the side of their parents, and out of the same dish.

A Bedouin, in his tent, is the most lazy of all creatures; while the women are employed in manual work and laborious occupations, the men do nothing but smoke their pipes, and play at the game called *Sheidje* or *Syredje* (a kind of draughts); thus they pass away all their leisure hours. This game, which is general throughout every part of Arabia, has likewise found its way into Egypt, and (from Egypt probably) among the black inhabitants of Nubia, where I have seen it played almost as frequently as in Arabia.

The Bedouin mode of life may have some charms even for civilised men; the frankness and uncorrupted manners of the Bedouins must powerfully attract every stranger; and their society in travelling is always pleasant. But after a few days' residence in their tents, the novelty subsides; and the total want of occupation, and the monotony of scenery, efface all the first impressions, and render the life of a Bedouin insupportable to any person of an active disposition. I have passed among Bedouins some of the happiest days of my life; but I have likewise passed among them some of the most irksome and tedious, when I impatiently watched the sun's disk piercing through the tent from its rising to its setting; for I knew that in the evening some songs and a dance would relieve me from my draught-playing companions.

Slaves, both male and female, are numerous throughout the Desert: there are but few sheikhs or wealthy individuals who do not possess a couple of them. After a certain lapse of time, they are always emancipated, and married to persons of their own colour. There is not, perhaps, any place which affords more instances of the fidelity of slaves, than the Desert. The Bedouin mode of life is in some respects congenial with that to which the negro slaves were accustomed in their own country; they therefore easily attach themselves to it, and soon become as it were naturalised among the tribe. Among the Wahabys, female slaves are not allowed to veil their faces; but the free Arab females in Nedjd are very strict in that respect with regard to themselves. In Hedjaz, black slaves are very common among the Bedouins, but I never saw any Abyssinians there; for these are generally reckoned less able to work or endure fatigue than the aboriginal blacks of Africa.

General Character.

My first view of the Bedouins in their own habitations on the Desert was recently after my arrival from Europe, while the impressions which I brought with me were still very strong. Whatever preference I might give in general to the European character, yet I was soon obliged to acknowledge, on seeing the Bedouins, that, with all their faults, they were one of the noblest nations with which I ever had an opportunity of becoming acquainted. Since that time, a residence of seven years in the East has rendered my European impressions more faint; and instead of drawing, as I then did, a comparison between Bedouins and Europeans, which in many respects was favourable to the former, I now compare them principally with their neighbours, the Turks, and in this point of view the Bedouins appear to still greater advantage. The influence of slavery and of freedom upon manners, cannot any where be more strongly exemplified than in the characters of those two nations. The Bedouin, certainly, is accused of rapacity and avarice, but his virtues are such as to make ample amends for his failings; while the Turk, with the same bad qualities as the Bedouin, (although he sometimes wants the courage to give them vent,) scarcely possesses any one good quality. Whoever prefers the disorderly state of Bedouin freedom to the apathy of Turkish despotism, must allow that it is better to be an uncivilised Arab of the Desert, endowed with rude virtues, than a comparatively polished slave like the Turk, with less fierce vices, but few, if indeed any, virtues. The complete independence that Bedouins enjoy, has alone enabled them to sustain a national character. Whenever that independence was lost by them, or at least endangered by their connexion with towns and cultivated districts, the Bedouin character has suffered a considerable diminution of energy, and the national laws are no longer strictly observed.

We may readily suppose that among a warlike nation such as the Bedouins, public spirit and patriotism are universal. Their primary cause is that sentiment of liberty, which has driven and still keeps them in the Desert, and makes them look down with contempt upon the slaves that dwell around them. Fully conscious that his own condition is far preferable to any other that can be his lot, the Bedouin exults in the advantages he enjoys; and it may be said, without any exaggeration, that the poorest Bedouin of an independent tribe smiles at the pomp of a Turkish Pasha; and, without any philosophical principles, but guided merely by the general feelings of his nation, infinitely prefers his miserable tent to the palace of the despot. Among Turks and Arab settlers, the feelings of patriotism are almost wholly extinct. The Turkish empire is too extensive, and composed of too many different nations and heterogeneous parts, to render it probable that a general spirit of patriotism should ever be equally diffused among all its members. A few provinces, inhabited by particular races, are distinguished, however, by their patriotic sentiments;

but the Arnaut and Albanian feel for their own provinces merely, and not for the empire at large, of which they form a portion. In Egypt and in Syria (with perhaps an exception of the Libanon mountains), I can venture to affirm that patriotism is altogether extinct. Fanaticism, in some places, might supply it in any contest with Christians; but no proofs are even given now of public spirit, except the absurd praises bestowed on different towns by the natives or inhabitants of them.

Bedouins are not only solicitous for the honour of their own respective tribes, but they likewise consider the interests of all other tribes as more or less attached to their own; and frequently evince a general *esprit de corps*, which reflects great honour upon their national character. The successes of Mohammed Aly's army, however coincident with the interests of those Bedouins who had shaken off the Wahaby yoke, were generally deplored all over the Desert, and even by those very allied tribes, being considered as prejudicial to the national honour, and endangering independence. For the same reason Bedouins lament the losses of any of their tribes occasioned by attacks from settlers or foreign troops, even though at war with those tribes. As to the attachment which a Bedouin entertains for his own tribe, the deep-felt interest he takes in its power and fame, and the sacrifices of every kind that he is ready to make for its prosperity—these are feelings rarely operating with equal force in any other nation; and it is with an exulting pride of conscious patriotism, not inferior to any which ennobled the history of Grecian or Helvetian republics, that an Aeneze, should he be suddenly attacked, seizes his lance, and waving it over his head exclaims, "I am an Aeneze!" On my journey from Palmyra to Damascus I was accompanied by a single guide, a man of the tribe of Sebaa, the chief of the Fedan Arabs, Ibn Ghebeyn, with whom I had left Aleppo, having declined the journey to Palmyra. Early in the morning on the day after we had set out from Palmyra, my guide, all of a sudden, leaped off his camel, and desired me, mounted on a horse, to prepare for defence. I could not discern any enemies; but the sharp-sighted Bedouin had already perceived four horsemen galloping towards us. We had no chance of success in resistance, yet my guide thought it shameful to surrender. When one of the horsemen approached so near that they might hear his voice, he shook his lance over his head and exclaimed, "I am a Sebaa! I am a Sebaa!" According to the Bedouin law of nations, these horsemen were justifiable, by this exclamation, in treating my guide with all the rigour of war; while, if he had laid down his lance, he might have been certain of personal safety at least. Fortunately, the horsemen proved to be friends; and after they had left us, my guide informed me, that if he had thrown away his lance without a show of resistance, the sneers of those horsemen would have for ever dishonoured him among his own people.

I must repeat my former acknowledgment, that the Bedouins are most greedy of gain, and by no means of good faith in common pecuniary transactions. In proportion as they reside near to a town, this avaricious spirit becomes more general among them; and all that has resulted to the Bedouins from their intercourse with towns, is an increase of wants, and a decrease of virtues; nor is there any feature in the character of those Asiatics who inhabit towns, by adopting which, as their own, the Bedouins could be improved. If a Bedouin finds his interests hurt, or if he is in pursuit of some advantage or gain, he allows of no check to his passionate temper, but that which is prescribed by the law of dakheil. Whenever he feels himself strongest, he oppresses the inoffensive peasant, or the peaceable traveller, with unceasing demands; and no promise can bind him to limit his rapacity. It is for this reason that the Bedouins are so defamed in Egypt and in Syria, because they are only known in those countries as levying contributions on the cultivators and on caravans, and committing acts of hostility against the individuals of every district who do not readily consent to become their tributaries. In the general curse which the peasant imprecates upon his oppressors, he forgets that the indolence and erroneous measures of his own government are as much to be condemned as the hostility of a foreign nation, the declared and open enemy of all settlers, and therefore using, as it were, the rights of conquest.

The governments of Mesopotamia and Syria are too weak to check the depredations of the Bedouins, and all the frontier villages towards the Desert are left to their fate. Mohammed Aly, in Egypt, has contrived to rescue his villages from the hands of the Bedouins, on both banks of the Nile. The Libyan or Maggrebyn Arabs had become particularly troublesome, and from Siout down to Alexandria they had exacted tribute from all the villages, besides attacking and robbing almost every unprotected individual whom they met on the road. The Pasha having laid hold of many young male children belonging to these tribes, detained them as hostages in his castle at Cairo; and the amount of the ransom paid for their liberation in horses, sheep, and camels, reduced the strength of the most powerful among those tribes. They were obliged to renounce the custom of levying tribute on the peasants; but continued still so formidable, that the Pasha agreed to pay them part of that tribute out of his own treasury, while he receives the whole of what was formerly given to the Bedouins. About thirty villages are still in his hands, and their friends remain quiet.

Before the reign of Mohammed Aly Pasha, the Arabs of Sinai were the protectors of Suez, where every Christian, and even all the principal Turkish merchants engaged one of them as his guard, whom he was obliged to recompense with a yearly stipend and occasional presents. The Arab guardian was called *ghafeyr*, and the person protected, *hasnay,* because he gave *hasneh,* or presents. These Arabs had become so insolent, and were so dreaded by the people of Suez, that a young Bedouin girl, placed alone at the wells, which are almost two hours distant from the town, would sometimes not allow the water-carriers to take any water from the wells until they had given her some presents.

The sociable character of a Bedouin when there is no question of profit or interest, may be described as truly amiable. His cheerfulness, wit, softness of temper, good-nature, and sagacity, which enables him to make shrewd remarks on all subjects, render him a pleasing and often a valuable companion. His equality of temper is never ruffled or affected by fatigue or suffering; in which respect he differs materially from the Turk, who is of a changeable, fickle, and capricious disposition. The finest trait in the character of a Bedouin (next to good faith) is his kindness, benevolence, and charity—his peaceful demeanour whenever his warlike spirit or wounded honour does not call him to arms. Among themselves, the Bedouins constitute a nation of brothers; often quarrelling, it must be owned, with each other, but ever ready, when at peace, to give mutual assistance. Not accustomed to the cruel scenes of blood which harden the hearts of Turks from their very youth, the Bedouins delight to foster within their breasts those sentiments of mercy and compassion, which often cause them to forget that an unfortunate person is, perhaps, an enemy.

In their domestic quarrels the Bedouins are more reserved, and, on the other hand, more rancorous than the inhabitants of towns. The lowest, and even the middle classes of the latter, in Syria and Egypt, exclaim against each other upon trifling occasions, in the meanest and most opprobrious language; and I have often witnessed conversations, which would shock and astonish those who have entertained the false notions generally received concerning

Eastern decorum: the terms used on these occasions would be found worthy of a Billingsgate vocabulary; but it most commonly ends in words—blows seldom follow, because the first striker is always condemned by the kadhy. Weapons are used only upon extraordinary emergencies, and in cases where soldiers take a part in the fray. Among Bedouins, on the contrary, insults are offered in language more moderate, and at the same time more manly; and those disgusting expressions are not used which, among towns' people, evince the gross depravity of a debauched imagination. The Bedouins content themselves with such phrases as "Blindness to thy eyes, thou dog!" "A shot to thy heart!" "Disease upon thee!" "Perdition to thy family!" and other expressions common in the Desert, which, although scarcely justifiable, are in savage minds the natural effusions of anger. A Bedouin, however, in the greatest paroxysm of rage, abstains from the use of language which could never be forgiven. To call his adversary a liar, a traitor, or an inhospitable wretch, would be an insult punishable by the dagger; as sometimes has been the case. If such violent language is not used, a quarrel among Bedouins seldom lasts half an hour, and the parties become reconciled; but for insulted honour no excuse or apology can ever be accepted.

Salutation.

The general mode of saluting throughout the Desert is, after the "*salám aleyk*," to ask "*tayb*," or "well?" Shaking hands and kissing, after a long absence, are every where practised. The Bedouins know nothing of those numerous cant phrases and ceremonious expressions current in the towns. To inquire after a person's health, the reason of his long absence, and to describe the great pleasure felt on seeing him again, these are all questions and phrases, to each of which there is a precise and regular form of reply; and a person would be thought ridiculous or ill-bred, who attempted to answer in any other manner. Thus there are twenty different modes of wishing good morning to an acquaintance in Cairo; and if a person says, "May your day be white," there is not absolutely any answer left but "May yours be like milk." All these superfluous and teazing phrases of compliment are unknown to the Arab, who simply wishes a good morning when he meets, or a farewell when he leaves his friend upon the road. Among the Bedouins about Mekka, (and still more as I heard among those of Yemen,) it is usual, after the salutation has passed, to quote a passage either of the Koran, or of Mohammed's sayings, to which an answer is returned in a corresponding passage. Illiterate as the Bedouins are, it is said that in Yemen they learn by heart a considerable portion of their scriptures.

A Bedouin who does not know the person interrogating him, will seldom answer with truth to questions concerning his family or tribe. The children are taught never to answer similar questions, lest the interrogator may be a secret enemy, and come for purposes of revenge. Among the Bedouins themselves it is regarded as a shame to ask another what is his tribe, as they think that the origin of a man ought to be recognised by his accent, dialect, and appearance. My guide in the Desert was much displeased at my asking strangers to what tribes they belonged; and in fact, I seldom obtained a satisfactory answer on that subject, except in those places where they found that I was too well acquainted with the neighbouring tribes to admit of imposition or deception. Those who accost a stranger in the Desert, and ask him concerning water, or the nearest road, or similar matters, generally entitle him "uncle," to which he replies by styling the querist "brother:" thus one hears, "Ha, uncle, walking there, have you any water with you?" "In truth there is some, my brother, you are welcome to it."

Language.

The Bedouin dialect is every where different from the Arabic spoken in towns and villages, even among those tribes whose territories adjoin the inhabited places, and who mix in frequent intercourse with town's-people. The Bedouins use a dialect much more pure, and in its construction much more correct and grammatical than the low language of the Syrian and Egyptian mob, which is wholly excluded from the encampments of the Desert. There is, however, among the Bedouins themselves, a great variety of dialects; and the language spoken by a Nedjd Bedouin is as different from that of a Sinai, as the dialect of the latter is from an Egyptian Bedouin's; but they all agree in pronouncing each letter with much precision, expressing its exact force or power, which, with respect to the letters, ث, ذ, ض, ظ, is never the case among the inhabitants of towns. The Bedouins also agree universally in using, as common, many select words, which in the towns would be called "literal terms" (كلام نحوي), and in speaking always with grammatical accuracy. They likewise refuse to admit into their colloquial speech many of those cant phrases and terms by which the Arabic of Syria and Egypt is so materially corrupted. I shall here venture to affirm, that by far the best Arabic is spoken in the Desert, and that Bedouins are as much distinguished from other Arabs, by the purity of their language, as they are by that of their manners. That they have thus preserved, during so many centuries, the purity of their language, without books or writings, may with probability be ascribed to the frequent practice of learning by heart and reciting poetry. Young persons are thus accustomed to the use of select and elegant expressions; and there are always in the camps some old men who take delight in explaining the recondite meanings and other difficulties that may occur in the poems.

Sagacity in tracing of Footsteps; or "Athr."

Here I must offer some observations on a talent which the Bedouins possess, in common with the free Indians of America—the faculty of distinguishing footsteps, both of men and beasts, upon the ground. In the American woods the impression is made upon grass, in Arabia upon sand; and in the examination of these impressions, the Americans and the Arabs are, perhaps, equally skilful. Although it may be said, that almost every Bedouin acquires, by practice, some knowledge in this art, yet a few only of the most enterprising and active men excel in it. The Arab, who has applied himself diligently to the study of footsteps, can generally ascertain, from inspecting the impression, to what individual of his own, or of some neighbouring tribe, the footstep belongs; and therefore is able to judge whether it was a stranger who passed, or a friend. He likewise knows, from the slightness or depth of the impression, whether the man who made it carried a load or not. From the strength or faintness of the trace he can also tell whether the man passed on the same day, or one day or two days before. From a certain regularity of intervals between the steps, a Bedouin can judge whether the man whose feet left the impression was fatigued or not; as, after fatigue, the pace becomes more irregular, and the intervals unequal. Hence he can calculate the chance of overtaking the man.

Besides all this, every Arab knows the printed footsteps of his own camels, and of those belonging to his immediate neighbours. He knows by the depth or slightness of the impression whether a camel was pasturing, and therefore not carrying any load, or mounted by one person only, or heavily loaded. If the marks of the two fore feet appear to be deeper in the sand than those of the hind feet, he concludes that the camel had a weak breast, and this serves him as a clue to ascertain the owner. In fact, a Bedouin, from the impressions of a camel's or of his driver's footsteps, draws so many conclusions, that he always learns something concerning the beast or its owner; and in some cases this mode of acquiring knowledge appears almost supernatural. The Bedouin sagacity in this respect is wonderful, and becomes particularly useful in the pursuit of fugitives, or in searching after cattle.

I have seen a man discover and trace the footsteps of his camel in a sandy valley, where thousands of other footsteps crossed the road in every direction; and this person could tell the name of every one who had passed there in the course of that morning. I myself found it often useful to know the impression made by the feet of my own companions and camels; as from circumstances which inevitably occur in the Desert, travellers sometimes are separated from their friends. In passing through dangerous districts the Bedouin guides will seldom permit a townsman or stranger to walk by the side of his camel. If he wears shoes, every Bedouin who passes will know by the impression that some townsman has travelled that way; and if he walks barefooted, the mark of his step, less full than that of a Bedouin, immediately betrays the foot of a townsman, little accustomed to walk. It is therefore to be apprehended, that the Bedouins, who regard every townsman as a rich man, might suppose him loaded with valuable property, and accordingly set out in pursuit of him. A keen Bedouin guide is constantly and exclusively occupied during his march in examining footsteps, and frequently alights from his camel to acquire certainty respecting their nature. I have known instances of camels being traced by their masters, during a distance of six days' journies, to the dwelling of the man who had stolen them.

Many secret transactions are brought to light by this knowledge of the *Athr* (اثر), or "footsteps;" and a Bedouin can scarcely hope to escape detection in any clandestine proceeding, as his passage is recorded upon the road in characters that every one of his Arabian neighbours can read.

General Reflections.

In examining the Bedouin laws, and especially those which are determined with scrupulous nicety, a question naturally arises, how that code of law, which in its main points there is reason to believe general among all Bedouins of Arabia, (and which I know to be common among several of them,) was originally given to that nation. We can scarcely suppose that it arose from the natural wants of the tribes, which slowly and partially adopted certain customs; and that these, by practice and common consent, in process of time became the universal law. The political institutions of the Bedouins, the nature of the offices of their sheikhs and elders, the rules which they observe in war and in negotiating peace—rules founded on the very spirit of their free and wandering life—might probably be traced to such an origin. They are so well adapted, so natural, and so simple, that every nation, not yet reduced to slavery, if thrown at large upon the wide Desert, might be expected to observe the same rules and usages. But quite contrary is the case with their civil institutions, which it is difficult to imagine could ever have originated in chance, or the consent gradually obtained of a wild and warlike multitude.

The general law by which the right of blood-revenge is determined to rest within the *khomseh*, and which limits hospitality towards a fugitive to three days and one third of a day; the rules of *dakheil*, of the *rabiet*, of several of the laws relating to divorce; the nice distinctions made in estimating wounds and insults; to which may be added the nature of the agyd's office; all these seem so many arbitrary regulations, that, in my opinion, indicate the work of a legislator. Any reader conversant with the Turkish laws will have seen, on perusal of these papers, how much the Bedouin civil code differs from that most general throughout all Muselman empires. The great eastern legislator, Mohammed, seems to have been much less successful in forcing his laws upon his own nation, the Bedouins of Arabia, than in establishing them by their assistance in all the surrounding countries. He obliged the Bedouins to renounce their idolatry, and to acknowledge the unity of a Divine Creator; but although they acquiesced in adopting a few religious rites, and in performing some outward ceremonies, the civil laws which he promulgated as having been communicated immediately from heaven, seem to have never made any lasting impression upon them; while their ancient customs, which did not actually clash with the religious creed, continued to be steadily observed. A more intimate acquaintance, than I could obtain, with the great tribes of Yemen and Nedjd, would undoubtedly bring to light many other laws and customs corresponding with those which they had in the time of *Djáhelye*, or Ignorance, as the Muselmans style those ages that preceded Mohammed.

If, therefore, the civil laws of the Bedouins originate with Mohammed, and if since his time history does not mention any legislator of the Desert, we must seek for one in more remote ages of antiquity; but throughout Arabia, every thing is involved in darkness and uncertainty; and we have no reason to imagine that any Arab chief or king who flourished at that early period, and of whom we know little besides their names, had extended his authority over the desert parts of Arabia, or ruled over the Bedouins. The ancient code of one Bedouin tribe only has reached posterity; but the Pentateuch was exclusively given to the Beni Israel; and we remain totally unacquainted with the internal laws of the numerous nations that surrounded the chosen race.

Perhaps a discovery may yet be made of Arabic manuscripts capable of throwing light upon those points; for, notwithstanding all the literary treasures contained in our libraries, not one tenth of the Arabian historians have hitherto found their way to Europe. Perhaps the discovery of ancient monuments and inscriptions in Nedjd and Yemen may lead to a disclosure of new historical facts; but even though posterity should be left in ignorance on those subjects, the present state of the great Bedouin commonwealth of Arabia must be considered a most interesting field for inquiry, as it offers to our contemplation, the rare example of a nation which, notwithstanding its perpetual state of warfare, without and within, and the frequent attempts made for its subjugation, has preserved for a long succession of ages its primitive laws in all their vigour, the observance of which has been enforced merely by the national spirit and uncorrupted manners of its rude but patriotic members.

ADDITIONS

TO THE

CLASSIFICATION OF BEDOUIN TRIBES.

A CONSIDERABLE portion of the *Wold Aly* tribe reside above *Khaibar*, in the Southern Desert of Arabia.

The tribe of *el Hessenne*.—Their chief is named *Mehanna*, having been born in the "low-grounds," so called in the Desert, between Tedmor and Anah. Those low grounds, which are denominated "wádys," and of which the Bedouins distinguish eight as the principal in this direction, are the pasturing places of all the great Aeneze tribes in winter time, and extend for a distance of five days' journies from west to east. Wady Hauran, which has been mentioned in a preceding account of this Desert, forms a part of those wadys. During the last century this ground was the continual scene of conflict between the Mowaly Arabs, who were then very powerful, but at present inhabit the desert about Aleppo, and the Beni Khaled tribe from Basra. On those grounds both tribes were accustomed to meet in winter, and contend for the right of pasture.

The Djelás, or el Rowalla.

This third branch of the great Aeneze nation is not properly named Rowalla, but *Djelás*, and these are divided into two principal tribes.

1. *El Rowalla* (a name which should not be applied to the whole branch): their minor tribes are *el Ktaysán, el Doghama, el Feregge*, and *el Naszyr*.

2. The *Omhallef*, whose sheikh is *el Maadjel*.—To these belong the tribes of *Abdelle, Fersha, el Bedour*, and *el Sowaleme*.

Most of the great Aeneze tribes, as I have already remarked, are entitled to passage-money from the Syrian hadj, or pilgrim caravan. Thus, for instance, the El Ahsenne take a yearly *surra* or tribute of fifty purses (or about one thousand pounds), dividing it among a number of their individuals. A surra to the same amount is taken by the Wold Aly. The Fedán, who at present are one of the strongest Aeneze tribes, receive nothing from the pilgrims.

The Djelás were, in former times, perpetually wandering about Nedjd. They are known in Syria principally, since the battle which they fought with the Baghdad troops in the year 1809, upon a piece of ground formed into a corner or angle by the river Euphrates and the Khabour, opposite to Rahaba. Having taken several small guns and some tents, they carried them to Derayeh, the capital. About five hundred horses which became their property as plunder, they sold to Asyr Arabs of Yemen. Those Djelás are the most wild and warlike tribe of the Desert between Syria and Basra. By their great numbers and strength, they have latterly been enabled to extort tribute from many Syrian villages.

The Besher, or Bisher.

These divide themselves into two great branches.

1. The *Tana Mádjed* Arabs, to whom belong, as minor tribes, the *Fedán* and the *Sebaa*.

2. The *Selga* Arabs. Of these the greater part occupy the district of *el Hassa* on the Persian Gulf, belonging to the Wahabys. Of those Selgas there are three ramifications, the *Medheyán, Metarafe*, and the considerable tribe called *Oulád Soleymán*. The Selga sheikh is Ibn Haddal, a strenuous supporter of the Wahabys. He was present in almost every battle fought from the year 1812 to 1815 in Hedjaz against the army of Mohammed Aly; and it was chiefly through his exertions that Tousoun Pasha was kept completely in check on his progress in spring, 1815, from Medina towards Kasym.

The *Fedan* Arabs have latterly become very powerful, and defeated the Hessenne under Mehanna in many encounters on the Syrian frontier.

The *Oulad Soleymán* are descendants from the ancient tribe of *Djaafere*, which is now almost extinct. Another small tribe claiming descent also from Djaafere is named *Owádje*. These people generally encamp with the Wold Aly in Hauran, and occupy above two hundred tents; they do not belong to the nation of the Aenezes. Of these Djaafere, a part went over to Egypt at the time of the Muselman conquest; their descendants are now settled on the western banks of the Nile in Upper Egypt, among the numerous villages between Esna and Assouán. It may be remarked as an extraordinary circumstance, that the women descended from this tribe of Djaafere are celebrated both in Egypt and Arabia for their frequent production of twins. The usual dwelling-place of the Oulad Soleyman is on the vicinity of Khaibar; they constitute a very strong and warlike tribe, occupying about five thousand tents.

The Sebaa Arabs, who at present live on the Syrian frontiers, had their residences formerly in Nedjd. They left that country about twelve years ago, that they might be less exposed to the extortions of the Wahaby chief.

Ahl el Shemál.

This denomination is used by the Syrian Arabs only with relation to their own position. Among the Arabs of Hedjáz, the whole Aeneze tribe is classed among the *Ahl el Shemál*, or " northern nations." The great ancestor of the Aenezes was *Wayl*, and his descendants, the Beni Wayl, are known in historical records as the contemporaries and the enemies of Mohammed. Not much more than one hundred and twenty years have now elapsed since the Aenezes came from Khaibar and Nedjd into Syria. For the extraordinary increase of this numerous nation and their great abundance of cattle, the Bedouins account in the following manner. They relate that Wayl, their illustrious forefather, by some fortunate chance happened to ascertain the exact moment of the *Leilet el Kader* (the twenty-fifth or twenty-seventh night of the fast Ramadhan), when the Almighty is always disposed to comply with the prayers of mortals. Wayl, placing his hands on certain parts of his she-camel and of his own person, implored the divine blessing, with respect to those objects which he touched: his prayers were favourably heard; he was blest with a numerous family of sons and daughters; and his people became rich in a multiplicity of camels. This story is related, and firmly believed by every person of the Aeneze tribe.

El Mowaly.—The celebrated sheikh of this tribe, *El Gendj*, one of the bravest men in Syria, was treacherously killed by the Pasha of Aleppo in his own *harám*, in the year 1813; and his son, a boy of sixteen, invested with the office of guardian of the Desert of Aleppo. They were formerly sole masters of the open country about Aleppo and Hamah, and were entitled to a considerable *surra*, or annual tribute, from the hadj of pilgrims passing through their territory. Of these advantages they have been dispossessed by the Aenezes, and are now reduced to small numbers, and very limited extent of patrimony.

The *Fehely* Arabs of Damascus are certain tribes who labour under the imputation of being persons of bad faith; and in general it is found that this unfavourable opinion, which all the Bedouins entertain respecting them, is but too justly applicable to numerous individuals among them. They endeavour to extenuate their faults by an exercise of hospitality. Thus in Syria, the Mowalys and Fehelys are notorious for treachery; but, on the other hand, are celebrated for treating their guests with a profusion of victuals. The Fehelys, in particular, are despised, because they do not scruple to steal from the tents of their friends.

The *Howeytát* derive their origin from the ancient tribe of *Beni Atye*; from whom likewise are descended the *Heywát* (also entitled *Leheywát*), the *Terabein*, the *Maazy* (in the deesrt between Suez and Cosseir), and the *Tyaha*. Those Arab tribes dwelling on the eastern gulf of the Red Sea, generally receive their supplies of provisions from the country about Khalyl. Should the harvest in Syria not have been abundant, those Arabs travel a journey of fourteen or fifteen days to Cairo, and there furnish themselves with the necessary stock of corn.

The *Omran*, although connected by alliance with the Howeytát, do not in fact belong to them, but form a distinct tribe in themselves. They inhabit the mountains between Akaba and Moeyleh, on the eastern coast of the Red Sea. The Omran are a strong tribe of very independent spirit. Their frequent depredations render them objects of terror to the pilgrims proceeding to Mekka, who are under the necessity of passing through their territory. At the time when Mohammed Aly, Pasha of Egypt, had reduced all other Bedouins on the Egyptian hadj road to complete subjection, the Omran still proved obstinate. In the year 1814 they attacked and plundered a detachment of Turkish cavalry near Akaba; and in 1815 they pillaged the whole advanced corps of the Syrian pilgrim caravan, on their return from Medinah to Damascus. Among their principal tribes are the *Hadnán*.

The *Debour* and *Bedoul* are tribes that reside in the vicinity of the Akaba; they are in alliance with the tribes of Omran and Howeytat: in the same quarter also dwell the *Seyayhe*.

Among the Arabs of Khalyl, or Hebron, are, *el Tyáha*—whose principal tribe is called *el Hekouk*—the *Terabein*—who conduct the caravans from Ghaza and Hebron to Suez; of their tribes one is the *Azazeme*—the *Wahydy* (or *Wahydát*), among whose tribes are the *Oulad el Fokora*. There is also a small tribe about Ghaza and Hebron, called *Reteymát*, and another, the *Khanasera*. These Arabs of Ghaza and Khalyl repair in spring time to the borders of the canals on the river Nile, in the Sherkieh, where they pasture their cattle on the fine herbage produced by the inundation.

The Arabs of Tor, or Towara.

These inhabit the peninsula of Sinai, and are divided into three branches—the *Sowaleha, Mezeyne,* and *Aleygat*.

1. The *Sowaleha*, who are subdivided into four tribes, viz.—the *Oulad Sayd*, the *Owareme*, the *Geráshy*, and the *Rahamy*. Those whom I have here named *Geráshy* are descended from the ancient *Gereysh* of Mekka, as the Arabs pronounce the name قريش, which Europeans generally express by *Koreish*. The Sowaleha can muster about three hundred matchlocks, but they have not any horses, and, like all the Towara tribes, maintain very little intercourse with their eastern neighbours.

2. The *Mezeyne*—descended from a tribe of the same name

residing eastward of Medinah. The Mezeyne and Aleygát tribes remain in the eastern and southern parts of the peninsula.

3. The *Aleygát*. These, with the Mezeyne tribe, can form together a force of three hundred matchlocks. The Aleygáts settled in Nubia, below *Derr*, are acknowledged by the Sinai Aleygáts to be of the same original stock. Besides the three tribes above mentioned, the Tyaha and Terabein likewise pasture their flocks in the northern parts of the peninsula of Mount Sinai. There are remnants of two tribes found in this country, originally from Barbary; the *Beni Wászel* and the *Beni Soleymán*. Some of the Beni Wászel live in Upper Egypt, on the eastern bank of the Nile, opposite Mirriet, where they have become cultivators. None of the Tor Bedouins have at present any horses.

To complete this review of the Eastern Bedouins, the names of those tribes that wander about in the neighbourhood of the eastern frontiers of the Egyptian Delta are subjoined—

Arabs of the Sherkyeh of Egypt.

These were once very powerful tribes, which the fertility of the country had attracted from various parts. During the time of the Mamelouk reign in Egypt, it might be said that they were the sole masters in the province of *Sherkyeh*: they exacted a tribute from all the villages; indeed many villages belonged to them, so that the peasants were obliged to divide the produce with these owners. The confined space of ground in which they moved, and their intermixture with the peasants (to whom they bestow their girls in marriage), rendered the conquest of them more easy to Mohammed Aly, Pasha of Egypt, who not only subdued, but almost wholly exterminated them; in doing which he very materially served his own Egyptians, who had been always extremely ill-treated by those tribes, of whom the principal are:—

El Sowaleha—related to those of the Sinai peninsula above noticed.

The *Ayayde*, who about one hundred years ago formed a tribe of six hundred horsemen. They sometimes encamp in the mountains between Suez and Cosseir, but are more commonly found in the flat country not far from Cairo. They occupy about one hundred tents; their minor tribes are, *Salatene*, *Djerabene* and *Maazy*, but these must not be confounded with others bearing the same name. The Ayayde are perpetually at enmity with the Howeytát. Some of their encampments are seen on the Syrian road, leading towards El Arish.

The *Howeytát*—related to those of the east, but become so degenerate in consequence of their intermixture with the peasants that they can scarcely be distinguished from them. They are principally engaged in the transport business between Cairo and Suez. Their branch-tribes are, *el Mowalle*, *Ghanayme*, *Shedayde*, *Zeráyne*, amounting all together to about six hundred tents.

The *Heteym*.—Of this wide-spread nation, of which individuals are found in every corner of Arabia, considerable numbers have reached Upper Egypt, where they encamp above *Gous*, and *Goft*, or Coptos.

The *Djeheyne*.—These came from Hedjaz, where their main tribe still exists.

The *Bily*—likewise eastern: all these tribes come either as fugitives, or for the purpose of benefiting by the advantages which robbers may derive from the neighbourhood of so rich a country as Egypt. These Arabs of the Sherkyeh have all (with the exception of the Maazy) adopted the Egyptian dialect; and this circumstance alone would be sufficient to render them despicable in the opinion of all true Arabian Bedouins. The small Bedouin tribes of Syria, on the contrary, who were never out of the inhabited parts, surrounded by Syrian peasants, still retain the Bedouin dialect in all its purity. The Bedouins of Syria have never mixed so much with the inhabitants of that country as the Egyptian Bedouins have done with the Fellahs, among whom they reside.

The *Aleygât*—a kindred tribe of those in the mountains of Sinai. They derive their origin from the Syrian Desert.

The *Azayre*, belonging to the *Heteym*. Several camps of the Azayre are found in Upper Egypt.

The tribe of *Amarât*.

The *Maazy*. These sometimes pasture their flocks near the Nile, but generally reside in the mountains between Cairo and Cosseir; they are most commonly employed in the transport trade between Cosseir and Genne. These Maazy are the only Egyptians of their race who have preserved the language, dress, manners, and institutions of the Eastern Bedouins in all their original purity. They were formerly stationed southward and eastward of the Omrán, about Moeyleh, where their brethren still remain. In the course of the last century, having been much annoyed by various enemies, they abandoned their homes and sought refuge in Egypt. Those who undertook their journey by land, were, for the greater number, killed during their passage through the territory of the Howeytats. Others came over by sea to Tor, and arrived safely in Egypt, where, finding that the Sherkye was fully peopled with Bedouins, they retired to the mountains eastward of the river Nile. Having been frequently at war with the Beys of Egypt, and latterly with the *Pasha*, their numbers are considerably reduced. At present, the utmost of their force does not exceed two hundred horsemen. They are constantly at variance with the Ababde Bedouins, who reside on the south of the Cosseir route. Within the last twenty or thirty years, those Sherkye tribes have been rendered more numerous by the addition of—

The *Hanády*, a tribe of Moggrebyn Bedouins, who have adopted the dress and customs of the Barbary and Libyan Arabs. They were formerly established in the Beheyre province of the Delta, and in the Desert extending from the Pyramids towards Alexandria. Having been overpowered by the Oulad Aly, another Moggrebyn tribe of the same province, much superior to them in numbers, they were obliged to abandon the right of tribute which they had exacted from the villages of Beheyre, and leaving it to their more powerful rivals, they retired across the river Nile towards the Sherkye, where they now reside. From five to six hundred horsemen constitute the utmost force of all those Sherkye tribes. Thirty years ago they were able to muster at least three thousand, if we may believe their own reports. The Pasha of Egypt levies a tribute on them at present, and observes their movements with so much vigilance that they are not even permitted to make war against each other; the most galling predicament in which a Bedouin can possibly be placed. The district between Belbeis and Salehye is the most frequented by these Bedouins, to whose number may be added the three tribes, *el Howámede, Oulad Mousa* and *Lebádye*.

Returning from the limits of Egypt towards the eastern borders of the Red Sea, I shall continue to trace the different tribes as far south as Mekka and Tayf.

The *Howeytát* and *Omrán*, (who have been already mentioned) extend as far as the neighbourhood of Moeyleh. Among them, in the mountains not very remote from the sea, are likewise some encampments of the Bily and Heteym tribes; and at a distance of two days' journies southward of Akaba, in the fertile wady called *Megna*, which is remarkable for its abundance of date-trees, reside the Megana Arabs, who are partly husbandmen or cultivators.

Eastward of Akaba and Megna, towards the Syrian hadj road, we find the *Maazy* tribe, who are in a state of constant warfare with the Omran. They constitute a force of about four or perhaps five hundred matchlocks, and are the brethren of the Egyptian Maazys.

The *Beni Okaba*, the same as that tribe which inhabits the vicinity of Kerek; they possess the small town of Moeyleh and the surrounding country. Parties of the Mesayd Arabs are likewise found in the neighbourhood of Moeyleh.

El Bily. These Arabs inhabit the country between Moeyeleh and the castle of *Wodje*, and the wady bearing the same name, a principal station on the hadj road, being abundantly supplied with excellent water. The castle of Wodje is situated on the mountain, about three miles distant from the sea, where there is a good harbour; the garrison consists of about a dozen Moggrebyn soldiers: this seems to be the original abode of the Bily: those of the same tribe who live in Syria and Egypt are *advenæ*. In spring time, many of these Arabs cross with their sheep and goats in small boats over to the islands within sight of the shore, where the winter rains have produced vegetation, and continue there as long as they can find rain-water remaining in the rocks of these islands. Some Howeytáts are found southward of Moeyleh; they are called *Howeytát el Kebly*, to distinguish them from their brethren of the north.

Heteym. To the distance of three days' journies from Wodje, in a southern direction as far as the promontory and mountain of *Hassány*, the country is inhabited by the Heteyms. Of the innumerable tribes who people the deserts of Arabia, none is more dispersed, nor more frequently seen in all parts of that country, than the Heteym. In Syria, in Lower and Upper Egypt, along the whole coast of the Red Sea down to Yemen, in Nedjd and Mesopotamia, encampments of the Heteym are always to be found. Perhaps it is from this wandering disposition that they are much less respected than any other tribe. For one Bedouin to call another "Heteymy," is considered as a very serious insult; for the Heteyms are despised as a mean race of people, and in most provinces the other Bedouins will not intermarry with them. They are, besides, obliged almost every where, to pay tribute to the neighbouring Bedouins for permission to pasture their cattle; and I believe that, with the exception of this territory bordering on the Red Sea, where the property of the land is peculiarly their own, they are no where regarded as owners of the place which they inhabit, while the contrary is the case with all genuine and true-born Bedouins. Thus in Egypt, Syria, and Hedjaz, the Heteyms pay a tribute in sheep to all their neighbours. Conscious of the little esteem in which they are universally held, these Heteyms have renounced all their martial spirit, and have become of a peaceable character, but extremely shuffling, which renders them still more disliked.

The Heteym women have the reputation of being very beautiful, and licentious in their manners; and the Arabs say that the slave of a Heteymy will never attempt to run away, because his mistress never hesitates about admitting him to her embraces. It must, however, be allowed, that the Heteyms are commended for generous conduct and hospitality towards strangers; but these virtues have been forced upon them by the necessity of endeavouring to conciliate, in some degree, the amity of their neighbours. Like all the other Bedouins on this coast, they are active fishermen: they sell their dried fish to the crews of ships coming from, or going to Hedjaz. The Heteyms also fish for pearls near several of the islands. They purchase their provision of corn at Moeyleh and Wodje; but they live principally on milk, meat, fish, and wild honey. They possess but few camels, and are altogether without horses; but their flocks of sheep are very numerous, and they take them for sale to Tor and Yembo. In general the Bedouins on this side of the Red Sea are poor, because their land does not afford good pasturage; and they live at such a distance from towns, that no advantage can be derived from any intercourse with the inhabitants.

The *Beni Abs.*—A few families of this ancient and celebrated tribe, among which the famous Antar was educated, still continue to inhabit the Djebel Hassany, (from three to four days' journey north of Yembo,) and an island opposite to it, called *el Harra*. They are the only Bedouins of Arabia who preserve the name of *Abs;* although there still exist many tribes who claim descent from that illustrious nation, but are known by other denominations. Like the Heteyms, these people of the Abs tribe are held in much disrepute; and the name of *Absy* is applied to a stranger with the intention of insulting him, in the same manner as the name of *Heteymy*. The Abs possess several small ships, in which they carry provisions to Hedjaz and Suez; and when the rains cease, they pasture their few sheep upon the island of *Harra* above mentioned. In the beginning of the last century these Abs were still a numerous tribe: even at present, the few remaining families of them are entitled to a tribute from the Egyptian pilgrim caravan; a tribute which, in very remote ages, their ancestors had enforced.

Djeheyney.—To the south of Djebel Hassany (northward of Yembo as above described), begin the dwelling places of the great tribe of *Djeheyne*, extending along the sea-coast as far as below Yembo, and eastward to Hedye, a station of the Syrian Hadj road. From Yembo, in the direction of Medinah, these Djeheyne possess the ground to a distance of about twelve or fifteen hours. The cultivated vallies of *Yembo el Nakhel* also belong to them. Part of this tribe are cultivators, but the greater number continue Bedouins. They constitute the chief portion of the population of Yembo; and although they possess but a few horses, it is said that they can muster a force amounting to eight thousand matchlocks.

They are constantly at war with the neighbouring tribe of Beni Harb; through whose assistance the Wahaby chief, Saoud, was enabled to subjugate them, while all the other tribes above mentioned, southward of Akaba, had invariably refused to submit; and Saoud had not thought it expedient to attack them in their mountains, contenting himself with detaching occasionally some plundering parties against them. The Djeheynes nominally acknowledge the supremacy of the Sherif of Mekka: they proved very serviceable to the Pasha of Egypt at the taking of Medinah, in the year 1812.

Like all the Bedouins before mentioned, dwelling southward of Akaba, the Djeheyne are entitled to surra, or passage money, from the pilgrims of the Egyptian hadj. Of their branch tribes I cannot give any account.

Returning to the latitude of Akaba, I shall now proceed to enumerate the Bedouin tribes of the Eastern Desert, towards Nedjd, and thence on to Medinah.

Bedouins of the Desert between Akaba el Shámy (or the Syrian Akaba) and Medinah, comprising those of Nedjd.

I can speak of these tribes merely from hearsay, and well-authenticated reports; while I myself have seen individuals of almost every other tribe enumerated in these pages, from the river Euphrates, down to Mekka and Tayf. The tribes which I am now about to describe are all Wahabys, continuing to profess themselves such even after the campaign of Mohammed Aly Pasha against these sectarians.

The Desert southward of Akaba, as far as Hedjer, is almost wholly inhabited by Aenezes. But the watering-places of that Desert are few, and on that account the Bedouins seldom remain stationary on the hadj route, but take up their abode in the eastern parts, towards Djebel Shammar, and Kasym. The Aeneze tribes encamped in these districts are—

The *Oulud Soleymán*, a tribe of Besher: they have about five thousand tents in the neighbourhood of Khaibar.

The *Rowalla* of the *Djelás*, who are likewise established at Khaibar.

El Fokara, belonging to the Wold Aly, at Hedjer.—These Fokara are much celebrated for their bravery. All the tribes here mentioned are rich in horses, and exact a tribute from the pilgrim caravan.

Bedouins of Djebel Shammar.

The *Beni Shammar*—whose sheikh, Ibn Aly, is a man of considerable influence at the Wahaby court. These Beni Shammar possess but few horses; they are, however, able to muster from three thousand to four thousand men, all armed with matchlocks. Some of them are Bedouins, and others cultivators. Part of their tribe is in Mesopotamia, where they have always proved themselves great enemies of the Wahabys.

The most numerous branch of the Beni Shammar are the *Degheyfát*.

El Djaafar.

El Rebaay—These are descended from the ancient tribe of *Beni Deyghám*; whose chief, Orar el Deyghámi, is often mentioned in Bedouin tales.

The *Zegeyrát*—descended from the same Beni Deygham, are cultivators in the vicinity of Imam Hosseyn. There are in the Djebel Shammar and Nedjd several other Bedouin tribes, besides those above mentioned, but I have not been able to ascertain their names.

Bedouins of Kasym, and other parts of Nedjd.

There is scarcely any great tribe of the Arabian Desert which has not always some encampment in Nedjd. The inhabitants of all the towns and villages in that country are descended from Bedouin tribes, whom they much resemble in their manners and institutions. Of those tribes who wander about this part of the country during the whole year are—

The *Selga*—one of the great branches of the Bisher Arabs, belonging to the Aenezes. Their chief, Ibn Haddal, a man in high favour with the Waháby government.

The *Sahhoun*—celebrated for their bravery and activity as horsemen; of whom they can muster to the number of three hundred.

The *Beni Lam*—related to those bearing the same name, who pasture their flocks on the banks of the Shat el Arab: they form but a small tribe.

The *Heteym.*—Here we again find this tribe, as every where else throughout Arabia.

The *Beni Hosseyn*—a tribe of wandering Arabs, who, like the Persians, are disciples of Aly. They professed to adopt the Wahaby doctrines, but continued secretly attached to their Persian, or *Shya*, creed.

The *Zaab*—an inconsiderable tribe, residing in Nedjd and El Hassa.

The *Ageyl.*—In former ages these were a very powerful tribe, descended from the Beni Helál. They now are scattered about in small numbers among the villages of Nedjd. But another tribe called also Beni Ageyl, has lately sprung up since the reign of Sultan Murad. All the Arabs of Nedjd, whether settlers or Bedouins, who repair to Baghdad, and establish themselves there, become members of the tribe of Ageyl of Baghdad, which enjoys considerable influence at that place, and is, in fact, the strongest support of the Pasha in his wars with the surrounding Bedouins, and against the rebels of that city. The chief of these Ageyls of Baghdad is always some native of Derayeh, chosen from among themselves, and confirmed by the Pasha. These Ageyls are celebrated for their bravery. They conduct the caravans from Baghdad to Syria, and have frequently repulsed very superior forces of the Wahabys. They divide themselves into two classes at Baghdad.

1. The *Zogorty*—comprising the poorer individuals and pedlars.
2. The *Djemamyl*, who conduct the caravans. Among these classes of Ageyls are found persons belonging to many different tribes and districts, such as El Hassa, El Aaredh, El Kasym, and Djebel Shammar. Those settlers of the *Zedeyr* district (forming part of Nedjd,) who come to Baghdad, are not admitted as members of this body. Individuals of the southern tribe of Dowasyr, near the frontiers of Yemen, are likewise not to be found among these Ageyls.

Meteyr (or, as they are sometimes denominated, *Emteyr*).—These are a strong tribe, consisting of twelve hundred horsemen, and from six to eight thousand matchlocks. They live in Nedjd, chiefly in Kasym, and from thence on towards Medinah. They branch off into four principal tribes—1. The *Alowa*, whose sheikh, Dowysh, was an ally of Tousoun Pasha in his wars with the Wahabys. 2. The *Boráy;* their sheikh is called Merykhy. 3. *El Harabeshe;* and 4. *El Borsán*. Some of the Meteyr are likewise to be found in Mesopotamia: they are all inveterate enemies of the Aenezes.

From Kasym towards Medinah and Mekka.

Except the space occupied by the Meteyr, and some encampments of the Heteym, this whole extent of country is inhabited by the mighty tribe of *Harb*, which in numbers only yields to the Aenezes, and next to them constitutes the most formidable association of Bedouins in Arabia.

The Beni Harb.*

From the aggregate of this tribe, there might probably be formed a body comprising between thirty and forty thousand men armed with matchlocks; and such is the numerical strength of their main tribes, that each of them is rather to be considered as a distinct body; yet the ties which connect the whole body together are much stronger than those by which the numerous Aeneze tribes are united. Some of the Harbs are settlers; some are Bedouins. Almost every tribe has adopted both modes of life. They derive considerable profit from the Syrian and Egyptian pilgrim caravans, and may be styled the masters of Hedjaz. They were the last tribe in these countries that yielded to the Wahabys. They have few horses southward of Medinah, but every boy is armed with a matchlock. The Arabs belonging to this tribe of Harb frequently make plundering excursions against the Aenezes in their camps, as far as the plains of Hauran near Damascus.

* It may be here remarked that the word *Harb* in Arabic signifies "war."

Of the Harb tribe, east of Medinah, are

The *Mezeyne,* who can muster between four and five hundred horsemen, and about two thousand matchlocks. These became Wahabys long before the other tribes of Harb submitted: they are all Bedouins.

The *Wohoub,* and the *Gharbán.*

The *Djenáyne.*—Some of these are settlers, and cultivators of fields among the hills eastward of Medinah to the distance of between two and three days' journeys: from this they probably derive their name.

Beni Aly.—These are of the Persian creed, and followers of Aly. In numbers they amount to five hundred matchlocks. A few of them are settlers. They possess some watering-places, situated in fertile spots, where they sow corn and barley; but continue to live under tents, and pass the greater part of the year in the Desert.

Of the Harb tribe near Medinah, eastward and southward.

Beni Safar—Beni Ammer. This is a tribe amounting to between two and three thousand matchlocks, and three hundred horsemen; they live on the east and south of Medinah, and have the character of being cowardly and of bad faith; many of them are cultivators. The district of *El Fera,* (from which dates are exported all over Hedjaz, and which is said to be very fertile,) is in their possession. Their sheikh, Doſny, first joined the Turkish army, but in Kasym went over again to the Wahabys.

El Hámede—Likewise on the east and south of Medinah; equal in strength to the Beni Safar above-mentioned. Among them very few are cultivators; their sheikh, Mohammed Ibn Motlab, is considered at present as chief of all the Beni Harb. He succeeded to Djezye, who was treacherously murdered at Medinah, in the year 1814, by the Turkish governor.

The Beni Harb between Medinah and Mekka are entitled to a considerable tribute, or surra, from the Syrian as well as from the Egyptian hadj caravan. The tribute of the latter is said to be about eight thousand dollars, which the sheikhs divide among themselves and many individuals.

The Harb, southward of Medinah.

The *Beni Salem*—Among the vallies of Djedeyde and Safra, where they live in houses amidst plantations of date-trees; but few of these are Bedouins. They muster two thousand five hundred matchlocks, and are reported to be excellent soldiers; they receive a considerable tribute from the Syrian hadj, as the pilgrims belonging to it pass through their territory.

The *Howáseb*, to whom belongs *el Hamra*, a village with fields and gardens, between Djedeyde and Safra. The greater part of these Howáseb are Bedouins.

The *Sobh*.—These can assemble two thousand five hundred men, armed with matchlocks, and reckoned the most warlike among the tribes of Harb. To them belong Beder, and the surrounding country. I have seen them sit during the day-time in their small shops at Beder (where a market is held), and in the evening mount their camels that they might return to their families in the Desert. Some of them are permanently settled at Beder; the greater number inhabit the mountain of *Sobh*, eastward of Beder, which is inaccessible to enemies, and was the refuge of the Harb tribe against the Wahabys, who could never dislodge them from it. Upon that mountain grows the balm-tree and Senna in great abundance. They subdivide themselves into the three tribes of *Shokbán*, *Rehalát*, and *Khadhera*.

El Owf, the wildest of the Harb tribes. They occupy the mountains southward of Djebel Sobh toward Rábegh, and were never completely subjugated by the Wahabys. The name of Owf is dreaded as far as Mekka, and particularly by all pilgrims; for they are most enterprising robbers, and parties of them amounting to three or four hundred men have been known to carry off at night, by force, valuable loads out of the midst of the encampments of the hadj. They are accustomed to follow the hadj upon its return by night, to a distance of several days' journeys beyond Medinah, in hopes of cutting off the stragglers.

El Haib, a branch of the Owf, has emigrated (as I have already mentioned) into Syria, and occupies with its camels the fertile pasture-ground on the summit of Mount Libanon.

Dwy Dhaher.—These extend from Rábegh towards Mekka. Several encampments of them are likewise found in the vicinity of Medinah; they occupy the country as far as Wády Fatme. Their sheikh, Ghánem, rendered considerable services to the Turkish army at Medinah.

Beni Harb (in the low country, or Tehama or el Ghor, between the Mountains and the Sea).

Zebeyde.—These are in possession of the coast from the vicinity of Yembo, down to Djidda and Leith. (From Djidda southward, in the direction of Leith, encampments of the Heteym may likewise be seen.) Of the Zebeyde tribe many are settlers. The market-place of Kholeys with its fertile neighbourhood, at the distance of two days' journies northward of Djidda is their principal station. But as their territory is in general poor, they are obliged to seek for other means of subsistence than what can be derived from pasture alone. They are very active as fishermen: many of them are sailors, and serve as pilots between Yembo and Djidda. Their intimate connexion with the inhabitants of the towns of Hedjaz, and the trade in which they engage, have caused the other tribes of Harb to look upon them with disdain. A man of the Sobh or Beni Sálem tribe would resent it as a serious insult if any one were to call him a "*Zebeyde.*" Some of that same tribe of Zebeyde are said to be established on the Shat el Arab, below Baghdad. Among the Harb, from Medinah to Mekka, horses are very scarce; a few only are in the possession of their principal persons.

With most of the Harb tribe above mentioned I was personally acquainted; and the names of others of the same nation were familiar to me, although I do not exactly recollect their respective places of residence, but have reason to think them in the latitude of Medinah; their names are, *Sedda*, *Djemmela*, and *Saadyn*.

Bedouins from Medinah towards Mekka and Tayf, eastward of the great chain of Mountains.

The *Beni Harb* reside upon those mountains, and westward of them, towards the sea. To the east of that chain are the plains inhabited by the powerful tribe of *Ateybe*, whose territory extends as far south as Tayf. Their pasturing grounds are excellent. They possess great abundance of camels and sheep: they have also horses, and are in good reputation for bravery, being constantly at war with all their neighbours. They were, before the time of the Wahabys, the most inveterate enemies of the Harb tribe, and derived profit from the pilgrims of the hadj, whenever they passed through their territory; there being two hadj routes—one in a western direction from Medinah to Mekka, through the Harb country—the other, in an eastern direction through their own. With their different branches I am not acquainted. Their force cannot be less than six thousand matchlocks, and may amount to ten thousand.

Bedouins of Mekka.

Between Mekka and Djidda live the Bedouins called *Lahhyán*: these are related to the Hodheyl and Metarefe, and occupy the two principal stations on that road, *Hadda* and *Bahza*, places where a few of them reside in huts, and where travellers halt. The others pasture their flocks in the neighbouring mountains. Altogether they can muster about two hundred and fifty matchlocks. The Bedouins about Mekka are all poor, from the sterility of the ground which they inhabit, and the high price of all commodities and provisions in that country. Those of Tayf are much more at their ease.

From Mekka southward, in Tehama, or the "Low Country."

Here dwell the *Beni Fahem*, who supply Mekka with charcoal and sheep. They are celebrated for having retained in its purity the Arabic language. Of men armed with matchlocks they can assemble about three hundred.

The *Beni Djehádele* occupy the country southward of the Fahem, towards Wady Lemlem. In time of peace they conduct the caravans from Mekka to the coast of Yemen.

From Mekka eastward, in the direction of the great chain of Mountains.

In the Wady Fatme, and Wady Zeyme or Wady Lymoun, reside some Sherifs of the Sherif families of Mekka, belonging to the tribe of Dwy Barakát, who cultivate those fertile vallies, and encamp likewise in the neighbouring desert.

The *Koreysh.*—Of this famous tribe only three hundred matchlock-men now remain: they encamp about Mount Arafát. Notwithstanding their great name and ancient celebrity, they are but little esteemed by the other Bedouins. Mekka derives from them supplies of milk and butter.

The *Ryshye.*—This is a small tribe: it cannot muster above eighty matchlocks. The Ryshye engage in the transport trade between Mekka and Djidda. They are of recent origin, a kind of *advenæ*, held in little repute. Their small camps are pitched in the Wady Noman, on the way from Arafát towards Tayf; and in that wady they cultivate some fields.

The *Kabákebe.*—These reside in the vicinity of Sheddád, a station beyond Arafát, eastward; their numbers amount to about one hundred and fifty matchlocks.

The *Adouán.*—About forty years ago these formed a considerable tribe, mustering one thousand matchlocks. Their continual wars with every neighbour had reduced them to little more than one hundred families, and latterly they have been nearly exterminated by Mohammed Aly Pasha. They were an ancient and noble tribe, unequalled by any in Hedjaz for bravery and hospitality, and they occupied the first rank in public esteem. They were the intimate friends of the Sherifs of Mekka. The reigning Sherif, and all the families of the other Sherifs, were accustomed to send their children when eight days old to be educated among Bedouins, and principally among the tribe of Adouán, with whom they remained until they had learned to manage a horse with dexterity. It is well known that Mohammed himself was brought up in a similar manner among the tribe of Beni Sad. Their present system of politics has made them hostile to Mekka. Their late sheikh, Othman el Medhayfe, the brother-in-law of Sherif Ghaleb (who took him prisoner and beheaded him at Constantinople), had been named, by the Wahabys, chief of all the Bedouins of Mekka and Tayf. On his death the tribe fell into decay; and the few remaining families of the Adouáns have taken refuge among the Ateybes.

The Adouáns formerly had not any fixed pasturing places, but encamped all over the country from Djidda to Tayf. Such was their high reputation, that a man of the Hodheyl tribe said to me one day—"Where shall we now look for models of generosity and courage, since the Adouáns are gone?" A small branch of this tribe, called *el Harreth*, were all Sherifs, of the Beni Hashem race. In Nedjd also are found some branches of those Adouáns, not very numerous, but bearing the same names.

Bedouins of Tayf.

These are comprised under the denomination of *Thekyf*, and among them the Hodheyl are sometimes reckoned; but in general the Hodheyl are not included under that title.

The *Hodheyl* occupy the steep mountainous region on the road from Mekka to Tayf, and especially about the *Djebel Kora*. They muster one thousand matchlocks, and are reputed the best marksmen in the whole country. They are a famous tribe, eminent for their bravery. The Wahabys killed above three hundred of their best men before the tribe would submit. They have but few horses or camels; their sheep and goats, however, are numerous. They are subdivided into the three small tribes of *Alowyein*, *Nedowyein*, and *Beni Kháled*.

The *Toweyrek*. These live southward of the Hodheyl upon the same mountain; in numbers they amount to about five hundred matchlocks. They have the character of being expert thieves; which charge is not made against the Hodheyl, although these latter are very daring highway-robbers.

The *Thekyf*. This is a very powerful tribe, possessing the productive country about Tayf, its gardens, and other equally fertile spots on the eastern declivity of the great Hedjaz chain of mountains. Many of them are settlers. Half of the inhabitants of Tayf belong to this tribe: others of them continue to dwell in tents. Like all those mountaineers, they have few horses or camels, but are rich in flocks of sheep and goats.

The principal tribes of the Thekyf are *Beni Sofyán*, who live altogether as Bedouins; they can muster from six to seven hundred matchlocks. Two minor tribes, the *Modher* and *Rabýa*, reside with the Thekyf and participate in their interests, although I doubt whether they properly belong to them. It is these Beni Rabýa, whose emigrants have peopled a considerable part of Nubia, and whose descendants are the *Kenouz* (erroneously called *Berabera* in Egypt), above the first cataract. The Thekyfs can raise two thousand matchlocks; they defended Tayf against the Wahabys.

Tribes from Tayf toward Szana in Yemen.

Of these I can only speak from report, and shall here merely notice the tribes whose territories are more particularly described in my Arabian Travels.

From Tayf along the South-eastern plain in the direction from North to South.

Proceeding eastward from Tayf, we find at Ossoma a tribe of *Ateybe*, and at Taraba, the strong tribe of *el Begoum*. From thence southward, on the back of the great chain of mountains, we find the *Beni Oklob*. At Ranye are the *Beni Sabya*, and about Wady Beishe the *Beni Sálem*, whose numbers amount to five thousand matchlocks. Southward of them are the *Beni Kahtan*, a large tribe; the strongest and most considerable between the Ateybe and Hadramaut. They possess a good breed of horses, and their camel-riders are the best soldiers of the southern plains.

The *Beni Kahtan* are subdivided into two tribes: *Es-Sahámba*—whose sheikh, *Gormola*, was very much the friend of Saoud—and the tribe of *el Aasy*, whose sheikh, Hesher, is the most renowned warrior in the whole country.

The *Beni Dowaser*, a wild tribe, but little connected with any settlers. They are great hunters of ostriches.

Of the tribes above mentioned, the Begoum, Sabya, and Beni Sálem, are partly cultivators. The Kahtan and Dowaser are exclusively Bedouins. The Kahtan are more rich in camels than any Bedouins of the Eastern Desert. A person of the middle class sometimes possesses one hundred and fifty camels, and a man is reckoned poor who has only forty. Their camels are all of a black colour.

The *Beni Kelb* are described as being half-savage.

The *Beni Yám* are cultivators in the Wády Nedjrán; a warlike tribe whom the Wahabys could not find means to subdue. Some of their members profess the Persian creed; the more orthodox among them are subdivided into the minor branches of *Okmán* and *el Marra*. There is a saying recorded of Mohammed, that " the worst of all names are Harb and Marra."

The *Beni Kholan*, bordering upon the territory of the Imám of Szana.

From Tayf along the Mountains southwards.

The *Beni Sad*. Of them and of the Kahtan Arabs (whom I mention together, as they border upon each other in a southern direction) Masowdy says, in his work entitled "The Golden Meadows," that they are the only remnants of the primitive tribes of Arabia. Most of the other tribes about Mekka, Tayf, and Medinah, are well known in Arabian history since the propagation of Islám; others, such as Hodheyl, Koreysh, Thekyf, Fahem, Mezeyne, Harb, prior to Mohammed. But the two tribes above mentioned, the Beni Sad and Kahtan, are famous in the most remote antiquity, when Arabian history, for the greater part, is covered with complete darkness.

The *Nászera, Beni Málek, Ghámed,* and *Zohrán*. Of these three last mentioned tribes, each can raise from five hundred to one thousand matchlocks; the Zohrán as many as fifteen hundred.

The *Shomrán*, a very strong tribe: these extend likewise into the eastern and western plains. The *Asábely*, the *Ibn el Ahmar*, the *Ibn el Asmar*, and *Beni Shafra*.

The *Asyr*, forming the most numerous and warlike tribe of those mountains, and exercising considerable influence over all their neighbours. They can assemble fifteen thousand men armed with matchlocks.

The *Abyde*, the *Senhán*, the *Wadaa* (a strong tribe), the *Sahhár*, and the *Bágem*.

Here begins the territory of the Imám of Szana, and the road leads to that town through the tribes of Sofyán, Háshed, Omrán, and Hamdán.

The tribes of these mountains are all cultivators, but many individuals of them live in tents, and in spring time descend into the neighbouring plains to pasture their flocks; they possess but few horses or camels; the produce of their ground, however, is abundant, and they sell it on the coast of Yemen.

HORSES, CAMELS, AND LOCUSTS OF ARABIA.

Horses. (See p. 115.)

It is a general but erroneous opinion that Arabia is very rich in horses; but the breed is limited to the extent of fertile pasture grounds in that country, and it is in such parts only that horses thrive, while those Bedouins who occupy districts of poor soil rarely possess any horses. It is found, accordingly, that the tribes most rich in horses are those who dwell in the comparatively fertile plains of Mesopotamia, on the banks of the river Euphrates, and in the Syrian plains. Horses can there feed for several of the spring months upon the green grass and herbs produced by the rains in the vallies and fertile grounds, and such food seems absolutely necessary for promoting the full growth and vigour of the horse. We find that in Nedjd horses are not nearly so numerous as in the countries before mentioned, and they become scarce in proportion as we proceed towards the south.

In Hedjaz, especially in the mountainous regions of that country, and thence on towards Yemen, but few horses are to be seen, and these few are imported from the north. The Aeneze tribes on the frontiers of Syria have from eight to ten thousand horses; and some smaller tribes roving about that neighbourhood possess, probably, half as many. To the single tribe of Montefek

Arabs, in the Desert watered by the river Euphrates, between Baghdad and Basrah, we may assign at least eight thousand horses, and the tribes of Dhofyr and Beni Shammar are proportionably rich in those noble quadrupeds; while the province of Nedjd, Djebel Shammar, and Kasym, (that is from the vicinity of the Persian Gulf, as far as Medinah,) do not possess above ten thousand.

Among the great tribes on the Red Sea, between Akaba and Mekka, and to the south and south-east of Mekka as far as Yemen, horses are very scarce, especially among those of the mountainous districts. In the eastern plain between Beishe and Nedjrán, horses are rather more numerous. The tribe of Kahtan, residing in that quarter, is celebrated for its excellent studs; and the same may be said of the Dowaser tribe.

The settled inhabitants of Hedjaz and Yemen are not much in the habit of keeping horses; and I believe it may be stated as a moderate and fair calculation, that between five and six thousand constitute the greatest number of horses in the country from Akaba or the north point of the Red Sea, southwards to the shores of the ocean near Hadramaut, comprising the great chain of mountains and the lower grounds on the west of it, towards the sea. The great heat of the climate in Oman is reckoned unfavourable to the breeding of horses, which are there still more scarce than in Yemen. When I affirm, therefore, that the aggregate number of horses in Arabia, (as bounded by the river Euphrates and by Syria,) does not exceed fifty thousand, (a number much inferior to what the same extent of ground in any other part of Asia or in Europe would furnish,) I am confident that my calculation is not by any means under the true estimate.

In this part of the East, I know not any country that seems to abound more in horses than Mesopotamia; the tribes of Curdes and Bedouins in that quarter probably possess greater numbers than all the Arabian Bedouins together, for the richness of the Mesopotamian pasture contributes materially to augment the breed.

The best pasturing places of Arabia not only produce the greatest number of horses, but likewise the finest and most select race. The best koheyls of the khomse are found in Nedjd, on the Euphrates, and in the Syrian deserts; while in the southern parts of Arabia, and particularly in Yemen, no good breed exists but those which have been imported from the north. The Bedouins of Hedjaz have but few horses, their main strength consisting in camel-riders and foot-soldiers, armed with matchlocks only. In all the country from Mekka to Medinah, between the mountains and the sea, a distance of at least two hundred and sixty miles, I do not believe that two hundred horses could be found; and the same proportion of numbers may be remarked all along the Red Sea, from Yembo up to Akaba.

The united armies of all the southern Wahaby chiefs who attacked Mohammed Aly Pasha in the year 1815, at Byssel, consisting of twenty-five thousand men, had with them only five hundred horsemen, mostly belonging to Nedjd, and the followers of Faisal, one of Saoud's sons, who was present with the troops.

Both the climate and pasture of Yemen are reckoned injurious to the health of horses: many of them die from disease in that country, where they never thrive; indeed, the race begins to fall off in the very first generation. The Imám of Sana, and all the governors of Yemen, derive an annual supply of horses from Nedjd, and the inhabitants of the sea-coast receive considerable numbers by way of Sowakin from the countries bordering on the Nile. The horses taken in 1810, by the Rowalla Arabs, from the defeated troops of the Pasha of Baghdad, were all sold by them to the horse-dealers of Nedjd, and by the latter to the Arabs of Yemen; who are not, it may be here observed, by any means so nice and fastidious in choosing blood horses, as their northern neighbours.

During the government of the Wahaby chief, horses became more scarce every year among his Arabs. They were sold by their owners to foreign purchasers, who took them to Yemen, Syria, and Basra; from which last-mentioned place the Indian market was supplied with Arabian horses, because they feared that Saoud or his successor might have seized them; for it had become the custom, upon any slight pretext of disobedience or unlawful conduct, to confiscate a Bedouin's mare as a forfeit to the public treasury. The possession of a mare, besides, imposed an obligation on the Bedouin of being in constant readiness to attend his chief during his wars; therefore many Arabs preferred the alternative of being altogether without horses.

In the district of Djebel Shammar, many encampments have been lately seen without a single horse, and it is well known that the Meteyr Arabs (between Medinah and Kasym) reduced the number of their horses, within a few years, from two thousand to twelve hundred. The late Sherif of Mekka possessed an excellent stud of horses: the best stallions of Nedjd were taken to Mekka for sale, and it became a fashion among the Bedouin women going on a pilgrimage to Mekka, that they should bring their husbands' stallions as presents to the Sherif, for which, however, they received in return, silk stuffs, ear-rings, and similar articles.

From all that has come to my knowledge, on the very best authority, I have no hesitation in saying, that the finest race of Arabian blood horses may be found in Syria; and that of all the Syrian districts, the most excellent in this respect is the Hauran, where the horses may be purchased at first cost, and chosen among the camps of the Arabs themselves, who occupy the plains in spring time. The horses bought up at Basra for the Indian market are purchased at second hand from Bedouin dealers, and an Arab will rarely condescend to offer a good horse at a distant market without a certainty of selling it. True blood horses of the khomse, as I have been credibly informed, seldom find their way to Basra; and most of the horses purchased there for the Indian market belong to the Montefyk Arabs, who are not very solicitous about giving a pure breed. It might perhaps be advisable for the great European powers to have persons properly qualified, employed in purchasing horses for them in Syria, as the best mode of crossing and ennobling their own studs. Damascus would be the best position for the establishment of such persons. I am induced to suspect that very few true Arabian horses, of the best breeds, and still less any of the first rate among them, have ever been imported into England, although many horses of Syria, Barbary, and Egypt, have passed under the name of Arabs.

The Bedouins are of opinion that an Egyptian mare coupled with a blood Arabian produces a good breed, much better than that of the indigenous Syrian mares, whose breed is not considered of any value, even though crossed by the Koheyl. It would be erroneous to suppose, that the horses of the khomse, or the noble breed, are all of the most perfect or distinguished quality and beauty. Among the descendants of the famous horse Eclipse may be found mere hacks; thus I have seen many koheyl that had little more to recommend them than their name, although the power of bearing considerable fatigue seems common to all of the Desert race. The fine horses, however, of the khomse are far more numerous than the common horses belonging to the same breed; but still, among those fine horses, there can be found only a few worthy of being entitled "first rate," in respect to size, bone, beauty, and action; perhaps not above five or six among a whole tribe. It seems a fair and probable calculation to say, that the Syrian deserts do not furnish more than two hundred of that pre-eminent description, each of which may be estimated, in the Desert itself, at from one hundred and fifty to two hundred pounds. Of these latter, I believe that very few, if any, have ever found their way to

Europe, although it is through them alone that any successful attempt could be made to ennoble and improve the European race, while the horses usually exported are all of the second or third quality.

The Hedjaz Bedouins are accustomed to purchase mares from the Egyptian pilgrim caravan, and the fillies produced between these mares and good stallions they sell to the Arabs of Yemen. I never saw any geldings in the interior of the Desert.

In Egypt itself, on the borders of the Nile, there is not any breed of horses particularly distinguished. The finest of that country are produced in those districts where the best clover grows; which is in Upper Egypt, about Tahta, Akhmim, and Farshiout, and in Lower Egypt, in the territory of Menzaleh. Very few Arabian blood horses ever come to Egypt, a circumstance not surprising, since their remarkable quality, the power of supporting fatigue, is but little requisite on the fertile borders of the Nile.

The Egyptian horse is ugly and of a coarse make, resembling more a coach horse than a racer. His chief defects are, clumsy legs and knees, a short and thick neck. The head is sometimes fine; but I never saw an Egyptian horse having handsome legs.

They are not able to bear any considerable fatigue; but those that are well fed display much more brilliant action than the Arabian horses: their impetuosity renders them particularly desirable for heavy cavalry, and it is from this quality of the horse that the Egyptian cavalry have always founded their claim to celebrity. In their first onset the Egyptian horses are much superior to the Arabian; but when long marches become necessary, and the duties of light cavalry required, the Egyptians prove themselves infinitely less useful than the Koheyl.

The Libyan Bedouins derive their supplies of horses from their own breeds, as well as from Egypt. In the interior of the Desert, and towards Barbary, they are said to have preserved the ancient breeds of Arabian horses; but this is not the case in the vicinity of Egypt, where the peculiar races are as little distinguished as among the Egyptians. Like the Arabian Bedouins, those Libyans exclusively ride mares.

Respecting the pedigrees of Arabian horses I must here add, that in the interior of the Desert the Bedouins never refer to any among themselves; for they as well know the whole genealogy of their horses, as they do that of the owners. But when they take their horses to market at any town, such as Basra, Baghdad, Aleppo, Damascus, Medinah, or Mekka, they carry along with them a written pedigree, which they present to the purchaser; and it is only on such occasions that a Bedouin is ever found to possess the written pedigree of his horse; while, on the other hand, in the interior of the Desert itself, he would laugh at being asked for the pedigree of his mare. This may serve to correct an erroneous account, elsewhere given, on the subject of such pedigrees.

In Upper Egypt the Maazy and Heteym Arabs, occupying the Desert between the Nile and the Red Sea, have preserved among them the breed of the khomse. As in Arabia, horses are possessed by them in partnership. They divide each horse into twenty-four shares, or *kerat* (according to the division of landed property in Egypt, which is always by kerats), and different persons buy three, four, or eight kerats of the mare, and share proportionably in the benefits arising from the sale of the young breed. So little is known concerning the true breed of horses among the soldiers in Egypt, that when in the year 1812 Ibrahim Pasha's troops took ten Koheyl horses belonging to Heteym, the soldiers sold them one to another, as if they had been common Egyptian horses; while their former possessors valued them at least three times beyond that amount.

For a hundred Spanish dollars a good cavalry horse may, at

any time, be purchased in Egypt. The highest price paid for an Egyptian horse is three hundred dollars; but for this horse a Bedouin would not give fifty dollars. The Mamelouks formerly esteemed the Koheyl of the Desert, and expended considerable sums in propagating their breed in Egypt. The present masters of this country have not the same passion for fine horses as their predecessors; who, in many respects, had adopted Arab notions, and had made it a fashion among them to acquire a competent knowledge of horses, and to keep their stables upon a most extravagant establishment.

Here may be added to the names of Arabian breeds already mentioned:—

El Thámerye, of the Koheyl race.

El Nezahhy, a breed of the *Hadaba*. Some tribes reckon the Nezakhy stallions among the number of blood horses.

The *Manekye* and *Djolfe* are not considered as belonging to the khomse by the Arabs of Nedjd.

The Hadaba and Dahma breeds are much esteemed in Nedjd.

The horses of the Mesenna breed (of the Koheyl race) are never used in Nedjd as stallions.

The Bedouins use all the horses of the khomse exclusively as stallions. The first horse produced by a mare belonging to a race not comprehended within the khomse, would, notwithstanding its beauty, and perhaps superior qualities, never be employed as a breeder. The favourite mare of Saoud, the Wahaby chief, which he constantly rode on his expeditions, and whose name, *Keraye*, became famous all over Arabia, brought forth a horse of uncommon beauty and excellence. The mare, however, not being of the khomse, Saoud would not permit his people to use that fine horse as a stallion; and not knowing what to do with it, as Bedouins never ride horses, he sent it as a present to the Sherif.

The mare, Keraye, had been purchased by Saoud from a Bedouin of the Kahtan Arabs for fifteen hundred dollars.

A troop of Druses on horseback attacked, in the summer of 1815, a party of Bedouins in Hauran, and drove them into their encampment, where they were in turn assailed by a superior force, and all killed except one man, who fled. He was pursued by several of the best mounted Bedouins; but his mare, although fatigued, continued her speed for several hours, and could not be overtaken. Before his pursuers gave up the chase they cried out to him, promising quarter and safe conduct, and begging that he would allow them to kiss the forehead of his excellent mare. Upon his refusal, they desisted from pursuing, and, blessing the generous creature, they exclaimed, addressing her owner, "Go and wash the feet of your mare, and drink up the water." This expression is used by the Bedouins to show their great love for such mares, and their sense of the services which they have rendered.

The Bedouins in general do not allow their mares to breed until they have completed their fifth year; but the poorer classes, who are eager for the profits arising from the sale of foals, sometimes wait no longer than the completion of the fourth year.

The price paid in Nedjd, when a stallion is occasionally hired, merely for the purpose of breeding, is one Spanish dollar; but the owner of the horse is entitled to decline the acceptance of this dollar as payment: if he think fit, he may wait until the mare brings forth. Should she produce a filly, he may claim a she-camel of one year; if the offspring prove male, he takes, in like manner, a young he-camel, as payment for the use of his stallion.

The Bedouins never allow a horse, at the moment of its birth, to fall upon the ground: they receive it in their arms, and so cherish it for several hours, occupied in washing and stretching its tender limbs, and caressing it as they would a baby. After this they place it on the ground, and watch its feeble steps with particular attention, prognosticating from that time the excellencies or defects of their future companion.

In Nedjd, the people feed their horses regularly upon dates. At Derayeh, and in the country of El Hassa, dates are mixed with the *birsím,* or dried clover, and given to them as food. Barley, however, is the most usual provender throughout all parts of Arabia. The wealthy inhabitants of Nedjd frequently give flesh to their horses, raw as well as boiled, together with all the fragments of their own meals. I know a man at Hamah, in Syria, who assured me that he had often given to his horses roasted meat before the commencement of a fatiguing journey, that they might be the better able to endure it. The same person also related to me, that fearing lest the governor of the town should take a liking to his favorite horse, he fed it for a fortnight exclusively upon roasted pork, which excited its spirit and mettle to such a height, that it became absolutely unmanageable, and could be no longer an object of desire to the governor.

I have seen vicious horses in Egypt cured of the habit of biting, by presenting to them, while in the act of doing so, a leg of mutton just taken from the fire: the pain which a horse feels in biting through the hot meat causes it, after a few lessons, to abandon the vicious habit. Egyptian horses are much less gentle in their temper than the Arabian; they are often vicious —the Arabians scarcely ever—and require to be constantly tied, while the Arab horses wander freely and quietly about the camps like camels. Egyptian grooms are celebrated all over the East for their treatment of horses; insomuch that the Pashas and grandees throughout Asiatic Turkey make it a rule to have always a couple of them in their service. They curry the horse three or four times a day, and devote so much of their time and trouble to it, that it is usual in all parts of Egypt to have as many grooms as horses in the stable, each groom having the peculiar charge of one horse only.

The Wahaby chief, who possesses, indisputably, the finest stud of horses in the whole East, never allows his mares to be mounted until they have completed their fourth year. The common Bedouins, however, frequently ride them even before they have attained their third year.

It has been forbidden by the Wahaby chief, that his Arabs should sell one third of a mare, as frequently is practised by the Northern Aenezes. He alleges, that this custom often leads to unlawful and cheating tricks: but he permits the selling of one half of the mare. (See the preceding remarks on horses, p. 115.)

Camels.—(See p. 110.)

Between the races of camels in the northern and southern countries, there is a considerable difference. In Syria and Mesopotamia they are covered by thick hair, and in general attain to a much greater size than in Hedjaz, where they have very little wool. The Nubian camel has short hair like a deer, as likewise the Nubian sheep which prevents the Bedouins of that country from living under tents, (fabricated in Arabia from goat's and camel's hair), they are therefore obliged to construct portable huts made of mats and reeds; the Arabian camels are generally brown: many black camels are seen also among them. The further we approach the south in Egypt, the lighter becomes the colour. Towards Nubia the camels are mostly white, and I never saw a black one in that country.

The largest camels are those from Anadolia, of the Turkman

breed: the smallest that I have seen are those from Yemen. In the Eastern Desert the camels reputed best for carriage, are those of the Beni Tay, in Mesopotamia, near the river Euphrates. In mountainous countries camels are certainly scarce; but it is an erroneous opinion to think that camels are not capable of ascending hills. Thus in Hedjaz their numbers are very limited, because pasture is scanty. The country most rich and abundant in camels, is undoubtedly Nedjd, entitled on that account *Om el Bel*, or "The mother of camels." It furnishes Syria, Hedjaz, and Yemen with camels, which in those countries are worth double the price paid originally for them in Nedjd. During my residence in Hedjaz, a good camel was there estimated at the price of sixty dollars; and such was the want of pasturage and scarcity of provisions, that within three years, upon a moderate calculation, there died thirty thousand camels belonging to the Pasha of Egypt, at that time commanding in Hedjaz.

The Turkmans and Kurds from Anadolia purchase, every year, eight or ten thousand camels in the Syrian deserts, of which the greater number are brought there by dealers from Nedjd. They use them in propagating the breed of Turkman camels called *Maya* (see the former account).

No country in the East is so remarkable for the rapid propagation of camels as Nedjd, during years of fertility. The Nedjd camels are likewise less susceptible of epidemic diseases (and especially the *Djam*, which is much dreaded in various quarters of the Desert,) than any others; and on that account principally they are preferred by the Bedouins, who from the most distant parts of Arabia repair to Nedjd that they may renew their flocks.

Among the Bedouins, female camels are always more esteemed and dearer than the males. In Syria and Egypt, on the contrary, where the camels are chiefly wanted for their strength in bearing heavy loads, the males are most valued. The people who inhabit the towns and villages of Nedjd ride only she-camels on their journies, because these support thirst better than the males; but the Bedouins generally prefer he-camels for riding. The common load of an Arabian camel is from four to five hundred pounds upon a short journey, and from three to four hundred pounds on a journey of considerable distance. The camels employed between Djidda and Tayf in the year 1814, or 1815, for carrying provisions to Mohammed Aly, had loads not exceeding two hundred and fifty pounds. The well-fed and well-watered Egyptian camels are equal in strength to the Anadolian; those of the largest size at Cairo will carry three bales of coffee, or fifteen hundred weight, from the town to the water side, about three miles distant. From Cairo to Suez, the same camels will carry ten hundred weight; and that space is a journey of three days. The longer the journey to be undertaken, and the fewer wells to be found on the way, the lighter are the loads. The Darfur camels are distinguished for their size and great strength in bearing fatigue under heavy loads; in this latter quality they surpass all the camels of North-Eastern Africa. Those which accompany the Darfur caravan to Egypt, are seldom loaded with more than four quintals. The Sennár camels generally carry three and a half, and are not equal in size to those of Darfur.

The capability of bearing thirst varies considerably among the different races of camels. The Anadolian, accustomed to cold climates, and countries copiously watered on all sides, must, every second day, have its supply of water; and if this be withheld in summer-time until the third day, on a journey, the camel often sinks under the privation. During the winter, in Syrian latitudes and in the Northern Arabian Desert, camels very seldom drink unless when on a journey; the first succulent herbs sufficiently moisten their stomachs at that season of the year. In summer-time the Nedjd camel must be watered on the evening of every fourth day; a longer exposure to thirst on a journey would probably be fatal to him.

I believe that all over Arabia four whole days constitute the utmost extent to which camels can stretch their capability of enduring thirst in summer; nor is it necessary that they should be compelled to thirst longer, for there is no territory in the route of any traveller crossing Arabia where wells are farther distant than a journey of three entire days, or three and a half. In case of absolute necessity, an Arabian camel might perhaps go five days without drinking, but the traveller must never reckon upon such an extraordinary circumstance; and after the camel has gone three whole days without water, it shows manifest signs of great distress.

The indigenous Egyptian camels are less qualified to endure fatigue than any others that I know: being from their birth well watered and fed on the fertile banks of the river Nile, they are but little accustomed to journies in the Desert of any considerable length; and during the pilgrims' march to Mekka, several of them daily perish. There are not, of any race, camels that bear thirst more patiently than those of Darfur. The caravans coming from that country to Egypt, must travel nine or ten days' journies on a route which does not furnish any water; and over this extent of ground they often pass during the heats of summer. It is true that many of the camels die upon the road, and no merchant undertakes such an expedition without a couple of spare camels in reserve; but the greater number reach Egypt. There is not the slightest probability that an Arabian camel could ever perform such a journey, and still less a Syrian or Egyptian. The camels in most parts of Africa are more hardy than the Arabian.

Although I have often heard anecdotes related of Arabs, who on their long journies were frequently reduced to the utmost distress by want of water, yet I never understood that a camel had been slaughtered for the sake of finding a supply in its stomach. Without absolutely denying the possibility of such a circumstance, I do not hesitate to affirm that it can have occurred but very seldom; indeed the last stage of thirst renders a traveller so unwilling and unable to support the exertion of walking, that he continues his journey on the back of his camel in hopes of finding water, rather than expose himself to certain destruction by killing the serviceable creature. I have frequently seen camels slaughtered, but never discovered in the stomachs of any, except those which had been watered on the same day, a copious supply of water. The Dàrfur caravans are often reduced to incredible suffering by want of water; yet they never have resort to the expedient above mentioned. It may perhaps be practised in other parts of Africa, but it seems unknown in Arabia; nor have I ever heard, either in Arabia or Nubia, that camel's urine mixed with water was used to allay the creature's thirst in cases of extreme distress.

What is called in Egypt and Africa *hedjein*, and in Arabia *deloul*, (both terms signifying the camels trained for riding,) is in fact the same race with the heavy carrying beast, distinguished from the latter only as a hunter is from a coach-horse. Whenever an Arab perceives in one of his young camels any indication of its being small and extremely active, he trains it for the purposes of riding; and if it be a female, he takes care to match her with a fine well-bred male. For the temporary use of a male camel on such occasions the price is one dollar, among the Arabian Bedouins; being the same price that is paid for the similar services of a hired stallion. The breeds which I have mentioned are those of heavy transport camels, as well as the lighter kind destined for the saddle.

In Arabia, the best camels for riding, those of the most swift and easy trot, are said to be in the province of *Oman*. The *deloul el Omány*, is celebrated in all the songs of the Arabs. While I was at Djidda, Mohammed Aly Pasha received two of those camels as a present from the Imám of Maskat; they were sent by sea. In their appearance it would not perhaps have been easy to distinguish them from other Arabian camels; their legs, however, were somewhat more straight and slender; but there was in their eyes a noble expression, and something in the whole deportment, by which, among all animals, the generous may be distinguished from the common breed. Of other *delouls* in Arabia, the breeds most esteemed are those belonging to the tribes of Howeytat, of Sebaa (an Aeneze family), and of Sherarat. In North-Eastern Africa, where the deloul is called *hedjein*, the Sennár breed and that of the Nubian Bedouins are much preferred to any others for riding. The Darfur camels are by much too heavy to be used as hedjeins for the purposes of saddle-riding.

The good Nubian hedjeins are so very docile, and have so swift and pleasant an amble, that they supply the want of horses better than any other camels; most of them are whitish. In swiftness they surpass any of the various camels that I have seen throughout those parts of the East.

The name of *oshāry* (implying a camel that travels in one day a ten days' journey) is known in Egypt and Nubia, where incredible stories are related concerning a race of camels that were accustomed to perform very wonderful expeditions. I have reason to doubt whether they ever existed but in the imagination of fanciful Bedouins. Were I to repeat the tales of Arabian and Nubian Bedouins on this subject, the circumstances would appear similar to those which too credulous travellers report of the Barbary camels, or a particular breed of them; circumstances which I shall never believe until they can be ascertained beyond doubt, and proved to be facts. An Ababde Bedouin told me once, at

Assouan, that his grand-father went on some occasion from that place in one day to Siout, a journey of at least two hundred and fifty miles; and that the camel which had performed such an expedition, was not in the slightest degree fatigued. But I never could positively ascertain an instance of greater swiftness than what I shall immediately mention, and am persuaded that very few camels in Egypt or Nubia are capable of such an exertion.

The greatest performance of a hedjein that ever came to my knowledge, satisfactorily ascertained on credible authority, is that of a camel belonging to a Mamelouk Bey of Esne, in Upper Egypt, which he had purchased from a Bisharein chief for one hundred and fifty Spanish dollars. This camel was to go for a wager, in one day between sun-rise and sun-set, from Esne to Genne and back again, the whole distance being equal to a space of one hundred and twenty-five miles. It arrived about four o'clock in the afternoon at a village sixteen miles distant from Esne, where its strength failed, after having travelled about one hundred and fifteen miles in eleven hours, and twice passed over the Nile in a ferry-boat; this passage across the river requiring at least twenty minutes. A good English trotting mare could do the same, or perhaps more, but probably not in such a warm climate as that of Egypt. Without so much forced exertion, that camel would probably have gone a distance of one hundred and eighty or even two hundred miles within the space of twenty-four hours; which, according to the slow rate of caravan-travelling, might be reckoned as equivalent to ten days' journies; therefore, the boast above mentioned, of performing a journey of ten days in one day, may not appear altogether extravagant.

But it would be absurd to suppose any beast capable of running ten times, for an entire day, as a man could go on foot during the same space of time; and the swiftness of a camel never approaches, for short distances, even to that of a common horse. The gallop of a camel (which is not that quadruped's natural pace) it can never sustain above half an hour, and its forced exertion in galloping never produces a degree of speed equal to that of an ordinary horse. The forced trot of a camel is not so contrary to his nature, and he will support it for several hours without evincing many symptoms of being distressed. But even of that forced trot I must here remark, that it is much less expeditious than the same pace of a moderately good horse, and I believe that the rate of twelve miles an hour is the utmost degree of celerity in trotting that the very best hedjein can accomplish; it may perhaps gallop at fullest speed eight or even nine miles in half an hour, but it cannot support so violent an exertion for any longer time.

It is not, therefore, by extreme celerity that the hedjeins or delouls are distinguished, however surprising may be the stories related on that subject, both in Europe and in the East. But they are perhaps unequalled by any quadrupeds for the ease with which they carry their rider during an uninterrupted journey of several days and nights, when they are allowed to persevere in their own favourite pace, which is a kind of gentle and easy amble, at the rate of about five miles or five miles and a half in the hour. To describe this pleasant ambling pace, the Arabs say of a good deloul, " His back is so soft that you may drink a cup of coffee while you ride upon him." At the rate above mentioned, if properly fed every evening (or in case of emergency only once in two days), the strong camel will continue ambling for five or six days. I know of camels that went from Baghdad to Sokhne (in the Desert of Aleppo) within the space of five days. This is a caravan journey of twenty-one days. Messengers sometimes arrive at Aleppo on the seventh day after they have left Baghdad, distant a journey of twenty-five days, according to the common calculation; and I have known couriers go from Cairo by land to

Mekka (forty-five days' usual journies) in eighteen days, without even changing their camels.

The first thing about which an Arab is solicitous respecting his camel, when going to undertake a long journey, is the hump. Should he find this well furnished with fat, the Arab knows that his camel will endure considerable fatigue even with a very moderate allowance of food, because he believes that, according to the Arabic saying, "The camel, during the time of that expedition, will feed upon the fat of its own hump." The fact is, that as soon as the hump subsides, the camel begins to desist from much exertion, and gradually yields to fatigue. After a long journey the creature almost loses the hump, and it requires three or four months of repose and copious nourishment to restore it; which, however, does not take place until long after the other parts of the body have been replenished with flesh. Few animals exhibit so rapid a conversion of food into fat, as camels. A few days' rest and plentiful nourishment produce a visible augmentation of flesh, while, on the contrary, a few days employed in travelling without food reduce the creature almost immediately to little more than a skeleton, excepting the hump, which resists the effects of fatigue and starvation much longer.

If a camel has reached the full degree of fatness, his hump assumes the shape of a pyramid, extending its base over the entire back, and occupying altogether one fourth of the creature's whole body. But none of this description are ever seen in cultivated districts, where camels are always, more or less, obliged to work. They are only found among the wealthy Bedouins in the interior of the Desert, who keep whole herds of camels merely for the purpose of propagating the breed, and seldom force more than a few of the herd to labour. In spring time, their camels, having been fed for a couple of months upon the tender verdure, increase so much in fat, that they no longer seem belonging to that species of the hard-labouring, caravan or peasant camel.

After the fore teeth of the camel have reached their full length, the first pair of back teeth appear in the beginning of the sixth year; but two years more must elapse before they attain their greatest size. Early in the eighth year the second pair of back teeth, standing behind, and quite separate from the other teeth, make their appearance; and when they are complete, in the tenth year, the third and last pair push forward, and, like the former, grow for two years. The camel, therefore, has not completed its full growth before the twelfth year, and then it is called *rás*. To know the age of a camel under that period, the back teeth are always inspected. The camel lives as long as forty years; but after twenty-five or thirty his activity begins to fail, and he is no longer capable of enduring much fatigue. If a camel that has passed his sixteenth year become lean, the Arabs say that he can never be again rendered fat; and in that case they generally sell him at a low price to the peasants, who feed their cattle better than the inhabitants of the Desert.

The common hedjein saddle in Egypt (very slightly differing from a horse-saddle) is called *ghabeit*. The hedjein saddle of the Nubians, imported likewise into Egypt, and very neatly worked in leather, is called *gissa*. The pack-saddle of the Egyptian peasant, different from that of the Arabians and Syrians, is called *shaghour*. (From this word the Arabians derive an opprobrious appellation, which they bestow upon the Egyptian peasants, whom they style *shaghaore*). The pack-saddles of the Libyan, Nubian, and Upper Egyptian Bedouins are called *Hawýe*, and are the same as those of the Arabians.

The deloul saddle is, throughout every part of Arabia, called *shedád*. The asses in Hedjaz are saddled with the *shedád*, differing only in proportionable size from that used with the deloul.

In Hedjaz the name of *shebrýe* is given to a kind of palanquin, having a seat made of twisted straw, about five feet in length, which is placed across the saddle of the camel, with ropes fastened to it. On its four sides are slender poles, joined above by cross bars, over which either mats or carpets are placed, to shade the traveller from the sun. This among the natives of Hedjaz is the favourite vehicle for travelling, because it admits of their stretching themselves at full length, and sleeping at pleasure.

Similar machines of the palanquin kind, but on a shorter and narrower scale, are placed lengthways on both sides of the camel's saddle, and then called *shekdef*. One person sits in each of them, but they do not allow of his stretching out at full length. Both of these shekdefs are covered, likewise, with carpets thrown across; and this vehicle is principally used for the conveyance of women.

Different from that is the *taht roán* (or rather *takht raván*, as the Persians, from whom the term is borrowed, call it); a litter carried by two camels, one before, and the other behind. In this kind of vehicle the great pilgrims travel: but it is more frequently used by the Turks than by the Arabians.

It is the fashion in Egypt to shear the hedjein as closely as a sheep is shorn; and this is done merely from a notion that it improves the beast's appearance. The French, during their occupation of Egypt, had established a corps of about five hundred camel-riders, whom they selected from the number of their most brave and excellent soldiers, and by means of whom they succeeded in checking the Bedouins. Many horsemen among the troops of the Pasha of Egypt have been ordered by him to keep hedjeins; and his son, Ibrahim Pasha, has about two hundred of his men mounted in that manner.

The hedjeins of Egypt are guided by a string attached to a nose-ring. Those of Arabia are very seldom perforated in the nose; and are more obedient to the short stick of the rider than to the bridle.

The Arab women, on all occasions, make a great display in the fitting-out of their camel-saddle. A woman of Nedjd would think herself degraded, were she to ride upon any other than a black camel; but, on the contrary, a lady of the Aenezes much prefers a grey or white camel.

The practice of mounting upon camels small swivel-guns, which turn upon the pommel of the saddle, is not known in Egypt. I have seen them in Syria; and they appear to be common in Mesopotamia and Baghdad. Although of little real service, yet against Arabs these small swivel-guns are a very excellent and appropriate weapon, more adapted to inspire them with terror than the heaviest pieces of artillery.

The price of a camel is found to vary in almost every place: thus, in Egypt, according to the abundance and cheapness of provisions, the price of the same camel may fluctuate from twelve to forty dollars. A good dromedary, or hedjein, from Nubia, sometimes will cost at Cairo eighty dollars. In Hedjaz very high prices are paid for camels; fifty and sixty dollars are sometimes given for a deloul of the most common kind. There is a considerable demand in Nedjd for delouls of the first quality. Saoud has been known to pay as much as three hundred dollars for an Omán camel.

The Arabs distinguish in their camels various defects and vices, that very much affect their value. The principal defect is called *el asaab*: this is in the camel's fetlock; and they regard it as incurable, and a proof of great weakness. The next is *el fekeh*, a strong tremor in the hind legs of the camel when it couches down, or rises up: this, likewise, is considered as a proof of weakness. *El serrar*, ulcerations below the chest; *el hellel, el fahoura*, and many others. Most of the caravan camels are broken-winded (or *sedreh khorbán*) from excessive fatigue, and the carrying of too heavy loads. When this circumstance occurs, the Arabs cauterise the camel's chest. They resort also to the same process, cautery, in cases of wounds on the camel's hump, and of injuries frequently occasioned by bad pack-saddles, and burdens of too great weight. Towards the close of a long journey scarcely any evening passes without the cauterising operation, yet the next morning the load is placed again upon the part so recently burnt: but no degree of pain induces the generous camel to refuse the load, or throw it on the ground. It cannot, however, be forced to rise, if from hunger or excessive fatigue its strength has failed.

Locusts.

It has been remarked in my different journals, that these destructive creatures are found in Egypt, all along the river Nile as far as Sennar, in the Nubian, and in all parts of the Arabian deserts. Those that I have seen in Upper Egypt came all from the north; those that I saw in Nubia were all said to have come from Upper Egypt. It seems, therefore, that such parts of Africa are not the native places of the locusts. In the year 1813, they devoured the whole harvest from Berber to Shendy in the Black countries; and in the spring of that same year I had seen whole flights of them in Upper Egypt, where they are particularly injurious to the palm-trees. These they strip of every leaf and green particle, the trees remaining like skeletons with bare branches.

In Arabia the locusts are known to come invariably from the

East, and the Arabs accordingly say that they are produced by the waters of the Persian Gulf. The province of Nedjd is particularly exposed to their ravages; they overwhelm it sometimes to such a degree, that having destroyed the harvest they penetrate by thousands into the private dwellings, and devour whatever they can find, even the leather of the water vessels. It has been observed, that those locusts which come from the East are not considered so formidable, because they only fix upon trees, and do not destroy the seed; but they soon give birth to a new brood, and it is the young locusts, before they are sufficiently grown to fly away, that consume the crops. According to general report, the locusts breed as often as three times in the year.

The Bedouins who occupy the peninsula of Sinai are frequently driven to despair by the multitudes of locusts, which constitute a land plague, and a most serious grievance. These animals arrive by way of Akaba (therefore from the East), towards the end of May, when the Pleiades are setting, according to observations made by the Arabs, who believe that the locusts entertain a considerable dread of that constellation. They remain there generally during a space of forty or fifty days, and then disappear for the rest of the year.

Some few are seen in the course of every year, but great flights every fourth or fifth year; such is the general course of their unwelcome visits. Since the year 1811, however, they have invaded the peninsula every successive season for five years, in considerable numbers.

All the Bedouins of Arabia, and the inhabitants of towns in Nedjd and Hedjaz, are accustomed to eat the locusts. I have seen at Medinah and Tayf locust-shops, where these animals were sold by measure. In Egypt and Nubia they are only eaten by the poorest beggars. The Arabs, in preparing locusts as an article of food, throw them alive into boiling water, with which a good deal of salt has been mixed; after a few minutes they are taken out, and dried in the sun; the head, feet, and wings are then torn off, the bodies are cleansed from the salt and perfectly dried; after which process whole sacks are filled with them by the Bedouins. They are sometimes eaten broiled in butter; and they often contribute materials for a breakfast, when spread over unleavened bread mixed with butter.

It may here seem worthy of remark, that among all the Bedouins with whom I have been acquainted in Arabia, those of Sinai alone do not use the locusts as an article of food.

MATERIALS

FOR A HISTORY OF

THE WAHÁBYS.

MATERIALS

FOR A HISTORY OF

THE WAHÁBYS.

INTRODUCTION.

RESPECTING the Wahábys, various contradictory and erroneous statements have been given in the few accounts hitherto published. Some anecdotes of those remarkable sectaries, collected from the best sources of information to which I could obtain access in the East, may prove interesting to many readers. I must, however, regret, that during my residence in Hedjáz this country was, on account of the war with Mohammed Aly, closed against the people of Nedjd, who, above all others, were qualified to give faithful and accurate details of the Waháhys; while those Bedouins of the common classes, who had adopted the new faith, were, in general, wholly ignorant of its true import and doctrines.

The religion and government of the Waháhys may be very briefly defined, as a Muselmán puritanism, and a Bedouin government, in which the great chief is both the political and religious leader of the nation, exercising his authority in the same manner as the followers of Mohammed did over his converted countrymen. The founder of this sect is already known: a learned Arabian, named *Abd el Waháb*, who had visited various schools of the principal cities in the East (as is much the practice with his countrymen even now), being convinced by what he had observed during his travels, that the primitive faith of *Islám*, or Mohammedism, had become totally corrupted, and obscured by abuses, and that the far greater part of the people of the East, and especially the Turks, might be justly regarded as heretics.

But new doctrines and opinions are as little acceptable in the East as they are in the West; and no attention was paid to *Abd el Waháb* until, after long wanderings in Arabia, he retired with his family to Derayeh, at the period when Mohammed Ibn Saoud was the principal person of the town. This man became his first convert, and soon after married his daughter. These two families, therefore, must not be mistaken for each other. Abd el Waháb, the founder of the sect, was, by birth, of the tribe of *Temym*, and of the clan called El Wahábe. The Beni Temym are, for the greater part, husbandmen in Nedjd; their principal place of abode is at El Howta, a village five days' journey from Derayeh, southerly, in the direction of Wady Dowasyr, and the birth-place of Abd el Waháb. Another colony of the Temym inhabit the town of *Keffár*, in the province of Djebel Shammar, and are the descendants of families who fled from Howta, in order to escape the consequences of the blood-revenge. A third colony are husbandmen, under the jurisdiction of the Pasha of Baghdad, in the villages between Helle and Meshed Aly. The Beni Temym are noted for their lofty stature, broad heads, and thick beards; characteristics which distinguish them from other Bedouins.

But the family of Saoud, the political founder of the Waháby government, is of the tribe of *Messálykh*, a branch of the Wold

Aly, and therefore belonging to the Aeneze. The clan of the Messálykh, called Mokren (مكرن) or, as the Bedouins also pronounce it, *Medjren*, to which Saoud belonged, had settled at Derayeh, and acquired influence there; and it was to them that Abd el Waháb addressed himself. Mohammed Ibn Saoud was the first who assumed the title of *Emír*; but his force was then so small, that in his first skirmish with some enemies, as it is related, he had only seven camel-riders with him.

To trace the history of this sect, is to record facts similar to those which are daily occurring in the Desert. A tribe is fortunate, rises into power, takes booty, and extends its influence over its neighbours. By unwearied exertions and efforts, Abd el Azyz and Ibn Saoud, the son and grandson of the first leader, Mohammed, succeeded in carrying their arms to the remotest corners of Arabia; and while they propagated their religious tenets, they established a supremacy of power conformably with these tenets, which taught the Arabs to acknowledge a spiritual and temporal leader in the same person, as they had done on the first promulgation of Islám. I shall resume their history, though I am unable to give with accuracy very few dates prior to the campaign of Mohammed Aly. But it seems necessary to begin by explaining the principles upon which the religion and government were founded.

The doctrines of Abd el Waháb were not those of a new religion; his efforts were directed only to reform abuses in the followers of Islám, and to disseminate the pure faith among Bedouins; who, although nominally Muselmáns, were equally ignorant of religion, as indifferent about all the duties which it prescribed. As generally has been the case with reformers, he was misunderstood both by his friends and his enemies. The latter, hearing of a new sect, which accused the Turks of heresy, and held their prophet, Mohammed, in much less veneration than they did, were easily persuaded that a new creed was professed, and that the Wahábys were consequently not merely heretics, but *káfirs*, or infidels. They were the more confirmed in this belief, first by the artifices of the Sherif Gháleb of Mekka, and secondly, by the alarm raised among all the neighbouring Pashas. The Sherif of Mekka, who had always been a determined enemy of the growing Waháby power, had an interest in widening the breach between the new sectaries and the Turkish empire, and therefore artfully and unremittingly spread reports of the Wahábys being really infidels, in order to render abortive all attempts at negotiation with them. The Pashas of Baghdad, Damascus, and Cairo, who were nearest to the dreaded Bedouins, were no less eager in representing under the blackest colours, the designs of these enemies of the Turkish abuses, and as they consequently inferred, of the Turkish faith. They had either to conduct, or to send an escort with the pilgrim caravans to the holy cities, and it became their interest to magnify the dangers on the road, in order to be excused if any accident should befall the caravan, or to be justified in keeping it back, which they secretly wished to do, as the departure of the caravans subjects all these Pashas to very great expenses. Added to this, were the reports of many hadjys or pilgrims who had gone by sea to Djidda and Mekka, and had suffered from the insolence of the Waháby soldiers, and in some instances were not permitted to perform the pilgrimage. Upon their return, they exaggerated their sufferings, and a description of the Waháby could not, certainly, be given by them with impartiality. We need not, therefore, be surprised if it became generally believed throughout the East, that the Waháby were endeavouring to establish an entirely new religion, and that they treated all Turks with increased cruelty because they were Muselmáns—a belief which the conduct of the great body of the Waháby themselves was not calculated to invalidate. These were Bedouins who, before they knew Wahábyism, had been almost wholly ignorant of Islám, and whose notions of it now were very imperfect. The new doctrines were therefore likely to appear to them as a new religion, and especially so, when they learned the different customs and tenets of the Turkish hadjys, and the Arabian inhabitants of towns, and compared them with their own. The spirit of fanaticism which their chief fostered by all the means in his power, did not permit them to draw nice distinctions in a matter about which they had themselves very imperfect notions; and this satisfactorily explains, how it happened that they accused the Turks of being infidels, and were in their turn treated by the latter as such. The few intelligent Syrians or Egyptians, who, having been on the pilgrimage, had found opportunities to converse with the well-informed sectaries, might probably be convinced that the Bedouin creed was that of Islam; and although the opinions of both parties might not agree in all points, yet they felt the injustice of calling the Wahábys infidels. But the testimony of such persons, if they ever dared to give it, without exposing themselves to the charge of being bad Muselmáns, was unavailing in the general outcry; and especially after the year 1803, when the hadj caravans were finally interrupted, an opinion prevailed generally, that the Wahabys were determined enemies of the Muselmán religion. In two short treatises on the Wahabys, written at Baghdad and Aleppo, about 1808,* by M. Rousseau, it is positively asserted, that the Wahabys have a new religion, and that although they acknowledge the Koran, yet they have entirely abolished the pilgrimage to Mekka. This was certainly the vulgar opinion about that time at Aleppo; but more accurate information might have easily been obtained from intelligent pil-

---

* The first is the "Description of the Pashalick of Baghdad," the other a Memoir in the "Mines de l'Orient."

grims and Bedouins even in that town; and it is surprising that it should not, as the author was professedly giving a description of the Wahabys, and as he states that he derived part of his information "du Chapelain de Saoud," implying an office in the court of Derayeh, respecting the nature of which I am not able to form any exact notion.

Since the army of Mohammed Aly established itself in Hedjaz, and the intrigues of Sherif Gháleb became no longer of any avail, direct communications too having been opened with the Waháby chiefs as well as with the inferior leaders, and the pilgrim-caravans having resumed their ancient route, the real character of the Wahábys is better known, even in the distant parts of the Turkish dominions; and the gratitude which the people of Mekka express towards their temporary masters, is likely to impress with the most favourable ideas, every pilgrim who there inquires after the new sect.

If farther proof were required that the Wahabys are very orthodox Muselmáns, their catechism would furnish it. When Saoud took possession of Mekka, he distributed copies of this catechism among the inhabitants, and ordered that the pupils in public schools should learn it by heart. Its contents are nothing more than what the most orthodox Turk must admit to be true. Saoud entertained an absurd notion, that the town's-people were brought up in entire ignorance of their religion, and therefore wished to instruct those of Mekka in its first principles. Nothing, however, was contained in this catechism which the Mekkans had not already learned; and when Saoud found that they were better informed than his own people, he desisted from further disseminating it among them.

The chief doctrines of the Wahabys, it will be seen, correspond with those taught in other parts of the Muselman empire. The Koran and the traditions of Mohammed (*Sunne*) are acknowledged as fundamental, comprising the laws; and the opinions of the best commentators on the Koran are respected, although not implicitly followed. In the attempt, however, to exhibit the primitive practices and pure dogmas of the original founder of Islám and of his first followers, as established upon these laws, they were naturally led to condemn a number of false opinions and corruptions which had crept into Islám as at this day taught, and also to point out the numerous cases in which Turks acted in direct opposition to the precepts they themselves acknowledged to be indispensable. I am not qualified by a sufficient knowledge of the controversy, to present my reader with full details on this head, and shall therefore confine myself to the notice of a few instances, which are considered as the chief points of dispute between the two parties: the Wahábys reproach the Turks with honouring the prophet, in a manner which approaches adoration, and with doing the same also to the memory of many saints. In this they seem not to be much mistaken. By once admitting the Koran as their revealed law, the Turks were obliged to believe implicitly the numerous passages wherein it is expressly declared that Mohammed is a mortal like themselves: but the fanatic love for their prophet could not be content with this modest declaration; their learned men proved with sophistical subtlety that the prophet, although dead and buried, had not shared the common lot of mortals, but was still alive; that his access to the Almighty, and his being dearly beloved by him, rendered it easy for him to protect or recommend any of his faithful adherents. Though Turks never address any distinct prayers to their prophet, yet they pronounce his name, as if to invoke him, in the same manner as we say "O Lord!" and this was enough to draw upon them the severe reprehension of the Wahabys. They moreover visited his tomb, with the same devotion as they do the great temple of Mekka, and, when standing before it, uttered aloud their impious invocations, as the Wahabys called them; so that they fully deserved the opprobrious appellation of infidels, who associate an inferior divinity with the Almighty.

In similar respect are held many sheikhs, or saints, but not to the same extent. In every Turkish town are many tombs; and in almost every village at least one tomb of some renowned saint, whose exemplary life, (that is, great cunning or hypocrisy,) and sometimes great learning, had procured for him the reputation of sanctity. Their countrymen thought it incumbent on them to honour their memory, by erecting small buildings, with cupolas or vaulted roofs over their tombs, and in these places particularly to offer up their prayers to the Divinity, in the belief that the saint would thus be more inclined to second their supplications before the throne of the Almighty. In fact, the Mohammedan saints are venerated as highly as those of the Catholic church, and are said to perform as many miracles as the latter. The people of the East are extremely attached to their sheikhs; and in every town and village there is annually, on a fixed day, a festival in honour of its particular patron.* The Wahabys declared, that all men were equal in the eyes of God; that even the most virtuous could not intercede with him; and that it was, consequently, sinful to to invoke departed saints, and to honour their mortal remains more than those of any other persons. Wherever the Wahabys carried their arms, they destroyed all the domes and ornamented tombs; a circumstance which served to inflame the fanaticism of their disciples, and to form a marked distinction between them and their opponents, which it has always been the policy of every founder of a sect to establish, and which was the more necessary

---

* Saints were formerly as much venerated in the Desert as in the towns. The Bedouins were accustomed to kill victims in honour of a saint, and to visit his tomb in a manner not much different from the pagan sacrifices to idols.

with the common mass of the Wahabys, who are not capable of judging accurately on the other points of dispute.

The destruction of cupolas and tombs of saints became the favourite taste of the Wahabys. In Hedjaz, Yemen, Mesopotamia, and Syria, this was always the first result of their victory; and as many domes formed the roofs of mosques, they were charged with destroying these also. At Mekka, not a single cupola was suffered to remain over the tomb of any renowned Arab: those even covering the birth-place of Mohammed, and of his grandsons, Hassan and Hosseyn, and of his uncle, Abou Táleb, and his wife, Khadydje, were all broken down. While in the act of destroying them, the Wahabys were heard to exclaim, "God have mercy upon those who destroyed, and none upon those who built them!" The Turks, who heard of these ravages, naturally believed that they were committed through disrespect for the persons to whose honour they had been erected, and disbelief in their sanctity. Even the large dome over the tomb of Mohammed, at Medinah, was destined to share a similar fate. Saoud had given orders that it should be demolished; but its solid structure defied the rude efforts of his soldiers; and after several of them had been killed by falling from the dome, the attempt was given up. This the inhabitants of Medinah declared to have been done through the interposition of Heaven.

The negligence of the far greater part of the Turks towards their religious laws, except what relates to prayer, purification, or fasting, was another subject against which the founder of the Wahaby sect inveighed. Alms to the poor, as enjoined by the law; the sumptuary regulations instituted by Mohammed; the severity and impartiality of justice, for which the first Khalifahs were so much distinguished; the martial spirit which was enjoined by the law to be constantly upheld against the enemies of the faith, or the infidels; the abstaining from whatever might inebriate, unlawful commerce with women, practices contrary to nature, and various others, were so many precepts not only entirely disregarded by the modern Turks, but openly violated with impunity. The scandalous conduct of many hadjys who polluted the sacred cities with their infamous lusts; the open license which the chiefs of the caravans gave to debauchery, and all the vices which follow in the train of pride and selfishness; the numerous acts of treachery and fraud perpetrated by the Turks, were all held up by the Wahabys as specimens of the general character of unreformed Muselmáns; and presented a sad contrast to the purity of morals and manners to which they themselves aspired, and to the humility with which the pilgrim is bound to approach the holy Kaaba. Enthusiastically attached to the primitive doctrines of his religion, justly indignant at seeing those doctrines corrupted by the present Muselmáns, and feeling, perhaps, no small degree of spite at having been treated with scorn in the Turkish towns, wherever he preached against disorders, Abd el Waháb, the founder of the sect, professed nothing but a desire to bring back his adherents to that state of religion, morals, and manners, which, as he had learnt from the best historical and theological works of his nation, prevailed when Islám was first promulgated in Arabia. As this code of law was evidently framed for Bedouins, the reformers found it the more easily re-adapted to the same people; and thus showed how little the foreigners, or Turks, had sacrificed their own northern manners to the true spirit of Islam. Not a single new precept was to be found in the Wahaby code. Abd el Waháb took as his sole guide the Koran and the Sunne (or the laws formed upon the traditions of Mohammed); and the only difference between his sect and orthodox Turks, however improperly so termed, is, that the Wahabys rigidly follow the same laws which the others neglect, or have ceased altogether to observe. To describe, therefore, the Wahaby religion, would be to recapitulate the Muselmán faith; and to show in what points this sect differs from the Turks, would be to give a list of all the abuses of which the latter are guilty. I am strongly warranted in giving this statement, by the opinion of several of the first olemas of Cairo. In the autumn of 1815, two envoys were sent to that city by the Wahaby chief, one of whom was a perfect Wahaby scholar. Mohammed Ali Pasha wished them to give an explanation of their tenets to the principal learned men of Cairo; they, in consequence, met repeatedly; and the Wahaby had invariably the best of the controversy, because he proved every proposition by a sentence of the Koran, and the Hadyth, or Tradition, the whole of which he knew by heart, and which were of course irrefragable authority. The olemas declared, that they could find no heresy in the Wahabys; and as this was a declaration made in spite of themselves, it is the less to be suspected. A book had also been received at Cairo, containing various treatises on religious subjects, written by Abd el Wahab himself: it was read by many olemas, and they declared unanimously, that if such were the opinions of the Wahabys, they themselves belonged altogether to that creed.

As the fanatic mob of a new sect can seldom be impressed with the true spirit of its founder, it happened that the greater part of the followers of Abd el Wahab considered as chief points of doctrine such as were rather accessories, and thus caused their enemies to form very erroneous notions of the supposed new religion. Next to the war which they declared against saints, their fanaticism was principally turned against dress, and the smoking of tobacco. The rich Turkish costume is little in accordance with the precepts of the Sunne, where silk is absolutely prohibited, as well as gold and silver, except the latter, in small quantity. The Wahabys beheld the gaudy robes of the Turkish pilgrims with disdain; and as they knew that the Prophet had worn an abba like them, and had prohibited sumptuous apparel, they considered it to be as necessary to follow his mode of dress, as his moral precepts. It was by the dress that Wahabys could be immediately recognised in Arabia. An Arab who had not embraced this creed, would assuredly have some part of his dress of silk; either the kerchief round his head would be interwoven with silk, or his gown would be sewed with silk. Respecting the smoking of tobacco, it is well known that many Turkish olemas have repeatedly, in their writings, declared it to be a forbidden practice. One of the four orthodox sects of the Muselmáns, the Malekys, have declared it "hateful." A great number of olemas in every part of Turkey abstain from it on religious principles. The Wahaby wished also to prevent the smoking of intoxicating plants, much used in the East, being directly against the Koran, but which could not well be prevented, while the pipe was suffered. He must, at the same time, have been aware, that his followers, in making so great a sacrifice as abstinence from smoking, would naturally become the more bitter enemies to all those who still indulged in that luxury, and had not yet embraced their creed. The prohibition of tobacco has been one of the principal means of inflaming the minds of the Wahabys against the Turks: it has become a rallying word to the proselytes; but of all the precepts taught by the reformers, it has been the most reluctantly complied with by the Arabs. Another prohibited act is praying over the rosary, a general practice with moslems, though not founded on the law. The Wahabys declared it to be an unwarrantable practice, and abolished it. It has been stated that they likewise prohibited the drinking of coffee; this, however, is not the fact, they have always used it to an immoderate degree.

It is much to be doubted whether Abd el Wahab, when he preached reform at Derayah, had any idea of establishing a new dynasty to reign over the proselytes of Arabia. The strength of his own and of his relations' families did not authorise him in undertaking such a measure, which seems to have gained ground only during the life of Abd el Azyz, the son of Mohammed Ibn Saoud. In delivering his new doctrines to the Arabs, it cannot be denied that Abd el Waháb conferred on them a great blessing; nor was the form of government that ensued unfavourable to the interests and prosperity of the whole Arabian nation. Whether the commonly received doctrine considered as orthodox, or that of the Wahabys, should be pronounced the true Mohammedan religion, is, after all, a matter of little consequence; but it became important to suppress that infidel indifference which had pervaded all Arabia and a great part of Turkey, and which has a more baneful effect on the morals of a nation than the decided acknowledgment even of a false religion. The merit, therefore, of the Wahabys, in my opinion, is not that they purified the existing religion, but that they made the Arabs strictly observe the positive precepts of one certain religion; for although the Bedouins at all times devoutly worshipped the Divinity, yet the deistical principles alone could not be deemed sufficient to instruct a nation so wild and ungovernable in the practice of morality and justice.

A desire of reducing the Arabs to the state in which they were when the founder of their religion existed, naturally induced Abd el Waháb and his successors to alter likewise their political condition as soon as they perceived that their proselytes increased. Mohammed, and after him the Khalifahs, were the spiritual as well as the political leaders of their nation; and the code of Muselmán law shows in every page how necessary is the existence of a supreme chief in religious and in civil affairs. Nedjd, which became the principal seat of the Wahaby power, was divided into a number of small territories, cities, and villages, totally independent of each other, and constantly engaged in warfare. No law but that of the strongest was acknowledged either in the open country or within the walls of towns, and personal security was always purchased at the price of individual property. Besides this, the wild freedom of the neighbouring Bedouin tribes, their endless wars and predatory expeditions, rendered Nedjd and the surrounding country a scene of perpetual disorder and bloodshed. It was not until after many hard struggles that Abd el Azyz extended at last his religion over the whole of Nedjd; and being then no longer the chief of a tribe, but of a province, he assumed the supreme power, and assimilated his authority to that which was exercised by the first followers of Mohammed.

To enslave his countrymen would have been a fruitless attempt; he left them in the enjoyment of their freedom, but obliged them to live in peace, to respect property, and to obey the decisions of the law.

Thus in process of time the Wahaby chief became governor of the greater part of Arabia; his government was free, because it was founded upon the system of a Bedouin commonwealth. He was the head of all the sheikhs of tribes whose respective politics he directed, while all the Arabs remained within their tribes completely independent and at liberty, except that they were now obliged to observe the strict sense of the law, and liable to punishment if they infringed it. Formerly an Arab acknowledged no rule but his own will; he was forced by the Wahaby chief to obey the ancient Muselmán laws. These enjoined him to give tithes or tribute to the great chief, and that he should be at all times ready to join his ranks in any expedition against heretics or infidels. It was not allowed, that in a dispute with his neighbours an appeal should be made to arms, and a tribunal was fixed, before which all litigations should be decided. Such were the main objects of the Wahaby chiefs. Tribute, military conscription, internal peace, and rigid administration of justice. They had completely succeeded in carrying these measures into execution, and seemed to be firmly established, when the efforts of Mohammed Aly, and his gold, rather than the valour of his troops, weakened their power and reduced them to the state in which they had been several years before. I shall now enter into further details concerning this interesting government; details founded on the most accurate statements that I could obtain from many well-informed people in Hedjaz.

Of Saoud's person and family.

Saoud, chief propagator of the new doctrine, was eldest son of Abd el Azyz, who was assassinated in the year 1803. Besides Saoud, his mother, the daughter of Abd el Wahab, had two sons, Abderrahman and Abdallah. Saoud died, aged forty-five or fifty, in April 1814, of a fever, at Derayeh; and to his death may be attributed the misfortunes which befel his nation soon after. He is said to have been a remarkably handsome man, with one of those fine countenances for which his family has been distinguished. He wore a longer beard than is generally seen among Bedouins, and so much hair about his mouth that the people of Derayeh called him *Abou Showáreb*, or the " Father of Mustachios."

All the Arabs, even his enemies, praise Saoud for his wisdom in counsel and his skill in deciding litigations; he was very learned in the Muselmán law; and the rigour of his justice, although it disgusted many of his chiefs, endeared him to the great mass of his Arabs. From the time that his reign began, he never fought personally in battle; but always directed his army from a position at some distance in the rear. It is related by the Arabs, that he once fought in a battle when only twelve years old, by the side of his father Abd el Azyz.

By his first wife, now dead, he had eight children; of these the oldest is Abdallah, who during his father's life-time occupied the second place in his dominions, and after his death succeeded to the supreme government. It is related that at the early age of five years Abdallah could gallop his mare; and he is more eminent for courage than his father, as he made it a constant rule to fight every where in person. During the life of Saoud, the mental qualities of his son, Abdallah, were described as of the first order, and he was regarded as a prodigy of wisdom and sagacity; but the measures which he adopted in opposing Mohammed Aly seem to prove that he by no means possessed such abilities as his father in those respects. He is esteemed in the Desert on account of his liberality and his social manners. He married a girl of the Záb Arabs, in the province of Hassa. Of his brethren, the most celebrated among the Arabs, is *Faysal*, reputed the handsomest man in Derayeh, and the most amiable. To him the Arabs are much attached. He has fought many battles in Hedjaz against the Turkish troops. *Nászer* was the favourite son of Saoud; he fell in an expedition against Maskat. *El Turky* often commanded flying corps of Wahabys in Irak and towards Syria. By his third wife, Saoud had three sons, *Omar, Ibrahím*, and *Feheyd*.

Saoud never permitted his children to exercise any influence in public affairs, except Abdallah, who participated in all his counsels. But he was extremely attached to them. The inhabitants of Mekka still relate with pleasure, that at the time of the pilgrimage, Saoud was once sitting under the gate of the Kaaba, while his people were covering that edifice with the new cloth, and numerous pilgrims were engaged in their sacred walk around it. At that moment the wife of his son Feheyd appeared, holding in her arms one of his young children. She had just arrived at Mekka for the pilgrimage, and hastened towards Saoud that she might present to him the infant whom he had not before seen. He took it from her, kissed it affectionately, and in presence of all the assembled pilgrims pressed it to his bosom for a considerable time.

Besides his wife, Saoud had, according to the custom of great people in Nedjd, several Abyssinian female slaves or concubines; he resided with all his family in a large mansion built by his father on the declivity of the mountain, a little above the town of Derayeh. All his children, with their families, and all his brothers had their separate ranges of apartments in that building. Of his brothers he is said to have entertained some jealousy; he never appointed them to any post of confidence, nor did he permit them to leave Derayeh. In this house he kept his treasures, and received all those who came on business to Derayeh. There the great emírs, or chiefs of considerable tribes, were lodged and feasted on their arrival, while people of inferior rank resided with their acquaintances in the town; but if they came on business they might dine or sup at the chief's house, and bring from it a daily allowance of food for their horses or camels. It may easily be conceived, that the palace was constantly full of guests.

Saoud granted ready admission to every person; but to obtain a private interview without his especial desire, was rather difficult. He had several Egyptians who served as porters, and for a bribe would admit people into the interior apartments at unusual hours. The surest mode of obtaining private access was to wait before the inner apartment until some great sheikh passed, and to enter with his attendants. Saoud gave public audiences early in the morning, between three and six o'clock in the afternoon, and again late in the evening. After supper he regularly assembled in the great room all his sons who happened to be at Derayeh;

and all those, who were desirous of paying court to him, joined this family circle. One of the olemas then read a few pages of the Koran, or the Traditions of Mohammed, and explained the text according to the commentaries of the best writers. After him, other olemas delivered lectures in the same manner, and Saoud himself always closed the meeting by taking the book and explaining every difficult passage. It is said that he equalled, or perhaps excelled, any of the olemas in his knowledge of religious controversy and of the law in general. His eloquence was universally admired; his voice remarkably sonorous and sweet at the same time, which made the Arabs say, that " his words all reached the heart." Upon those occasions, Saoud was the only speaker; but it often happened that points of law were to be discussed, and these sometimes excited his impatience and induced him to argue with great vehemence, deriding his adversary, and taunting him for his ignorance in controversy. Thus, having continued about an hour, Saoud generally concluded by saying, " *Wa Allahou aálem*"—" God knows best ;" and those who had no particular business understood that expression as the signal for departure, and persons who had business with him remained until two hours after sun-set: these assemblies took place every evening.

Saoud was extremely indignant when any Arab endeavoured to deceive him by a falsehood. On such occasions, he sometimes seized a stick, and belaboured the man himself; but of these passionate fits he soon repented, and desired the by-standers always to interpose and prevent him from striking any person whenever they should see him angry; this was frequently done, and he expressed his thanks for the interference.

During his residence at Derayeh, Saoud very rarely left his house, except when he went on Fridays to the neighbouring mosque. The Arabs imputed this seclusion to fear, supposing that he apprehended the fate by which his father perished—

assassination; and he certainly had enemies enough among the Arabs, anxious to avenge the blood of relations shed by him, and ready to conspire against his life, if they could see any possibility of succeeding in their attempts to kill him. But his friends declared, that he was occupied the whole day at home in study. It is well known, that for several years after the death of his father, Saoud constantly wore a coat of mail under his shirt. The inhabitants of Mekka relate, that during his stay in that city he was always surrounded by a chosen guard, and that no stranger dared to approach him alone. He would not even go to the great mosque, nor perform the circuit of the holy Kaaba without a numerous train of followers: and he chose his seat during prayers in the mosque, not as persons of distinction generally do, in the *Mekám el Hanbaly*, but mounted the roof of the *Bír*, or Well of *Zemzem*, as a more safe position, and he prayed upon that roof which forms the *Mekám el Shafey*.

Not only in his own palace, but throughout his dominions, he desired that persons should remain seated when he appeared; and at his evening assemblies (*madjlis*), every body sat down where he could find a convenient place, although it was generally understood that the great emírs should take their seats next to Saoud. His younger sons sat among the crowd, paying due attention to all that was said, but never speaking themselves. The Arabs who entered, usually shook hands with Saoud, having previously hailed him with the salutation of peace, and he politely inquired after the health and affairs of all whom he knew in the room. The great sheikh on arriving at Saoud's residence, exchanged a kiss with him, according to Bedouin custom. In addressing him no pompous title was used; the people merely said, "O Saoud!" or " O father of Abdallah!" or " O father of Mustachios!" he, too, called every man by his name without any ceremonious or complimentary phrases, which are so numerous among Eastern nations in general.

In his dress, Saoud did not affect any distinction from his own Arabs; he only wore an abba, a shirt, and a keffie, or head-kerchief: yet it is said that he chose these articles from among the finest that Derayeh could afford; that he was scrupulously clean, and had his keffie constantly perfumed with civet.

The principal expense of Saoud's establishment was for his guests and his horses; he is said to have kept no less than two thousand horses and mares as his own property. Of these, three or four hundred were always at Derayeh, and the others in the province of El Hassa, where the clover pasturage is excellent. The finest mares of Arabia were in his possession. Some of those he had taken from their original owners, either as a punishment for misconduct, or as a fine, but he had purchased many at very considerable prices; it is known that he paid for one mare a sum equivalent to five hundred and fifty or six hundred pounds sterling.

To each of his sons he allowed a retinue of one hundred or a hundred and fifty horsemen. Abdallah, during the life of his father, had above three hundred. To these may be added numerous *delouls*, or swift camels, of which Saoud kept the best breed in Arabia.

The members of his own household and the strangers whom he fed every day, amounted to between four and five hundred persons. Rice, boiled corn (*borghol*), dates, and mutton, constituted the principal dishes. Saoud permitted his grown-up sons and the great sheikhs to eat with himself: their usual food was rice and mutton; common strangers were treated with borghol and dates. From all that I could learn of his manner of living and the prices of provisions in Nedjd, it would appear that his whole establishment (exclusive of the body-guard which is paid out of the public treasury) cost him annually from ten to twelve thousand pounds sterling. Contrary to Turkish and Bedouin customs, Saoud never celebrated any circumcision feasts in his house, because, as he said, no such feasts ever took place at the first propagation of Islám. Yet he allowed his Arabs to amuse themselves on those occasions. He also observed with great splendour the nuptials of his children. When his son, Feheyd, married his cousin, the wedding-feast at Derayeh lasted for three days. On the first day, the girl's father, Saoud's brother, treated the guests, consisting of all the male inhabitants of the town and a number of strangers, with the meat of forty she-camels and five hundred sheep. On the second day, Saoud himself slaughtered for his guests one hundred she-camels and eight hundred sheep. On the third day, another of his brothers entertained all the company.

Saoud kept a number of black slaves in his house. He never would permit any of his wives or concubines to suckle their own male children; but for that purpose had always in readiness some wet-nurses, generally chosen among his Abyssinian slaves. A similar practice is prevalent among the sherifs of Mekka, who educate their little children among the neighbouring Bedouin tribes, never keeping them above eight days in their own father's house. After the same fashion, Mohammed was educated among the tribe of *Adouán*.

Wahaby Government.

This is an aristocracy, at the head of which stands the family of Saoud. He divided his dominions into several governorships, which included the Arab tribes who have become settlers. Every great Bedouin tribe has also a governor or sheikh; and subordinate to them are various minor chiefs. The great Bedouin sheikhs, to whom the minor tribes are obliged to pay deference, receive from the Wahaby chief the honorary title of *Emír el Omera*. The principal governorships are those of the districts *el Hassa el Aredh*, (which Saoud took into his own hands, Derayeh being the capital of that province,) *el Kasym, Djebel Shammar, el Harameyn*, (Mekka and Medinah,) *el Hedjáz*, (signifying in the Bedouin acceptation, the mountains southward of Tayf,) and *el Yemen*. The governors or emírs of those provinces execute public justice, but are not the judges; for Saoud has every where placed his own kadhys. The authority of those emírs over the Arabs is very limited, not much exceeding that which an independent Bedouin sheikh possesses, except that he can enforce obedience to the law by imprisoning the transgressor and fining him for non-compliance. If he himself commit injustice, an appeal is made to the great chief; hence Derayeh is constantly filled with Arabs coming from the remotest quarters to plead against their sheikhs. The principal duty incumbent on the latter (besides the execution of justice) is to recruit troops for the Wahaby army, and to assist the tax-gatherers.

In the time of war, the chiefs of these provinces, as well as the great Bedouin sheikhs, form a council; in time of peace, Saoud consulted none but the olemas of Derayeh. These belong principally to the family of Abd el Wahab, founder of the sect; they are numerous at Derayeh, and possess considerable influence. That family is called "*Oulad es' Sheikh*." I do not exactly know what positive rights or privileges they possess; but it is certain, that Saoud communicated to them every important affair before a final decision was given. The Wahaby chief may seem an absolute master, but he knows too well the spirit of his Arabs to attempt governing with despotic sway. The liberties of individuals are maintained as in former times; but he appears to administer justice rather as a potent sheikh than as the lord of Arabia. He is, in fact, under the control of his own governors, all persons of great influence in their respective provinces, who would soon declare themselves independent were he to treat them with injustice Instances of this kind have maintained that spirit of resistance against arbitrary power, to which the Bedouins never yield. The governors of provinces are controlled in their authority by a number of lesser sheikhs; and we accordingly find many small clans always ready to defend their cause against the tyranny of the great chief, who, in uniting them all under one system of government, has succeeded, after violent struggles, in establishing an order of things in Arabia, equally advantageous to public security and to private interests.

The Waháby government is now (1816) hereditary in the family of the Saouds. While Abd el Azyz lived, the principal sheikhs were required to swear allegiance to his son Saoud, who succeeded to the supreme authority, on his father's death, without opposition. In the same manner the sheikhs afterwards swore fidelity to Abdallah, while his father Saoud was still living. The Arabs, however, do not think it necessary that the chieftainship should descend from father to son. Saoud might have nominated one of his brothers to succeed him, and so far we may presume that the same system prevails at Derayeh as all over the Desert in electing the sheikh of a tribe.

The chief Waháby appoints and removes at his pleasure the sheikhs of cities, districts, and tribes; but he generally confirms the election made by the Arabs themselves; and if a sheikh proves attached to his cause, he always permits his son or brother to succeed him.

Administration of Justice.

All the open country of Arabia, and all the towns of the interior were formerly subject to the same disorderly state of law which still prevails among those tribes that have not submitted to the Wahabys, and which I have described in my account of the Bedouins. Abd el Azyz and Saoud taught their Arabs to obey the law, to maintain public peace, and in their disputes to abide by the decision of a tribunal, without any appeal to arms. Abd el Azyz was the first who sent kadhys into all the districts under his sway. He chose them among the most able and upright of his learned men, and assigned to them annual allowances from the public treasury, forbidding them to accept fees or bribes from contending parties. Those kadhys were to judge according to the laws of the *Korán* and the *Sunne*. All the Arabs were to state their subjects of litigation before them, but might afterwards appeal to the supreme chief.

The next step was to secure the country against robbers. Before Abd el Azyz had acquired sufficient power, the whole of Nedjd, and, indeed, of Arabia, was overrun in every direction by hostile parties, and the great number of independent states rendered it impossible to establish a firm internal peace. Abd el Azyz, and, still more, his son Saoud, made the Arabs responsible for every robbery committed within their territory, should the robber be unknown; and those who were sufficiently strong to repel or resist a hostile invasion of a camp or town, and wanted the inclination or courage to do so, were punished by a fine equivalent to the amount of cattle or other property taken away by the robbers. Thus every tribe was rendered vigilant in protecting its neighbours, as well as strangers passing through their territory. So that both public and private robberies almost totally ceased among the settlers as well as Bedouins of Arabia, who formerly delighted in nothing so much as in pilfering and plundering. For the first time, perhaps, since the days of Mohammed, a single merchant might traverse the Desert of Arabia with perfect safety, and the Bedouins slept without any apprehension that their cattle would be carried off by nocturnal depredators.

The two Wahaby chiefs seem to have been particularly anxious that their Arabs should renounce the long-established custom of taking into their own hands the punishment of an enemy, and inflicting retaliation. They, therefore, constantly endeavoured, more especially Saoud, to abolish the system of blood-revenge, and to render the Arabs content with a stipulated price, payable for the blood of a relation. But in this respect, the chief was never able to obtain complete success; he has frequently compelled the sufferer's family to accept the fine, if offered by the homicide's party; but if any act of revenge has taken place before he can give orders respecting the fine, he does not punish the man who availed himself of the old Arab rights.

If disputes arise among his people and occasion blows, and if the relations of both parties espouse respectively the cause of their friends (as is usual in Arabia), shedding blood in the affray, Saoud without any mercy condemns all those who meddled on the occasion, and punishes them either by taking away their horses, camels, and arms, or else by the confiscation of their property to the public treasury.

In a quarrel among Arabs, should one draw his dagger and wound another, Saoud levied a heavy fine upon the by-standers for allowing the matter to proceed so far. If, notwithstanding the laws against war, two tribes commence hostilities, Saoud immediately sends messengers to the sheikhs, and insists upon a reconciliation, levying a fine from each tribe, and obliging them to pay

2 P

to each other the price of blood for the lives of those who perished in the first onset. Tribes were commanded to bring their public disputes always before the tribunal of Saoud, whose authority was so dreaded, that a single Negro slave of his household has been known to arrest, by his order, some great sheikh in the midst of his own camp, and bring him as a prisoner to Derayeh.

Saoud was acknowledged to be a man of incorruptible justice; but in his sentences against transgressors rather too severe. His great penetration enabled him soon to discover when a witness prevaricated; and this he punished always in an exemplary manner. His punishments, however, were not cruel; and I have been assured that, since the death of his father, only four or five men have been put to death at Derayeh. As the Bedouins rarely possess any money, he fines them in horses, camels, and sheep. It is this severity which has excited against him so many enemies among his own Arabs. He never respects the protection given to a delinquent by other Arabs. He abolished the laws of dakheil (or protection) all over his dominions, as far as they might be used in screening a person from the hand of justice. If an Arab has killed another, he may seek dakheil at a friend's, to save himself from the immediate vengeance of the deceased man's relations; but he can remain under that protection only until the law claims him, and he must then be given up.

The great sheikhs grant a kind of protection to delinquents accused of petty crimes. An Arab, in such a case, and afraid of appearing before Saoud, places himself under the protection of some sheikh who possesses influence with the chief. This sheikh intercedes, and generally prevails on Saoud to remit the punishment, or commute it for a small fine.

The offence which Saoud had most frequently to punish was the intercourse of his Arabs with heretics. At the time that the Wahaby creed was first instituted, the most positive orders had been given to interdict all communication between the Wahabys and other nations who had not yet adopted the new doctrine; for it was said, that the sword alone was to be used in argument with the latter. As the inhabitants of Nedjd, however, were much in the habit of visiting Medinah, Damascus, Baghdad, and the adjacent countries, they continually disobeyed those orders; so that at last Saoud found it necessary to relax his severity on that subject. He even tacitly connived, in the last period of the Syrian hadj, at his Arabs transporting provisions for the caravans, and took himself one dollar for every camel, belonging to his people, so employed; but except in this carrying business of the hadj, he never would allow any of his Arabs to trade with Syria or Baghdad until after 1810, when the Egyptian expedition began. Yet the law existed, that if a Wahaby, whether Bedouin or merchant, should be found on the road going towards any heretic country, (which the direction of the road, and nature of the loads would prove,) his whole property in goods and cattle should be confiscated to the public treasury. But in returning from the heretic country, his property is respected.

Those arbitrary impositions, called *avanias* in the Levant, are wholly unknown in the Wahaby dominions, where no individuals were ever required to pay more than what he owed to the tax-gatherers, or a fine to the treasury for some offence. Wealthy individuals are perfectly secure from the rapacity of government; and this perhaps is the only part of the East where such is the case. The rich merchants of Mekka, whose warehouses contained the finest Bedouin clothes, were never obliged to pay the smallest sum, nor even to give any valuable presents to Saoud.

The Arabs, however, murmur at a kind of forced requisition, in the frequent orders of their chief to join him on his expeditions against the heretics. In this case the Arabs must find their own food and camels, or horses, and receive in return no emolument but whatever booty they may be able to take. Such expeditions, are therefore very expensive to them. On the other hand, any man who has incurred the displeasure of Saoud, by some minor offence, is sure to conciliate him by joining in his expeditions.

The great security which resulted from this rigid administration of justice, naturally pleased those who were most exposed to depredations and disorders of any kind. The settlers, therefore, of Nedjd, Hedjaz, and Yemen, became most sincerely attached to the new system, because they had suffered most from the defects of the old. Caravans of any extent, loaded with the produce of the ground, passed unmolested through those parts of the country; nor were the people ever afraid that their crops should be cut up, or destroyed by the wandering tribes. The latter, on the contrary, who had always lived by robberies and attacks on others, found it much more difficult to obey a government whose first principles directly opposed their mode of subsistence. It is therefore not surprising that some of the great Bedouin tribes hesitated to adopt the Wahaby creed, until it was forced upon them by a superior power; and they have proved, by frequent revolts, how impatient they are of the check which they have experienced in their manner of living; to which must be added, their repugnance with respect to paying the tribute.

If Saoud was known to be a very severe judge in cases of transgression, and implacable towards his enemies, he was equally celebrated for the warmth and sincerity of his friendship, and his regard for old and faithful adherents. Any sheikh who has evinced his attachment to Saoud, might rely on his constant protection and help under all misfortunes, even to the full indemnification for every loss, however considerable, that he might incur in his service.

The greatest punishment inflicted by order of the Wahaby chief is the shaving of the culprit's beard. This is done only with persons of distinction, or rebel sheikhs, and is to some a disgrace more intolerable than death. An Arab thus shaved endeavours to conceal himself from view until his beard grows again. An anecdote related on this subject shows the real character of an Arab. Saoud had long wished to purchase the mare of a sheikh belonging to the tribe of Beni Shammar, but the owner refused to sell her for any sum of money. At this time, a sheikh of the Kahtán Arabs had been sentenced to lose his beard for some offence. When the barber produced his razor in presence of Saoud, the sheikh exclaimed, "O Saoud, take the mare of the Shammary as a ransom for my beard!" The punishment was remitted; the sheikh was allowed to go and bargain for the mare, which cost him two thousand five hundred dollars, swearing that no sum of money could have induced him to part with her, had it not been to save the beard of a noble Kahtány. But this is a rare example; for Saoud frequently refused considerable offers of money, to remit the punishment of shaving.

I shall here notice some Wahaby laws, founded upon the Korán, and sayings of Mohammed.

A haramy, or robber, is obliged to return the stolen goods, or their value; but if the offence is not attended with circumstances of violence, he escapes without further punishment, except a fine to the treasury. If a door be broken open in committing the robbery, the thief's hand is cut off.

One who kills his antagonist in a dispute with dagger or pistol is condemned to death: if he kills him by a blow of a stick or stone, it is deemed man-slaughter; and he only pays the price of blood, as having not been armed with any deadly weapon.

The price of blood among the Wahabys is fixed at one hundred she-camels, according to the rate established by Abou Beker. Saoud valued every camel at eight Spanish dollars; and the fixed sum is now eight hundred dollars.

Whoever curses a Wahaby, or calls him "infidel," incurs very heavy penalties. The terms of insult are measured among the Wahabys with great exactness; the worst (not amenable to the law) is to call a man "dog." The common insult is to say, "O doer" (that is, doer of evil or mischief), or "O leaver-off" (that is, O leaver-off of religious and social duties).

The stocks, called *debabe,* in which the feet of prisoners are confined, is only for the lower class. Saoud has a prison in his own mansion for persons of quality; those especially who, having been sentenced to pay a certain sum, plead poverty, and refuse to comply. In some cases, they are imprisoned until they pay.

The neglect of religious duty is always severely punished. I have already mentioned the penalty for omission of prayers. When Saoud took Medinah, he ordered some of his people, after prayers in the mosque, to call over the names of all the grown-up inhabitants of the town who were to answer individually: he then commanded them to attend prayers regularly; and if any one absented himself two or three times, Saoud sent some of his Arabs to beat the man in his own house. At Mekka, when the hour of prayer arrived, he ordered his people to patrol the streets, armed with large sticks, and to drive all the inhabitants by force into the mosque; a harsh proceeding, but justified by the notorious irreligion of the Mekkans. Saoud has always been extremely punctual in performing the pilgrimage to Mekka. Whenever it was in his power he repaired to that holy place, accompanied by thousands of his Arabs, men and women. His last pilgrimage was performed in the year 1812.

Saoud endeavoured to check among his people the frequent practice of divorce, so pernicious to social and moral habits. Whenever he heard an Arab say, "I swear by the divorce" (that is, from my wife), he ordered that the man should be beaten. To break the fast of Ramadhan, without some legitimate excuse, subjected a man to capital punishment. Abd el Azyz (who was, however, more rigid than his son) once put an Arab to death for that offence. The smoking of tobacco publicly is forbidden; but it is well known that all the people of Nedjd continue this practice in their houses; and even the Wahabys, in their camps, at night. On the capture of Mekka, Saoud ordered all the inhabitants to take their Persian pipes (called *shíshe* by the Arabs) to a green piece of ground, before the house where he resided; and having formed them into a vast heap, he set them on fire, together with all the tobacco that could be found in the shops. Some time after, one of his retinue informed him in public, that the Mekkans disregarded his orders, and still smoked. "Where did you see them smoke?" asked Saoud. "In their own houses," answered the informer. "Do you not know," replied the chief, "that it is written, 'do not spy out the secrets of the houses of the faithful?'" Having quoted this sentence of the Koran, he ordered the informer to be bastinadoed, and no further notice was taken of the private smoking.

The Mekkans still remember, with gratitude, the excellent police observed by Saoud's troops during his frequent visits to Mekka; especially on his first taking the town. With the same vigilance he watches over his soldiers on an expedition; and whoever receives from him the word *Amán*, or safe-conduct, may be perfectly secure from any misconduct of the troops. It was mentioned, as an instance of the Wahabys' good faith, that some of them were often seen in the temple at Mekka, looking out for the owners of lost articles which they had found, and were desirous of returning.

Saoud always protected trade in his dominions, provided that it was not carried on with those whom he called heretical Muselmáns. The principal trade of Nedjd is in provisions; and there the tribes from the interior of the Desert purchased what they required; and as years of dearth often occur, the rich people hoard up great quantities of corn. With these Saoud never interfered; and in times of scarcity he allowed them to sell at their own prices, however they might distress the poor; for he said, that Mohammed never forbade merchants to derive from their capitals as much profit as they possibly could obtain.

Usury, and even lending money on interest (which is not uncommon among the Bedouins), he prohibited under severe penalties, as contrary to the express tenor of the law. If money was lent, the conditions were generally to share the chances of loss, and to take one half of the profits.

The Wahabys have no particular coin. Dollars are in general currency; and articles of little value are estimated by measures of corn, or purchased with old copper money of the imáms of Yemen. Venetian zequins are likewise taken, but no Turkish coin whatever. During the late war in Hedjaz, when the Wahabys killed and stripped any Turkish soldiers, and found some piastres in their pockets, they always threw them with indignation on the ground.

Revenues.

The Wahaby revenues have been established upon a plan similar to that which prevailed in the time of Mohammed. They consist in—

1. One fifth of the booty taken from the heretics. This portion must be set aside for the chief, whether he or one of his officers was present on the expedition; and the sheikh of the most distant

tribe is answerable for the remittance of it, however small or considerable the amount may be. Saoud never attempted to withhold from his soldiers the remaining four fifths. In common warfare with Arabs (when cities are not plundered), the booty consists generally of horses, camels, and sheep; those are sold to the highest bidder immediately after the battle. The money thus obtained is distributed among the troops. A cavalry soldier has three shares (one for himself, and two, as the Arabs say, for his mare); every camel-rider has one share, (before Saoud's time he had two,) every foot-soldier one share. If in battle a Wahaby should kill a trooper of the enemy, and get possession of his mare, he is allowed to keep it as his own property, and the recompence of his valour. I need not here repeat, that Mohammed took the fifth part of all booty.

2. The tribute; or, as it is called by the Wahabys, "the Alms." A fundamental law of Islam is the giving of these alms. Mohammed regulated the amount which is observed by the Wahaby legislator. Similar alms are prescribed to the Turks also, but the distribution is left to every man's own conscience; whereas the Wahabys are obliged to deliver them, for distribution, to their chief. The Muselman law has minutely fixed what proportion the alms are to bear with respect to the property; and the Wahabys have not made any alteration in this arrangement. The sums paid in proportion to horses, sheep, and camels, are according to the precepts of the Sunne, and may be seen detailed in D'Ohhson's excellent work. Saoud divided the tribute from his subjects into two parts; that from the Bedouins flows wholly into his private treasury; but the alms from inhabitants of towns, or cultivators, are appropriated to the public treasury, or "*Beit el Mál.*"

From fields watered by rains only, Saoud takes a tithe of the produce; from fields fertilised by the water of wells or of fountains, which it is laborious and expensive to draw, he takes but one twentieth of the produce.

The merchants pay yearly two and a half per cent on their capital, and are obliged to state its amount upon oath to the collector. It is, however, well known that they seldom return an account of more than one fourth of their property. A merchant of Khadera, in the province of Kasym, had been robbed of three thousand dollars in cash. He applied for assistance to Saoud, who directed the clerk of the Beit el Mál, or treasury, at Khadera, to ascertain how much the merchant had reported his property to be worth; and it appeared that he had only stated it as being one thousand dollars. For this false return, Saoud confiscated the merchant's mare and camels.

These alms, or *zeka*, are peculiarly galling to the Arabs under Saoud's authority, as they were formerly free from taxes of any kind. Distant tribes have frequently revolted on account of them, and driven away the collectors. Nothing but compulsion or necessity could ever induce a Bedouin to admit of taxation. It is likewise the exemption from these zekas which rendered the Hedjáz Bedouins less hostile to the cause of Mohammed Aly Pasha than they otherwise might have been; for his first measure was to declare, that not only the Bedouins, but all the settled inhabitants of Hedjaz, should be wholly free from taxes.

3. The most considerable portion of the Wahaby chief's revenues are derived from his own domains. He has established it as a rule, that whenever any of his districts or cities rise in rebellion, he plunders them for the first offence; for the second rebellion, he not only plunders but confiscates them, and all their land, to the public treasury. He then bestows some parts of them on strangers, but leaves most in the hands of the former proprietors, who now become merely his farmers, and are obliged to pay, according to circumstances, either one third or one half of the produce. The

property of those who took the most active part in the rebellion is farmed out to others, while they themselves either fly or are put to death.

As the Arabs did not adopt the Wahaby system until after repeated struggles, considerable districts were thus confiscated to the chief, and if ever he resume his power in Hedjaz, he will seize in like manner on the property of all who had joined Mohammed Aly. At present most of the landed property in Nedjd belongs to the Beit el Mál, or treasury; that of Kasym, whose inhabitants have been constantly in rebellion, is entirely held in farm; and many villages of Hedjaz, and the mountains towards Yemen, are attached also to the treasury.

4. Fines levied for trespasses against the law. The crime of disobedience is generally expiated by pecuniary fines. It is a maxim in the Wahaby courts, that an Arab who falsely accuses another must pay a fine to the treasury.

All these revenues, except the alms, or zeka, from the Bedouins, are deposited in the public treasury, or Beit el Mál. Every city or village of any note has its own treasury, into which the inhabitants pay their quotas. Every treasury has a writer, or clerk, sent by the Wahaby chief with orders to prevent the sheikh of the place from partaking in illicit gain from the revenue. The sheikhs are not allowed to collect nor to account for the money paid. These funds are appropriated to public services, and are therefore divided into four parts. One fourth is sent to the great treasury at Derayeh; one fourth is dedicated to the relief of paupers in the district of the Beit el Mál; for the pay of olemas who are to instruct the kadhys and the children; for keeping the mosques in repair, digging public wells, &c. One half is expended for the benefit of indigent soldiers, who are furnished with provisions when they set out on an expedition, or, in case of necessity, with camels; also for the entertainment of guests. The money thus allowed for guests is paid into the hands of the sheikhs, who keep a sort of public houses, where all strangers may halt and be fed gratis; it is thought just that the whole community should contribute towards their expenses. Thus Ibn Aly, the sheikh of Beni Shammar, in Djebel Shammar, has every year from the treasury of his province, two hundred camel-loads of corn, two hundred loads of dates, and one thousand Spanish dollars; with this money he purchases meat, butter, and coffee; and the whole is expended in the entertainment of from two to three hundred strangers of all descriptions, who are received and fed every day in his public rooms.

From the great treasury of Derayeh, sums are applied to the relief of Saoud's faithful subjects, whose property had been taken by the enemy. Derayeh is always full of Arabs who apply to Saoud for the restitution of some part at least of their lost property. If Saoud knows the man to be a sincere Wahaby, he generally pays him to the amount of one third. Other sums are given from that treasury to Arabs who have lost their cattle through disease or accidents. If upon an expedition the mare or camel (deloul) of a soldier has been killed, or dies, and that booty has been taken, Saoud most commonly gives another mare or camel to the soldier; if no booty has been taken, the Arab must bear the loss.

Besides what is paid to the sheikhs of districts, towns, or villages, for the entertainment of guests, the Bedouin sheikhs receive annual presents from the treasury of Derayeh as tokens of Saoud's good-will. These donations vary from fifty to three hundred dollars, and are bestowed in imitation of a similar practice of Mohammed.

The collectors of revenue (called *nawáb*, or *mezekki*, or *aámil*) are sent every year from Derayeh to the different districts or tribes, and receive a certain sum for their trouble and expenses on the journey. Thus every collector sent from Derayeh to the Bedouins of the Syrian Desert, receives seventy-five dollars. The sheikhs, as I have already mentioned, are not allowed any concern in the taxes. When the collector goes to receive the alms, some Arab of those who are going to pay, is employed to write a statement of the sums payable, and another collects those sums, which he hands over to the collector: thus they endeavour to prevent peculation. The collector then gives a receipt to the district or tribe for the amount that has been paid.

The Bedouins must pay this tribute immediately after the first spring month, when the camel and sheep have produced their young. The collector and the sheikh agree in appointing a certain spot, some watering-place, where all the Arabs of the tribe are directed to repair. Thus in the year 1812, Saoud collected tribute from the Bedouins about Baghdad at the watering-place called Hindye, two or three days' journey distant from that town. In the same year, the Djelás Arabs paid their tribute at a watering-place twelve hours' distant from Aleppo.

Out of his private treasury, Saoud pays the expenses of his establishment and of his life-guard.

It cannot be denied, that the Wahaby chief shows great avidity in dealing with his subjects; his income is much more than sufficient to defray the public expenditure, which is not considerable, as his army costs him nothing. The Arabs complain, that if a man has a fine mare, Saoud will find out some charge of misconduct to justify him in taking the mare as a fine. The great riches that he has accumulated have increased his desire of more: and the Arabs declare that since the taking of Imám Hosseyn, where much booty was obtained, and the sacking of the Yemen towns, the character of Saoud has suffered considerable deterioration, and he has become daily more avaricious. I have not heard, however, a single instance of his depriving the meanest Arab of his property without a legal cause. The avarice of Saoud had alienated the sheikhs from his interests, long before Mohammed Aly attacked Hedjaz; and if Saoud had, on that occasion, behaved as prudently as the Pasha, in distributing money among the sheikhs, Mohammed Aly would have found it impossible to gain any firm footing in that country.

Saoud did not deny, that he had been guilty of injustice in punishing culprits too severely; and he was often heard to say, that were it not for his own and his friends' evil doings, their religion would long since have found its way to Cairo and Constantinople.

Many exaggerated statements have been made respecting the Wahaby revenue. Some well-informed Mekkans, who enjoyed frequent access to the person of Saoud and to his family, and had the best opportunities of knowing the truth and no reason for concealing it, told me, that the greatest amount ever received by Saoud into his own, or the public treasury of Derayeh, in one year, was two millions of dollars; but that in general it did not exceed one million of dollars annually. This does not include the sums received by the treasuries in the districts and towns; which, however, are generally expended, leaving no surplus at the end of the year.

His private expenses being very moderate, the chief may be supposed extremely rich in cash, which he has secreted in his mansion at Derayeh. Yet with so much wealth and power, neither Saoud nor his father were able to subjugate the free-born Arabs; they were forced to leave them in possession of their individual liberty; nor is it to be presumed, that the Arabs will ever submit to any more absolute master, and still less to a foreign invader, who may, perhaps, pass rapidly through their country, but can never bind them in lasting chains. At present their obedience is rather to the law than to Saoud, who is, in fact, but the great sheikh, not the master of Arabia; and however they may dislike the exacted tribute, they know that much of it is expended for purposes connected with their own interests: a consolation which the peasants in Turkey can never enjoy.

Military Affairs of the Wahabys.

Between the Wahabys and the Bedouins there is but little difference in military matters. Without any standing army the sheikh of a tribe collects the warlike Arabs of his camp for an excursion against the enemy, and the corps is dissolved again as soon as they return. Such is also the case with the Wahabys. Except a few hundred chosen men kept at Derayeh, neither Saoud nor his father had ever any regular army or body of troops. If the chief meditates an attack, he orders the sheikh of tribes and of districts to be on a fixed day at some certain spot, generally a well in the Desert. Sometimes the chief asks a certain number of soldiers from the sheikh, who then levies them by a kind of conscription from every village and camp under his control. Thus, if one thousand men be required from the sheikh of Kasym, every town of that province is obliged to contribute in proportion to its population. The inhabitants of towns (or in camps the Bedouins) then settle the matter amicably among themselves. All those who possess *delouls*, or camels fit for the saddle, divide into two bodies; one set goes to the war now, the other on the next summons. All from the age of eighteen to sixty must attend, whether married or unmarried, or fathers of families. All who possess mares must join the party on every summons, unless it be specified in such summons that cavalry is not required; if a man abscond, the chief takes away his mare, or camel, or some sheep, as a fine. Saoud was very severe in the exaction of these fines; and the heavy military duties imposed on those possessing horses induced them to sell those valuable creatures, and thus reduced considerably their number in the territories under his dominion.

A general requisition for troops was sometimes made without any mention of the numbers: in this case, all who possessed a deloul were obliged to attend. On some occasions the chief merely said, "We shall not count those who join the army, but those who stay behind:" every man, therefore, capable of bearing arms, felt himself obliged to go, the poor being furnished by the rich with camels and weapons, or by the Beit el Mál. When a very distant expedition was proposed (as that against Damascus in 1810, or against Oman), Saoud commanded his chiefs to attend him with the *Sylle* only (that is, the most select horsemen and camel-riders). In that case, not more than one out of twenty joined the army. But, on all occasions, some Arabs contrive to abscond, or evade the conscription, although they know the certainty of incurring a heavy fine. This they prefer to the great expense of equipping themselves for the expedition, and providing a stock of food for forty or fifty days, each from his own purse.

One hundred pounds weight of flour, fifty or sixty pounds of dates, twenty pounds of butter, a sack of wheat or barley for the camel, and a water-skin, are the provisions of a Wahaby soldier. Dates mixed with flour, kneaded into a cake, and baked in ashes, form the morning and evening meals. The price of those provisions, the time spent on the expedition, which might be employed more profitably, the injury done to the camel by forced exertions (which kill many on the road); all these considerations render the military attendance very irksome to a poor Arab. If the summons, however, be not general, a man may hire a substitute, allowing him from eight to ten Spanish dollars for an ordinary expedition of about forty days, besides his provisions.

If camels are scarce, a man mounted upon one takes a companion (*meradíf*) behind him.

A statement formerly made, respecting some landed properties held in bail, under obligation of military attendance, I now find to have been erroneous. All the male Wahabys are so far soldiers, that the great chief may call upon them to serve at any moment; and thus, at a fortnight's notice, assemble an army of excellent troops. But this system, though favourable to rapid movements towards an enemy's territory, or against invasion, does not suit a project of distant and permanent conquest.

The Wahaby religion prescribes continual war against all who have not adopted the reformed doctrine. As nearly the whole extent of Arabia had been reduced to submission by the Wahabys, their expeditions were chiefly directed towards their northern neighbours, from Basra, along the Euphrates, to Syria. It does not appear that they ever wished to extend their dominions beyond the limits of Arabia: so that they only attacked Irak, Mesopotamia, and Syria, for the sake of plunder. Sudden invasions were the most favourable to such an object; and no other kind of warfare has ever been practised by the Wahabys. Their chief undoubtedly wished to render himself sole master of all Arabia and its tribes; and those who rejected his invitation to become true Moslims, were exposed on all sides to attacks from his people, who damaged their fields and date-trees, or carried off their cattle; while their neighbours, who had embraced the new faith, continued unmolested by the Wahabys. Multitudes, therefore, affected to conform, that they might save their property and themselves from constant annoyance; but few provinces, or tribes, that had been outwardly converted, felt any real interest in the Wahaby cause. Many leagues were formed with the Sherif of Mekka for resisting the power of Saoud's family; and the Bedouins at first considered their subjection as they would an alliance with a stronger neighbouring tribe, which they might dissolve at any hour, and convert into a war. Provinces, strong by position and population, such as the mountains of Shammar, Hedjaz, and Yemen, and others distant from the chief seat of Wahaby power in Nedjd, soon became relaxed in their obedience to the great chief's orders, and irregular in the payment of tribute. At first, he reminded them of their duty by a parental exhortation, which they regarded as a proof of weakness, and then proceeded to open rebellion. In this case, the chief informs all his sheikhs, that "such Arabs have become enemies; and that without his further orders, every person is at liberty to attack them." He then sends three or four flying expeditions against them; and they are soon reduced to obedience, by the fear of losing their crops and their cattle. Saoud was often heard to say, that no Arabs had ever been staunch Wahabys until they had suffered two or three times from the plundering of his troops.

Some very strong and distant tribes have, however, successfully resisted the payment of tribute, although, in other respects, they profess themselves Wahabys. Thus in 1810, when Saoud's power was unshaken in Arabia, the northern Aenezes refused to pay tribute; and the chief did not think it prudent to attempt the subjection of them by main force, but continued to correspond with their sheikhs, who paid him a nominal obedience, but acted according to the interests of their own tribes, whenever they came in contact with partisans of the Wahabys.

It will be easily perceived, that the Wahabys are generally in a state of warfare. Saoud's constant practice was to make every year two or three grand expeditions. The neighbourhood of Basra (being rich in cattle and dates), and the banks of the Shat el Arab, and of the Euphrates, up to Anah, were the scenes of his annual attacks. His troops even forded the Euphrates, and spread terror in Mesopotamia, and, on the southern side of his dominions, the still unconquered provinces of Yemen, Hadramaut, and Omán, presented fertile fields of booty. Saoud did not always accompany these expeditions himself, but sent one of his sons as commander, or some distinguished sheikh; and we have even seen his black slave, *Hark* (حرك), at the head of several Wahaby corps.

When the chief plans an expedition, the object of it is known to himself alone. He assembles his emírs at a certain watering-place, which is always selected in such a manner as to deceive the enemy whom he designs to attack. Thus if the expedition be intended for the northward of Derayeh, his army is assembled at a place many days' journies distant southward of Derayeh. He then actually sets out in a southern direction, but soon wheels about, and by forced marches falls upon the enemy, who is generally taken by surprise. This stratagem is very necessary, for the news spreads like lightning through Arabia, that Saoud had summoned his troops to meet at a certain spot; and if from the position of that spot any conjecture might be formed of the intended object of attack, the enemy would have time to prepare for resistance, or to fly.

The expeditions of Saoud were planned with much prudence and foresight, and executed with such celerity, that they seldom failed. Thus, when he invaded the Hauran plains in 1810, although it required thirty-five days to arrive at the point of attack, yet the news of his approach only preceded his arrival by two days; nor was it known what part of Syria he meant to attack; and thirty-five villages of Hauran were sacked by his soldiers before the Pasha of Damascus could make any demonstrations of defence.

Of the bravest and most renowned warriors among his Arabs,

Saoud has formed a body-guard (*mendjyeh*), which he keeps constantly at Derayeh, and which are the only standing troops of his army. Whenever he hears of any distinguished horseman, he invites him to Derayeh, and engages him in his service, by agreeing to furnish him and his family with an annual provision of corn, butter, and dates. He gives to the man also a mare, or a good *deloul* camel. This guard constantly attends the chief on his expeditions. The name of this body-guard is dreaded by all enemies of the Wahabys, for they have never forfeited their high character for bravery. Saoud always kept them as a kind of reserve in battle, detaching small parties of them in support of his other troops. They amount to about three hundred in number, and for the greater part they fight in complete armour. Their horses are covered by the *lebs*, (a sort of quilted woollen stuff, impenetrable to lances or swords). As their service is quite voluntary, Saoud always placed great confidence in this body-guard.

Besides the *mendjyeh*, or body-guard, Saoud took with him to Derayeh many of the *agyds*, or war-chiefs of Bedouin tribes (mentioned in another place, see page 168). He lessened the power of these tribes, in carrying off their chiefs, and strengthened his own party by the accession of those renowned men; to whom, if he saw them sincerely attached to his interests, he often entrusted the direction of his expeditions.

The Wahabys make their attacks in every month of the year, even in the holy month of Ramadhán. Saoud has always shown a great predilection for the month *Zul hadje*, and his adherents pretend that he never was defeated in any expedition undertaken during that month. As Saoud, in the time of his prosperity, performed annually the pilgrimage, his enemies, especially the strong Arabian tribes of Mesopotamia, always took the opportunity of his absence at Mekka to make inroads on his territory.

If Saoud was embarrassed respecting the choice of two measures which seemed equally advantageous, he often resorted to the practice recommended by Mohammed, which is, to address a short prayer to the Almighty before going to sleep, and to interpret the next morning whatever dream he might have had either for or against the measure. He seldom allowed the sheikhs to know any thing of his plans.

On the march every emír or sheikh has his standard. Saoud himself has several of different colours. His tents are very handsome, made at Damascus and Baghdad; but his people have only the common black Arab tents, and most of them have not any tents. Saoud's provision and baggage are carried upon two hundred camels. He takes a considerable supply on distant expeditions, that he may be able to relieve those of his troops who lose their own; and whenever he passes through any district inhabited by settlers or Bedouins, it is expected that he should treat all arriving guests in the same manner as he does at Derayeh. If the army marches at night the chief and all the great sheikhs have torches carried before them. Night marches are only practised when the point of attack is fixed, and a space of four or five days is traversed in two. The Wahaby army is always preceded by a van-guard of thirty or forty horsemen (called *el Sabr*). They generally go before, a march of one day or perhaps of two days. The Bedouins have a similar custom of sending on a vanguard some hours in advance.

Approaching an enemy, the army always divides into three or four corps, one behind another. The first which attacks is composed of horsemen, as being the principal strength of the army. They are supported by the second line, consisting of camel-riders, who advance if the horsemen should be routed. Saoud for a long time had ceased to fight in person, and remained in the rear. The superiority of his troops over the enemy's generally enabled him to send fresh reinforcements to his people engaged in battle, and the victory was seldom disputed for any length of time. It was a favourite stratagem of Saoud to fly before the enemy, and rallying suddenly, to fall with his chosen horsemen upon the fatigued pursuers.

To all his troops who die fighting, Saoud insures the enjoyment of paradise, according to the doctrine of the Korán. Whenever a sheikh is killed in battle, and his mare (as generally happens) gallops back towards the ranks of the troops, which she knows, the report of his death is made to the chief as tidings of glad import; because the sheikh has certainly gone to paradise. On this occasion the expression is, "Joy to you, O Saoud! the mare of such a man is come back!"

Whenever the flying corps of Wahabys plunder an encampment of Arabs, the women are obliged to strip themselves naked, while the Wahabys turn away and throw them some rags for the sake of decency. No further insult is ever offered to a female. When the plundering has ceased, the commanding emír distributes some clothes amongst them, and gives to every family a camel and sufficient provision for their journey to some camp of relations or friends. As their husbands may have been killed, or escaped by flight, it sometimes happens that women belonging to plundered camps remain during several days with the plunderers, and march in their company for the sake of being protected on the road.

In propagating their creed, the Wahabys have established it as a fundamental rule to kill all their enemies found in arms, whether they be foreign heretics (such as Syrian, Mesopotamian, or Egyptian soldiers or settlers), or Arabs themselves, who have opposed the great chief, or rebelled against him. It is this practice (imitated from the first propagators of Islám) which makes the Wahaby name so dreaded. During their four years' warfare with the soldiers of Mohammed Aly Pasha, not a single instance is recorded of their having ever given quarter to a Turk. When Kerbela (or Meshed Hosseyn) and Tayf were taken, the whole male population was massacred; and in the former town the *Haret el Abasieh,* or quarter of the Abasides, was only spared because Saoud had a particular veneration for the memory of the Abaside khalifahs. Whenever Bedouin camps are attacked, the same circumstance occurs; all who are taken with arms are unmercifully put to death. This savage custom has inspired the Wahabys with a ferocious fanaticism that makes them dreadful to their adversaries, and thus has contributed to facilitate the propagation of their faith.

But the Wahaby chief is easily induced to grant safe conduct to his enemies if they voluntarily surrender; and to this they are often inclined, as it was never known that the chief on any occasion had broken his word. Here the good faith of Bedouins towards an enemy may be recognised; a noble trait in their character. The reputation of Saoud for strict observance of a promise is allowed by his bitterest enemies, and particularly celebrated by his friends since the war with Mohammed Aly Pasha, as contrasted with the treachery of the Turks.

If the threatened Arabs surrender to Saoud before his vengeance can reach them, he usually gives to them the " *Amán ullah,*" or "God's security," with the condition of the "*halka,*" which excludes from the safe conduct all horses, camels, shields, matchlocks, lances, and swords, and all copper vessels, which must be given up as booty to the Wahabys; the rest of their property remains untouched with the owners.

Sometimes the *Amán* is given unconditionally, and then extends over persons as well as property. All commanders of Wahaby troops have strict orders to accept any offer of submission from an enemy, and to observe inviolably the promised " Amán."

Having subdued a rebellious tribe, or province, Saoud always sent (soon after peace was concluded) for the sheikhs of the rebels, and established them with his own family at Derayeh, or in some neighbouring district, furnishing them amply with provisions. Thus he weakened their influence among their own people; replacing them by chiefs on whose attachment he could depend, chosen from those powerful families which had formerly been at variance with the sheikhs of the subdued parties. Great numbers of chiefs from all parts of Arabia are thus assembled at Derayeh and in Nedjd. They are not, by any means, close prisoners; but cannot escape from the district assigned to them. An Arab sheikh is so well known to all inhabitants of the Desert, that he can scarcely hope to remain "incognito" for any length of time.

After the taking of Medinah, Saoud found it necessary to keep there a constant garrison of Wahabys; no other instance of that kind occurred during his government. For he never thought it advisable to garrison any district that he had subdued, but relied upon the sheikh whom he had placed over it, and the dread of his own name, to keep the vanquished in subjection. Yet he commanded his new sheikhs in some districts south of Mekka to build small castles, or towers, for the defence of their residences. At Medinah, an important hold, where he knew that the people were hostile to his religion and his person, he kept a garrison of Arabs from Nedjd and Yemen armed with matchlocks, paying to each man seven dollars every month, besides rations of flour and butter. These, inhabitants of the towns of Nedjd, who are all furnished with matchlocks, form the most select corps of the Wahaby army. To them are entrusted the most difficult enterprises. It was these troops that stormed the town of Kerbelá.

Gháleb, Sherif of Mekka, and the Turkish Pasha of Baghdád, at war with the Wahábys.—The holy cities, Mekka and Medinah, taken by the Wahábys.

During my residence in Arabia I made repeated inquiries after a written history of the Wahabys, thinking it probable that some learned man of Mekka or Medinah might have composed such a work; but my search proved fruitless. Nobody takes notes of daily occurrences, and the dates of them are soon forgotten. Some few persons, well informed of what has passed in their own neighbourhood, know but little of distant transactions; and before a complete and satisfactory account of the Wahaby affairs could be compiled, it would be necessary to make a journey through every part of Arabia. Baghdad, from its vicinity to Nedjd, the centre of the Wahaby dominion, is, under present circumstances, the place where probably the most accurate statements might be collected.

I shall here give but few details respecting the history of this extraordinary people before the Turks re-conquered Hedjáz; an event which I can describe with more accuracy, having myself resided in that country while the war still continued.

The Wahabys had for nearly thirty years established their doctrines, made numerous proselytes, and successively conquered Nedjd and subdued most of the great Bedouin tribes, who feed their cattle there in spring and retreat afterwards to the Desert. Yet war had not been declared, nor did the Wahabys encroach upon the rights of the two governments nearest to them; that of Baghdad on the north, and that of Hedjaz towards the south. The pilgrim-caravans passed from Damascus and from Baghdad without any molestation through their territory. Their increase of power, and the assiduity with which they propagated their doctrines, seem first to have excited the jealousy of Sheríf Ghâleb. Under his authority, and partly under his influence, were placed all the tribes settled in Hedjaz, and several on the frontiers of that country. The attempts made by Abd el Azyz to gain over these latter to his party after he had subjugated their neighbours, could not be viewed with indifference by Ghâleb, whom we may consider rather as a powerful Bedouin sheikh than an eastern prince; and the same causes that produce constant wars between all great neighbouring tribes of the Desert, sowed the seeds of contest between him and the Wahabys. A few years after his succession to the government of Mekka, Ghâleb first engaged in open hostility with the Wahabys, about the year 1792 or 1793. This warfare he continued until the final surrender of Mekka. His party was then strengthened by the southern tribes of Begoum (at Taraba), Beni Salem (at Beishe), Ghâmed (in Zohrán), and the numerous Bedouins bordering on Tayf. These wars were carried on in the Bedouin style, interrupted only by a few short-lived truces. Sudden invasions were made by both parties on their enemy's territories; and booty was taken reciprocally, without much loss or advantage. Ghâleb, who was then in regular correspondence with the Porte and received every year the pilgrim caravan, left no means untried for prejudicing the Turkish government against his enemies. He represented them as infidels, and their behaviour towards the Turkish hadjys, or pilgrims, did not remove this unfavourable opinion. The Porte listened more readily to these representations as the pashas of Baghdad had made statements of a similar nature. Like the Sherif of Mekka, the Pasha of Baghdad exercises influence over numerous Bedouin tribes in his neighbourhood. Several of these were already at war with the Wahabys, whose expeditions were dreaded all along the banks of the Euphrates. The country about Basra was almost every year visited by a host of these sectaries, who slaughtered many of the Arab settlers on the southern side of the river, who were subjects of the Baghdad government.

The Persian hadjys, who went to Mekka by way of Baghdad and Derayeh, complained moreover, at their return, of the great vexations they had experienced from the Wahabys, to whose chief they were obliged to pay a capitation, or passage-toll, to a considerable amount.

To direct an attack against Derayeh, no city on the Arabian border seems so well adapted as Baghdad. The pasha of this place, however, has so few pecuniary resources, and his authority so imperfectly acknowledged even within the limits of his own province, that until the year 1797, actual hostilities could not be undertaken. An invasion of Derayeh was then planned. Soleyman Pasha was at that time governor of Baghdad, a personage distinguished for bravery, energy, equity, and those talents which are necessary to a Turkish grandee, desirous of retaining his post. His lieutenant-governor was charged with the management of the expedition which marched from Baghdad. The army consisted of four or five thousand Turkish troops, and twice that number of allied Arabs of the tribes of Dhofyr, Beni Shammar, and Montefek. Their march lay parallel with the Persian Gulf, through a desert country where wells are found at every station. It was directed, in the first instance, towards the province of El Hassa, the richest and most productive part of the Wahaby dominions.

Instead of advancing from that place at once towards Derayeh (only distant five or six days' journey), they laid siege to the fortified citadel of El Hassa, which they expected to take without difficulty. The resistance was prolonged above a month; and the arrival of a strong Wahaby force under Saoud, the son of Abd el Azyz, who remained at Derayeh, excited strong doubts of success, and the Turks resolved to retreat. Saoud anticipated this measure, and, starting before them, encamped with his troops at one of the wells called *Thádj*, at the distance of three days from El Hassa. The other well of that watering-place, about two miles further off, he rendered useless by throwing into it several camel-loads of salt, which he had brought with him for that purpose. The Baghdad troops halted at this well, and it may be conceived how much both men and cattle suffered from the quality of the water; nor was it thought advisable to march, as Saoud might have fallen upon the army by surprise. On the other side, this Wahaby chief did not venture to attack the Turks, whose artillery was very formidable to him and his Arabs. Thus the two armies continued three days within sight of each other, in opposite ranks; only a single horseman from each party skirmishing occasionally in the plains between the two camps. A parley having been established, peace was concluded for six years between Saoud the Wahaby, and the pashalic of Baghdad, after which both armies returned quietly to their respective homes.

The failure of this expedition was the first cause of the misfortunes which soon after befell the Turkish party on all sides, as the Wahabys had now learned to despise the Osmanly troops. The peace was soon broken. A Persian caravan of pilgrims, escorted by a Wahaby guard, was attacked and almost totally plundered between Helle and Meshhed, by Arabs, under the Turkish jurisdiction of Baghdad. The neighbourhood of Basra was again visited by plundering parties of the Wahabys; and the sacking of Imám Hosseyn, in 1801, spread terror among all true Muselmáns, as much as it elated the sectaries. The veneration paid to that tomb of Mohammed's grandson was a sufficient cause to attract the Wahaby fury against it. Five thousand persons were massacred in the town. Old men, women, and children were spared; and the quarter called Haret el Abbasye was respected on account of the Wahaby regard for the memory of its founders. The cupola of Hosseyn's tomb was destroyed; but the treasures of that mosque, as well as those of Meshhed Aly had been secreted and afterwards removed towards Baghdad. The Wahabys, having placed trunks of palm-trees against the wall which defended the town of El Hosseyn, escaladed it, and during five or six days were engaged in the massacre and plunder of the inhabitants, after which the invaders retired and attacked the Arab settlers on the river Shat el Arab; but they were repulsed by the Zebeyr Arabs, and also by the people of Meshhed Aly. They carried off, however, all the booty previously taken, and returned to their homes.

After the plundering of Imám Hosseyn the Wahabys seem to have considerably extended their views, especially as a second expedition in the neighbourhood of Baghdad had failed. The Montefek sheikh, *Thoeny*, accompanied by his own people and the tribes of Dhofyr, Shammar, and Beni Kab, with a troop of Turkish soldiers, had marched against Nedjd. Without halting at El Hassa they passed on at once towards Derayeh, and reached the well *Szebeyhy*, distant one day's journey from the much-frequented watering-place called *el Koweyt*, within five or six days of Derayeh. While the troops were encamped there, Thoeny, the commander, was murdered by a slave belonging to Beni Khaled, a fanatic Wahaby. Saoud immediately approached, and the Baghdad soldiers fled; but several thousands of them, not knowing the roads, were slain, although most of the Bedouin troops escaped. Many of the former returned on the following night to the well of Szebeyhy that they might obtain water, hoping also either to pass unnoticed or to be treated as prisoners. But Saoud would not depart from his established custom; he ordered his Arabs to kill them all.

The Arabs of Nedjd, and of the Northern Desert, evinced more humanity than the others; they secreted in their tents many of their unfortunate enemies, gave them water for the road, and dismissed them before day-break; while, on the contrary, the southern Bedouins (principally those of Kahtan and Ateybe) unmercifully put to death all who halted at their tents. Yet even then, whatever might be their fanaticism or the commands of their chief, the Bedouins could not wholly suppress their feelings; and an eye-witness assured me that every straggler was permitted to allay his thirst before he received the mortal blow. I have already mentioned that the Wahaby chief allows no right of *dakheil*, or protection, in favour of any individual devoted to death by the Wahaby law as an enemy found in arms.

Saoud's father, Abd el Azyz, in 1801, began to attack Hedjaz and Sherif Ghaleb, with more perseverance and zeal than he had demonstrated before. Ghaleb in his campaigns against the Wahabys had been alternately victor and vanquished; he had once penetrated into Nedjd, and for a whole year kept possession of the small town called Shaara, in the province of Kasym. Another time, being surrounded by the Wahaby troops, he fought his way through them by night, and with a few followers only escaped to Beishe. The Wahabys, during some years, had extended their arms and faith among most of the mountain tribes southward of Tayf towards Yemen, people of considerable strength; and *Abou Nokta*, sheikh of Azyz was appointed commander of all. Even the Arabs near Tayf were, in 1801, obliged to yield. Ghaleb's brother-in-law, Othman el Medhayfe, a sheikh of the Adouan tribe inhabiting those parts, had been for several years at enmity with him; and as he was distinguished for all the qualities necessary to a Bedouin chief, Abd el Azyz, having subdued the country, named him chief of the tribes of Tayf and Mekka, and thence northward halfway towards Medinah. Ghaleb was now closely hemmed in, yet did not lose his energy; he collected the remainder of his faithful Arabs, and once more attempted the invasion of Nedjd but with little success.

In 1802, Othman el Medhayfe besieged Tayf; and this pretty town, the summer residence of all the rich Mekkans and the paradise of Hedjaz, as the Arabs call it, was taken after a vigorous resistance, and shared the fate of Imám Hosseyn, with this difference, that Othman's enmity to the Sherif induced him to ruin most of the good buildings, and, in the general massacre, his soldiers were not commanded to spare either the infirm or the infants. In the course of the same year, Medhayfe also took Gonfode, a harbour on the Red Sea, seven days southward of Djidda, and belonging to the Sherif.

These successes had rendered the Wahabys very bold. Hitherto the Syrian and Egyptian caravans of pilgrims had proceeded regularly to Hedjaz, although Sherif Ghaleb had done all in his power to produce open warfare between the Porte and the Wahabys. Djezzar Pasha of Acre, while he was Pasha of Damascus, had sometimes conducted the caravan himself to Mekka in a pompous style; and so, likewise, did Abdallah, Pasha of Aden. The latter had repeatedly met at Mekka, on the plain of Arafat, during the hadj, the whole host of Wahaby pilgrims; and presents had been exchanged between him and Abd el Azyz. In refusing to let the caravans pass, the Wahabys appear to have acted from religious motives, for they knew that the soldiers who accompanied them would not attempt any hostile measures in a country where they might be at once cut off from all supplies and reinforcements. But the hadjys, or pilgrims, composing those caravans had always acted in so indecorous a manner, their chiefs had so openly sanctioned the vilest practices, and the ceremonies of the hadj itself had been so polluted by the conduct of the devotees, that the Wahabys, who had long insisted upon a reform of these disorders, resolved to terminate them. The Syrian caravan performed its pilgrimage for the last time in 1802.

In the northern parts of Hedjaz, the Wahabys attacked the strong and warlike tribe of Beni Harb, and blockaded Medinah.

In 1803 the Wahabys effected the total conquest of Hedjaz, and their power was then extended beyond all former bounds. Saoud, the son of Abd el Azyz, and Othman el Medhayfe, had collected early in that year a strong force at Tayf, and, after several battles with Sherif Ghaleb, the Wahaby host approached Mekka and fixed their head-quarters at the village of El Hesseynye, where the Mekkans had many pleasant summer-houses, one hour and a half distant from Mekka towards the south. Their light troops beset the town on every side; they attacked the eastern suburb called *el Moabede*, of which they kept possession for a while, together with the Sherif's palace in that quarter; from this place they made frequent irruptions into the town, which is not defended by walls. Ghaleb, undismayed, bravely resisted. He laid a mine near his palace, which though not completely successful, yet obliged the enemy to retire.

They now cut off the supply of sweet water which the canal from Arafat conveys to the town, and the inhabitants were reduced to the necessity of drinking from the brackish wells. After two or three months' siege the inhabitants began to suffer extremely both from bad water and scarcity of provisions. Ghaleb himself and his soldiers had some stores at their disposal; but nothing was distributed among the lower classes, who were therefore obliged to venture out at night to collect dry grass upon the neighbouring mountains for the Sherif's horses, receiving in return a handful of corn at the Sherif's residence.

When all the cats and dogs of Mekka had been devoured, and the Sherif's provisions became scarce, he left the town with his own people, carrying off the whole of his family and baggage, having previously set fire to such furniture of his palace as was not easily portable. He retired to Djidda, and Mekka was left to its fate. On the next morning the chief inhabitants went out to capitulate, or rather, to surrender at discretion; and Saoud entered on the same day. These events occurred in April and May, 1803. The Mekkans still remember with gratitude the excellent discipline observed by these wild Wahabys on their entering the town. Not the slightest excess was committed. On the next day all the shops were opened by order of Saoud, and every article which his troops required was purchased with ready money. Saoud declared that he might have taken the town by assault long before, but that he wished to avoid disorder and excesses; and he told the olemas in full council that he had seen Mohammed in a dream, who threatened him that he should not survive three days if a single grain of corn were forcibly taken from the holy city.

The people of Mekka now became Wahabys; that is, they were obliged to pray more punctually than usual, to lay aside and conceal their fine silk dresses, and to desist from smoking in public. Heaps of Persian pipes, collected from all the houses, were burnt before Saoud's head-quarters, and the sale of tobacco was forbidden. The brother of Ghaleb, *Abd el Mayen*, was placed by Saoud at the head of the Mekkan government; and a learned man from Derayeh, called *Ibn Name*, was appointed kady of the town. So upright was this Bedouin judge that his sentences have become almost proverbial, and the Mekkans now say in derision of their venal Constantinopolitan kady " There goes Ibn Name!" At this time the prayers for the sultan, usually recited in the grand mosque, were abolished.

From Mekka Saoud turned his arms against Djidda, where Sherif Ghâleb had taken refuge. The town was besieged for eleven days, but the inhabitants fought bravely; and Saoud, despairing of being able to force the walls, retreated. Many persons affirm that Ghâleb, who had made preparations on board a large ship in the harbour, for escaping by sea, induced Saoud to retire, by a bribe of fifty thousand dollars. The Wahabys now moved back towards the Northern Desert. Ghâleb issued from Djidda, and resumed the government of Mekka (in July 1803), where the small Wahaby garrisons of the two castles capitulated, and Abd el Mayen, a man of peaceable character, again submitted to his brother; but Ghâleb himself, soon after, knowing that he could not defend the place for any time, compromised with Saoud, and surrendered to that Wahaby chief. The details of this war, although it had occurred only eleven years before my travels in Hedjaz, were related to me with different circumstances, by various persons.

Ghâleb enjoyed, on this occasion, more favourable conditions than those usually granted to other proselyte chiefs. He was left in possession of his towns and their incomes. Several Bedouin tribes were permitted to remain under his influence; and in consideration of his high station, and the respect due to those who inhabited the holy city, neither himself, nor the Mekkans, were required to pay tribute to the great chief. On the other hand, the Sherif renounced the custom duties at Djidda from all true Wahabys.

The capture of Mekka was the signal for other advantages in Hedjaz. The tribe of Harb was obliged to yield, but not without a severe contest, which so exasperated the Wahabys, that they treated them more rigorously than any other Bedouins of the country. A branch of the Harbs, called *Beni Sobh*, successfully maintained themselves in their steep mountains, and were never reduced to submission. Yembo surrendered when the Beni Harb and Djeheyny (another large tribe of that neighbourhood) had joined the Wahaby party; and Medinah soon after (early in the spring of 1804) followed its example. The principal man of this city, Hassan el Kaladjy, had usurped a despotic power, and been guilty of the greatest injustice during the general distress, while all supplies were withholden from the town by the Wahabys. He at last seized upon the treasure attached to the tomb of Mohammed, and divided part of it among his adherents; after which, he proposed to surrender. The inhabitants of Medinah, who are much more inclined to the Turkish interest than the Mekkans, and live wholly upon the profits derived from those who visit their mosque, were not so leniently treated as the people of Mekka had been. The usual tribute was required, but private property was not plundered. The chief Turkish officer of the town, the Aga el Haram (appointed by the sultan), was obliged to leave Medinah, with many Turkish hadjys; and El Medheyan, whom the Wahaby chief had nominated sheikh of the whole tribe of Harb, was appointed governor of Medinah.

Here the Wahabys enforced, with great strictness, the regular observance of prayers. The names of all the adult male inhabitants were called over in the mosque after morning, mid-day, and evening prayers; and those who did not obey the call were punished. A respectable woman, accused of having smoked the Persian pipe, was placed upon a jack-ass, with the pipe suspended from her neck, round which was twisted the long flexible tube, or snake: in this state she was paraded through the town. Hassan el Kaladjy still retained some influence under the Wahabys, and continued to annoy the inhabitants.

Saoud soon after visited Medinah, and stripped Mohammed's tomb of all the valuable articles that it still possessed (the gold vessels had been previously taken away). He also endeavoured to destroy the high dome erected over the tomb, and would not allow Turkish pilgrims to approach Medinah from any quarter; and several of them, who attempted to pass from Yembo to the town, were ill treated; their beards also were cut off, as the Wahabys, who themselves have short scanty beards, declared, that the prophet did not wear so long and bushy a beard as those of the northern Turks. This was done by the low classes of Wahabys in derision of the Turks, and not in obedience to any law, or command.

The Wahabys, however, continued always to visit Medinah in honour of Mohammed; and they paid a devout visit also to the mosque of that prophet, but not, like other Muselmáns, to his tomb, situated in that mosque. The tomb was left uninjured; but Saoud regarded as idolatrous any visits, prayers, or exclamations, addressed to it, and therefore he prohibited them. But it is false to assert, as the Turks have done, that the pilgrimage to Medinah was abolished by the Wahabys.

Even before the capture of Medinah, the great pilgrimages by caravans had ceased. The Syrian caravan, commanded by Yousef Aga, an officer of Abdallah Pasha, had not been able (in 1803) to reach Medinah, but retreated when within a few hours' distance. They were not molested on their return. The Egyptian hadj of that year did not venture to take the land route, as the tribes of Harb and Djeheyne had now become Wahabys; but the Mahmal, and a few pilgrims, went by sea to Djidda, with about four or five hundred soldiers, under the command of Sherif Pasha, whom the Porte had named governor of Djidda. The Persian hadj, too, had been kept back since 1802; and the same was the case with the Yemen caravan of pilgrims: so that, after 1803, no regular hadj caravan arrived at Mekka, where a few only succeeded in finding their way. The Mahmàl was detained at Djidda, and Sherif Pasha died in 1804 in Hedjaz. It was suspected that he had been poisoned by order of Ghaleb.

Abd el Azyz survived the taking of Mekka, but did not witness that of Medinah. He was assassinated in the latter end of 1803 by a Persian, whose relations the Wahabys had murdered. Abd el Azyz was succeeded by his eldest son, Saoud, superior to his father in the necessary qualities of a religious leader of Bedouin warriors. He had for many years conducted all the wars; and to him may be ascribed the conquest of Hedjaz.

While Medinah was compelled to admit within its gates the northern Wahabys, those of the south were not idle in extending the influence of their arms. Abou Nokta, the sheikh of Asyr, had been for some time at war with the Sherif Hamoud, who at that time governed the Yemen coast from near Gonfode southward to Beit-el-Fakyh, a country which he had himself detached from the jurisdiction of his nearest relation, the Imam of Szana. Hamoud relying upon the walls of his town, and five or six hundred cavalry in his service, had always refused to adopt the Wahaby faith. Near the close of the year 1804, Abou Nokta, with a numerous body of his Arabs, descended from the mountains, and spread over the coast such multitudes of Wahabys, that Hamoud was obliged to fly. The richest towns on the Yemen coast, Loheya and Hodeyda, were plundered; but Abou Nokta did not venture to remain in them long with his army; he retreated again to the mountains, thence keeping in check the whole coast of Yemen. Hamoud again declared his adherence to the new faith.

Although Hedjaz was now conquered, the Sherif's power continued to be very great. His name and venerable office; his great talents for intrigue; and his personal influence over many Bedouin tribes, that still resisted the authority of Saoud, and the valuable presents made to the latter, whenever he visited Mekka, caused the Wahaby chief to connive at several of Gháleb's proceedings. When Saoud approached Mekka for the annual pilgrimage (which he regularly performed, with great numbers of his Arabs), a whole caravan of camels, loaded with presents from the Sherif, came to meet him at Zeyme, two days distant from the city. The presents comprised all sorts of choice provisions, clothes, and other articles, besides several camel-loads of Indian muslin, to serve for the *ihram*, or mantle, in which the pilgrims enter the sacred territory. All his officers received similar presents. The women and children had all new suits of clothes, and quantities of sweetmeats. Such, indeed, was the liberality of Gháleb on these occasions, that Saoud often said, it made him blush, and rendered it impossible for him to treat the Sherif as he otherwise should have done.

At Mekka the power of Gháleb was thus always balancing that of Saoud, and at Djidda the authority of the former continued in full force. A good garrison was constantly kept in that town, which the Wahaby troops never entered, although the inhabitants were obliged to profess their conversion to the new faith, whenever any of Saoud's officers visited them on business. In the course of 1805, Medhayfe, who still continued his hostility against Gháleb, made several attempts to seize Djidda with his own Arabs, and without any formal authority from the Wahaby chief. He took possession of the wells belonging to the town; but the inhabitants, including foreigners who happened to be there, took up arms and frustrated his design.

Although the hadj caravans were now interrupted, great numbers of pilgrims flocked every year to Mekka from all parts of the Turkish empire. They came by sea to Djidda, and no orders were even given by Saoud to prevent them from going on to Mekka. These pilgrims of course were obliged to comply with all the Wahaby precepts; but those who conducted themselves accordingly, and with decency, experienced no harsh treatment. I knew in 1810, at Aleppo, a native of that town, who informed me that he had for the last six years annually performed the pilgrimage by way of Cairo and Cosseir, without any molestation. Pilgrims from Yemen, India, and the Negro countries arrived as before at Djidda by sea, about the month of the hadj; but they found it expedient to leave their arms at Djidda, as the wearing of any weapons at Mekka exposed foreigners to suspicion, and often to ill-usage. The pilgrimage, therefore, was never abolished, either with regard to Arabs or Turks; and had the great Syrian and Egyptian caravans placed confidence in the safe-conduct of the Wahabys, they might have crossed the Desert with security, but without any armed force.

Hedjaz was now tranquil. The communication being opened with all the interior, and few foreigners arriving, provisions were abundant and cheap; but the inhabitants of the holy cities had lost their principal means of subsistence, derived from their intercourse with foreign merchants coming to the pilgrimage.

In this state Hedjaz continued during the years 1806, 1807, and 1808. The Sherif's power was daily declining, and Saoud's authority was acknowledged over the far greater part of Arabia. In the years above mentioned, this Wahaby chief made several incursions against Basra and Mesopotamia. One of his attacks on Basra about this time proved unfortunate. His troops were engaged in plundering the villages about that town in small parties, when they were overpowered by a strong body of Kab and Montefek Arabs, and upwards of fifteen hundred of the Wahabys were slain. A Negro slave of Saoud, called *Hark*, at the head of a strong troop, made various expeditions into the Syrian Desert, and frightened the Bedouins in the very vicinity of Aleppo. The Euphrates was forded by Wahaby detachments, and the wealthy camps of the Mesopotamian tribes were attacked and plundered, even in the neighbourhood of Baghdad. In the south, Abou Nokta continued to harass Yemen by rapid incursions and frequent plundering. Sana, however, does not seem to have been ever made the object of attack. Saoud, who knew the jealousy prevailing between Hamoud, the governor of the coast, and Abou Nokta, chief of the mountains, alternately promised to each of them the plunder of that rich city, which, from its feeble means of defence, could not have resisted a slight attack; but he never actually ordered either to undertake the conquest of it; and this, it was supposed, he wished to reserve for himself.

During those years the Porte remained almost inactive. Saoud had come to open hostilities with the Turkish government, since he forbad the people to pray in their mosques for the welfare of the Sultan, as was usually done on Fridays. This was effected by the artful contrivance of Sherif Ghâleb, who wished to cause an irreconcileable rupture between Saoud and the Porte. A brave warrior, Yousef Pasha, had been placed at the head of that government; and it was expected that he could lead the pilgrim caravans by force through the Desert. But the sums destined for that caravan (which are assessed upon the income of Damascus), he applied to his own use. Nor did the Syrian Bedouins, who usually escort the caravan, show any great desire to be concerned in so hazardous an enterprise.

Yousef Pasha made, in the year 1809, some faint preparations of attack against the district of Djof, consisting of several villages on the road from Damascus to Nedjd, twelve days distant from Damascus. But it was only a vain demonstration of his zeal, and never took place. The greatest loss which the Wahabys ever experienced was, in the course of that year, the destruction of their fortified harbour on the Persian Gulf, called *Râs el Kheyme*, which was laid in ashes by an English expedition sent from Bombay; as its piratical inhabitants of the *Gowasim* or *Djowasim*, tribe had committed numerous depredations upon the English commerce in that sea. A cousin of Saoud was among the killed on that occasion.

In the same year a fresh war broke out between Abou Nokta and Sherif Hamoud: the former descended from his mountains, and encamped in front of Abou Arysh. Hamoud sallied forth at night from that town with about forty horsemen, dressed as Wahaby Bedouins, and taking a circuitous route, arrived by dawn of day in the rear of his enemies; whose camp they entered without having excited any suspicion, for they were supposed to be friendly mountaineers. But in front of Abou Nokta's tent they shouted their war-cry, and Hamoud killed that chief with his own hand as he was starting up from his mat, and was fortunate enough to escape in the general disorder.

Sheikh Tamy, of the small Refeydha tribe (belonging to Asyr), was appointed by Saoud to succeed Abou Nokta. Hamoud again submitted; but his allegiance was always doubtful, and he never was punctual in remitting the tribute.

In 1810, Saoud struck terror into the heart of Syria, by attacking the neighbourhood of Damascus with about six thousand men. His arrival was unexpected; and Yousef Pasha's army was unable to check his progress. During three days he plundered thirty-five villages in the Hauran district, only two days distant from Damascus, and burnt all the corn wherever he passed; but he was not so unmerciful to the inhabitants as he had been on other occasions; and the lives of many peasants were spared. A Christian woman, made prisoner, and carried off as a slave, was some days afterwards released by order of Saoud. He might easily have taken the town, had he known the terror inspired by his approach among the inhabitants, who began to send off all their valuable property to the mountains of Libanon; but his plan was, undoubtedly, to make frequent plundering visits; so that Damascus, at least, would have been induced to surrender voluntarily. He returned with considerable booty.

A numerous caravan of Moggrebyns, which had come by land to Cairo, performed the pilgrimage this year. On their arrival in Hedjaz, they received permission to visit Mekka, as Saoud had always declared that the Moggrebyns behaved with decency, and were religious people. He met with the leader of this caravan, a son of the Emperor of Marocco, and presents were exchanged between them.

While the Pashas of Baghdad and of Damascus had, at different times, made hostile demonstrations against the Wahabys, Egypt remained a passive spectator of the fate of Hedjaz; and the small expedition of about five hundred men, fitted out in 1804 by Sherif pasha of Djidda, was the only feeble effort made on the part of Egypt to restore the Turkish influence over the holy cities. The turbulent state of Egypt—the division of power among the numerous Beys, who acknowledged but a nominal obedience to the pasha sent by the Porte—and the desire of those Beys to possess the money appropriated for the pilgrim-caravans, and for the holy cities—all these circumstances caused every faithful Sunny to despair of ever seeing the hadj revived, as long as Egypt should remain in that condition. For all parties knew, that from Egypt only could Hedjaz be conquered. The immense Desert extending between that country and Damascus, rendered impossible the transport of sufficient provision and ammunition for a regular campaign with an enemy, whose first measure would be to cut off all other communication. A strong body of troops, accompanied by a vast number of loaded camels, might perhaps, after many serious difficulties, succeed in reaching Medinah, and even Mekka: they might also take those towns; but all the troops and camels that they could muster would not enable them to keep the whole country in subjection, to defend it against an active enemy, and to render themselves independent of foreign supplies.

This last consideration alone showed, that from Egypt all efforts must be directed for liberating the country from its Bedouin masters. Hedjaz depends almost exclusively upon Egypt for every necessary of life, which may be carried there by sea, through Yembo and Djidda, the very gates of both the holy cities, without exposing them, during their passage, to any of the casualties attending a journey of thirty or forty days, over a barren and hostile desert, from Syria to Mekka.

The Wahabys did not refuse to admit pilgrims from all quarters into the holy cities: they had often publicly offered to allow their peaceable passage should they behave with decorum, and not assume any airs of supremacy in these countries, which the natural disposition and character of their inhabitants, as well their geographical position, had made an Arabian and not a Turkish province. After Mekka and Medinah had yielded to the Wahabys, after the Sherif himself had become a proselyte to their faith, and acted in open hostility against the Porte, and all Hedjaz followed his example, the most natural measure that presented itself was to cut off any farther supplies, by shutting the ports of Cosseir and Suez against all Hedjaz shipping. That such a step was not taken during the Mammelouk reign, when no general measure could ever be carried into effect in Egypt, where, besides, those Beys whose influence predominated, derived considerable profits from the Hedjaz trade, will not surprise us. But one might reasonably wonder at the neglect of this prohibitory system, under the government of Mohammed Aly, who, since 1805, possessed the port of Suez, and since 1808 that of Cosseir; and who had promised in the strongest terms, to his sovereign, that he would rescue Hedjaz from the Wahabys.

During all that time, and even in the beginning of 1810, when

Mohammed Aly made serious preparations for attacking the Wahabys, there were daily arrivals at Suez and Cosseir of ships from Djidda and Yembo, which went back loaded with corn and provisions for the Sherif, as well as for private adventurers; nor was that traffic discontinued until a few months before the sailing of the first expedition from Suez against Arabia, when fears were entertained of the ships being seized in that port for the conveyance of troops. To withhold all supplies from Hedjaz for a single year, would have produced most alarming consequences in that country, where it is not usual to lay by provisions for more than two months; and the scanty supplies brought from Nedjd and Yemen could not have prevented a famine. Had this actually occurred, the Wahaby chief would certainly have been induced to make terms with the governor of Egypt, highly in favour of the the hadj, and of the whole Turkish empire.

Although the Wahaby army occupying Hedjaz might always have been able to subsist upon supplies furnished by the interior, yet the miseries of famine in the sacred cities would have strongly affected those religious fanatics, who had frequently evinced their veneration for those places, and their regard for the inhabitants. The Sherif himself would have employed all his interest with the Wahabys (and even since his submission he possessed considerable influence) to terminate a state of things which, besides distressing his own people, (a matter perhaps of little consideration to him,) would have reduced a great part of his income, arising from trade and the duties levied upon merchandise going to Egypt, or coming from that country.

As so easy and so natural a measure was not attempted by Mohammed Aly, his partisans endeavoured to excuse his neglect by alleging that it would be a heinous sin to starve the Holy Land; but those acquainted with the pasha's character knew that such a consideration was of little weight with him, while persons conversant with the Red-Sea commerce believed that the gains which flowed into his treasury through this channel (partly by his own selling of corn and provisions at Suez and Cosseir, and partly by the custom duties,) were so considerable that he declined the execution of his sovereign's orders, which might have caused a reduction or cessation of those profits. All the nations of the Turkish empire united in execrating the Wahabys, and demanded an expedition, resembling our old crusades, against those heretics. Yet their ships were seen carrying the stores of Egypt from Suez to the barren soil of Hedjaz, thus supplying their own enemies, at the same time that caravans loaded with ammunition destined to be employed against those enemies daily arrived at Suez from Cairo.

The account of such absurd proceedings and miserable half-measures will scarcely be credited by an European reader; but a residence of some years in the Levant will prove, that whenever the smallest, or even temporary loss, is apprehended by a Turkish governor, nothing can induce him to adopt measures of general utility: his views never extend beyond the present moment, while he sacrifices the interests of his sovereign and the welfare of his subjects to any certainty of the most trifling pecuniary advantage. But his cupidity often overshoots its mark, and finally tends to his own ruin, or at least forms an impediment to his own operations.

Mohammed Aly, Pasha of Cairo, despatches his son Tousoun Pasha with a Turkish army to invade Arabia.—Thomas Keith, a Scotchman, (Ibrahím Aga,) commander of Tousoun's Mammelouks—His intrepidity—Ahmed Aga, surnamed Bonaparte—Medinah taken by the Turks, and Mekka surrendered to them.

WHEN Mohammed Aly in 1804, was appointed Pasha of Egypt, where for the last two years he had exercised all the influence which his numerous troops and his own subtlety could give him over the feeble remnant of the once formidable Mammelouks, the principal duty imposed on him by orders of the Porte was to attempt the re-conquest of the holy cities. He was aware that to disobey these orders would be punished with removal from the government; and the Porte, to stimulate his exertions, promised him the pashalik of Damascus for one of his sons, as soon as he should obtain possession of Mekka and Medinah; his own ambition also made that object highly desirable, as the deliverance of the holy cities would exalt him far above all other pashas of the Turkish empire, and add such celebrity to his name that the Porte might never afterwards be induced to oppose his interests. During the first years of his government, the pasha was constantly engaged in skirmishes with the Mammelouks; and it was not until 1810 that he came to a compromise, which made them abandon their pretensions upon all Lower and the greater part of Upper Egypt, engaged them to re-enter Cairo under a promise of safe-conduct, and caused the treacherous massacre of them soon after in the castle of that city.

Near the end of 1809 Mohammed Aly began seriously to prepare for his expedition. It was above all things necessary to have a sufficient number of ships at his command for the transport of troops and provisions. If he had seized upon a single *dow*, coming from Hedjaz, all others would have been frightened away, and an injury done to his undertaking. He, therefore, resolved to construct a flotilla, and during 1809, 1810, and in the beginning of 1811, twenty-eight large and small vessels (from one hundred to two hundred and fifty tons burden) were built at Suez, where about one thousand workmen, among whom were Greeks and other Europeans, found constant employment. The wood prepared at Boulak, near Cairo, was carried upon camels across the Desert, and large magazines of corn, biscuit, and other provisions, were about the same time formed at Suez. As it was not easy to transport in such vessels numerous bodies of cavalry across a dangerous sea, it was necessary to provide for their passage by land. The castles on the hadj road, between Cairo and Yembo, (Adjeroud, Nakhel, Akaba, Moeyleh, and el Wodj,) were all repaired and strengthened by new walls, and garrisoned principally with Moggrebyn foot-soldiers, well accustomed to treat with Bedouins, and those living in the vicinity of the castles were engaged by presents to go with their camels and bring back from Cairo provisions, which were to be placed in the store-rooms of those castles.

At the same time magazines of grain were established at Cosseir; but this port had not, in the beginning of the war, that importance which it afterwards acquired as the exclusive depôt of provisions, being considerably nearer to Hedjaz than Suez, which continued to be merely the mercantile port of Cairo.

When Ghâleb, the Sherif of Mekka, heard that such considerable preparations were made for the invasion of Hedjaz, and that Mohammed Aly possessed greater resources than any other pasha who attempted to force an entrance into that country, he thought it advisable to commence a secret correspondence with him, and to affirm that although irresistible circumstances had obliged him to adopt Wahabyism, yet he was ready to throw off the yoke at the first appearance of a respectable Turkish army on the shore of Hedjaz. In the course of this correspondence he added much information respecting the actual state and force of the Wahabys, the disposition of the Hedjaz Bedouins, and the best mode of attack.

To the first merchant of Cairo, *Seyd Mohammed el Mahrouky*, who had himself often been at Mekka and was deeply concerned in the Red Sea trade, were entrusted by Mohammed Aly the political conduct of the war, and all the necessary arrangement with the Bedouins of the Red Sea: and it cannot be doubted that he had a considerable share in the final success of this enterprise. Mohammed Aly was of too suspicious a character to place much confidence in the assurances of Ghaleb, whose artful and wily talents were well known; but it became necessary to soothe the apprehensions that Ghaleb might entertain of a foreign invader. The fairest promises were made to him, that his authority in Hedjaz should be respected; that the custom duties of Djidda (the chief source of his revenue) should be left in his hands; and the soldiers destined to embark on the expedition were encouraged by reports secretly spread, that Sherif Ghaleb, with all his force, would join them on their arrival.

The state of Egypt was not yet sufficiently tranquil to allow the absence of Mohammed Aly himself. In the southern part of Upper Egypt the Mammelouks still continued a teasing warfare with the pasha's troops. Tousoun Bey, the second son of Mohammed Aly, a youth of eighteen years, was placed in command of the first expedition against the Wahabys, which after much delay was ready for departure at the end of August, 1811. Tousoun Bey, while yet a mere boy, had given proofs of extraordinary courage in the Mammelouk war; and courage being so rare a quality among the present race of degenerate Osmanlys, and still more rare in the family of a pasha, his friends reckoned him competent to the most arduous undertaking. Ahmed Aga, the treasurer, or kheznedar, of Mohammed Aly, was sent with Tousoun as a commander of equal bravery and graver counsel. His butchering achievements in the wars against the Mammelouks and the Arabs in Egypt, had exalted him in the eyes of his master; his utter disregard of human life, his contempt of all moral principles, and his idle boasting had procured him the surname of *Bonaparte*, which afforded him much delight, and by which he was universally designated in Egypt.*

That he was a brave soldier cannot be denied; but drunkenness and lusts of the vilest kind had deprived his mind of all energy and judgment.

To these two commanders was joined El Mahrouky, above mentioned, whose department was the diplomatic negotiation with the Sherif and the Bedouins. Two great olemas of Cairo, Sheikh el Mehdy and Sheikh el Tahtawy, likewise embarked with the troops; that by their controversial learning, as it was said, they might convince the Wahabys of the errors which they had adopted in their new faith. The expedition consisted of two parts. The infantry, composed principally of Arnaut soldiers, amounting to fifteen hundred or two thousand effective men, under Saleh Aga and Omar Aga, embarked at Suez for Yembo, and took with them all the new-built ships carrying provisions.

* I have in my possession some original letters addressed to him by the Wahaby chief, in which he is styled "*Ahmed Aga Bonaparte.*"

The cavalry, with Tousoun Bey and Ahmed Bonaparte, forming a body of about eight hundred men, Turkish horsemen and armed Bedouins (under the command of Shedíd, sheikh of the Howeytát tribe) proceeded by land.

In October 1811, the fleet arrived near Yembo, the troops landed at a short distance from the town, of which they took possession, after a feeble resistance of two days, by capitulation. A fortnight afterwards, the cavalry arrived by land, not having met with any opposition from the Bedouin tribes, who had already been conciliated by considerable sums of money. The taking of Yembo was proclaimed as a first victory over the Wahabys, and a favourable omen for the future success of the expedition. The troops remained several months inactive; the infantry at Yembo, the sea-port; and the cavalry, with the Bedouins, at Yembo el Nakhel, distant from the sea-port six hours, and the chief station of the Djeheyne Arabs. This time was consumed in negotiations. Tousoun Bey found that Hedjaz was not by any means in such a state as he had expected from the representations which Sherif Ghaleb had made. The Bedouin inhabitants of that country, and especially the two great tribes of Harb and Djeheyne, whatever might be their dislike of the Wahabys, and their desire to participate again in the rich tribute and gains arising from the Turkish pilgrim caravan, were completely overawed by the power and vigilance of Saoud, the Wahaby chief; and they did not dare to stir as long as the Turks continued without some decided advantage, which might give them hopes of ultimate success in joining their party. The taking of Yembo alone could not be reckoned of much importance in the prosecution of the war, although it was highly useful for the Turks to have a safe place of anchorage for their vessels and a depôt for their stores.

At the time when the Turkish expedition arrived, Yembo was

not garrisoned by Wahabys; but the Sherif Ghaleb kept in it a governor and about one hundred soldiers. These had attempted some resistance; but the inhabitants obliged them to retreat, fearing that the town might be exposed to the assault of savage troops, and thinking it prudent to capitulate. The Sherif remained a quiet spectator of this commencement of war; he wrote letters to Tousoun Bey, in which he excused himself for not joining him on account of the smallness of his force and his dread of the Wahabys; but he again solemnly declared that he would throw off the mask, and openly attack the latter as soon as the Turks should gain any important advantage, which might at once bring over to their side all the Bedouins of Hedjaz. Meanwhile he strongly garrisoned Djidda and Mekka, and, when urged by Saoud to join him against the invaders, excused himself by expressing his fears of a sudden maritime attack on Djidda, which might lead to the capture of the more distant Mekka.

It was evidently the Sherif's plan either to temporise and to fall upon whichever party should suffer the first signal defeat, or to wait until the two parties were weakened by the war and then to drive them both out of his dominions. The only Hedjaz Bedouins whom Tousoun Bey was able to detach from the Wahabys, were a few branches of the Djeheyne, inhabiting the neighbourhood of Yembo, while the greater part of that tribe and the whole of the Harbs, who bordered upon their territories, remained insensible to his offers.

It became necessary, however, to begin a campaign, lest the people of Hedjaz, as well as the enemy, should regard inactivity as the result of fear, and negotiation as a proof of weakness. To march towards Mekka or Djidda would have obliged the Sherif who occupied those towns to declare himself at once decidedly for one party or the other. A decision which Tousoun Bey had more to dread than the Wahabys. He, therefore, wisely directed his views towards Medinah (six days distant from Yembo). Medinah was always considered the best walled town of Hedjaz, the rampart of that province against Nedjd, and the strong-hold of the Wahabys: the possession of it, therefore, might open or obstruct the passage of the Syrian hadj. The taking of Medinah would induce a number of Bedouins to join the army; and Sherif Ghaleb, when he learned that such was the design, formally promised to declare against Saoud whenever that event should take place.

Having left a garrison at Yembo, Tousoun Bey advanced with his troops in January, 1812, towards Medinah. After a slight skirmish he entered Beder, a small town two days distant from Yembo, and occupied by the tribe of Harb. Beder is situated at the entrance of those mountains which it was necessary to cross on the way to Medinah. Some resistance was expected from the Beni Harb, who held the passes through those mountains; but nothing was known of the presence of any Wahaby troops. Tousoun left a small garrison at Beder, and proceeded with his army to Szafra, a market-place of the Harb tribe (eight hours from Beder); there, after some short fighting, a body of that tribe, gave way. At four hours from Szafra, the road leads through a narrow passage (from forty to sixty yards across), between steep and rugged mountains, at the entrance of which, the village of Djedeyde is situated, among groves of palm-trees, the principal settlement of the Beni Harb; to whom, in former times, the Syrian pilgrim-caravan had often been obliged to pay considerable sums for the permission of passing unmolested.

In this defile, which extends lengthways about one hour and a half, the Turkish army was at once assailed by the united force of the tribe of Harb. After some skirmishing, the Turks, believing that they had obtained the advantage, were induced to pursue the Arabs into the very middle of that pass; when, on a sudden, the mountains, on both sides, were thickly covered with the Wahaby troops, who had arrived the day before from Nedjd, and of whom the Turks had not the slightest information. The Wahabys were commanded by Abdallah and Faysal, the sons of Saoud, and their number amounted to twenty thousand infantry and camel-riders, and from six to eight hundred horsemen. By retreating into the village of Djedeyde, and fortifying themselves there, the Turks might have withstood the attack, and obtained an honourable capitulation, as the number of the enemy rendered it impossible for them to remain long upon the same spot.

On the first cry of alarm, however, the Turkish infantry fell back, and the cavalry, ordered to cover their retreat, soon joined in the flight; while their nimble enemies, pressing them from behind, and outrunning them along the mountain side, poured incessant vollies upon them. Under such desperate circumstances, Tousoun Pasha did not forfeit his reputation for bravery, and acted as became the honour of a commander. Accompanied at first by two horsemen only of his own suite, after vain endeavours to rally his troops, he hastened to the rear, and plunged into the enemy's ranks, to make them desist from the pursuit.

Persons who were present assured me, that while tears gushed from his eyes, Tousoun exclaimed to the fugitive Turks, "Will none of you stand by me?" About twenty horsemen at last joined him; when luckily the Wahabys were, for a short time, engaged in seizing the baggage of the army, and this circumstance caused them to slacken their pursuit; and when the Turks had regained the open space beyond the entrance of the defile, their cavalry rallied, and in some degree protected the others. Had the Wahabys eagerly pushed forward over the mountains, the whole body of Turks would have been annihilated: they contented themselves, however, with taking all the Turkish baggage, four field-pieces, almost every one of their camels, and much booty, which they found in the girdles of the Arnauts, who had enriched themselves with the Mammelouk's spoils in Egypt. About twelve hundred were killed on that day. Tousoun Bey retreated to Beder, set the camp there on fire, not having any means of removing it, and abandoning, for the same reason, his military chest, returned to the sea-shore nearest to Beder, where several of his ships lay at anchor, in a bay called Bereyka. Here he embarked with very few attendants, and proceeded to Yembo by sea. The rest of his troops arrived some days after in great distress; but fortunately for them, the Wahabys, imagining that a strong Turkish corps was intrenched at Beder, did not immediately pursue their success; and thus all who were sufficiently strong to perform the journey, finally reached Yembo.

When the Wahabys knew that their enemies had secured themselves in Yembo, they sent out parties of troops to scour the country up to the very walls of that town. The Sherif, immediately after he received intelligence, that the Turkish expedition had failed, joined the Wahabys in person at Beder. It was at first proposed to storm Yembo; but this project was abandoned, from fear of the Arab inhabitants, who, no doubt, would fight with desperation, as they had espoused the Turkish interests with cordiality. The Wahabys found it unnecessary to blockade the town any longer, and retreated to the interior, ready to assemble again at a moment's notice, whenever the Turks should venture a second time to lead an army into the open country. On this retreat, they left the Harb Bedouins to harass the Turks, and cut off all supplies from the town.

Reverting to the account of those dangerous circumstances in which Tousoun Pasha was placed, when all his people had forsaken him except two horsemen, I must here record an anecdote respecting one of those brave soldiers, called Ibrahím Aga, acting as chief of Tousoun's Mammelouks (Anakder Agassy). This was a young man of about twenty years, a native of Edinburgh, named Thomas Keith. Having been taken prisoner at the last English expedition against Egypt, together with many others of his regiment, (the 72nd Highlanders,) in which he served as gunsmith, he became a Muselmán, and was purchased from the soldier who had made him prisoner, by Ahmed Bonaparte above mentioned. A favourite Sicilian Mammelouk of his master having insulted the young Scotchman, blows ensued; swords were drawn, and the Sicilian fell. Ibrahím Aga escaped from the wrath of Ahmed Bonaparte, and implored the protection of Mohammed Aly's lady, who befriended him and caused her son, Tousoun Bey, to engage him in his service. Tousoun, in one of those capricious fits of ill-humour to which Turkish despots are so often subject, gave orders that the young Scotchman should be put to death for some trifling neglect of duty; but the brave fellow with his sword defended the entrance of his room for half an hour against several assailants, then threw himself out of the window, and again escaped to his kind protectress, who soon reconciled him with his master. Tousoun Bey at length became sensible of Ibrahim's merit as a courageous soldier, made him chief of his Mammelouks, and, after his valorous conduct at Djedeyde, promoted him to the office of treasurer, the second post in rank at the court of a Pasha. He again fought bravely at Medinah and at Taraba (hereafter mentioned), was appointed governor of Medinah in April 1815, and two months after, when hastening with two hundred and fifty horsemen to the assistance of Tousoun Bey (encamped in the province of Kasym), was overtaken by a superior number of Wahabys, and shared the fate of his troops, who were all destroyed. In this last action the gallant Scotchman killed four Wahabys with his own hand; and Abdallah Ibn Saoud confessed, that Tousoun Bey and his faithful treasurer were the two bravest men of the Turkish army.

The losses which they had sustained, now completely disheartened the troops. Saleh Aga and Omar Aga, the two chiefs of infantry, both declared that they could not fight any longer in Hedjaz. Tousoun Bey therefore resolved to send them back: they returned to Cosseir, and, on their voyage to Cairo, recruited their corps with a number of individuals discontented with the Pasha. Having approached that city, they assumed such an imposing attitude, that Mohammed Aly found it necessary to exert all his art in inducing them by threats, as well as by presents, to quit Egypt. Both had formerly pillaged the richest districts of Upper Egypt, and embarked at Alexandria with considerable treasures.

The troops of Tousoun Bey had been much reduced in horses by the fatiguing land journey even before their arrival at Yembo, and they were forsaken by most of the Bedouin horsemen who had accompanied them. About two hundred horses were killed at Djedeyde; and when the army returned to Yembo, those that could be mustered did not exceed that number. Scarcity of food also obliged the owners of these remaining horses to sell them, and the men were sent back to Cairo that they might be fresh mounted. As soon as Tousoun's failure was known to his father, every effort was made to supply the loss and prepare for a new expedition. Mohammed Aly sent large sums of money to his son for distribution among the neighbouring Bedouin sheikhs, with the hope of detaching them from the Wahaby interests. The whole spring and summer of 1812 were spent in these endeavours, while daily reinforcements of troops and ammunition arrived at Yembo. Mahrouky succeeded at last, by the influence of gold, to gain over a considerable number of the Beni Harb, and principally the strong branches of that tribe called Beni Sálem and Beni Sobh, who occupied the pass of Szafra and Djedeyde. Even Sherif Ghaleb, when he was convinced that Mohammed Aly had resolved to prolong the contest, resumed his old system of policy, and assured

Tousoun Bey, that he had only joined the Wahabys at Beder from fear, renewed his offer of opening the gates of Djidda and Mekka to the Turkish troops, as soon as the latter should have taken Medinah.

In October, 1812, Tousoun thought himself sufficiently strong to make a second attempt upon Medinah. The Bedouins on the road had become his friends; many individuals of the Djeheyne tribe had enlisted under his banners; and information that the Wahabys remained inactive in Nedjd, encouraged his hopes of success. He transferred his own head-quarters to Beder, and Ahmed Bonaparte took the command of the troops; who, by the same pass which had been the scene of their former defeat, now advanced towards Medinah. They passed unmolested, left a strong garrison at Djedeyde, and arrived without a skirmish before the walls of Medinah.

A Wahaby garrison had occupied that town and its castle since the last year; and both were well stocked with provisions for a long siege. The chief, however, had remained in Hedjaz unaccountably inactive; but the victory at Djedeyde had extended his authority over all the Northern Arabs; and in 1812, he collected tribute from the Bedouins immediately near to Baghdad, Aleppo, and Damascus. Having sold at Mekka the plunder obtained at Djedeyde, he had returned to Derayeh; and his soldiers were so elated by their victory, and so much despised the Turks for their cowardly conduct at Djedeyde, that they considered it in their power, at any time, to defeat them again. Saoud probably expected that Medinah would make a long resistance, and that want of provisions would force the Turks at last to retreat; in which case he foresaw that the Beni Harb would abandon their foreign allies, who, in their turn, might be easily annihilated.

Some skirmishes with the Wahaby garrison took place before

Medinah, in consequence of which, Ahmed Bonaparte entered the suburbs, and drove the Wahabys into the inner town; from whence, on the approach of the Turks, they had expelled all the inhabitants, who now resided in the suburbs, and took an active part in the first skirmish against the Wahaby intruders. The inner town was defended by a strong and high wall, and a fortified castle; to batter which, the Turks had nothing but light field-pieces. After a siege of fourteen or fifteen days, during which the Wahabys made several sorties, the Turks laid a mine, but in so open a manner, that the Wahabys found means to counter-mine it, and destroy the work. A second mine was attended with greater success, in the middle of November, 1812; and while the Wahabys were engaged in their mid-day prayers, part of the wall was blown up, and the Arnauts rushed into the town. The Wahabys surprised, fled towards the castle: about one thousand of them were butchered in the streets; the whole town was plundered, and only fifty Turks were killed. The Scotchman above mentioned, Thomas Keith (or Ibrahim Aga), evinced his usual intrepidity on this occasion, being the first who entered the breach. About fifteen hundred Wahabys sought refuge in the castle, which the Turks were unable to take, not having proper battering artillery; and the building, situated on a solid rock, was proof against any mine. But after three weeks, their provisions being exhausted, the Wahabys capitulated, on the promise of Ahmed Bonaparte to grant them safe-conduct: he also agreed that they should carry off unmolested all their baggage; and that camels should be provided for those who wished to return to Nedjd.

When the garrison marched out from the castle, they found but fifty camels, instead of three hundred, that had been promised for their conveyance. Thus, they were obliged to leave behind the greatest part of their baggage, carrying on their own backs whatever was most valuable; but they had no sooner left the precincts of the town, than the Turkish soldiers pursued, stripped, and killed as many of them as they could reach; and few escaped, besides those who were mounted on camels. These Arabs were mostly of the Asyr tribe, residing southward of Mekka, who afterwards made such obstinate resistance against Mohammed Aly. One of their chiefs, Saleh Ibn Saleh, a man from Baghdad, was fortunate in returning to his own country. Masaoud el Medheyan, whom Saoud had made chief of all the Beni Harb, and had placed over several other tribes, not wishing to shut himself in the interior of the town, retired with his family, and forty of his men, to a garden-house, which he had fortified, in a date grove about an hour's distance from Medinah. When this town was taken, he capitulated, on condition of safe-conduct for himself, his family, his followers, and all their baggage; and a house was assigned for his accommodation in the suburbs, where he deposited his family and goods. But when the castle surrendered, and the garrison was so basely massacred, the Turks plundered his house, killed his sons and his attendants, and put himself in irons, and sent him to Yembo. On his passage through Beder, he contrived to escape at night into the mountains, and took refuge with some Bedouins of Beni Harb, who, after three days, were induced by Turkish gold to deliver him up. He was then sent from Yembo to Cairo, and afterwards to Constantinople, where his head was cut off. His fellow sufferer, on this occasion, was Hassan el Kaladjy, already mentioned, who had usurped the government of Medinah, before the Wahabys took the town.

The treacherous behaviour of the Turks at Medinah was an unwise measure, as they were contending with an enemy celebrated for the most scrupulous observance of good faith, in executing the promises of safe-conduct once given. It disgusted all the Bedouins; and with other transactions of a similar nature, which I shall hereafter notice, branded the name of Turk with infamy throughout Hedjaz. Ahmed Bonaparte, in the true style of a Vandal, collected the skulls of all the Wahabys killed at Medinah, and constructed with them a kind of tower, on the high road to Yembo. He stationed a guard near it: notwithstanding which, the Arabs, and even the people of Medinah, succeeded in removing, from time to time, most of those ghastly memorials; and when I arrived at Medinah in 1815, very few of them remained.

On the taking of Medinah, an expedition of one thousand horse, and five hundred foot-soldiers, who had gone by Yembo, advanced towards Djidda and Mekka. They were commanded by Mustafa Bey, the brother-in-law of Mohammed Aly. Like Ahmed Bonaparte, this man had formerly distinguished himself by his barbarous severity towards Egyptian rebels, against whom Mohammed Aly had such frequent occasion to contend. He was named governor of the province of Sherkieh, where he exterminated whole camps of Bedouins, and burnt many villages; and he was often heard to boast, that more men had died under the sticks of his *kowas* (or executioners), than could have come into the world, had some one of his women produced a male infant every day in the year.

Sherif Ghaleb had been intimidated by the fall of Medinah: perhaps he actually wished to shake off the Wahabys, and for the present, at least, preferred the Osmanlys. He sent messengers to Mustafa Bey, inviting him to his towns. A few hundred men were detached to Djidda, while the principal corps advanced towards Mekka, where El Medhayfe was then commander of the Wahaby forces; but he found himself not sufficiently strong to offer battle, and retired towards Tayf, a few hours before Mustafa Bey made his entry, in January, 1813. The property of the Mekkans was respected, as it had formerly been by the Wahabys; and Ghaleb now joined the Turks with above one thousand Arabs and black slaves. A fortnight after the deliverance of Mekka, an attack was made on Tayf (three days distant eastward), and some skirmishing occurred before the town; El Medhayfe fled; and Sherif Ghaleb, with Mustafa Bey, entered the place, which the Wahabys had held during ten years, and which had suffered more than any other town in Hedjaz.

Mohammed Aly Pasha proceeds from Egypt with an army of Turks—Arrives at Djidda and Mekka—Arrests Sherif Ghálveb, and sends him prisoner to Cairo—Ghálveb's troops assemble at Turaba.

MUSTAFA BEY, intoxicated with success, and with the raisin wine of Tayf, considered himself alone able to subdue the Wahabys. The town of Taraba, distant from Tayf about seventy or eighty miles, in an easterly direction, was one of the principal strong-holds that connected the Wahabys of Nedjd with those of the Yemen mountains. At Taraba resided the Begoum Arabs; and since the Wahaby wars with Sherif Ghaleb, they had fortified their town with a wall and a ditch; and the thick forest of date-trees in which it was situated, served as an additional defence. Mustafa Bey pushed on towards Taraba, but was opposed in the mountainous country, and obliged to return, with a loss of four or five hundred men, to Tayf. Othman el Medhayfe, with his light cavalry, was not inactive in the mean while: he scoured the country in every direction, cut off many stragglers, often intercepted the communication with Mekka, and, during the whole summer of 1812, greatly embarrassed the garrison of Tayf. Sherif Ghaleb, who had, like Othman, his Bedouin horsemen, offered five thousand dollars as a reward for the capture of Medhayfe. Personal enmity to his brother-in-law, who had been the main cause of all his misfortunes with the Wahabys, here overcame his judgment; and he did not reflect, that if the Bedouins about

Mekka should lose that chief, the Turks would find it easy to establish themselves firmly in the country, and to deprive himself of his authority.

In one of his excursions Medhayfe halted at Byssel, a small castle which he had built in the mountains, four or five hours eastward of Tayf. The Sherif, informed of his being there, detached a strong party of troops from Tayf, who surrounded the castle and soon after set it on fire. Medhayfe with about thirty followers, all dressed like Bedouins of the poorest class, rushed upon the enemy and cut their way through them; a wound, however, disabled his mare, and she could not carry him far. He then proceeded on foot and escaped from his pursuers; but next day, seeking refuge in the tent of an Ateybe Bedouin, he was seized and carried before the Sherif, who paid the promised reward to the Bedouin and loaded his prisoner with chains. Medhayfe was then despatched to Djidda and Cairo, and finally to Constantinople, where the youngest son of Mohammed Aly presented the noble captive to his sovereign, with the keys of the holy cities and many valuable offerings. As may be supposed, Medhayfe was, soon after his arrival, beheaded; and thus the Wahabys lost their most active and daring partisan in Hedjaz. He was made prisoner in September 1812.

Hedjaz was now reduced to obedience, and the holy cities were free. The pilgrim-caravan from Cairo arrived at Mekka in November 1812, with all its usual pomp, and performed the hadj with due ceremony. The caravan from Syria could not as yet attempt to pass through the Desert, as the castles in the hadj route and the reservoirs attached to them had not been repaired, nor had stores been provided. Ahmed Bonaparte had returned to Cairo; Tousoun Bey, created Pasha of Djidda, had come to Mekka as a hadjy in the winter of 1812, leaving the Diwan Effendi, an officer of Mohammed Aly's court, as governor at Medinah.

Although the five cities of Hedjaz were now in the hands of the Turks, yet the Wahaby power was unbroken. All the tribes eastward of those mountains that traverse that country from north to east parallel with the sea, still acknowledged the supremacy of Saoud. The Turks, whenever they encountered the Bedouins in the open country, were always defeated; and the Sherif's conduct by no means inspired his allies with confidence. Under these circumstances, Mohammed Aly Pasha thought it necessary to visit in person the scene of action, and strike a signal blow that might establish his authority on a permanent footing in Hedjaz, and enable him to claim for himself the whole merit of the conquest. It was known that his sovereign had peremptorily commanded him to place himself at the head of the troops in that country; and as Egypt, since 1811, was under complete subjection, he had not any excuse for disobedience. The feeble remnant of the Mammelouks had been expelled from Upper Egypt, and had retired to Dongola. Ahmed Aga Lás, a celebrated Arnaut chief, governor of Genne, the only person of influence among the soldiers, and of whose designs the Pasha entertained suspicions, was enticed to Cairo; and his execution was a farther proof (if any were requisite) of the little respect in which Mohammed Aly held his own most solemn pledges of safe-conduct. At his departure from Cairo, Mohammed Aly left Hosseyn Bey as governor of the city and of Lower Egypt, and Ibrahím Pasha, his eldest son, as governor of Upper Egypt, both men of considerable talents; Hosseyn Bey in the military, and Ibrahím Pasha in the civil administration.

Mohammed Aly embarked at Suez with two thousand infantry, while a corps of cavalry equal in numbers, accompanied by a train of eight thousand camels, proceeded by land about the same time. Tousoun Pasha was employed in collecting his troops at Mekka, when his father arrived at Djidda in September 1813. Sherif

Ghâleb happened to be there, and repaired on board the Pasha's vessel to compliment him even before his landing. It was on this occasion that they swore upon the Korán, never to attempt any thing contrary to the interest, safety, or life, one of the other—a vow which they solemnly and publicly renewed some weeks after in the holy temple at Mekka, by express desire of the Sherif, who had not yet learned that no promise could be devised sufficiently sacred to bind an Osmanly. The Sherif likewise settled with the Pasha some difficulties which had arisen between him and the Turkish governor of Djidda; for since the conquest of Hedjaz in the sixteenth century by the Turks, it was an established law that the customs of Djidda should be divided between the pasha of that place and the governor of Mekka. Ghâleb had appropriated them to his own use exclusively, and the Pasha had promised not to interfere with his possession of them.

Mohammed Aly having arrived at Mekka, bestowed presents on the olemas, and distributed alms to the poor. He began to repair the great temple, and invested large sums for the service, as well as for the ornaments of it. But his first, and most urgent business at that time, was to provide for the transport of necessary supplies from Djidda to Mekka and to Tayf. Djidda had become the great depository of provisions and ammunition for the army. The whole shipping of that port, and of Yembo, (which is considerable,) was employed in that transport business; and Mohammed Aly had contracted with the Imám of Mascat for the hire of twenty ships during one year.

The Pasha had wished that a small frigate, the only ship of war belonging to him, and which was at Alexandria, should have been taken round by the Cape of Good Hope, into the Red Sea; but the English government would not grant permission, knowing that the ship, badly manned as it was, would probably be lost in seas unknown to Turkish navigators, and the loss attributed by the suspicious Turks, to the secret orders of the English. An Englishman, who had resided for some time in Egypt, proposed to convey the ship, at high water, to Cairo, and then upon rollers across the Desert to Suez. He seemed confident the undertaking was practicable; but his project deviated too much from the usual routine of things to be adopted by the Turks.

It was found more difficult to convey provisions the short distance between Djidda and Mekka, than to send them from Egypt to Djidda. Most of the camels that attended the expeditions to Hedjaz, perished soon after their arrival. By the continual passage of caravans, the herbage in the road was soon consumed, and the camels had no food, except a small quantity of beans in the evening; and of this scanty allowance, some was purloined by the drivers, Egyptian peasants, who had been forced from their homes, and sold the beans to the Hedjaz Bedouins. Of the eight thousand camels which Mohammed Aly had sent by land, five hundred only remained alive three months after their arrival. To inspect the details of his commissariat, was beneath the dignity of Mohammed Aly; nor could he have made any salutary arrangements without changing the whole administration of his army, in which every individual, from the lowest to the highest, was engaged in peculation. The Bedouins who espoused the Turkish interest were poor in camels, as are all those who live in mountainous districts: few of them ventured to offer their beasts for the service of the army; and during the whole Turkish war there was not, at any time, the number of five hundred Hedjaz camels collected. Under these circumstances, the Pasha found himself crippled in his operations. The actual number of camels could scarcely supply the daily wants of the troops at Mekka and Tayf; and the Pasha offered so little money to the Bedouins, that few of them would employ their camels in his service.

On his arrival, however, at Mekka, finding the necessity of the case urgent, he pressed the Sherif to use all his influence with the neighbouring Arabs, and induce them to furnish as many camels as possible; and for this purpose a large sum of money was advanced, to be distributed among the sheikhs. But a Bedouin chief has no despotic power in his tribe, nor can he forcibly take away the camel of his meanest Arab. The Sherif promised fairly; so did the Arab sheikhs. A second advance of money was demanded from the Pasha, but still no camels appeared.

The Pasha, who during his first residence at Mekka had visited the Sherif on friendly terms, now became cool in his demonstrations of amity. The Sherif, on his side, complained that the customs of Djidda, notwithstanding the promises of Mohammed Aly, were withheld from his officers; and each party soon accused the other of planning insidious machinations. The intimate connexion of the Sherif with all the neighbouring tribes, who, since the capture of Medhayfe, looked upon him as their protector against both Wahabys and Osmanlys, excited additional suspicion in the Pasha's mind; and he became persuaded, that as long as the Sherif retained his authority, he himself could have no chance of pursuing his operations with success. Mohammed Aly had received a firmán from the Sultan, allowing him to act towards the Sherif as he should think expedient; and either to leave him at the head of the government, or to depose and take him prisoner. So, at least, the Pasha publicly declared, after the imprisonment of Sherif Ghál">eb.

It now became his principal object to arrest and imprison the Sherif; but this was a difficult undertaking. Ghaleb had with him at Mekka about fifteen hundred fighting men, and other troops at Tayf, and at Djidda. The neighbouring Arabs were all more inclined to favour Ghaleb than the Pasha, against whom it would have been easy to excite their hostility. At Mekka, the

Sherif inhabited a strongly-built palace, on the slope of a hill, upon which was a castle, that communicated with the palace by a subterraneous passage. The castle had been built by his elder brother, Serour, and newly fortified by himself, when he heard of Mohammed Aly's preparations for invading Arabia. The castle was well supplied with provisions; the water was abundant in its cisterns; and a garrison of eight hundred men, with a dozen of heavy guns, constantly defended it. The whole town was commanded by this castle, which might be deemed impregnable with respect to the means which Mohammed Aly could employ towards the capture of it by a regular siege. Many other of Ghaleb's troops, such as sherifs of Mekka, with their attendants, several armed slaves, and mercenary soldiers from Yemen, remained quartered in the town itself, or acted as his body-guards. He soon became aware that Mohammed Aly entertained some treacherous designs against him.

It is certain, that if he had violated his solemn promise, and attacked the Pasha (who had, at that time, but twelve hundred men at Mekka), he might, with the assistance of the Bedouins, have driven him from the town. But whatever accusations may have been made against the Sherif for despotism, his bitterest enemies could never prove him guilty of having broken a promise; although the Turks insinuate, that he had laid a plan against the person of Mohammed Aly.

Ghaleb no longer visited the Pasha on a familiar footing as before. Whenever he went to see him at his residence (a large school-house, near the great mosque), he was accompanied by several hundred soldiers; and at last, he discontinued his visits altogether, never quitting his palace but on Fridays, when he went to prayers in the mosque. Mohammed Aly in vain attempted to throw him off his guard. He visited him twice, attended only by a few officers, thinking that Ghaleb would return this visit in a similar manner: he had even resolved to seize him in the very mosque, but was dissuaded from so strong a measure by the kadhy, recently arrived from Constantinople, who strenuously maintained the inviolability of that sacred asylum. This circumstance I state on the best authority.

Nearly a fortnight elapsed, during which Mohammed Aly made daily efforts, but in vain, to accomplish his design. At last he devised a stratagem, which proves the great experience he had acquired in the art of entrapping. He directed his son, Tousoun Pasha, who was then at Djidda, to come at a late hour, on a certain evening, to Mekka. Etiquette rendered it necessary that the Sherif should go to salute him; for the omission of such a ceremony would, according to the Turkish notions, have been equivalent to a declaration of war. Ghaleb wishing to pay his visit before any new plans could be devised against him, went at an early hour on the morning after Tousoun's arrival, and called at his house, attended only by a small party. This had been foreseen; and on the day before his son's arrival, Mohammed Aly ordered about a hundred soldiers to conceal themselves in different rooms, adjoining the court-yard of the house where Tousoun was to halt; this they did in such a manner as not to excite any public observation. When Ghaleb arrived, the attendants conducted him up stairs, under pretence that Tousoun was fatigued by his journey; and the Sherif's principal officers were directed to stay below. He entered the Pasha's room and conversed with him for some time, but, when preparing to depart, was informed by *Abdín Bey* (a commander of the Arnauts) that he must remain their prisoner; resistance would have been unavailing; the hidden soldiers rushed from their lurking-places, and Abdín Bey, with Tousoun Pasha, obliged the Sherif to show himself at a window, and order his people below to return home, as no harm was intended.

When this was publicly known, the two sons of Ghaleb took refuge with their troops in the castle and prepared for defence. The Sherif manifested great coolness:—"Had I proved a traitor myself, this would not have happened," said he to Tousoun Pasha, in presence of his officers; and when a firman (whether true or forged has not been ascertained) was exhibited, requiring his appearance at Constantinople, he replied, "God's will be done: I have spent my whole life in wars with the Sultan's enemies, and cannot therefore be afraid to appear before him." As long as the castle remained in the hands of Ghaleb's sons, the business was but half done. The Sherif was accordingly forced to write a note to his sons, ordering them to surrender the castle to Mohammed Aly; but he did not sign this order until he was threatened with the loss of his head.

Next day the Turks entered the castle, and the garrison dispersed themselves among the neighbouring Bedouins or went to join the Wahabys. The kadhy, with an officer of the Pasha, and another belonging to the Sherif, were appointed to make an inventory of the whole property of the Sherif, and for this purpose his different palaces at Mekka were closely searched. The amount of all that they found was estimated at about sixteen purses, or two hundred and fifty thousand pounds sterling.

After a few days' captivity at Mekka, the Sherif was sent (in November) to Djidda, where he was detained on board a ship in the harbour, and then embarked for Cosseir. I happened to be at Genne, in Upper Egypt, when he arrived there from Cosseir on the first of January 1814, and had an opportunity of seeing him. His spirits seemed unbroken, he spoke boldly and with great dignity, but never mentioned the name either of Mohammed Aly or of his son. He had with him a dozen of eunuchs, a few Arab servants and two of his sons, who had voluntarily joined him at Djidda. Among the few articles of his baggage, I remarked a handsome chess-board, and it was said that he passed some hours every day in playing chess with his favourite eunuch.

At Cairo he met his women, who had been sent by way of Suez, together with his whole property as it was found in his palaces at Mekka; for Mohammed Aly had received orders not to withhold any part of it. One of his sons died at Alexandria; the other followed his father to Salonika, which the Porte had assigned for his residence, and where he received a monthly pension corresponding to his rank. Some female slaves, a younger son, and a sister of Ghaleb remained at Mekka. The Sherif himself and all his family died of the plague at Salonika in the summer of 1816. Abdallah Ibn Serour, a cousin of Sherif Ghaleb, was seized at Mekka the day after that chief's imprisonment, and forwarded likewise to Cairo. He succeeded in escaping, but was retaken and brought back by the Bedouins of Suez. As he had always been at enmity with Ghaleb, no motive could be assigned for his seizure, but that he had a strong party at Mekka. By orders of the Porte he was soon after liberated.

Sherif Ghaleb, during his government of Mekka, had evinced considerable bravery in fighting against the Wahabys, as well as against his own relations, who often opposed him. His profound cunning, and his intimate knowledge of the Bedouins and their politics, his eloquence and penetration, eminently qualified him for the government of Mekka; but he was rapacious and unjust in making demands of money and levying great fines for the smallest offences, and his avarice had caused him to be generally disliked. During a reign of eight-and-twenty years, he must have accumulated considerable treasures in Mekka, where he lived at little expense. As nothing was found on his removal besides the property above mentioned, many persons suspected that he had privately remitted considerable sums of money or articles of value to the East Indies, particularly to Bombay, with which port he was long engaged in commercial intercourse. Mohammed Aly insinuated that the Sherif had intended to take refuge at Bombay; the care however with which he fortified and stored his castle at Mekka, rather proved that he was determined to resist and even to fight the Turks within the precincts of that holy city.

The capture of Sherif Ghaleb spread terror among all the Mekkans and Bedouins. Several chiefs of the latter, whom he had introduced to Mohammed Aly, and with whom a negotiation had commenced, fled from Mekka, and returned to Taraba, the watering-place of the Wahabys. All Ghaleb's friends at Mekka, and several powerful Sherif families with their adherents, left the city and took refuge in the tents of their neighbours, not knowing whether the Pasha did not design to extirpate the whole Sherif race. Among these was *Sherif Rádjeh*, a distant relation of Ghaleb, and a man the most conspicuous in Hedjaz for courage, judgment, and liberality. To him Mohammed Aly had given the command of a few hundred Bedouins, and had charged him to procure others as recruits in his service. On the day when Ghaleb was seized, Rádjeh left Mekka, and proceeded with all his people to Derayeh, the residence of Saoud, who was glad to be joined by a man of such influence and talent; gave him a considerable sum of money, and appointed him in the room of Medhayfe, to be *Emír el Omera*, or chief of the chiefs of the Hedjaz Bedouins.

The imprisonment of Ghaleb caused a stagnation in all the political affairs of the country. Such open treachery alienated from the Turks even those who were most strongly opposed to the Wahabys, and Mohammed Aly's situation became critical. The best-informed persons thought, that if he had resolved to seize upon the Sherif, he should have waited until some powerful

Bedouin sheikhs had joined him, and engaged them to commit actual hostilities against the Wahabys, which might have rendered it difficult or impossible for them afterwards to abandon the Pasha's cause. Mohammed Aly, no doubt, judged of the Sherif's intentions by his own; and feared that he should himself fall a victim to treachery, were he to allow Ghaleb time for the execution of his designs.

But in this he was wrong. Ghaleb was certainly no friend of the Osmanlys; but, on the other hand, he equally disliked the domination of the Wahabys. His project was to weaken both parties; but he never thought of personal treachery towards the Pasha, to preserve whose safety he had made a solemn vow.

A man of the Sherif race, Yahya, distantly related to Ghaleb, and formerly his antagonist, was appointed governor of Mekka by Mohammed Aly, who knew him to be without talents or reputation, and meant that he should be nothing more than a cipher. The Pasha took into his own hands all Sherif Ghaleb's income at Djidda and Mekka, allowing to Yahya a monthly stipend of thirty purses; so that he became, in fact, little more than one of Mohammed Aly's own officers.

At this time, Mohammed Aly had no other object than to forward provisions from Djidda to Mekka and Tayf. Having collected a small quantity at the latter place, he resolved to strike a decisive blow against his enemies, who had been emboldened by his long inactivity, to carry off camels from the very gates of Tayf and of Mekka, while the Bedouins began to show contempt for the power of the Pasha, whom they already detested for his treachery. Among the enemies of the Turks near Mekka, none had evinced more determined hostility than the Begoum Arabs, who inhabited Taraba, and, on a former occasion, had defeated Mustafa Bey. Most of Ghaleb's troops had taken refuge in Taraba after the capture of their master; and Sherif Rádjeh had fixed his head-quarters there, and was joined by Aly el Medhayfe (brother of Othman above mentioned), a man of influence in this country. So that Taraba became the point of union for all the southern Wahabys, as Derayeh was of the northern.

The Begoum Arabs headed by a woman, regarded as a sorceress by the Turks, who are defeated at Taraba—Mohammed Aly takes Gonfode—Discontent of the Turkish troops—Death of Saoud—His son Abdallah declared chief of the Wahabys.

The Begoum Arabs, of whom some are shepherds, and some cultivators, were headed by a widow named *Ghálye*, whose husband had been one of the chief men at Taraba. She herself possessed more wealth than any Arab family in the neighbourhood. She distributed money and provisions among all the poor of her tribe, who were ready to fight the Turks. Her table was open to all faithful Wahabys, whose chiefs held their councils in her house; and as the old lady was celebrated for sound judgment, and an accurate knowledge of the interests of the surrounding tribes, her voice was not only heard in council, but generally prevailed; and she actually governed the Begoums, although they had a nominal chief, or sheikh, called *Ibn Khorshán*. From the first defeat of Mustafa Bey, near Taraba, the name of Ghálye had spread over the whole country. The Turkish soldiers' fears soon magnified her influence and importance: they regarded her as chief of the united Wahabys, and reported the most absurd stories respecting her powers as a sorceress, bestowing her personal favours on all the Wahaby leaders, who, by her means, were rendered invincible.

These reports served to discourage the Osmanlys, and inspired the Bedouins with additional confidence; thus contributing very materially to cause the failure of Tousoun Pasha's expedition. Mohammed Aly had finally determined to try a second attack; and Tousoun was despatched from Tayf about the end of October, or beginning of November, 1813, with two thousand men, to take possession of Taraba. The country between that town and Tayf was in the hands of hostile tribes, the Beni Sad, El Nasera, and particularly the Ateybe. These had appeared neutral while the Sherif governed; and several of their sheikhs had even come to Mekka, that they might negotiate with the Pasha; but as soon as he seized the Sherif, they all fled back to their mountains, and began to make incursions against Tayf, and the Turkish troops, whom they upbraided with the Pasha's treachery.

When Tousoun marched from Tayf, he took with him provisions for thirty days, of which time he consumed the greater part in a fatiguing warfare against the Ateybes, whom he hunted about in their mountains, reducing some of their branch tribes to subjection. On his arrival before Taraba, he had but three days' allowance of provisions remaining. The troops were immediately ordered to attack the place; but the Arabs defended their walls with spirit, being animated by the presence and exhortations of Ghalye; while the Turks, having no prospect of a rich booty, and fatigued by previous exertions, were easily repulsed. Tousoun commanded a second attack to be made on the next day, but his troops openly refused to contend with Ghalye; and his officers represented the exhausted condition of the army, and the want of provisions, stating, that in case of a second repulse, they should all perish from famine. They thus induced him to change the order for attack into one for a retreat towards Tayf. The Bedouins, aware of his embarrassing situation, as soon as he began to retreat, issued from the town, pressed closely upon his soldiers, gained the passes through which his road lay, and harassed them so severely, that at last the Turks commenced a running fight, and abandoned their baggage, tents, guns, and provisions.

Here Thomas Keith, the Scotchman above celebrated, distinguished himself; with a few of his horsemen he retook a gun, and pointed it so well, that he gave the fugitives time to cross a defile, where otherwise they would probably have been all destroyed. Upwards of seven hundred men were killed in this retreat; many died from mere want of water and provisions; for even before Taraba, a pound of biscuit had risen to the price of a dollar. The army was saved from annihilation by about a hundred horsemen, who accompanied Tousoun. The Bedouin infantry were unable to withstand the charge of this heavy Egyptian cavalry, which, however, had but few opportunities of acting with effect in these hilly and rocky districts. The nimble and hardy sons of the Desert possessed great advantages over the clumsy Turkish foot soldier, who is not capable of enduring much fatigue.

After four days of considerable hardship, and many hair-breadth scapes, Tousoun Pasha arrived with the remains of his army from Taraba at Tayf. The failure of his expedition may be chiefly ascribed to the want of camels, for the transport of his men, as well as provisions. Nor were any spare camels left at Tayf, to furnish him with fresh supplies of both. With no other advantage than experience derived from misfortunes, Mohammed Aly was obliged, after this signal defeat, to resume his former occupation, of sending caravans backwards and forwards between Djidda, Mekka, and Tayf, being convinced that any operations against his enemies could best be directed from the last-mentioned place.

The Wahabys having pursued the Turks within a day's journey from Tayf, returned to Taraba, and again practised their system of harassing, by flying excursions, the Pasha's caravans; which could never effect their passage through the country without such numerous guards, as consumed one-third of the food before their arrival at the place of destination. Mohammed Aly passed his time at Mekka and at Djidda.

In November 1813, the pilgrimage was performed with great pomp. Soleyman, Pasha of Damascus, had come with the Syrian caravan through the Desert without any obstacle; but the Bedouins, through whose territories his road lay, obliged him to pay the passage tribute for the whole space of ten years, during which there had been a suspension of the Syrian hadj to Hedjaz. Great numbers of pilgrims from Asia Minor and Constantinople had come by Suez and Djidda to Mekka, and the inhabitants of the holy cities rejoiced to see the revival of those profits which they had formerly derived from the presence of the pilgrims, and of which they had been partly deprived by the Wahabys. Several thousand camels were sent from Cairo with the hadj caravan to the Pasha, also a considerable reinforcement of troops, while Mustafa Bey was ordered back to Egypt, that he might thence procure fresh horses in place of the vast numbers that he had lost. During the winter of 1813 and the beginning of 1814, the Turkish army remained perfectly inactive.

Every expedition against the enemy having failed, (except that in which Medinah was taken,) the Pasha thought it necessary to attempt a diversion on a new plan, the success of which might encourage his troops, and draw off the attention of the Wahabys from the main point of attack. A naval expedition was fitted out at Djidda, accompanied by fifteen hundred foot-soldiers, and numerous transports loaded with provisions. Hosseyn Aga and Saym Oglu were entrusted with the command of this force. They proceeded to Gonfode, a sea-port, seven days southward of Djidda, and formerly part of Sherif Gháleb's territory, but during the last five years in the possession of Támy, sheikh of the Asyr Arabs, the strongest of the mountain tribes south of Mekka, and the most enthusiastic adherents of the Wahabys. The position of Gonfode seemed advantageous in directing attacks against the mountaineers in concert with the garrison of Tayf; and as the place might be easily supplied with provisions, and was a step towards the conquest of Yemen, the riches of which no doubt had strongly attracted Mohammed Aly, the plan was altogether not injudiciously contrived. Gonfode, where Tamy kept only a small garrison, was taken in March 1814, without bloodshed; but most of the inhabitants had fled. A corps of four hundred cavalry set out for Djidda on the sea-shore, as soon as the capture of the town became known. Gonfode was sufficiently defended by a wall to resist an enemy who wanted guns, like the Wahabys; but it has no water within its precincts, and the wells which supply it are three hours distant near the mountains. Fortifications should have been constructed about these wells, and the road from them to the town of Gonfode protected by a line of towers or batteries, as the Turks had abundance of artillery with them; but similar precautions never occur to the stupid and improvident mind of an Osmanly chief: thus the wells of Djidda, which are at half an hour's distance from that town, were always left without the slightest defence.

One hundred and fifty Arnauts were placed near the wells of Gonfode; not so much to guard them against the enemy as to prevent the neighbouring Arabs and country people from watering their cattle. After the Turks had remained at Gonfode about one month, perfectly inactive, they were surprised early in May by a corps of from eight to ten thousand Wahabys, under the personal command of Támy. The Arnauts near the wells were first attacked. Some of them fought bravely till night, the others fled towards the town and spread a general consternation. Without attempting resistance from within the walls, the panic-struck commander and most of his troops ran towards the ships that lay in the harbour, while the Wahabys entered the town and killed numbers of soldiers and servants belonging to the Turkish army, who could not save themselves in boats and who were not able to swim. Many were actually slain in the water close to the vessels, by the Wahabys who swam after them; and the Turkish commander was no sooner safe on board ship himself, than he ordered the sails to be hoisted, and abandoned to certain death all who could not escape by sea.

The Wahabys had never found such booty as rewarded them at Gonfode. The whole baggage, considerable stores, and all the guns became their property, few of the Turks carrying away more than the clothes which they wore. But the most valuable part of the plunder was four hundred horses and a considerable number of camels.

The ships being badly supplied with water or provisions, many of the Turkish soldiers and sailors died on the passage to Djidda. Yet it was insinuated that the commander, Saym Oglu, regularly washed his hands with fresh water, while his unfortunate attendants were expiring from thirst. He was, however, on the arrival of the expedition at Djidda, appointed governor of the place. The few soldiers who had fought during the day at Gonfode, contrived to escape by night, and twelve of them reached Mekka, where they were rewarded by Mohammed Aly, and allowed to enter another corps, as they had resolved never to serve again under the command of Saym Oglu.

About the time of the expedition to Gonfode, Mohammed Aly had gone to Tayf on account of its healthy climate, and that he might be nearer to the scene of action and to the residence of the Bedouins, with whom he again wished to establish an amicable intercourse. In June 1814, a body of fifteen hundred soldiers, the best infantry of Egypt, arrived from Cairo under Hassan Pasha, a celebrated Arnaut chief, and a faithful adherent of Mohammed

Aly, whose fortunes he had shared even before he became Pasha of Egypt. Hassan and his brother Abdín Bey, above mentioned, had reduced Upper Egypt to subjection, and had afterwards cooperated with Mohammed Aly in the massacre of the Mammelouks at Cairo, which was perpetrated wholly by Arnaut soldiers. He had lately shown his zeal, during a short revolution that occurred while the Pasha was absent from Cairo. In December 1813, (or the following January,) Latíf Pasha had excited some suspicion. This man, once a Mammelouk of Mohammed Aly, had been sent with Ismayl Pasha to present the keys of Mekka and Medinah to the Grand Sultán, by whom he was created a pasha of two tails, in compliment to his patron Mohammed Aly. A report became current at Cairo that Mohammed was dead, and the conduct of Latíf Pasha gave reason to suspect that he intended to seize upon the government. It was publicly rumoured that he had received from the Porte a firmán, authorising him to do so whenever an opportunity should offer. The deputy-governor, with Hassan Pasha, immediately adopted measures to check this revolution; and for three days they besieged the palace of Latíf Pasha, who was soon after taken in the dress of a peasant, and beheaded; thus they restored tranquillity.

On his arrival in Hedjaz, Hassan Pasha was sent by Mohammed Aly to establish his head-quarters at Kolach, a small village eight or nine hours eastward of Tayf, on the road to Taraba, situated in a plain beyond the great chain of mountains. Numerous wells rendered this Kolach an important position; and it was in some degree fortified. Tousoun Pasha, who had incurred his father's displeasure, by his inconsiderate attack on Taraba, remained stationed at Mekka.

It was about this time that I myself arrived at Djidda from Sowakin. The state of Turkish affairs in Hedjaz did not by any means promise a favourable issue of the contest. Discontent, and a kind of panic, were universal among the soldiers. The repeated victories gained by the enemy, and the certain death that awaited all Turkish prisoners, rendered the very name of Wahaby a terror among the Pasha's troops. The pay, which in Egypt sufficed for a soldier's comfort, scarcely enabled him in Hedjaz to keep himself from starvation. At Tayf and Medinah the prices of all necessary articles rose to such a height, that the soldier could barely afford to purchase enough of bread and onions as his only food; and three or four months' pay was always in arrear. Even at Djidda and Mekka, every thing was by two hundred and fifty per cent dearer than in Egypt; so that every man, who had saved a little money before his arrival in Hedjaz, was obliged to expend it in procuring the mere necessaries of life. They were paid, besides, in Egyptian piastres, bad coin, and so much less valuable in Hedjaz than at Cairo, that they lost by this money one-third of their pay. Many sold their fire-arms and clothes, and all, in general, suffered much distress; to relieve which, Mohammed Aly never troubled himself. Many soldiers, camel-drivers, servants, and artists, forfeited their pay, and embarked at Djidda and Yembo for Cairo; but the Pasha soon forbade such a proceeding, under severe penalties. By this prohibition they were much annoyed. A Turkish soldier is at all times a volunteer, and may retire from the service whenever he pleases; but in Hedjaz they found themselves treated as prisoners. Many left their quarters at Tayf and Mekka, and came privately to Djidda, hoping that they might escape on board some vessel. When detected, they were marched back, in chains, to headquarters; and I myself met once, on the road from Djidda to Mekka, above thirty of them, fastened together by their arms to a long rope; an ignominy which those haughty Osmanlys could never forget.

To these causes of complaint must be added the unwholesome

air, and the bad water, which render the low coast of Hedjaz one of the worst climates I know: very few soldiers escaped its influence; and at a moderate calculation, one-fourth of them were unable to do duty. Despondency, arising from illness, without any hope of relief, became general; and Mohammed Aly neglected the only means of encouraging them, and reviving their spirit, which was, to increase their pay, and distribute rewards among the few who had distinguished themselves. But their pay was not increased; and there existed such disorders in the financial department of the army, that every chief was able to curtail his inferiors of some part of their allowance; for which injustice no redress could ever be obtained. From the want of Turkish recruits, numbers of Egyptian Fellahs had been dressed up by the officers, with whom they lived as servants, to fill the ranks.

Mohammed Aly was perhaps the only person of his own court and army who, under these circumstances, did not despair of ultimate success; knowing that his downfall and expulsion from Egypt must be certain, if he should not gain some signal advantage in Arabia. Since his arrival at Tayf, he had endeavoured to re-open a friendly intercourse with the Bedouins; and in this respect partially succeeded, by means of money and patience. In August, 1814, the tribes of Hodeyl, Thekyf, Beni Sad, and part of the Ateybe, entered into a new alliance with him; the three first residing between Mekka and Tayf, and the Ateybe farther eastward. Their sheikhs had come to head-quarters, and about five hundred of their Arabs had enlisted under the banners of Mohammed Aly, who allowed to them nearly double as much pay as his own soldiers received. During my stay at Tayf, in August 1814, when I frequently was at head-quarters, Bedouin chiefs daily arrived, and were sure of being presented with a suit of clothes. The great sheikhs received money whenever they came. Many of them took the money, returned to their tents, and informed the Wahabys of all they had seen at Tayf; others remained neutral; and the Pasha, for the sake of gaining over a few, thought it right to give good words and presents to all. He listened to the discourses, and often deceitful assurances of the Bedouins, with a degree of patience, and seeming good-humour, unusual in an Osmanly of any rank.

Those sons of the Desert addressed him in the most blunt and unceremonious manner, calling him merely by his name, Mohammed Aly. One day an Ateybe Bedouin presented himself before the Pasha, kissed his beard, and exclaimed—"I have abandoned the religion of the Moslims" (or 'True Believers,' as the Wahabys style themselves); "I have adopted the religion of the heretics," (so the Wahabys entitle all those Mohammedans who are not of their own creed); "I have adopted the religion of Mohammed Aly." This unintended blunder caused a general laugh; and the Pasha answered through his interpreter (for he but imperfectly understood Arabic), "I hope you will always be a staunch heretic."

But the Pasha and his principal officers continued almost wholly ignorant of the strength, the interests, and private history of the surrounding tribes, and had no local knowledge of their territories; so that the Bedouins could not place much confidence in any measures of their new ally. Still the Pasha's party daily acquired influence. The profusion with which he scattered dollars around him, was felt in the heart of the Wahaby host; and although I doubt whether any Bedouin was ever sincerely attached to his cause, yet numbers affected to be so; and at least abstained from hostility, that they might partake of his bounty. Even Sherif Rádjeh, who had taken the lead among his enemies, and had personally distinguished himself on the Wahaby side, during the attack of Tousoun Pasha on Taraba, now made proposals of returning to Mohammed Aly, having reason to be discontented with his brother chiefs.

Hitherto the Pasha's conduct showed that Sherif Ghaleb was the only individual personally disliked by him among the chieftains of Hedjaz, and Rádjeh could clearly prove, that he merely abandoned the Pasha's cause, from the fear of sharing Ghaleb's fate. In September he came to Tayf, and Mohammed Aly received him most graciously, and again placed him at the head of his Bedouin soldiers.

Besides the condescending policy adopted in his intercourse with the Bedouins, Mohammed Aly had done all in his power to conciliate the inhabitants of Hedjaz. Many small duties levied by the Sherif were abolished; the customs at Djidda upon various articles, particularly coffee, were diminished; great sums distributed among the needy and poor of all descriptions, besides quantities of corn. The learned men, and those who held offices about the mosques and schools, received donations; the holy places at Mekka were repaired, and, during his residence there, the Pasha observed most scrupulously the minute and tedious rites prescribed to those who visit the Kaaba, which at Cairo would have afforded him subject for derision; indeed, at Cairo he never took any pains to conceal his sceptical or rather atheistical principles. The Turkish soldiers throughout Hedjaz were ordered to abstain from any insulting language towards the natives; and even severely punished, whenever they indulged in those tyrannical acts so frequently practised in Egypt. No soldier could venture to take things by force, or at half-price, from the market; for, on complaint to the Pasha, or his officers, the natives were always the favoured party. Thus, the strong prejudice of the Arabs against all foreigners became gradually weaker, and the Pasha obtained credit for justice and charity; qualities to which, in Egypt, he could not have made the slightest pretension.

In May 1814 Saoud died of a fever, a disease very prevalent in Nedjd. By this the Wahabys lost an indefatigable leader, possessing all the necessary talents for the eminent situation which he held. It is said that his last words were addressed to his son Abdallah, advising him, "never to engage the Turks in open plains"—a principle which, if strictly followed, would undoubtedly have insured to his people the recovery of Hedjaz. Abdallah, his eldest son, to whom the principal Wahaby chiefs had already paid obeisance during Saoud's life-time, became heir to the supreme authority. Some dispute, however, arose. Saoud had several brothers, who claimed part of his treasures, and one of these brothers, Abdallah, was supported by a strong party of the olemas of Derayeh. But after some short hostilities Abdallah, the son of Saoud, was acknowledged the Wahaby chief. With respect to courage and skill in war, his reputation exceeded that of his father; but he knew not so well as Saoud how to manage the political interests of the tribes under his command, the great sheikhs of which began to assume airs of independence. This impaired the general strength. The southern Wahabys, who were now most exposed to attacks, did not find support from the northern tribes, whose cavalry might have materially assisted them; and even the southern sheikhs were at variance with each other, and the Pasha had to contend against single tribes, rather than a combined force. This want of union, perhaps, may be ascribed to the contempt in which the Turkish troops were held by their enemies.

Distribution of the Turkish forces in Hedjaz—Massacre at Bahra—Mohammed Aly sends his son Tousoun Pasha to Medinah—The Turks defeated by the Wahabys in Zohrán — Mohammed Aly marches from Mekka towards Byssel — The Wahabys defeated there.

In September 1814 the Pasha's forces were distributed as follows:—About two hundred men were with Ibrahím Aga, the Moherdar, or seal-bearer of Mohammed Aly, at Mekka, where also were one hundred and fifty Arabian soldiers, under Sherif Yahya. Between three and four hundred men, commanded by Diván Effendi, were at Medinah; one hundred formed the garrison of Yembo, and two hundred were stationed at Djidda. Tousoun Pasha, with three hundred and fifty men, was encamped between Yembo and Medinah. Mohammed Aly had with himself at Tayf three hundred Turks, of whom about one hundred were cavalry. Hassan Pasha commanded the position of Kolach with one thousand of his Arnauts; and his brother, Abdín Bey, commanded the advanced posts of the army, consisting of twelve hundred Arnauts and four hundred cavalry, who had just arrived from Cairo. These advanced posts had pushed forwards three or four days' journies southward of Tayf, into the territory of the Beni Naszera tribe, and towards the district of Zohrán, where sheikh *Bakhroudj*, chief of the Ghamed Arabs, was principal opponent of the Turks. They had the advantage of being quartered in a fertile country, furnishing a sufficiency of corn and barley for their wants: thus they became independent of the magazines at Tayf.

The forces above enumerated may appear very inconsiderable to the reader; yet I am confident that they are here rather over-rated than underrated. According to the reports of the Turks, even of the Pasha himself, twenty thousand men were actually under the command of Mohammed Aly. The numerous stragglers attending a Turkish army; the multitude of Turkish merchants and hadjys scattered over Hedjaz, who affected the dress of soldiers, from whom they could scarcely be distinguished; an immense train of camel-drivers, grooms, and other servants accompanying the army—all contributed to swell its apparent numbers; and the Wahabys themselves had probably never a clear idea of the real strength of their enemies. Daily reinforcements arrived from Egypt, but were scarcely sufficient to recruit the ranks which had been so much weakened by disease, and by unsuccessful encounters with the Wahabys. The number of troops which Mohammed Aly had in Egypt was too small to admit of many draughts for Hedjaz. While the total amount of troops in this country was five thousand men, those in Egypt never exceeded from six to seven thousand effective soldiers; nor could the Pasha lessen that number without exposing the country to attacks, which he apprehended at once from Constantinople, from the Mammelouks in Dongola, or from England: at that time especially from the last-mentioned quarter.

When it became known in those countries which furnish the greater proportion of soldiers to the Turkish Pashas, namely Albania, Romelia, and the coast of Asia Minor, that the campaign in Hedjaz was so extremely distressing to the troops engaged in it, very few recruits came over to Egypt; and ever since 1813, Mohammed Aly was obliged to keep in those countries his own recruiting officers, who could not accomplish their object without expending considerable sums. I heard the Pasha himself state at Tayf, that his army consisted of 35,000 men; 20,000 of whom were in Hedjaz, and 15,000 in Egypt; and this statement was generally regarded as correct.

To defend the holy cities, and overawe the neighbouring provinces, the small force of between four and five thousand men was quite sufficient, with the help of four hundred Bedouin soldiers, collected from different tribes, and whose pay was twice as much as that allowed to the Turks; but with this army, the Wahabys could not be conquered. Yet it seems that the Pasha, at his departure from Cairo, had solemnly promised to his sovereign, that he should bring them under subjection. Notwithstanding all the Pasha's efforts, the want of camels had not been supplied; the road from Tayf to Mekka, and thence to Djidda, literally strewed with the carcasses of dead camels, showed that a continual renewal of the baggage-train was absolutely necessary. In the suburb of Mekka, called Moabede, where the caravans from Djidda and Tayf halted, so pestilential a stench was produced by the hundreds of dead camels, that on application made by the inhabitants, numerous poor negro pilgrims were hired to fetch dry grass from the adjoining mountains: a quantity of this was piled over each dead camel, and set on fire; so that the carcasses were consumed to ashes. At a moderate calculation, from the beginning of the war in 1811, up to this period, thirty thousand camels belonging to the army had perished in Hedjaz. But few remained in Egypt. Large supplies had been sought in the Negro countries as far as Sennar; but the transport of provisions from Genne to Cosseir, and from Cairo to Suez, required such numbers that few, comparatively, could be spared for the Hedjaz service. The Pasha had sent an officer to Damascus, that he might purchase camels among the Syrian Bedouins. These camels were expected at Mekka with the next pilgrim caravan; and Ibrahim Pasha had done all in his power to collect among the Libyan tribes as many as could be procured; which were likewise to be sent with the Egyptian hadj to Hedjaz.

Until the time of their arrival, mere defensive measures were adopted. About five hundred camels had been hired from the Harb Arabs for carrying provisions from Djidda to Tayf; but their owners positively refused to advance a step farther towards the east or the south, lest their camels should be taken by the Wahabys. The garrison at Tayf, as I learned there from good authority, had only provisions for ten days; and their distress was so great some weeks after, that the corn brought by caravans was immediately distributed, and never put into store-houses. On the advanced-posts at Kolach, and in Zohran, the troops had no means of grinding the corn; but every soldier received a daily portion of grain, which he was himself obliged to pound between stones, and to bake in the ashes.

Meanwhile the Wahabys made frequent incursions towards Tayf, and against the tribes which had espoused the cause of the Pasha; who, on his side, harassed the enemy's country, by means of his cavalry, sent in small detachments. Sherif Yahya, with his Arabs, made (in August 1814) an expedition over the mountains towards Gonfode, and brought back a valuable booty in camels and sheep. He had no sooner returned to Mekka, than Tamy avenged himself, by sending a corps of six hundred camel-riders of the Kahtan tribe towards Djidda. I myself narrowly escaped from these partisans. Having had occasion to go from Mekka to Djidda with a small caravan of camels, we arrived about midnight at a watering-place called Bahra, half way between the two towns, where a small camp of horsemen was stationed to guard the road. These men we found in a state of alarm, some Bedouins from the south having just informed them, that the enemy was approaching.

Our caravan immediately went off towards the northern mountains, and by a circuitous route arrived at Djidda the next day; but we had scarcely left Bahra, when the Wahabys rushed into it. We heard the discharges of musketry, and were soon after informed, that the invaders massacred all the inhabitants whom they could find, pillaged the camp and baggage, and carried away a small caravan, which had halted at Bahra some time before our arrival. All this time the eighty horsemen never offered the least resistance, but galloped off towards Mekka, where they spread the greatest consternation.

The intercourse between Djidda and Mekka was thus interrupted during a whole week; but the Wahabys, having accomplished their purpose, retreated to their homes. They had set out from a distance of at least fifteen days' journies to plunder on this road; and their exact knowledge of the country enabled them to take such a route, as brought them suddenly on their prey. In this kind of warfare the Bedouins have always been distinguished; and their invariable success in such enterprises terrified the Turkish soldiers more than the loss of a regular battle could have done; because they never thought themselves secure for one moment, as soon as they had left the precincts of the towns.

Ever since the taking of Medinah, the Turkish troops had remained there completely inactive, as the supplies sent to them from Yembo were scarcely sufficient for their daily use, and for the inhabitants of the town. The tribe of Harb continued on amicable terms with the Turks; and their sheikh, *Djezye*, who had mainly assisted in taking the place, had gone, in June 1814, on business to the Divan Effendi, commanding there. Being one day seated in full council with the latter, and unable to endure the vain Turk's idle bragging, he exclaimed in hearing of the whole company—"Be silent, O Divan Effendi, as every body knows that it was I who paved the way for your entrance into this town; and were it not for this blade (here he clapped his hand upon his sword), no Turk would have ever entered Medinah." The Turkish commander was incensed at this address, insulted Djezye with the most opprobious terms, struck him, and caused him to be put in chains; and next day it was reported, that he had killed himself in prison, certain proofs having been obtained that he was carrying on a treasonable correspondence with the Wahabys. The consequence of such an event might have easily been foretold. As soon as the Beni Harb knew that their sheikh was killed, they shut the road through their mountains against the caravans from Yembo; and without actually joining the Wahabys, they committed partial hostilities upon the Turkish out-posts.

In hopes of settling these disturbances, Mohammed Aly ordered his son, Tousoun Pasha, (in August 1814) to proceed towards Medinah. He arrived in September at Beder, and found that the Harb Arabs had strongly garrisoned the pass of Djedeyde, and were resolved to oppose his entrance by force. They boldly demanded the life of the Divan Effendi, as an expiation of the murder of their sheikh. Fortunately the Divan Effendi died at that very time, not without strong suspicion of poison, and the Arabs became more inclined to a reconciliation. Their new sheikh and minor chiefs received valuable presents; the price of Djezye's blood was paid to his relations, in compliance with the Bedouin custom, and peace was again concluded with the Beni Harb. Having passed the defile, Tousoun Pasha arrived at Medinah in October 1814, with about three hundred foot-soldiers and five hundred horse; most of the latter had just come from Cairo. The horsemen took up a position two or three days' journies in advance of Medinah, at Hanakye, whence they made several excursions towards the territories of the northern Wahaby tribes.

About this time, the affairs of the Turks assumed a favourable aspect throughout Hedjaz; and hopes were entertained, that after the reinforcement of men and camels, expected with the hadj, should arrive, the Pasha might be enabled to conduct in person some grand enterprise against the enemy; when another defeat still farther humbled the pride of the Turks, which, notwithstanding their cowardice, and their failures in war, they had never relinquished. Abdín Bey, with his Arnauts, occupied, as I have said, some districts in the province of Zohran, south of Tayf. To prevent the daily attacks of his enemies, he had laid waste the country within forty miles, and totally destroyed whatever might be serviceable for the passage of troops. He was encamped on one side of this artificial desert, and Bakhroudj was posted on another (the southern) side of it. With the usual negligence of Turkish commanders, no intrenchments were thrown up, no advanced posts nor sentinels placed towards the enemy; whose general was thus enabled, at the head of his own, and several allied tribes, and a strong detachment of infantry from Tamy, to surprise the Turks. Bakhroudj, early one morning in September, fell upon the sleeping Arnauts, who scarcely waited to fire one shot, but abandoned their camp, and all that it contained. Some little resistance was made by a few hundred soldiers from Romelia, under Mahou Beg, the Pasha's most active chief in Hedjaz; but they could not long contend against the overwhelming force of the Wahabys; and the whole army owed its escape from destruction to a corps of cavalry commanded by a Syrian chief, named Hosseyn Bey, who covered their retreat, in which Bakhroudj pursued them during two days. The Turks once more lost all their tents, artillery, baggage, and provisions: eight hundred Turkish foot-soldiers, and eighty horsemen, were killed; and it was not until the remainder of the army arrived at Lye (about four hours from Tayf) that they ventured to take up a position. Here Abdín Bey received some reinforcements from

Tayf and Kolach; and as it was known that the Arabs had returned home, he advanced a second time, by the Pasha's orders, towards Zohran. But such a panic had seized the Turkish troops, that one half of them deserted, and came to Tayf; and Abdín Bey was obliged to fix his head-quarters at a short distance in advance of Lye, wanting the necessary complement of men.

This last defeat had a very depressing effect on the spirits of the troops. Abdín Bey had hitherto enjoyed the highest reputation for skill and courage, and his troops were certainly the best of the whole army; but the late disasters convinced his soldiers, already not much inclined to fighting, that further resistance against such numerous enemies as the Wahabys would be vain, and there was not a man among the Turks who did not long to find himself again safe in Egypt. As the Turks however understand better almost than any other nation "faire bonne mine à mauvais jeu," they described their last defeat as a victory, because the horsemen had brought the heads of about sixty Wahabys with them to Tayf; and while the army trembled within the walls of that town, guns were fired at Djidda to announce a victory; Cairo, also, was illuminated three days, to celebrate the glorious exploit of Abdín Bey.

Soon after this event, a very seasonable reinforcement of cavalry arrived from Cairo. Horsemen had been drawn from all the Libyan tribes of Bedouins who encamp during summer in the neighbourhood of the Nile valley, and eight hundred of them had been despatched to Hedjaz. These were themselves Bedouins, well accustomed to the system of warfare prevalent among the Wahabys, their horses were equally trained to fatigue as the riders, and every horseman had a camel with him, carrying provisions for the most distant expedition. Half of these horsemen had joined Tousoun Pasha on his way to Medinah, the others advanced to Tayf, and had no sooner arrived there, than they distinguished themselves by daring excursions against the Wahaby tribes, situated several days' journies eastward of Taraba, being accompanied by Bedouin guides of those countries. They were all armed with guns and pistols, and known as good marksmen; circumstances which rendered them very formidable to their enemies. In one of their excursions they brought away eight thousand sheep from a Wahaby encampment.

The pilgrim-caravans arrived in November from Syria and Egypt. With the former came three thousand camels, which Mohammed Aly had purchased from the Syrian Bedouins, Tousoun Pasha having taken at Medinah, from the caravans passing, one thousand of the original number, four thousand to relieve his own want of transport-camels, as much felt at Medinah as in the southern parts of Hedjaz. The Egyptian caravan likewise brought about two thousand five hundred camels, besides a reinforcement of one thousand Turkish horsemen. And that these might be all employed for military purposes, the whole caravan was detained at Mekka, and the mahmal sent, after the pilgrimage was over, by sea back to Suez. This caravan, I must here remark, was entirely composed of soldiers or public officers; all the private pilgrims having been ordered to proceed by sea.

The Pasha came down from Tayf to assist in the ceremony of the hadj, and to meet Soleyman, Pasha of Damascus, who had again accompanied the caravan from Syria. Mohammed Aly's favourite lady, the mother of Tousoun, had come by sea to perform the pilgrimage. Her retinue was as splendid as the wealth of Egypt could render it. Four hundred camels transported her baggage from Djidda to Mekka, and her tent, pitched at the foot of Mount Arafat, equalled in size and magnificence any thing of which we read in fairy tales or Arabian romances. Several personages of high rank had come from Constantinople to visit the Kaaba; and the pilgrimage of this year, at which I myself assisted, was performed by about eighty thousand persons of all descriptions and nations. After the ceremony, the Syrian caravan generally remains a few days at Mekka. Mohammed Aly, however, on this occasion protracted their stay ten days beyond the usual term, by requiring all their camels (amounting to above twelve thousand) for the purpose of carrying provisions between Djidda and Mekka to supply his troops.

When he had collected his whole effective strength between Mekka and Tayf, and the state of his storehouses and the number of his camps excited his hopes of success against the enemy, he declared his intention of placing himself at the head of the army, which served to raise in some degree the spirits of his troops. Taraba was again pointed out as the first object of attack. A well-appointed artillery, consisting of twelve field-pieces, encouraged the soldiers to believe that the walls of Taraba could not long remain standing, and that no man should be required to scale the wall, as had been the case when Tousoun Pasha made his attack. Five hundred axes were provided for cutting down the palm-trees which impeded the approach to Taraba. Twenty masons and as many carpenters were attached to the army for the purpose of opening a mine which was to blow up the enemy at once. That the soldiers might be rendered sure of success, a load of water-melon seeds was brought from Wady Fatme and carried in pomp through the town of Mekka, it being intended, after the total demolition of Taraba, to sow these seeds on the spot where it had stood. But these preparations, so far from tranquillising the minds of the soldiers, increased their uneasiness, as they proved what vast importance was attached to the taking of that place, and the difficulty of the enterprise.

The enemy laughed when it was reported that Mohammed Aly considered the taking of Taraba as certain; and about this time the Pasha received a letter from Sheikh Bakhroudj, written in that sneering and taunting style, of which Arabian history affords many examples. He told him, that he had already sufficient proofs of what the Wahabys could do; that if he resolved to fight with them, he ought to provide better troops than those which he now commanded; but that his wisest plan would be, to return again into Egypt, and indulge in the sweet water of the Nile. Bakhroudj, as will hereafter appear, atoned, by an ignominious death, for this affront to the dignity of a Turkish Pasha.

As an encouragement to the army, thirteen Bedouins of the Ateybe tribe, captured on the Djidda road, and accused of being Wahaby robbers, (although it afterwards appeared most clearly, that they had gone to Djidda for the purchasing of provisions,) were executed on a plain near Mekka, before an immense multitude of people. One man of the same party, at the moment when his hands were untied, and a Turkish soldier prepared to inflict the deadly blow, knocked him down, and escaped through the crowd. He might ultimately have saved his life, had he sought refuge in the mountains, instead of continuing to run along the plain, where he was overtaken, and cut down, by a Turkish hadjy, who happened to be there on horseback. On this occasion the lower classes of the natives evinced their strong dislike of the Turks; they loudly hissed, and cursed the soldiers, who cruelly mangled their unfortunate victims: the fugitive was encouraged in his attempt to escape by shouts of applause; while the hadjy who killed him was abused in most opprobrious terms, and loaded with execrations.

Every thing being now prepared for the expedition, which was to decide the fate of this campaign, Ahmed Bonaparte left Mekka with the greater part of the infantry on the 15th of December, 1815, and proceeded at once to Kolach. The Pasha intended to follow him with about twelve hundred cavalry, on the 24th; when intelligence arrived, that a strong Wahaby force had been seen in the neighbourhood of Gonfode, advancing towards Djidda. This report excited great alarm. Bedouin scouts were despatched to obtain information; and at Djidda considerable disorder prevailed, for it was expected that the Wahabys, if they should not attack the town itself, would cut off its communication with Mekka. For some time water had been extremely scarce at Djidda; the government cisterns were now hastily filled by compulsory measures; and the inhabitants drew their scanty supply from wells at a distance of three hours. Every kind of provisions in Mekka rose thirty per cent. on the first rumour; but the people recovered from their panic, when it was known that a small troop only of Tamy's soldiers had pitched their tents near Gonfode.

A few days after, news arrived that Bakhroudj had made an incursion into the territories of the Naszera Arabs, allies of the Pasha, and had completely sacked the fortified village of *Bedjíle*, their principal hold, where a garrison of Arnauts had been stationed. It was once the head-quarters of Abdín Bey. News likewise arrived, mentioning that Taraba was in a state of considerable preparation, and that reinforcements were hastening from all quarters towards that town, to defend it against the threatened attack.

On the 26th of Moharram, 1230, (or the 7th of January, 1815,) Mohammed Aly Pasha marched from Mekka with all the troops and camels that he could muster, proceeding towards Kolach, where Hassan Pasha, Abdín Bey, Mahou Bey, Ahmed Bonaparte, Topous Oglou, Sherif Radjeh, and other chiefs of his army were already assembled, and where sufficient provisions for fifty or sixty days had been collected. When he arrived at Zeyme (which is the second station on the northern road from Mekka to Tayf) and Kolach, express messengers, sent in great haste from the last-mentioned place, informed him that a considerable body of the enemy had seized upon Byssel, between Tayf and Kolach, intercepting the communication between these places, while another hostile corps had made an incursion eastward of Kolach against the Ateybe Bedouins, allies of the Turks. Mohammed Aly hastened his march towards Kolach, where he arrived on Wednesday, and despatching Sherif Rádjeh with his Bedouin soldiers and the Libyan horsemen to support the Ateybe, advanced on Thursday himself with all his cavalry towards Byssel. He found the Wahabys encamped on the side of the mountains which open towards the plains of Kolach. They had possession of several fine watering-places, while the Turkish soldiers carried the water for their own use upon camels, from Kolach. The Wahaby force has been variously estimated; according to the best information, it amounted to about twenty-five thousand men, infantry, and a few cavalry; the mountains here being poor in horses, and the Wahabys when engaged in distant expeditions, seldom employing any considerable number of cavalry, depending chiefly on their camel-riders and matchlock foot-soldiers.

Their army was accompanied by five thousand camels, but wanted artillery of every kind. It consisted of men chosen among the southern Wahabys and a small band of the northern, the latter being themselves kept in check at present by the hostile demonstrations of Tousoun Pasha at Medinah. All the chiefs of the Yemen mountains, and of the south-eastern plain, were with the army, as was Faysal, the son of Saoud, and brother of the present Wahaby chief. Among the former, Tamy, sheikh of Asyr, and Ibn Melha, the agyd, or war-chief, of that tribe, held the first rank; and one-third of the army was composed of their Arabs; Ibn Katnan, sheikh of the Sabya Arabs, Ibn Khorshan, chief of Taraba, Ibn Shokban, chief of Beishe, Bakhroudj, sheikh of the Arabs of Ghamed and Zohran, Ibn Dahman, sheikh of the Shomran Arabs, Ibn Katamel, chief of that part of Ateybe, who remained attached to the Wahaby interest; Ibn Mahy, a chief of the Dowasir Arabs, who live far to the south-east, towards Hadramaut, and many other equally renowned and powerful leaders, commanded different bodies of this army. In making a diversion against Gonfode, they had endeavoured to draw off the Pasha's attention from the main object of attack, and fell quite unexpectedly upon Byssel, where they occupied a strong position in the very centre of the Turkish lines. When the Pasha's cavalry approached, they remained upon their mountains, and repulsed an attack made on a valley, where Mohammed Aly wished to plant one of his field-pieces. The whole of Thursday was consumed in several fruitless attempts made by the Turkish cavalry, of whom, in their last attack, above twenty were killed by the lances of the Wahaby horsemen.

Although but few lives were sacrificed this day, the Turks began to despair of success, while the Wahabys entertained sanguine hopes of weakening the enemy by repeated defeats, and finally destroying them. Fearing such a result, several Turkish soldiers, as well as Bedouins in the Pasha's service, deserted from the army and hastened back to Mekka, which they reached on the following Saturday night. Here they spread the news of a complete defeat, of the Pasha's death, and other disasters.

The terror caused by these reports in Mekka can scarcely be imagined. I resided there myself at that time, and can speak of it as an eye-witness. Numerous stragglers belonging to the army, and Turkish hadjys preparing to return home; also Turkish merchants and such soldiers as were in the town, all expected to suffer death on the first arrival of the victorious Wahabys. Four hundred piastres were offered for a camel to convey a person to Djidda; but the few Bedouins who possessed camels, removed them into the mountains on the first rumours of defeat. Several people left Mekka on foot that very evening, and endeavoured to reach Djidda by the next morning. Others joined the garrison in the castle, and put on Bedouin rags that they might not be supposed foreigners; but nobody prepared for defence, and Sherif Yahya himself, although he had not received any official report, was ready for a sudden flight to Djidda. For my own part, being convinced that if the Pasha had been defeated, the Wahaby light troops would intercept all fugitives on the Djidda road, and preclude the possibility of escape, I thought my safest asylum would be the great mosque, which, at all times, the Wahabys had respected as an inviolable sanctuary. Having put into a bag the few valuable articles that I possessed, along with a good provision of biscuit, I went accompanied by my slave and established myself in the mosque, where many poor hadjys had from the same motive taken up their residence. My biscuit, with the water of Zemzem found in the mosque, might have supplied my wants for some weeks. That the whole crowd of Turks did not follow this example, may be ascribed to their judging of the Wahabys by themselves; for they could never believe that in the hour of victory a soldier would regard any place as sacred.

But our apprehensions proved to be founded on imaginary disasters; and, after a night of considerable anxiety, we were surprised and gratified the next morning by the official account stating the total defeat of the dreaded Wahabys. Mohammed Aly Pasha had clearly seen, during the skirmishes on Thursday, that he could have no chance of success as long as the enemy remained upon the mountain; he likewise knew, that if unsuccessful on the following day, his career both in Hedjaz and in Egypt would probably close for ever. Therefore he sent, during the night, for reinforcements from Kolach, and ordered two thousand of his infantry, together with the artillery, to take a position in flank of the Wahabys. The next morning at an early hour he renewed the attack with his cavalry, and was again repulsed. He then assembled his officers, and commanded them to advance with their columns closer to the position of the Wahabys than they had done before, and, after firing off the guns, to retreat in seeming disorder. This was accordingly executed. The Wahabys seeing the enemy fly, thought that the fortunate moment for completely crushing them had arrived; they left their stronghold on the mountain side, and pursued the flying Turks over the plain. All happened as the Pasha had expected. When he thought the enemy sufficiently distant from the mountains, he rallied his cavalry, faced the pursuers, and the battle was soon decided in his favour.

The Turkish infantry now turned the position of the Arabs. Sherif Rádjeh who had just arrived with his corps, after having repulsed the enemy's false attack upon the Ateybe, joined Mohammed Aly, beset the valley through which the Wahabys were to retreat, and thus compelled them to fly in the utmost disorder. For pursuing a vanquished foe, the Turkish soldiers are pre-eminently qualified. As soon as Mohammed Aly saw the enemy running, he proclaimed among his troops, that six dollars should be given for every Wahaby's head. In a few hours five thousand were piled up before him: in one narrow valley fifteen hundred Wahabys had been surrounded and cut to pieces. Their whole camp and baggage, and most of their camels, became a prey to the Turks. Tamy himself escaped with only a few followers.

About three hundred Wahabys were taken alive, at the express command of Mohammed Aly, who ordered his men to offer them quarter, as very few of the enemy had condescended to beg for mercy. Sherif Radjeh was despatched with some cavalry in pursuit of the fugitives, and he was joined by many of the neighbouring Arabs, who would probably have exhibited as much zeal against the Turks, if the Wahabys had been victorious.

In this battle the Pasha fought personally, at the moment when he ordered his cavalry to wheel about and face their pursuers. He deserves great credit for his dispositions during the night previous to that attack, and for having known how to keep up a spirit of resistance in his troops, who had already relinquished all hopes of success. On his side, no man distinguished himself more than Sherif Radjeh; mounted upon a famous mare, and, armed with his lance, he galloped far in advance of the army, and among crowds of the enemy, towards the tent of Faysal, the most conspicuous in the whole camp, and, striking his lance into the ground before it, defended himself with his sword against a number of Wahabys, until his friends approached, and rescued him. When Mohammed Aly soon after passed near this spot, he inquired of Radjeh, to whom that tent belonged. "To Faysal," he replied. "Then take it," said the Pasha, "with all that it contains." Besides the camels, no booty of great value was taken by the army. Radjeh found in the tent of Faysal about two thousand dollars only. Many quarrels occurred between the Turkish soldiers and their allies, the Bedouins, who accompanied Radjeh, respecting the division of plunder. The Pasha seemed inclined to favour the Bedouins; and most of the camels fell to their lot. It was stated, that the Turks lost on this day between four and five hundred men.

The defeat of the Wahabys may be wholly attributed to their having descended from the mountain into the plain, where they had no means of resisting the Turkish cavalry. Saoud, in the last words which he addressed to his son, had cautioned him against such a proceeding. But the contempt in which the Wahabys held the Turkish troops, and the desire of terminating the campaign, and perhaps of securing the person of Mohammed Aly himself, made them forget the wise system of warfare which they had hitherto adopted; and their astonishment on finding themselves so suddenly overpowered, rendered them incapable of resistance.

Some anecdotes, however, are related of signal courage evinced by the Wahabys. Ibn Shokban, with a few hundred men, fought his way through the whole Turkish infantry, and escaped. Bakhroudj, one of the wildest of the Wahaby chiefs, killed with his own hand two of the Pasha's officers; and when his horse was shot under him, mixed among the Turkish cavalry until he found an opportunity of pulling a man from his horse, which he mounted, and by this means escaped. Whole parties of the Asyr Arabs were found upon the mountains tied with ropes together by the legs. On parting from their families, they had all sworn by the divorce (an oath common among Bedouins, and strictly observed, see p. 157), not to fly before the Turks, and if possible to return victorious. Being unsuccessful in battle, they resolved, at least, to prevent each other from running away. They fought as long as their ammunition lasted, and were then cut to pieces.

Turks elated with victory—their cruelty—their distresses on the march from Beishe—Mohammed Aly returns to Mekka—Makes proposals of peace to Abdallah Ibn Saoud.

MESSENGERS were immediately despatched to Constantinople and Cairo with intelligence of the victory; and throughout Hedjaz the Turks became elated, and resumed their national insolence and fierceness, which latterly they had, in some degree, laid aside. Meanwhile the natives of Hedjaz, although glad to be secured against a second Wahaby conquest, grieved to see Arabians vanquished by Turks, and shuddered at the cruelties which these victors had practised, both during and after the battle. The three hundred prisoners, to whom quarter had been promised, were sent by Mohammed Aly to Mekka. In the true style of a Turkish conqueror, he celebrated his triumph by causing fifty of them to be impaled before the gates of Mekka; twelve to suffer a like horrible death at every one of the ten coffee-houses, halting-places between Mekka and Djidda; and the rest before the Mekka gate of Djidda: there they were left until the dogs and vultures devoured their carcasses. If the Turks delighted in this disgusting and atrocious act, which they styled a martial triumph, all the Bedouins, their allies, expressed aloud the utmost indignation; and Sherif Radjeh remonstrated with the Pasha, but in vain.

Four days after the battle Mohammed Aly, with due activity, arrived before Taraba; from which Faysal fled at his approach.

The inhabitants, abandoned by their allies, capitulated; and the Pasha fixed his head-quarters at that place for some time. The Turks plundered a few houses, and carried off some handsome Arab women, who were, however, restored to their families by the Pasha's order. Ghalye had taken refuge with the Bedouins. She might have been sent as a trophy to Constantinople; but no proposals could induce her to return, or confide in the offers of the Turks. Immediately after the victory at Byssel, the Pasha directed Sherif Yahya to proceed by land with his Arabs to Gonfode; and he reinforced his corps with the troops of Mahou Bey. Orders also were sent to Djidda, that several transports, loaded with provisions, might be despatched to Gonfode. As the strength of his enemies lay in the southern countries, Mohammed Aly resolved to carry the war into their own territories, and completely to exterminate their party. Whatever provisions could be procured at Kolach, were loaded upon the five or six thousand camels, which the army had in its train on leaving Mekka, and upon almost as many which were taken after the battle.

The army proceeded from Taraba through the territory of the *Oklob* Arabs, in a southern direction, towards Rannye, over a level ground, two days distant, occupied by the Sabya Arabs, whose sheikh, Ibn Katnan, had fortified there a small castle, which surrendered. After four days' journies from that place, they arrived in the district of Beishe, a fertile country belonging to the powerful tribe of Beni Salem, whose chief, Ibn Shokban, was a leading man among the Wahaby party. Here two small castles had been built by the express command of Saoud, who had strengthened all the principal positions of these countries by similar structures. Ibn Shokban had taken refuge after the battle in the tents of some neighbouring Bedouins of the Kahtan tribe. One of those castles opened its gate: in the other, Ibn Shaban, a second chief of Beni Salem, defended himself for four days against the whole Turkish infantry, commanded by Hassan Pasha; while Mohammed Aly with his cavalry had taken post in the date-groves, on the southern side of Beishe.

Proposals for a capitulation were offered to Shaban, on condition of safe-conduct; these he unfortunately accepted; and with his garrison, of about sixty men, marched from the castle, and received camels for the carrying of his baggage. But having gone to pay his respects in the tent of Hassan Pasha, this fanatical Turk reproached him with heresy. Shaban boldly defended his opinions, and retorted upon the accuser, who became so enraged that when Shaban and his followers quitted the tent, he ordered his soldiers to fall upon them, and they were all cut to pieces. Of such infamous transactions, which frequently occur, no notice is ever taken by Turkish rulers.

The army remained about a fortnight at Beishe, the most important position in the country eastward of the Yemen mountains, and called by the northern Bedouins the key of Yemen. Here the Pasha was joined by many Bedouins. All those who were discontented with the Wahabys, and all the relations of those sheikhs who had been turned out of their situations, came now to seek redress from Mohammed Aly; who, imitating the system of Saoud, changed every where the chiefs of tribes, by which means a strong party in his favour was created. News reached him here, that Tamy had again assembled a considerable army in his mountains, and had resolved to try the chance of battle a second time. It was towards his territory that Mohammed Aly now directed his march, taking a western course from Beishe.

On this march his army suffered the extremes of hunger and fatigue. Half of the camels had already perished before the arrival of the troops at Beishe, and many horses had shared the same fate. The van-guard cleared the road of every particle of stubble or blade of grass; so that those who came after, found nothing but a barren desert. On the Turks' approach the Arabs fled in all directions, carrying off their cattle and provisions, while the Bedouins themselves, who followed the army, took advantage of the general disorder, and purloined many loads. At every halt a number of camels dropped, and their flesh was greedily devoured by the soldiers. The last biscuits had been distributed at Beishe, after which every man was left to supply himself as well as he could. The Pasha found it necessary to allow the troops an additional pay of one piastre per day, but this money was of little use in a place where as much corn made into bread, as would satisfy a man's appetite once, cost twelve piastres.

At two days' journey from Beishe, they entered the mountainous country, which had been almost totally deserted by the people. Among the Shomran Arabs, the Turks enjoyed a few days' repose. Hassan el Sulsan, a Bedouin chief, descended from an individual who, three centuries before, when Othman Pasha conquered Yemen, in the reign of Selim the Great, had been placed at the head of this tribe, was now reinstated by Mohammed Aly in the ancient rights of his family. Here in one day a hundred horses died: the soldiers became dissatisfied; but as they clearly saw that a retreat would lead to inevitable destruction, they still advanced. The Pasha commanded all his chiefs to dismount, and to march on foot at the head of their respective columns. To his soldiers he promised a glorious booty, in plundering the towns of Yemen, thus endeavouring to keep up their spirits. A market was established at every halt, just before the Pasha's tent, where the allied Bedouins sold to the troops whatever they had been able to carry off from the Arabs on the road. The Pasha himself presided, and enforced strict order.

Near the territory of Asyr the rugged mountains presented many obstacles to the passage of artillery. This territory the

Turkish army entered twelve or fourteen days after they left Beishe, halting near the castle called Tor, which stood upon an elevated ground, surrounded by mountains. It had been built by Abou Nokta, the predecessor of Tamy, and was deemed so strong, that no Arab force could possibly take it. Here Tamy had collected from eight to ten thousand men, whom the Pasha attacked: and as at Byssel, the Turkish troops were repulsed on the first day. The Asyrs fired incessantly, and three hundred Turks were killed. Tamy was seen on horseback in front of his men, animating them by war-songs. The field-pieces having been brought to bear on the second day, the Wahabys gave way. Tamy himself fled, but was the last who quitted the field. The battle was better disputed than that of Byssel, the number of Bedouins who accompanied the Turks rendering them more powerful than their enemies. In the castle were found considerable stores of provisions, which proved most serviceable to the army, likewise ammunition, the guns taken from Gonfode the year before, and a large stock of matchlocks, old Persian barrels, particularly esteemed by the Arabs.

After Radjeh had been sent in pursuit of Tamy, and a new sheikh of the Asyr, called Ibn Medry appointed, Mohammed Aly descended the mountains through steep passes to the sea-shore. It appears that he wished to advance towards Yemen, from the less mountainous country at the western foot of the high chain. Sherif Hamoud (surnamed Abou Mesmár) was in possession of the sea-coast. He had formerly been of the Wahaby party, after many contests with them, but when the Turks arrived in Hedjaz, he sent an envoy to the Pasha with rich presents, assuring him of his readiness to support the Turkish interest; the frequent defeats, however, of the Turks, caused his zeal to subside; he opened a communication with Tamy, and an envoy sent to his court by Mohammed Aly, found him engaged in active preparations for war. Little doubt existed that his design was to join the Wahabys if the Turkish expedition should miscarry. The Pasha had long eagerly wished to riot in the far-famed wealth of Yemen, which, however, is probably much overrated in the East. He might also have wished to get possession of the dollars which annually were sent in great sums from Cairo to purchase coffee; and it was reported in Hedjaz, that in case of success against the Wahabys, he had resolved to attack Hamoud. For this reason he had opened a correspondence with the Imam of Sanaa, who had sent presents to him, and was cordially interested in the favourable issue of his enterprise; as it would have delivered him from two dangerous neighbours, the Wahabys and Hamoud.

The army, however, after such a long, fatiguing, and perilous march, showed here strong symptoms of discontent, and openly declared their desire of returning to Mekka; it is certain that, as the means of tranquillising them, Mohammed Aly was obliged to promise that they should soon be sent back to Egypt, and replaced by fresh troops; and instead of proceeding southward, he now directed his march towards Gonfode. Tamy, after the battle which he had lost, took refuge in the neighbourhood of Arysh, at the house of a Sherif, his friend, and a relation of Hamoud. The Sherif thought this a favourable opportunity for warding off a hostile invasion, and of evincing his submission and repentance. Tamy was put in chains, and a messenger despatched to the Turkish head-quarters with a letter to Hamoud, in which the Sherif styled himself the "slave of Mohammed Aly," and asked how he should dispose of his prisoner. Sherif Radjeh, who was then roaming about the mountains in search of the fugitive, received orders to take him back to Gonfode, where the army now arrived, and found an abundant supply of provisions brought from Djidda by sea.

Mohammed Aly had sent off a body of troops from Rannye to

invade Zohran from the east, while Mahou Bey ascended the mountains from the east, and by a skilful manœuvre placed the Arabs of Bakhroudj between two fires, so that they were defeated, and Bakhroudj himself taken and carried to Gonfode. Here the Pasha remained several days, his two noble captives being lodged in tents close to his own. Tamy's conduct inspired the whole army with respect. The Pasha often conversed with him for amusement, as the tiger plays with his prey before he seizes it in his grasp; but Tamy's dignified behaviour subdued the ferocity even of this Turk, and he promised to write in his favour, and procure him permission from the Sultan to live in retirement in the mountains of Romelia. Tamy was a man of great natural powers; short in stature, with a long white beard, his eyes darting fire; sarcastic in general, but polite towards the Turkish chief. Bakhroudj, on the contrary, observed a sulky silence, convinced that Mohammed Aly would never forgive him for the letter he had once addressed to him, (see p. 393.) nor did the Pasha ever desire to see him. Finding his guards asleep one night, Bakhroudj seized a poniard, contrived to loosen his chains, and escaped from the camp, but was overtaken after he had killed two men and wounded another. Next day Mohammed Aly asked him, "by what right he had killed his soldiers:"—"Whenever I am not chained," replied Bakhroudj, "I act as I please:"—"I shall act in the same manner," said the Pasha; and to entertain his Turks, and at the same time gratify his revenge, he immediately caused the unfortunate prisoner, bound as he was in chains, to be placed in the midst of his body guards, who were directed to wound him slightly with their sabres so that his torments might be prolonged. He at last expired without having uttered one complaint: his head was sent to Cairo and Constantinople along with Tamy, who, upon his arrival in the latter city, was instantly beheaded.*

* In violation of the solemn promise made by Mohammed Aly, Tamy, when he ar-

From Gonfode the Pasha proceeded to Mekka, which he reached on the 21st of March, fifteen days after he had left that city. The nature of his expedition will be comprehended, when I state that out of more than ten thousand camels, originally with the army (half of which were taken at Byssel), only three hundred returned to Mekka; all the rest having perished on the road. Much of the baggage and ammunition was destroyed, there being no means of transporting it; and of the horses, only three hundred were brought back. Of four thousand Turks who set out from Mekka, only fifteen hundred returned, all of whom were, from the highest in rank to the meanest, worn out with fatigue, and without clothes or money.

Mohammed Aly, according to the promise extorted from him at Gonfode, permitted them all to embark at Djidda, except Hassan Pasha, whom he kept in Hedjaz with a few hundred Arnauts; and soon after, new reinforcements arrived from Egypt.

The strength of the Wahabys was now considerably reduced, particularly in the south. When the battle of Byssel took place, Abdallah Ibn Saoud was with a body of troops in the province of Kasym, ready to oppose the progress of Tousoun Pasha from the side of Medinah; but he returned to Derayeh on learning the defeat of his party, apprehending an attack from Mohammed Aly, who might easily have advanced from Taraba towards Nedjd.

Soon after his arrival at Mekka, the Pasha assembled all the chief men and olemas of the city, and read to them a letter which he had addressed to Abdallah Ibn Saoud, exhorting him to submission and offering terms of peace: he charged him to restore the treasures which his father had taken from the prophet's tomb at Medinah, if he did not wish to share the same fate as his friends

---

rived at Cairo, was loaded with an immense chain about his neck, placed upon a camel, and then paraded through the streets with the head of Bakhroudj in a bag suspended from his shoulders.

in the south. This letter was sent by a Turkish soldier, accompanied by some Bedouins, to Derayeh.

After a short stay at Mekka, Mohammed Aly, having appointed Hassan Pasha governor of that town, left Hosseyn Bey, a cavalry chief, and Sherif Radjeh, in garrison at Taraba and Beishe, and set out for Medinah, where he arrived unexpectedly on the 14th of April, with only thirty or forty attendants, mounted upon dromedaries, having performed the whole journey by land. Tousoun Pasha had already quitted Medinah. Thomas Keith, or Ibrahim Aga, before mentioned, acted meanwhile as governor of that place.

When the news of Mohammed Aly's success became known to the northern tribes, many of their sheikhs made proposals to Tousoun Pasha, who was then at Medinah, offering to join him against the Wahabys, whose power was more severely felt in the north than among the southern tribes. In March, most of the Kasym sheikhs came, one after another, to Medinah, and assured Tousoun Pasha of their readiness to assist him. He bestowed presents on them, and sent back with them four hundred cavalry, to garrison some of their villages. Tousoun himself now conceived hopes of conquering Nedjd. Notwithstanding his great personal courage so often displayed, he had been always unfortunate in his Hedjaz expeditions. He became anxious to emulate his father in the glory he had acquired by his late campaign; but, like most Turks, he did not calculate his means. Mohammed Aly had not entrusted to his son's management any considerable sums of money, knowing his liberality and generous disposition, and perhaps unwilling that any one besides himself should acquire renown in Hedjaz. Tousoun was much in want of camels, and of food, for the neighbouring Bedouins. The prices of all articles were higher at Medinah than at Mekka. Tousoun, however, resolved to try his fortune, and left Medinah at the end of March, setting out for Hanakye, a ruined village with walls, two or three days' journies on the road to Kasym. He had with him about four hundred camels carrying provisions, and between two and three hundred cavalry, with four hundred foot-soldiers. He was followed by a few hundred Bedouins, chiefly belonging to the tribes of Harb and Meteyr.

He remained some time at Hanakye, and was still there when his father arrived at Medinah. The reason of Mohammed Aly's visit to this sacred city was probably his wish to obtain information respecting the affairs of Northern Hedjaz, and pay his devotions at the Prophet's tomb. From Medinah he immediately sent orders, directing Tousoun Pasha to return from Hanakye, that he might concert measures with him for future proceedings. His son, however, had determined on the expedition; and as soon as he received Mohammed Aly's order, instead of obeying it he set out towards Kasym. As he was equal in rank to his father (being like him a pasha of three tails), the latter, perhaps, was wrong in making him feel too strongly his state of dependence; and we must not look for any thing like proper filial sentiments among Turkish grandees. The custom duties of Djidda, which by right belonged to Tousoun, had been transferred by the Porte to Mohammed Aly, for the expenses of the war. Tousoun Pasha received merely a certain allowance by the day, like all the other chiefs of the army; and in placing the north of Hedjaz under his command, Mohammed Aly had associated with him a person of his own court, named Kadery Effendy, through whom all business was to be transacted, and whom Tousoun was advised to consult upon all occasions, as if his father thought him unfit for the high situation that he filled.

Soon after their arrival at Medinah, Kadery Effendy, as might easily be supposed, rendered himself disagreeable to his pupil, who, in a fit of anger, caused him to be beheaded. Great disorder then prevailed in the administration of affairs. The interests of the Turks with the surrounding Arabs were ill managed: the soldiers committed depredations. Tousoun wanting camels seized all the cattle that could be found among the Bedouins; and Mohammed Aly, on his arrival, instead of taking offensive measures against the enemy, was fully occupied in repairing the mischief consequent upon the errors of his son. Two hundred and fifty horsemen, under the command of Thomas Keith (or Ibrahim Aga), were despatched after Tousoun Pasha, as was likewise a detachment of infantry, who had arrived from Yembo, having as their chief Ahmed Bonaparte, just returned from Cairo. Tousoun, early in May, after a march of ten or eleven days from Medinah, reached the province of Kasym. During this journey he attacked the Heteym Bedouins, and carried off five hundred of their camels, which he sent to Medinah for the transport of provisions from Yembo. Upon his arrival at *Rass*, one of the principal towns or large villages of Kasym, and defended by a wall, he was joined by the cavalry which had preceded him some time; and the sheikhs of different districts in Kasym came to concert measures with him: but the great chief of Kasym, *Hedjeylan*, did not attend him, having always been sincerely attached to Saoud, and even now to the interests of his son, in whose support he assembled the Arabs of his party at the town called Bereydha.

* In January 1815 I arrived at Medinah, and was soon confined to my bed by illness; at this time my slave frequently came home weeping and complaining that the Turkish soldiers had taken from him the meat which he had procured for my use, and beaten him because he had attempted to resist.

Abdallah Ibn Saoud enters Kasym with an army—Negotiations between him and Tousoun Pasha—Peace concluded—Mohammed Aly returns to Cairo—Despatches his son Ibrahim Pasha with an army to renew the war in Hedjaz.

In the mean while Abdallah Ibn Saoud had not neglected his duty; with an army composed of Bedouins and settlers of Nedjd, he, likewise, entered the province of Kasym, and fixed his headquarters at Shenana, only five hours distant from Khabara, where Tousoun Pasha had encamped. But here Tousoun found himself in a precarious situation. He heard that his treasurer, Ibrahim Aga (Thomas Keith), had been surrounded on the road, and, notwithstanding a most gallant resistance, had been cut to pieces, together with all his horsemen. The fertile district of Kasym might have supplied provisions for a much larger army than his, but the light troops of the Wahabys were hovering about the Turks, who depended wholly upon two or three villages for their daily food, which they foresaw must soon become extremely scarce. The road to Medinah was occupied by the enemy, and no intelligence could be obtained respecting the steps taken by Mohammed Aly.

Tousoun Pasha could not place much confidence in the Bedouins who were with him, knowing that they would readily join the other party on the first disaster of the Turks. He wished to terminate all suspense by a battle, but his officers and soldiery were not willing. The superior numbers of the Wahabys frightened them; they felt convinced that in case of defeat not one man could escape, and they thought it more prudent to compromise with the enemy than to fight; the more so as Mohammed Aly had empowered his son to make peace, if that could be done on favourable conditions. Some Bedouins were employed to sound the disposition of the enemy's chief, who, when he knew the circumstance, sent Habab, one of his people, to find out what were actually the designs of Tousoun, offering safe-conduct to any one who might be despatched to the Wahaby camp. However favourable these matters seemed to Abdallah, he foresaw that the destruction even of Tousoun's entire force of about twelve hundred men, would be of little real advantage to him. It would oblige Mohammed Aly to direct all his strength against that point, the consequences of which would be of more detriment to the Wahaby cause than the partial victory could be of service to it. He knew besides, that the resources of Egypt were such as would enable Mohammed Aly to prolong the campaign in Hedjaz for any time. The Turks had suffered many defeats, but had always repaired their losses and became stronger after each. They also possessed the means of bribery, and the Wahaby chief well knew that some of his present companions were in their hearts his enemies; by making peace he could insure the dependence of those tribes which had not yet joined the Turkish party.

Habab was well received by Tousoun, who immediately sent Yahya Effendy, his physician, a native of Syria, who spoke Arabic better than any of the Turks, to negotiate with Abdallah. He was the bearer of some presents, and remained three days in the Wahaby camp. As both parties desired peace, the negotiation was soon concluded, and one of Abdallah's courtiers waited upon Tousoun that he might ratify the treaty. In this, Abdallah renounced all claim to the possession of the holy cities—affected to style himself a dutiful subject of the Sultán, and obtained a free passage for all his party through the Turkish dominions, which would enable him to perform the pilgrimage at pleasure. Tousoun Pasha abandoned to Abdallah Ibn Saoud, those towns of Kasym which he held in his possession, and dismissed from his party all the sheikhs of that country who had already joined him. He likewise ceded to him all those Bedouin tribes whose pasture-grounds lay beyond Hanakye, reserving to himself those only which resided between Hanakye and Medinah, and in the territories of the holy cities. Nothing was said of the Southern Wahabys; in consequence of this, immediately after Tousoun went away, Abdallah punished the Bedouins (particularly the Meteyr tribe) who had joined his enemies. As both parties apprehended treachery, some difficulties arose respecting the priority of departure. Abdallah at length consented to break up his camp, but insisted that four of the Pasha's chief officers should be left with him as hostages until his arrival in a safe position, when he was to send them back. Tousoun, probably to conceal his own weakness, cavilled for some time on this point. A correspondence took place, and several of Abdallah's original letters are now in my possession. Most of them exhibit that frankness and boldness of language by which the Bedouins have always been distinguished, widely differing from the ceremonious and complimentary style usual among other eastern nations in similar cases. They were all written under the immediate dictation of Abdallah himself, expressing the unfeigned sentiments which he felt at the moment, and the hand-writing shows that but little time was employed in committing those sentiments to paper.

Tousoun Pasha then returned from Khabara to Rass, and, after a residence of twenty-eight days in the province of Kasym, arrived at Medinah about the end of June, 1815. With him were two

Wahabys, envoys from Abdallah to Mohammed Aly, bearing the articles of peace, and a letter from their chief to the Pasha, and another for the Grand Sultan.

Tousoun did not find his father at Medinah; for being convinced that the actual resources and means of war in those northern parts of Hedjaz were not sufficient to authorise hopes of success, Mohammed Aly resolved on leaving the doubtful chance to his son, rather than incur the risk of diminishing the reputation which he had himself acquired. On this occasion he evinced great want of paternal feeling. While Tousoun was absent, not one messenger was ever despatched to him; so that he remained ignorant of all that was passing at Medinah, and other places. Mohammed Aly, besides, thought so little of his son's necessities, that he left him without a single piastre; and when Tousoun arrived at Medinah, he was obliged to borrow money for his daily expenses. There was perhaps a cogent reason why Mohammed Aly quitted Medinah, and finally Hedjaz. In February and March, 1815, apprehensions were entertained in Egypt of an attack to be made upon Alexandria by the Capitan Pasha of the Grand Signor, who had arrived from the sea of Marmora with a strong fleet, and was cruising in the Archipelago. Alexandria and Rosetta were reinforced with numerous troops; and the Kechya Bey, governor of Cairo, sent messengers in haste, by land and sea, to acquaint Mohammed Aly of the circumstance.

On the 19th of May, some weeks after I had quitted Yembo, on my return to Cairo, Selim Aga, governor of Yembo, received an express from Medinah, ordering him, on pain of death, to have a ship ready for sailing on that very evening. Next day Mohammed Aly, with a few of his suite, mounted upon dromedaries, arrived at Yembo, and, without waiting for refreshment on shore, hastened to the ship, and immediately set sail. The Pasha would not allow the captain to keep along the coast, as is usual, although he knew that the ship was but scantily supplied with water, but made him stand out into the open sea, straight for Cosseir.

On his landing at that place, he could not procure either a horse or camel, but mounted, without loss of time, an ass, that he might proceed through the Desert to Genne, and hasten down the Nile. The dread of an attack upon Alexandria had, in the mean time, subsided: this he heard, and therefore travelled more leisurely towards his capital, which he reached on the 25th of June, 1815, after an absence of nearly two years, during which his health had considerably suffered from the climate of Arabia. He did not then know that peace had been concluded with the Wahabys; but that his arrival might be attended with éclat, the taking of Derayeh by Tousoun Pasha was announced, and the complete annihilation of the Wahabys.

In the month of August, after Mohammed Aly's return to Egypt, most of those very troops who had accompanied him in the Arabian campaign, showed symptoms of insurrection. The corps of Mahou Bey, and others, began to pillage the capital; and the Pasha found it necessary to shut himself up in his castle at Cairo. Those troops, to whom fine promises had been made in Hedjaz, now found that regulations were proposed, which would considerably reduce their pay, and increase their fatigues. The Pasha desired to introduce the *Nizám Jedíd,* or new system of discipline, a measure which had proved fatal to Sultan Selim; but the insurrection stopped its progress; and Mohammed Aly could not venture to punish the revolters. The reputation which he had acquired in Hedjaz was found to have caused a change in his character. The affability that had distinguished him from other Pashas was converted into haughtiness: instead of a simple soldier-like establishment, he began to indulge in pomp and show, and monopolised all the exports and imports for his own advantage, by which the labourers and manufacturers were materially injured.

The two envoys sent by Abdallah Ibn Saoud, in the train of Tousoun Pasha to Medinah, arrived at Cairo in August, during this insurrection of the soldiers. One of them, named Abd el Azyz, was a relation of the great founder of the Wahaby sect, Abd el Waháb: the other was an officer of Saoud. They presented to Mohammed Aly the treaty made with his son, Tousoun Pasha, and the letters before mentioned. Abd el Azyz was a very learned man; and several of the most able olemas of Cairo were directed by the Pasha to dispute with him on theological subjects. He inquired into every circumstance concerning the civil and military establishments of Egypt, its resources and commerce: he purchased several Arabic books, and at last excited the jealousy of Mohammed Aly, who ordered two or three soldiers to attend the envoys at all times, wherever they went. This conduct rendered their situation so unpleasant, that they soon demanded leave to depart. A suit of clothes, and three hundred dollars, were given to each as presents, with a letter to Abdallah Ibn Saoud from the Pasha, written in a most ambiguous manner, respecting peace or war; offering to confirm the treaty concluded with his son, provided the Wahabys would cede to him the province of Hassa, one of the most fertile and important of their dominions, being situated on the Persian Gulf.

It now became manifest, either that Tousoun Pasha had deceived the Wahabys at Kasym, or that Mohammed Aly had given a fresh proof of the contempt in which he held all engagements. Tousoun, equal in rank with his father, had concluded a treaty, binding his whole party; and he had enjoyed the full benefit of that treaty, in being allowed to save himself and his army from destruction. His father, however, seemed anxious to represent the matter under a different point of view at Constantinople; and as he had pledged himself to annihilate the Wahabys, by taking Derayeh, it was necessary to persuade his sovereign, that he had not yet abandoned that object; and that the treaty concluded by his son should be merely considered as a temporary armistice.

In September 1815 Sherif Rádjeh, the Arab hero, was brought to Cairo in chains. It was said, that he had quarrelled with Hassan Pasha, governor of Mekka, who suspected him of a treasonable correspondence with the enemy. But the fact was, that all the Osmanly party regarded him with jealousy, on account of the high renown he had acquired, and the general report, that the victory at Byssel was gained by his exertions. During the first months of his confinement at Cairo, he was treated like a common criminal; but in spring 1816, when preparations were made for an expedition against the Wahabys, he was released from prison, and Mohammed Aly affected to show him marks of distinction. On the 7th of November, 1815, Tousoun Pasha arrived at Cairo with a few hundred soldiers. After his return to Medinah, communication was restored all over Hedjaz with the Wahabys. Caravans came from Nedjd to Medinah and Mekka; and in December, many Wahabys attended the pilgrimage. No Turkish chief had exerted himself so much as Tousoun during this war, or displayed more personal valour; but his efforts had always been unsuccessful. He was welcomed at Cairo with all the honours due to his rank and bravery; but on paying a visit to his father at Alexandria, he was very coldly received.*

About the close of 1815, several Arab sheikhs from Hedjaz came to Cairo, claiming the Pasha's protection. They were rela-

* In September 1816 Tousoun Pasha died of the plague at Rosetta, where he commanded a large body of troops, encamped there for the defence of the coast. He was regretted as a man who showed great attachment to his friends, and was profuse in the expenditure of money.

tions of Ibn Medry, whom Mohammed Aly had appointed chief of the Asyr Arabs in place of Tamy; but when he returned to Cairo, Tamy's party obliged the new sheikhs to fly, Hassan Pasha being unable to support them. Mohammed Aly received them politely at Cairo, gave them some presents and sent them back to Mekka, but could not at that time spare any troops for Hedjaz; being seriously engaged in preparations for defending the Mediterranean coast against an attack, which, according to general report, the English intended. He had already heard, when in Hedjaz, of the first peace of Paris and the fall of Bonaparte, and had become apprehensive that England would send a large army from the south of France to Egypt, which he fondly supposed was the darling object of all European powers. These apprehensions were renewed by the second treaty of Paris, and still more when the English took possession of the Seven Islands, which he regarded as stepping-stones towards his own territory. He was confirmed in his opinion by the absurd reports of his own emissaries, and the whispers of flattering and servile Franks, or Pseudo-Europeans, who were all determined Anti-Anglicans. After some months the alarm subsided, and he again directed his views towards Hedjaz, intending to despatch a powerful expedition to that country, under his son, Ibrahim Pasha. Circular letters were written, in January 1816, to all the Arab sheikhs of Hedjaz, apprising them of Ibrahim's speedy departure, exhorting them to assist him; and assuring them, that he designed to revisit their territories himself in a short time, and crown his former victories by the taking of Derayeh. In these letters no mention was made of the treaty concluded with Abdallah Ibn Saoud; nor had any answer yet arrived from the latter, respecting Mohammed Aly's demand of the district of El Hassa.

In March 1816 intelligence arrived, that disturbances had broken out towards the south of Mekka. The Turkish cavalry stationed at Beishe, Rannye, and Taraba, had been withdrawn. Some Bedouins in the Pasha's service remained as the garrison of Taraba. The Wahabys seemed daily to gain strength in those quarters; nor does it appear that the southern districts had ever been included in the peace made with Abdallah Ibn Saoud.

In August 1816 Ibrahim Pasha left Cairo for Hedjaz, with orders, it was said, to attack Derayeh, taking the way of Medinah and Kasym. He was accompanied by about two thousand infantry, who went by Cosseir to Yembo, and fifteen hundred Libyan Bedouin horsemen, who proceeded by land: these horsemen he had himself chosen among the most warlike tribes of the Bedouins in Upper Egypt. In his suite were two French officers, one of whom, a chef d'escadre, had been with Bonaparte at Rochefort; but in consequence of orders to quit France, he repaired to Egypt, where Mohammed Aly received him in a very flattering manner, besides several other French emigrants of the year 1815.

APPENDIX.

APPENDIX.

No. I.

Lunar Months.—(See page 42.)

The following Table will show the names given by several Bedouin tribes, more particularly the Aenezes, to some of the Mohammedan months.

Moharrem, they call اشور—*Radjeb*, غُرة—*Shaban*, تصيير. The two months of *Shawál* and *Dsu el Kade*, they call (plurally) الافطار — *Shawál* (singly) فطر الاول; and *Dsu el Kade*, فطر الثاني. The month *Dsu el Hadj*, they call الصحير

No. II.

Warfare of the Bedouins.—(See page 177.)

While the battle rages, and horsemen or camel-riders contend in single combat, or mix in general fight, flying or pursuing, the Beni Atye (a considerable tribe of Arabs between Syria and the Red Sea, among whose numbers are the Omran, Howeytat, and Terabín) frequently utter with a loud voice the following verses:

"You birds with the bald-heads, you Rakham and Hadázy,
"If you desire human flesh, be present on the day of combat."

يا طير يا شايب الراس يا ابو رخم و حداذي
ان كان بدكم لحم ناس احضروا يوم الطرادي

The *Rakham* and *Hadázy* are birds of prey—the former an eagle, the latter a falcon. This battle-song is called by the Arabs *Boushán*, بوشان.

No. III.

Blood Revenge.—(See page 178.)

The origin of the *dye* (ديه), or fine for the blood of a man slain, amounting to one hundred camels, among several of the tribes, and ratified by the Wahabys, may be traced to the time of Abd el Motalleb Ibn Heshám (Mohammed's grandfather), who had made a vow to kill one of his ten sons in honour of the idol which was then worshipped in the Kaaba. The lot fell upon his favourite boy; but the intreaties of his friends, co-operating, we may suppose, with paternal affection, induced him to commute the sacrifice, and he immolated, in honour of the idol, one hundred camels, and this number thenceforward became necessary in atoning for blood. (See Azraky's History of Mekka.)

When a Bedouin of the tribes settled between Akaba and Cairo kills a man in blood-revenge, he exclaims, on cutting him down, "I take thy warm blood in revenge!" ناخذ بثارنا دمك الساخن

No. IV.

The Catechism (or Creed) of the Wahabys. (See page 278.)

Ibn Saoud to the inhabitants of Mekka the highly honoured.

Praise be to God, the only God! who has no co-partner—to whom belongs dominion, and who is omnipotent.

In the name of the all-merciful God! It is necessary that every chosen servant of God should have a true knowledge of the Almighty; for in the word of God (the Korán) we read, "Know that there is no God but one God!" *Bokháry*,[*] may God have mercy upon him! said, "First learn, then speak and act." If it be asked, "What are the three foundations of knowledge?" answer, "The servant's knowledge of his Lord, of his religion, and of his Prophet."

And first, as to the *knowledge of God*: if they ask of thee, "Who is thy Lord?" answer, "My Lord is God, through whose favour and grace I have been bred up; him I adore, and adore none but him." In proof of which we read (in the Koran), "Praise be to the Lord of all creatures! Whatever exists besides God, belongs to the class of creatures, and I myself am one of this created world." If they ask further of thee, "How didst thou know thy Lord?" answer, "By the signs of his omnipotence and the creation." In proof of which we read, "And of his signs are the night and the day, the sun and the moon; and of his creation, heaven and earth, and whatever is upon them and whatever they contain." And we likewise read, "Thy Lord is God, who created heaven and earth." If it be asked, "For what purpose did God create thee?" answer, "To adore him." In proof of this we read, "I created spirits and men to be adored by them." If it be asked, "What does God command?" answer, "The Unity; which means, to adore him exclusively and solely: and what he above all prohibits is the association with him, or the adoring of any other God besides himself." In proof of which we read, "Adore God, and do not associate with him any other thing or being."

---

[*] The celebrated compiler of Mohammed's traditions.

The adoration by which thou art to worship him, thou evincest by the *Islám;* by faith and alms, by prayers, vows, sacrifices; by resignation, fear, hope, love, respect, humility, timidity, and by imploring his aid and protection.

In proof of the necessity of prayers we read, "Pray, and I shall grant your wishes." Prayers therefore are true adoration. In proof of the necessity of making vows we read, "Fulfil your vows and dread the day of which the evils have been foretold." To prove the necessity of slaughtering victims, we read, "Pray to God, and kill victims." And the Prophet, may God's mercy be upon him! said, "Cursed be he who sacrifices to any other but God."

The second foundation of knowledge is the *religion of Islám*, which is submission to the Almighty. In proof of which we read, "The religion before God is Islám." And to this refers the saying of the Prophet, on whom be the peace of God! "The chief of all business is Islám." If they ask, "How many are the principal duties of our religion?" answer, "They are three: Islám, faith, and good works." Each of these is divided into different parts:—Islám has five, viz. the profession that there is no God but God, and that Mohammed is his prophet—the performance of the prescribed prayers—the distribution of alms—the observance of the fast of Ramadhán, and the pilgrimage to the holy house of God. In proof of the truth of the *profession of faith*, we read, "God declares that there is no God but himself;" and the meaning of the expression "there is no God but God," confirms that there is but one God, and that nothing in this world is to be adored but God. And in proof of the profession, that Mohammed is the prophet of God, we read, "And Mohammed is nothing but a prophet." Our duty is to obey his commands, to believe what he related, to renounce what he forbade; and it is by following his precepts that we evince our devotion to God. The reason for joining these two professions, viz. in saying, "There is no God but God, and Mohammed is his prophet," is to show our piety and perfect obedience. In proof of *prayers and alms*, we read, "Nothing was commanded but that they should adore God, with the true religion alone, that they should perform prayers, and distribute alms." In proof of *fasts*, we read, "O ye true believers, we have ordained for you the fasts!"

And in proof of the pilgrimage we read, "And God exacts the pilgrimage from those who are able to undertake the journey."

As a farther proof of these five fundamental parts of the *Islám*, may be quoted the tradition of Ibn Omar, who says, "The prophet, may God's mercy be with him, declared that the Islám rests upon five requisites: the prayers, the alms, the fast, the pilgrimage, and the profession that there is no God, but God." The second of the principal duties of religion, is the *faith*. It comprises seventy-nine ramifications.* The highest of them is the declaration, "There is no God, but God;" and the lowest, the removal of all deception from the road of the faithful. *Shame* (pudor) is one of those ramifications. The faith divides into six parts. These are: to believe in God and his angels, and the revealed books, and his prophets, and the last day, and the omnipotence of God, from whom all good and evil proceed. In proof of which we read: "This is not righteousness, to turn your faces towards the east or the west; † but he is righteous who believes in God, and the last day, and the angels, and the sacred book, and the prophets." And in proof of the omnipotence, it is said: "We created every thing through our power." The third of the principal duties of religion consists in *good works*. These are comprised within one single precept, which is: "Adore God, as if thou didst see him; and if thou canst not see him, know that he sees thee." In proof of which we read, "He who turns his face towards the Almighty and confides in him, he is the well-doer, he holds fast by the firmest handle."

The *third* foundation of knowledge, is the *knowledge of our prophet Mohammed*, may God's mercy and peace be with him! Mohammed the son of Abdellah, the son of Abd el Motalleb, the son of Hashem, the son of Menaf, whose parentage ascends to Adnan, who was himself a descendant of Ismayl, the son of Ibrahím, with whom and with our prophet may God's mercy dwell! Mohammed, may God's mercy be with him! is a delegate whom we dare not adore, and a prophet whom we dare not belie; but we must obey and follow him, for it has been ordained to spirits and to mortals to be his followers. He was born and appointed prophet, at Mekka; his flight and his death were at Medinah. From him, to whom may God show his mercy! we have the saying: "I am the

---

* The Arabic Ms. is not quite legible in this passage; it may be seventy-seven.
† Viz. to be exact in the ceremonial of praying.

prophet, this is no false assertion, I am the son of Abd el Motalleb!" If it be asked, "Is he *a mortal?*" answer, "Yes; he is a mortal." In proof of which we read: "Say, I am but a mortal like yourselves, to whom it is revealed that your God is but one God." If it be asked, "*Is he sent to any particular class of mankind?*" answer, "No; he is sent to the whole race." In proof of which we read: "O men, I am God's prophet sent to you all!" If it be asked, "Can any *other religion, but his, be acceptable?*" answer, "No other can be accepted:" for we read, "Whoever shall follow any other religion than Islám, will be rejected." And if it be asked: "Does any *prophet come after him?*" answer, "No prophet comes after him; for after him comes the last day." In proof of which we read: "He was father to none of your men, but the prophet of God, and the seal (that is the last) of all prophets."

No. V.

A Letter* of Mohammed Aly to the chief inhabitants of Medinah, acquainting them with the details of his great victory over the Wahábys, at Byssel. (January 1815.) (See p. 401.)

By the grace of the Most High!

To our worthy people, the inhabitants of Medinah the illustrious.

To the well worthy and noble primates, the neighbours of our prophet, (let God's mercy and peace be with him!) the first among the Sherífs and learned men, the praiseworthy, the venerable, the chiefs of the town, may God grant them his peace, take them under his care and custody, and pour out over them his full benevolence! Amen.

We give you our best salutation and greetings, and we announce to you that the Almighty, whose glory and power we celebrate, permitted us to accomplish the expectations of the Sultan of the Sultans of Islám, in prompting us to remove the army of true believers from Mekka, furnished

---

* This letter is a model of Arabic style. It was read before a general assembly in the great mosque of Medinah. (The original itself was in the possession of Mr. Burckhardt.)

with all necessary supplies of provisions, baggage, and ammunition, in order to transfer our head-quarters from thence to Kolach. We left for this purpose Mekka on Saturday the 26th of the month of Moharram, and arrived at Kolach on Wednesday, the last of that month. Our plan was to hasten towards Taraba, to encounter there the combined forces of the heretics, headed by their chief Faysal Ibn Saoud, accompanied by Ibn Shokban, Ibn Dohman, Ibn Katnan, and Ibn Mahy; also Bakhroudj and Ibn Hatamel, together with all the sheikhs of the Arabs of Beishe, and the Dowasir and Bekoom, and Oteban Arabs, and those of the countries of Hedjaz, Sebya, and El Aredh. They had been, moreover, reinforced by Tamy and ten thousand of the Asyr Arabs, which increased their strength to the number of forty thousand men. The devil then beguiled their councils, and they intended to attack us. They left Taraba, and arrived in our neighbourhood, near the celebrated village of Byssel. We advanced against them with fifteen hundred of our horsemen, chosen from the number of true believers, and two field-pieces, in order to reconnoitre. At our approach, they spread over the mountains and offered determined resistance. But our soldiers devoted themselves to their duty, and after great slaughter, drove them back to their strongest holds.* We continued then under an incessant fire to attack them, and to endeavour to draw them into the plain. Our soldiers were engaged from sun-rise till sun-set. Night at last put a stop to the battle. We then took possession of the passes through which they might attempt their retreat. God sent us strength and stratagems.† We sent now for a reinforcement of two thousand foot-soldiers from Kolach, with their field-pieces, and again attacked the enemy at the break of day.‡ They did not stand our first attack, they flew, and God permitted our swords to be drenched in their blood. They abandoned their encampment, and upwards of five hundred tents, and five thousand camels, dromedaries as well as beasts of burden,

---

* The truth is, that on this first day the Turkish cavalry was repulsed.

† This is particularly well expressed in Arabic الّي ان حال بيننا الليل و لزمنا دروب فرارهم و بالله القوة و الخيل

‡ Nothing is said here of the Bedouins in the service of the Pasha, who were principal actors among the infantry.

with all the baggage and provisions fell a prey to our troops, who thus became masters of all their camp and all their honour.* They pursued now the fugitives, who lost numbers, killed and taken prisoners; our allies the Arabs from Hedjaz likewise fell upon them in the narrow passes. Tamy himself escaped only with five horsemen and five camel-riders: God thus exterminated them by his power and strength. We left Kolach on Sunday, in hasty pursuit of the enemy, and arrived in the neighbourhood of Taraba on Tuesday. Faysal had taken refuge there with fifty horsemen and one hundred camel-riders, the remainder of his troops; but when he was apprised of our approach, he immediately fled. The people of Taraba, and the remaining part of its garrison, issued from the town to meet us and to beg for a safe-conduct. We promised to them security, and established our head-quarters in their town. All the neighbouring Arabs joined us here; and thus God permitted our wishes to be fulfilled in clearing these countries from their unjust and criminal oppressors. Let us address to him our most heartfelt thanks for the grace he has bestowed upon us, and the honour with which he covered our troops. If it please the Almighty, we shall leave this place in three or four days for Rannye and Beishe, and direct our march against the remaining Asyr Arabs, that we may establish order throughout the country, and destroy all rebels.

We wished to announce these good tidings, and to inform you how the Almighty in his bounteousness has granted to us the accomplishment of all our hopes. May he complete his grace, and purify the whole country of Hedjaz from the filth of the wicked, by exterminating them. We charge you to pray for us at the tomb of our Lord, the Redeemer; and may the Almighty, in his gracious assistance, continue to regard you with kind looks! This is the matter of which we wished to inform you.

God's mercy and peace be with our Lord Mohammed, his family, and his followers!

    On the 7th of the month of Safar,
      1230 of the Hedjra. (L. S.)

---

* A pun in Arabic; "camp and honour"—*Ordyhom* wa *Ardehom*, عرضهم و عرضيهم

No. VI.

A Letter from Abdallah Ibn Saoud to Tousoun Pasha, upon occasion of the latter's departure from Kasym towards Medinah. (See p. 414).

In the name of the all-merciful God!
Perfect peace, salutation, and honour to the Lord of Mankind, Mohammed, God's mercy and best blessings be with him! and then to the noble Ahmed Tousoun Pasha, may God prompt him to godly works! And next, thy letter reached us, may thou reach God's good graces! And we rejoiced at the news of thy welfare and good health. As to what thou allegest in justification of thy demands, thou possessest understanding and penetration; and thou surely knowest that thy demands are inadmissible, and contrary to peace. If we did not wish to preserve a permanent and sincere friendship, and to fulfil the promises we once made, we should have granted thy demand. But we are men of faith and of truth, and we do not recede from conventions; and we execute them, were we even convinced of having been deceived. With regard to thy departure, we trust thou wilt not think badly of us, nor lend thine ear to our enemies, and to intriguing deceivers. Ask the Bedouins who are with thee, if they choose to speak the truth they will tell thee, that were they even to kill one of Saoud's own family, and that I had promised them safe-conduct, they would never doubt of it, but trust to my word. We tread here upon our own ground; this is our own country. Let us advise thee not to suspect our intentions, and to trust to our good faith. By God, and the pledges he gave to mankind, I promise not to molest either thee or thy armies in any manner that might be disagreeable to thee. Thou art placed under the safe-conduct of God, and of myself. At the moment thou breakest up upon thy return, I shall likewise break up, and retreat with my army towards Aeneyzy.* But if thou believest the reports of thy enemies, and suspectest our sincerity, we shall even now break up forthwith towards Aeneyzy; and do this for the deference we pay to thee and

---

* A town of Kasym.

to thy father.* But we require that thou shouldest send us a letter, pledging therein the safe-conduct of God, and of the Sultan, and thy own, to all the Arabs on our side, whether settlers or Bedouins. And a second letter of safe-conduct to the inhabitants of Shenanne, Betah, and Nebhanye,† which we shall immediately forward to them. If it please God, we shall to-night receive thy answer; therefore do not cause our man to tarry with thee. If thou likest to send camel-riders about the affair Ahmed mentioned to us, we shall have no objection. For all this we pledge to thee our faith before God.

Whenever it shall come to an amicable compromise, nothing will set the hearts of the Moslims‡ at rest, and tranquillize them, with regard to their whole party, but hostages to be sent to us. They will be under my protection; and at thy arrival at Dat,§ they shall be sent back to thee; and thou shalt be well and honourably treated. Ibrahim will tell thee the names of these hostages: they are Mohammed Daly Bashy, Othman the Selehdar, Ismayl the Djokhadar, and Ahmed Aga. God's safe-conduct, and my own, is pledged to them. We shall cause them to be accompanied by some of our own people until they arrive at thy quarters. If they are sent to us, we shall, please God, forthwith break up. If on the contrary thou shouldst like to depart before us, we shall send to thee from our side hostages, who will follow thee. It is now for thee to choose. Either send us these people, and we shall depart, or start thyself, and take our own hostages. Let us have an answer to-day. We hope to God it will be such as to cause us joy. Be assured that the hostages shall be under my special care. God's mercy and blessing be with Mohammed, his family, and his followers!

From Abdallah Ibn Saoud. (L. S.)

---

* Literally: to you and to the one who is behind you, كرامة لخاطر كم و للي وراك

† Towns of Kasym.

‡ This expression is worthy of remark. The Wahabys call themselves by no other name but Moslims, (or true believers of the Islám,) distinguishing thus between themselves and the mere Turks. Here again, their party is called Moslims, which is as much as to say to the Pasha, "You are no Moslim." Perhaps it may be a mistake of the writer, as the letter, in its original, bears evident signs of great haste.

§ Dat is the village of Kasym nearest towards Medinah.

INDEX OF ARABIC WORDS.

PAGE
1. Aeneze, عنزه
2. Would Aly, ولد علي — El Teyar, الطيار
3. Meshadeka, مشادقا—Merreykhat, مريخات—Lahhawein, لححوين—Meshatta, مشطّا—Auadh, اواض—Hammamede, حمامده—Djedaleme, جدالمه—Tolouhh, طلوح—Hessenne, حسنه
4. Messaliekh, مسالخ—Raualla, رولّا—Djelaes, جلاس
5. Bessher, بشّر
6. Ahl el Shemál, اهل الشمال—Maualy, موالي
7. Hadedyein, حديديين—Turkman, تركمان—Arab Tahht Hammel Hamáh, عرب تحت حمّل حمّاه

PAGE
8. Szoleyb, صليب
9. Feheily, فحيلي
10. Serdye, سرديه
11. Ledja, لجا—Djolán, جولان
12. Kanneitera, قنيطره
13. Beni Szakhr, بني صخر—Abs, عبس
14. Belkaa, بلقا
15. Ghour, غور
16. Haueytat, حويتاط
17. Sherarat, شرارات
19. Dowar, دوار—Nezel, نزل—Fereik, فريق—Kabeile, قبيله—Fende, فنده—Tayfe, طايفه—Beni, بني
20. Sulf, سلف—Medhour, مضهور—Dhaan, ضعن—Ghazou, غزو
21. Shauke, شوقه—Kheroub, خرب
22. Matrek, متروك—Sefife, سفيفه—

3 I

INDEX OF ARABIC WORDS.

Rowak, رواق—Sefale, سفاله—Mereis, مريس—Khelle, خله—Kateaa, قاطع—Sáhhe, ساحه—Markoum, مرقوم
23. Redjoud, رجود—Roffe, رفه
24. Makszar, مقصر—Ketteb, كتب
25. Rawouye, راويه—Zeka, زقا—Udel, عدل—Harres, حرس
27. Mesoumy, مسومي—Meshlakh, مشلخ
28. Shauber, شوبر—Mekroune, مقرونه
29. Terkie, تركيه—Teraky, تراكي
30. Remahh san, رمح سان—Kennah, قناه—Harbe, هربه—Touman, تومان
31. Dora, درع—Kaldjak, قلجق
32. Dáfen, دافن—Lebs, لبس—Ftita, فتيته
33. Khafoury, خافوري—Ayesh, عيش—Behatta, بحته—Heneyne, حنينه—Khubz, خبز—Sadj, ماج—Burgoul, برغل
34. Kemmáye, كمايه—Khelásy, خلاصي—Jebah, جباه—Zebeidy, زبيدي
37. Szona, صنع—Oerk, عرق
38. Meghezel el souf, مغزل الصوف
41. Bakheil, بخيل—Wakhad helále, وخد حلاله

45. Khádhere, خاضره—Nekhouet, نخوة
46. Koualeh, قواله
47. Asamer, اسامر—El kheil djeitna, &c.
الخيل جيتنا يا ديبا
الخيل جيتنا حطيبا
الخيل ضوحي يا ديبا
Hodjeiny, حجيني
49. Szahdje, صهجه—Hadou, حدو
50. Moszana, مصنع
53. Sindián, سنديان
54. Hetout, حتوت
58. Welouloua, ولولوا
60. Zekawah, زكوه—Zeká, زكا
61. Talab, طلب—Kheteb, ختب
63. Ent tálek, انت طالقه
64. Tamehhe, طامحه
69. Mebesshae, مبشع
78. Metrás, متراس
111. Daly, دالي
131. Keffie, كفيه—Ares, ارس
133. Shebeyka, شبيكه
135. Mezrak, مزراق—Orar el Deyghemy, عرار الديغمي—Mashhour, مشهور—Ftita, فتيته—Medjelleh, مجلله—Merekeda, مرقده—Djereisha, جريشه—Nekaa, نقعه

INDEX OF ARABIC WORDS.

PAGE
- 136. Shyh, شرح
- 137. Kurs, قرص —Ayesh, عيش — Kahkeh, كهكه
- 138. Gharad, غرض —Dawíreh, دويره
- 139. Kahtan, قحطان
- 143. Rababa, رباب —Asamer, اسامر
- 144. "Get up, O camel," قوم يا جمل —"Walk fast," سوق —"The poor camel," &c. —"Come and take," &c. تعبان و عطشان قرب حتي نعلق لك
- 150. "None shall cover," &c. ما يغطيك الّا فولان
- 154. Ent taleka, انت طالقه
- 159. Rowadjeh, رواجح —Djaafere, جاعفره
- 164. Mebesshae, مبشع
- 166. Shahher, شحّر
- 167. Djerba, جربه —Beney, بنيّه
- 168. Agyd, عقيد
- 172. Kefyl, كفيل
- 177. "To dig up and to bury," الحفر و الدفن
- 178. Thar, ثار —Dye, ديه
- 179. "Were hell-fire," &c. النار و لا نترك الثار
- 181. Hhasnai, حسناي
- 183. Wallahy inny ma, &c. والله اني ما شقّيتُ جلدً و ما يتمتُ ولدً

PAGE
- Dhebahh, ذبح
- 186. Báikeh, بايقه
- 187. Zeben, زبن —Tezebbenet, تزبنت —Dakhelet, دخلت —Mezbene, مزبنه —Melha, ملحه
- 190. Othman el Medhayfe, عثمان المضايفه — El Medheyan, المضيّان
- 197. Abeyt, &c. ابيت وحيد و لا عند اولاد سعيد
- 202. Sheidje, شيجه — Syredje, سيرجه
- 207. Ghafeyr, غفير
- 208. Hasnay, حسناي — Hasneh, حسنه
- 209. Tayb, طيب
- 210. "May your day be white," "—نهارك ابيض May yours be like milk," نهارك لبني —"Ha, uncle," &c. يا عمنا الي ماشي معكم مويه
- 211. "In truth," &c. اه والله يا خوي مرحبابك
- 212. Athr, أثر
- 215. Djáhelye, جاهلية
- 217. Hessenne, or Ahsenne, الاحسنّه — Wády, وادي — Djelás, جلاس — Rowalla, روالّه

INDEX OF ARABIC WORDS.

218. Ktaysán, تتعبسان—Doghama, دغمه—Feregge, فريقّه—Naszyr, نصير—Omhallef, امحلّف—Maadjel, معجل—Abdelle, عبدالله—Fersha, فرشا—Bedour, بدور—Sowaleme, سوالمه—Tana Mádjed, طنا ماجد—Fedán, فدان—Sebaa, سباع

219. Selga, سلقا—Djaafere, جعافره—Owadje, عواجه

220. Wayl, وايل

221. Howeytát, حويطات—Atye, عطيه (plur. عطاونه)—Heywát, حيوات—Leheywát, لحيوات—Terábein, طرابين—Maazy, معازي—Tyaha, تياها—Moeyleh, مويلح

222. Hadnán, حدنان—Debour, دبور—Bedoul, بدول—Seyayhe, سيايحه—Hekouk, حكوك—Azázeme, عزازمه—Wahydát, وحيدات—Oulad el Fokora, اولاد الفقره—Reteymát, رتيمات—Khanasera, خناسره—Sowáleha, صوالحا—Sayd, صعيد—Owareme, عوارمه—Gerásh, قراشي—Gereish or Koreish, قريش—Rahamy, رحمي—Mezeyne, مزينه

223. Aleygát, عليقات—Wászel, واصل—Sherkyeh, شرقيه

224. Ayayde, عبايده—Salatene, سلاطنه—Djerabene, جرابنه—Maazy, معازي—Mowalle, (read *Mowaze*,) موازه—Ghanayme, غنايمه—Shedayde, شدايده—Zerayne, زرعينه—Heteym, هتيم—Djeheyne, جهينه—Bily, بلي

225. Azayze, عزايزه—Amarat, عمارات

226. Hanády, حنادي—Howámede, حوامده—Oulad Mousa, اولاد موسي—Lebadye, لباديه—Megna, مقنع

227. Okaba, عقبه—Mesayd, مساعيد—Wodje, وجه—Bily, بلي in the sing. Hassany, حسّاني—بلوي

229. Abs, عبس—(plur. عبوس)—El Harra, الحّره

231. Shammar, شمر—Degheyfat, دغيفات—Djaafer, جعافر—Rebaay, رباعي—Orar el Deyghami, عرار الديغمي—Zegeyrat, زقيرات

232. Selga, سلقا—Sahhoun, سحّون—Zaab, زعب—Ageyl, عقيل

INDEX OF ARABIC WORDS.

233. Zogorty, زقرتي — Djemamyel, جماميل — Meteyr, مطير — Alowa, علوي — Dowysh, دويش — Boráy, براي — Harabeshe, حرابشه — Borsán, برسان

234. Harb, حرب

235. Mezeyne, مزينه — Wohoub, وحوب — Gharbán, غربان — Djenayne, جناينه — Safar, سفر — Ammer, عمر — Fera, فرع — Doýny, ديني

236. Hámede, حامده — Salem, سالم — Howáseb, حواسب — Sobh, صبح

237. Shokban, شعبان — Rehalát, رحالات — Khadhera, خضره — Rábegh, رابغ — El Owf, العوف — Haib, حيب — Dwy Dhaher, دوي ظاهر — Ghor, غور — Zebeyde, زبيده

238. Sedda, سدّه — Djemmela, جمله — Saadyn, ساعدين — Ateybe, عتيبه (plur. عتبان)

239. Lahhyan, لحيان — Metarefe, مطارفه — Beni Fahem, بني فهم

240. Djehadele, جهادله — Dwy Barakat, دوي بركات — Koreysh, قريش — Ryshye, ريشيه — Kabákebe, كباكبه — Adouán, عدوان

241. Harreth, حرث — Thekyf, ثقيف — Hodheyl, هذيل

242. Djebel Kora, جبل كرا — Alowyein, علويين — Nedowyein, ندويين — Beni Kháled, بني خالد — Toweyrek, طويرق — Beni Sofyan, بني سفيان — Modher, مضر — Rabýa ربيعه

243. Ossoma, عسمه — Begoum, بقوم — Oklob, اقلب — Sabýa, سبيعه — Salem, سالم — Kahtán, قحطان — Es-Sahama, السحامه — Gormola, قرمله — Aasy, عاسي — Dowáser, دواسر

244. Yám, يام — Okmán, عكمان — El Marra, المرّه — Sad (or Saad), سعد — Nászera, ناصره — Málek, مالك — Gámed, غامد — Zohrán, زهران — Shomrán, شمران

245. Asábely, عسابلي — Ibn el Ahmar, ابن الاحمر — Ibn el Asmar, ابن الاسمر — Beni Shafra, بني شفره — Abyde, ابيده — Asyr, عسير — Senhán, سنحان — Wá-

INDEX OF ARABIC WORDS.

daa, وادعه—Sahhár, صحار—Bagem, باتم

253. Thámerye, ثامريه — Nezahhy, نزحي — Keraye, قريه

254. "Go and wash the feet of your mare," &c. &c. اغسل رجليه الفرس و اشرب مويتها

255. Birsim, برسيم

257. Om el Bel, ام البل—Djam, جعم

260. Hedjein, هجين

261. Osháry, عشاري (from عشر ten)

263 "His back is so soft," &c. ظهره ليّن تشرب عليه فنجان قهوه

264. "Will feed upon the fat of its own hump," ياكل في شحمه

265. Rás, راس—Ghabeit, غبيط—Gissa, تصعه — Shaghour, شغور—Shaghaore, شغاوره—Hawýe, حاويه — Shedád, هداد

266. Shebrýe, شبريه — Shekdef, شقدف—Takht raván, تخت روان

267. El Aasab, العصب— Fekek, فقف

268. Serrar, سرّر—Hellel, هلل—

Fáhoura, فاهوره—Sedreh khorban, صدره خربان

274. Abd el Waháb, عبد الوهاب — Temym, تميم — El Howta, الحوته — Keffár, كفار—Messalykh, مسالخ

284. "Hateful," حكروه

287. Abou Showáreb, ابو شوارب

288. Faysal, فيصل—Nászer, ناصر—El Turky, التركي

294. Oulad es' Sheikh, اولاد الشيخ

302. "O doer," يا فاعل—"O leaver-off," يا تارك

306. Zeka, زكي

308. Nawáb, نواب — Mezekki, مزكّي—Aámil, عامل

312. Sylle, سِله

313. Merádíf, مواديف

316. Mendjýeh, منجيه

317. El Sabr, السبر

319. Haret el Abasieh, حارت العباسيه — Aman Ullah, امان الله—Halka, حلقه

324. Thádj, تاج

325. Zebeyr, زبير—Thoeny, ثويني—Szebeyhy, صبيبحي—El Koweyt, القويط

326. Abou Nokta, ابو نقطه — Othman el Medhayfe, عثمان المضايفه

328. Moabede, معبده

INDEX OF ARABIC WORDS.

329. Abd el Mayen, عبد المعيّن—
   Ibn Name, ابن نعمه
330. Beni Sobh, بني صبح
335. Hark, حرك
336. Ras el Kheyme, راس الخيمه
   — Gowásim, (or Djowá-sin) قواسم
337. Refeydha, رفيضه
344. Seyd Mohammed el Mahrouky, سيد محمد المحروقي
371. Ghálye, غاليه — Ibn Khor-shán, ابن قرشان
380. "I have abandoned the religion," &c. تركت دين المسلمين و دخلت في دين الخوارج و دين محمد علي
383. Bakhroudj, بخروج
394. Bedjíle, بجيله
402. Oklob, الكلب
411. Rass, رصّ — Hedjeylan, حجيلان

THE END.

LONDON:
PRINTED BY A. J. VALPY, RED LION COURT, FLEET STREET.

LATELY PUBLISHED.

BURCKHARDT'S TRAVELS in ARABIA;

Comprehending an account of those Territories which the Mohammedans regard as Sacred. Second Edition, 2 vols. 8vo. with Map and Plans. 24s.

"This work is a valuable legacy from one of the most laborious, learned, and amiable of modern travellers. It contains an account of the Hedjaz, or Holy Land of the Musselmans, a territory hitherto but little known to Europeans, also a description of the cities of Mekka, Medina, and Yembo. The work cannot fail to excite the highest curiosity, when it is remembered that the author resided in the character of a Musselman among a people of whom travellers have never yet been able to give any account, from the circumstance of no unbeliever being permitted to remain in the country."—*John Bull.*

www.ingramcontent.com/pod-product-compliance
Lightning Source LLC
Chambersburg PA
CBHW080327170426
43194CB00014B/2493